Keynes and Macroeconomics after 70 Years

To the memory of
Hyman Minsky
Robert Heilbroner
Tom Asimakopulos
Robert Eisner
John Kenneth Galbraith

To Paul and Louise Davidson

Keynes and Macroeconomics after 70 Years

Critical Assessments of *The General Theory*

Edited by

L. Randall Wray

Center for Full Employment and Price Stability, University of Missouri–Kansas City, USA

and

Mathew Forstater

Center for Full Emploment and Price Stability, University of Missouri–Kansas City, USA

Edward Elgar

Cheltenham, UK • Northampton, MA, USA

Published by
Edward Elgar Publishing Limited
The Lypiatts
15 Lansdown Road
Cheltenham
Glos GL50 2JA
UK

Edward Elgar Publishing, Inc.
William Pratt House
9 Dewey Court
Northampton
Massachusetts 01060
USA

A catalogue record for this book
is available from the British Library

Library of Congress Control Number: 2008937108

PEFC
PEFC/16-33-111
CATG-PEFC-052
www.pefc.org

ISBN 978 1 84720 581 0

Printed and bound in Great Britain by MPG Books Ltd, Bodmin, Cornwall

Contents

Contributors

H. Sonmez Atesoglu is Professor of Economics at Clarkson University, Potsdam, NY, USA.

Joel Bonales is Professor and Researcher in Economics at the Universidad Latinamericana, the Universidad Panamericana, Mexico City, Mexico.

Luiz Carlos Bresser-Pereira is Professor Emeritus of Economics and Political Theory at the Getulio Vargas Foundation in São Paulo, Brazil. He is also editor of the *Brazilian Journal of Political Economy*.

Luciano Dias Carvalho is Assistant Professor of Economics at State University of the West of Paraná, Francisco Beltrão, Brazil.

Bokhyun Cho is Professor of Economics at the Hanbat National University, Daejeon, South Korea.

Jerry Courvisanos is Senior Lecturer in Innovation and Entrepreneurship in the School of Business at the University of Ballarat, VIC, Australia.

Cleomar Gomes da Silva is Professor of Economics of the Getulio Vargas Foundation in research at the Center for International Economics, São Paulo, Brazil.

Edwin Dickens is in the Department of Economics and Finance at Saint Peter's College, Jersey City, NJ, USA.

Mathew Forstater is Associate Professor of Economics at the University of Missouri–Kansas City, USA.

Paulo Gala is Assistant Professor at the São Paulo School of Economics, São Paulo, Brazil.

G.C. Harcourt is Reader in the History of Economic Theory and a Fellow of Jesus College at Cambridge University, Cambridge, United Kingdom.

Wenge Huang holds an MBA degree from China Europe International Business School and now serves as a Vice President of Beijing Jiuzhouding Investment Consulting Co., Ltd, Beijing, China.

Steve Keen is Associate Professor of Economics and Finance at the University of Western Sydney, Penrith, NSW, Australia.

Stephanie Kelton is Assistant Professor of Economics at the University of Missouri–Kansas City, Kansas City, MO, USA and a Research Scholar with the Center for Full Employment and Price Stability.

John E. King is Professor of Economics in the Department of Economics and Finance at La Trobe University, Melbourne, VIC, Australia.

Peter Kriesler is Associate Professor at the Centre for Applied Economic Research at the University of New South Wales, Sydney, NSW, Australia.

Edwin Le Heron is Professor at the Institute of Political Sciences in Bordeaux, France and President of the French Association for the Development of Keynesian Studies.

André Lourenço is Professor of Macroeconomics at Federal University Rio Grande do Norte in Natal, Brazil.

Jesús Muñoz is Professor and Researcher in Economics at the Universidad Latinamericana, the Universidad Panamericana, and at the Center for Economic, Managerial and Social Research at the National Polytechnique Institute, Mexico City, Mexico.

J.W. Nevile is Visiting Emeritus Professor at the Centre for Applied Economic Research at the University of New South Wales, Sydney, NSW, Australia.

José Luís Oreiro is Associate Professor of Economics at Federal University of Paraná, Curitiba, Brazil.

Carlo Panico is Professor of Economics in the Department of Economic Theory and Applications at the University of Federico II of Naples, Naples, Italy.

Colin Richardson is at Imperial College, London, England and the University of Abertay, Dundee, Scotland.

Lino Sau is a Senior Researcher of Political Economy in the School of Communication Studies at the University of Turin, Turin, Italy.

Abdelkader Slifi is Assistant Professor at the University of Picardie Jules Verne, Amiens, France.

L. Randall Wray is Professor of Economics at the University of Missouri – Kansas City, Kansas City, MO, USA.

Introduction

L. Randall Wray and Mathew Forstater

This volume contains a selection of the papers that were presented at the 9th International Post Keynesian Conference, organized by Jan Kregel, Mathew Forstater, and L. Randall Wray and held at the University of Missouri–Kansas City (UMKC) in September 2006. The conference was jointly sponsored by the *Journal of Post Keynesian Economics*, UMKC's Center for Full Employment and Price Stability (CFEPS), and the Economics Department of UMKC. The conference is normally part of a workshop that takes place every other year, carrying on the long tradition that was begun in the 1980s by Jan Kregel, Piero Garengnani, and Sergio Paranello. The workshops were originally held in Trieste, Italy, and were continued by Paul Davidson at the University of Tennessee–Knoxville before finally settling in Kansas City.

Traditionally, the workshop includes both a conference and a summer school, combined over a 10–14-day period. However, because the 2006 conference would be celebrating several significant anniversaries, it was scheduled for September, and the summer school was held separately in June. The summer school was a smashing success, with over 70 graduate students and faculty from around the world discussing not only a wide range of topics in Post Keynesian economics but also institutionalist, Marxian, and feminist economics. In addition, anthropology, sociology, and Black studies were included in the curriculum, reflecting the interdisciplinary nature of UMKC's PhD program. Many of the students and faculty would return to Kansas City for the conference in September.

We are most grateful to the members of the summer school faculty for volunteering their time: Morteza Ardebili, Barbara Bonnekessen, Robert Brazelton, S. 'Charu' Charusheela, Jerry Courvisanos, Colin Danby, Eliseo Fernandez, Mathew Forstater, Scott Fullwiler, Michael K. Green, John F. Henry, Jan Kregel, Frederic S. Lee, John Marangos, Donald Matthews, Jesús Muñoz, Christopher Niggle, Erik Olsen, Tanya Y. Price, Michael J. Radzicki, Jim Sturgeon, Linwood Tauheed, Pavlina Tcherneva, James Webb, and L. Randall Wray.

More than 150 economists from around the world attended the September conference, which celebrated: the 60th anniversary of Keynes's death, the Employment Act, the formation of the World Bank and the International Monetary Fund (IMF) and the Bretton Woods meeting; and the 40th anniversary of the Freedom Budget. Most importantly, it marked the 70th anniversary of the publication of Keynes's *General Theory*. The usual conference was followed by an extraordinary day-long series of keynote speeches by the world's foremost Keynes scholars. In recognition of the significance of the timing of the conference, we have selected those papers most closely related to Keynes and to *The General Theory* for this conference volume. Topics covered herein include the relations between Keynes and heterodox economics, the founding fathers of Post Keynesian economics, models inspired by the economics of Keynes, Keynesian policy, and modern developments and extensions of Keynes's economics. Obviously, these represent only a small fraction of the interesting papers that were presented at the 33 panels organized for the conference, and we would like to thank all of the other presenters whose papers covered a much wider range of topics than we could include in this volume.

As always, the editors would like to thank, in particular, Louise and Paul Davidson for their advice in the planning and organization of the conference. And we are grateful to Jan Kregel, who took time off from his busy schedule to help plan the workshop, teach at the summer school, and give a presentation during the conference Keynote Session.

The faculty and students of UMKC's Economics Department and the staff of CFEPS also played an important role in helping to make the conference possible. In particular, we thank Robert Brazelton, Karol Gil-Vasquez, Charlene Heinen, John Henry, Stephanie Kelton, Fred Lee, Ergun Meric, Gerald J.B. Mupingo, Michael Murray, Kelly Pinkham, Gianluca Rossi, Alla Semenova, Natalia Speer, Heather Starzynski, Jim Sturgeon, and Pavlina Tcherneva. Most of all, we thank Heather Starzynski for excellent editorial assistance in preparation of the manuscript and for keeping the authors to a tight schedule. Without all of her work, the volume would have been impossible.

In the remainder of this introduction, we shall summarize the main points of the chapters collected in this volume.

PART I: KEYNES AND HETERODOX ECONOMICS

1. King: What Are We Against?

In his chapter, Professor John King responds to claims by Bateman and Colander that heterodox economists are critiquing a straw man version of orthodoxy because they ignore the substantial changes made in the mainstream approach to macroeconomics over the past 40 years. According to the Bateman and Colander view, the now dominant new consensus macroeconomics (NCM) is solidly based on behavioral economics, having abandoned the older neoclassical synthesis with ad hoc assumptions, inadequate treatment of expectations formation, and a flawed view of the operation of monetary policy. The NCM adopts a reconfigured IS (investment–savings) curve, replaces the old LM liquidity curve with a Taylor-type monetary policy rule, and includes a short-run Phillips curve. It is supposed to be based on solid microfoundations, incorporating an intertemporal general equilibrium model immune to the Lucas critique and other problems that brought about the downfall of the neoclassical synthesis.

King examines the 'new' orthodoxy in detail and wonders why money is included in the models at all, since every conceivable state of the world is presumed known by agents in the models. He concludes that the newer approaches are not much different from the old ones. In some ways they are better, but in other respects they are much worse. For example, in the new approaches, there is no possibility of ever being out of equilibrium because markets clear continuously. King argues that the new approach to macro policy leaves virtually no room for behavioral economics – one of the advantages claimed by Bateman and Colander. Hence, 'Mainstream macroeconomics has not progressed very much in recent years, and where it has advanced it has been towards positions already established by heterodox (read: Post Keynesian) theorists'.

2. Muñoz and Bonales: Lakatosian Insight

Professors Muñoz and Bonales use Lakatosian methodology to identify the scientific research program (SRP) that is embedded in Keynes's *General Theory* to anticipate the direction he might have taken after 1937 if he had not become ill, with his time absorbed in important policy matters. They find that Keynes's SRP was based on a number of important concepts, such as animal spirits, market clearing as a special case, irreversibility, uncertainty, money non-neutrality, and liquidity preference. However, the most important of his insights was that equilibrium can be achieved without full employment. His probable directions after the publication of *The General Theory* would have included work in the area of endogenous money, inflation, open-economy macroeconomics, growth and cycles, and distribution. The authors doubt that Keynes would have pursued either microfoundations of macro (a trendy topic for the mainstream 40 years later), or imperfect competition (taken up by some of Keynes's followers). The authors conclude that Keynes would not have altered the fundamental vision of *The General Theory* in this later research – nor should he have done so, because its core has never been seriously challenged.

PART II: FOUNDING FATHERS OF POST KEYNESIAN ECONOMICS

3. Lourenço: Minsky and Keynes on Volatility

Professor Lourenço examines the emphasis placed by Keynes and by Hyman Minsky on the volatility of investment. Minsky proposed what he called the 'investment theory of the cycle' and the 'financial theory of investment'. Lourenço contrasts Minsky's 'two-price model' approach, which utilizes an investment 'demand price' curve and an investment 'supply price' curve to determine the level of investment, with Keynes's exposition that relies on the marginal efficiency of capital and the interest rate. He faults Minsky for barely distinguishing between the demand price for new investment and the market price for equity shares. Further, Minsky's analysis relies on shocks to explain the business cycle, rather than on endogenous generation of the cycle as in Keynes's approach. Minsky's analysis is thus criticized as more 'mechanistic'. Further, the economic agents in Minsky's model are more rational in the neoclassical sense, unable to deviate from strict profit maximization. However, because Minsky assumes that agents tend to hold homogeneous expectations, herd behavior leads to highly volatile investment – growing explosively in a euphoric boom or crashing when expectations reverse. On the other hand, Keynes recognized that economic stability requires heterogeneity of expectations – diversity of opinion helps to hold the economy in check so that it does not oscillate between one extreme and the other. While the editors of this volume believe that Lourenço has misinterpreted Minsky on some points and ignored the importance in Minsky's model of institutional 'ceilings and floors' in constraining the endogenous instability that is inherent in market economies that use sophisticated capital equipment and financing techniques, we include Lourenço's chapter in this volume to spark debate on this important and timely topic.

4. Sau: Two Founding Fathers

Professor Sau argues that Keynes and Kalecki are two founding fathers of the critique of the notion that markets are necessarily self-regulating in the sense that they are equilibrium seeking. In particular, they deny that wage and price flexibility will generate an equilibrium position with full employment. Indeed, the market forces can – in at least some significant situations – generate instability, moving the economy away from equilibrium. For example, if falling wages generate falling prices, this is likely to depress business expectations to the extent that prices are expected to be even lower in the future, thus reducing aggregate demand. By the same token, falling prices increase the burden of money-denominated debt; while creditors are richer in real terms, this is only true if debtors do not default. Hence, the net impact could be lower aggregate demand. Further, falling output prices would lead to falling asset prices – possibly to a Fisher debt deflation – and financial market instability. Kalecki rejected the so-called 'Pigou effect' (falling prices increase wealth through a real balance effect, stimulating consumption) on the basis that rising debt burdens would increase uncertainty and push up the long-term interest rate (falling investment could then more than compensate for any induced consumption). Hence, not only does price flexibility fail to move the economy toward equilibrium but it actually generates instability. Sau concludes the analysis by linking the arguments of Keynes and Kalecki to those made later by Tobin, Minsky, and Caskey and Fazzari.

5. Harcourt: On Asimakopulos

According to Professor Harcourt, Tom Asimakopulos came over to the heterodox side as a result of attending Robert Solow's lectures in 1965–66, apparently disgusted by the increasingly unrealistic assumptions adopted in what passed for economics in the name of Keynes at the centers of higher learning. Asimakopulos insisted that all economic discussions need to be grounded in a recognizable economy with history, institutions, and rules of the game, and with investment and consumption, wages and profits, and workers and capitalists. In his later work, he came to recognize the 'crucial organizing concept of the surplus', although he rejected long-period analysis and the notion that there is convergence to centers of gravity – both of which are adopted by many other economists who take a surplus approach. He linked the surplus to questions about distribution, effective demand, and employment. He always emphasized that, in discussion of a causal model, one must use historical time, not equilibrium – which can only describe equilibrium relations while merely assuming that there must be forces to move the economy to the position of equilibrium. In other words, equilibrium methodology is useless for matters of causation – which is what is usually of greatest interest. Of course, there was a close affinity between his argument and Joan Robinson's distinction between equilibrium and history.

Asimakopulos set off something of a firestorm of controversy in the pages of the *Cambridge Journal* and the *Journal of Post Keynesian*

Economics when he criticized Keynes's notion of the saving–investment relation. This was unintentional and surprising to Asimakopulos. One of the editors of this volume (Wray) recalls several later conversations with Asimakopulos, who was still hurt by the reaction and remained convinced that he had said nothing that should have been controversial. As Harcourt explains, Asimakopulos believed that Keynes's exposition was a *specific* theory, applicable only in the presence of unemployed resources and unused capacity in the financial sector, so that real resources could be mobilized for investment. Further, Keynes's argument was not a historical analysis, because it ignored the time required for the multiplier to raise income and induce saving. Only at the end of the historical process would investment have been able to create an equivalent amount of saving. Harcourt does not find Asimakopulos's argument to be completely comprehensible and so offers his own view on the relation: ' "Yesterday's" saving may influence "today's" investment, and "today's" saving may influence "tomorrow's" investment, but it is "today's" investment which is responsible for "today's" saving'. This is not the place to try to defend or criticize the position taken by Asimakopulos, but the editors note that Keynes very specifically addressed the issue concerning investment and the time required for the multiplier to operate in section IV of chapter 10 of *The General Theory* (pp. 122–5), which makes it quite clear that the saving–investment equality does not depend on any sleight of hand such as an instantaneous multiplier (or, as Asimakopulos believed, on ignoring history). In any case, Harcourt is correct in his argument that Asimakopulos stands as a giant among the second generation of the followers of Keynes.

6. Slifi: On Asimakopulos

Slifi also revisits Asimakopulos's critique of the Keynesian saving–investment relation. However, Slifi proposes a different, two-pronged solution. First, he argues that Keynes did want to use historical time but this created a tension with his short-period equilibrium approach; hence, he was forced to define a period as a length of time long enough to allow all income received to be spent. Clearly, this favors equilibrium analysis over historical analysis. If we drop this peculiar definition of period, then it is not true that investment equals saving no matter what the level of income happens to be, breaking the saving–investment identity. Slifi thus proposes to recast the formulation by combining the fundamental equations of the *Treatise on Money* with the identities from *The General Theory*, specified dynamically. The dynamic formulation (for example, spending this period depends on income from the last period) allows saving to deviate from investment except at the equilibrium level of income that is achieved only after the multiplier operates, resolving the problem identified by Asimakopulos in Keynes's presentation. While the editors are not convinced that there is any problem in Keynes's approach that requires correction, this chapter makes an interesting contribution to the controversy first spurred by Asimakopulos.

PART III: KEYNESIAN MODELS

7. Richardson and Courvisanos: Keynes and Kalecki

Colin Richardson and Jerry Courvisanos continue their important work on both Kalecki and the use of computer simulations in 'Modeling Keynes with Kalecki'. After rejecting the standard neoclassical interpretation of Keynes embodied in the IS–LM model, the authors argue that a Keynes–Kalecki synthesis can prevent the hijacking of Keynes by neoclassical economics, in part made possible by the remnants of Marshallian micro theory found in *The General Theory*. For Richardson and Courvisanos, the Kaleckian contributions that must be wedded to Keynes's framework are the dynamics of investment and profits and class-based income distribution. After laying out the model, the authors then subject it to computer simulations in three alternative institutional settings, with entrepreneurs, trade unionists, and Kaleckians in control of economic policy formulation.

The approach employed by Richardson and Courvisanos is Post Keynesian not only in its substance but in its method as well. Keynes's warnings about the pitfalls of overly formal and problematic mathematical techniques are well known, and the authors reject a standard econometric approach on these and related grounds. In its place, they employ a version of an approach increasingly popular in Post Keynesian circles: system dynamics. System dynamics complements rather than replaces verbal reasoning, and it can deal with both real-world complexity and disequilibrium (or non-equilibrium) dynamics, such as those characterized by cumulative causation.

Richardson and Courvisanos examine five different policies within the three institutional settings over what they call an 'era' (defined as 100 simulated short periods). Entrepreneurs promote moderate money wage growth and/or increased productivity. The first results in lower employment, a higher unemployment rate, and unacceptable excess capacity, as well as deflation. The last is only slightly better, with employment lower at the end of the era than at the beginning. Trade unionists back an approach based on money wage-led aggregate demand stimulus and/or job sharing. The first results in desirable employment and unemployment outcomes, but only with the attainment of an impossible negative excess capacity utilization rate, and severe price and wage cost inflation far outpaces increased profit margins. The latter policy does provide price and wage stability, but it also results in slow employment growth and an unacceptable unemployment rate. Kaleckians support a policy program comprising increased investment planning and an incomes policy. Their simulation shows that this approach provides full employment and price stability, with rising real wages and strong employment growth.

8. Atesoglu: A Model for the 21st Century

In his chapter, 'A Keynesian model for the 21st century', H. Sonmez Atesoglu, known to Post Keynesians for his empirical work, especially in the area of monetary policy, attempts to provide an alternative to both the standard neoclassical IS–LM and the Post Keynesian Weintraub–Davidson aggregate supply–aggregate demand models. For Atesoglu, such an alternative must include what he considers to be the fundamental Keynesian insights: the possibility of the economy being in macroeconomic equilibrium below the full employment level of output; monetary non-neutrality in the short and long runs; and aggregate demand driven by autonomous spending. Following his development of this model of output and employment, Atesoglu considers the policy implications and then introduces a monetary sector and uses it to discuss monetary policy in the United States.

The model of output and employment put forward by Atesoglu has some family resemblances to the 'Keynesian Cross', but there are some important differences. In the traditional version, there is no variable for employment, and both technology and labor productivity are considered given, so employment simply moves up and down with GDP in constant proportions. In Atesoglu's version, there is an explicit variable for employment, as well as for the employment–output ratio (inverse of labor productivity). The fiscal policy implications are standard Keynesian, with tax cuts and/or increases in government spending stimulating output and employment, given the likelihood of the economy operating below the full employment level of output. Atesoglu goes beyond this standard Keynesianism in considering the 'socialization of investment', however, and he makes the important point of citing important real-life examples, including the interstate highway system, aerospace, and the Internet.

In his model of the monetary sector, Atesoglu offers a partial equilibrium alternative to the general equilibrium IS–LM model. He also employs a 'neutral interest rate rule' as an alternative to the Taylor rule for monetary policy. Atesoglu admits that his results for the monetary model are not as reliable as those for his model of output and employment and that further work needs to be done, especially for understanding issues such as the determination of long-term interest rates.

9. Carvalho and Oreiro: A Post Keynesian Macrodynamic Model

Luciano Dias Carvalho and José Luís Oreiro offer a Post Keynesian macrodynamic model of capital accumulation, income distribution, technical progress and endogenous money. While there have been models of growth, distribution, and technical change, few have combined these with endogenous money, now one of the most widely accepted theoretical contributions in Post Keynesian theory. This allows the authors to include some highly original propositions in their model, such as the influence of technical progress on the banking mark-up. Carvalho and Oreiro then employ computer simulations to track the dynamic path of the economy according to their model. In this, they use real-world values where there exist reliable estimates and the correspondence principle where there do not.

Carvalho and Oreiro's model is an attempt to combine the so-called 'Cambridge' (that is, Kaldor–Pasinetti) model of growth and distribution with Post Keynesian monetary theory (associated with the endogenous money approach of Basil Moore, Randy Wray, and others). As already stated, one of their original contributions is to link technical change and the banking mark-up. The authors thus bring a Schumpeterian element into their model, with its important role for bank credit in technological innovation. In terms of the results of their simulations, one of the most interesting, perhaps, is that a low propensity to save is more important than a high rate of technical progress for macroeconomic stability. Thus, the paradox of thrift continues to be a prime feature of the model, demonstrating the continuing relevance of Keynes's insights in *The General Theory*.

PART IV: KEYNESIAN POLICY

10. Panico: Keynes on Control of Money Supply and Interest Rates

Panico examines Keynes's position concerning the ability of the central bank to control monetary aggregates and interest rates, as presented in *The General Theory*, the *Treatise on Money*, and elsewhere. Followers of Keynes have long stressed the accommodative nature of the money supply while focusing on the central bank's ability to achieve lower interest rates in order to stimulate effective demand. Basil Moore has gone even further, arguing that the central bank has no direct influence on the quantity of money, while the interest rate is said to be set exogenously by policy. Indeed, the money supply is supposed to be horizontal, with the quantity of money determined solely by borrowers. According to Panico, the position taken by Keynes is that the central bank *could* control the money supply if it adopted the appropriate procedures; however, he provided several caveats. In the *Treatise on Money*, he recognized that the supply of central bank reserves at the discount window would be mostly nondiscretionary ('horizontal' in modern parlance) in practice because the central bank sets a discount rate and then accommodates demand. In open market operations, the central bank has some control over reserves; however, this is attenuated by the necessity to respond to impacts on reserves arising from fiscal operations as well as from the external balance. At the time of the writing of the *Treatise on Money*, the government budget was generally in balance; hence, the main issue was the external balance of the nation operating on a gold standard. In this case, the interest rate is exogenously determined by the need to maintain external balance; thus the central bank would have to accommodate the demand for reserves at that interest rate. According to Panico, Keynes's conclusions on control of the money supply did not change with the publication of *The General Theory*: while it would be technically possible to control the supply of money, the central bank would instead choose to control the interest rate, in order to finance fiscal operations (internal balance) and achieve international objectives (external balance).

However, Keynes's approach to control of the interest rate did change substantially after the publication of the *Treatise on Money*. In that book, he argued that the central bank has the ability to identify the natural interest rate consistent with full employment and price stability. It would then set the policy rate at the natural rate, with short-term rates falling in line. Its ability to influence longer-term interest rates was believed to be more problematic because banks could resist central bank efforts to drive rates down. According to Panico, in *The General Theory*, Keynes abandoned the notion of a natural rate. (The editors would put this more precisely: in *The General Theory*, Keynes argued that there is a different natural rate for each level of effective demand, only one of which – the neutral rate – is consistent with full employment [*The General Theory*, p. 243].) So long as it is believable, it will be able to hit an interest rate target. However, again, the setting of the target will depend on international constraints; with a gold standard, the central bank's discretion is limited. Panico concludes that, while Keynes's *General Theory* analysis changed significantly from that of the *Treatise on Money* (most importantly, Keynes embraced a monetary theory of production), this did not require any major change to his views on the central bank's control over the money supply or interest rates.

Hence, the relatively new 'horizontalist' approach to money is not necessary in order to challenge neoclassical theory.

11. Bresser-Pereira and Gomes da Silva: Inflation Targeting

Professor Bresser-Pereira and Gomes da Silva offer a very interesting analysis of inflation targeting in Brazil. Rather than critiquing inflation policy in general, they argue that it can only be implemented in the proper economic environment. In Brazil's case, inflation targeting (IT) was adopted prematurely and has contributed to sluggish growth, fiscal constraints, high unemployment, and an overvalued exchange rate. While many credit IT for Brazil's recent lower inflation rate, the authors argue that the country could have had lower inflation with far lower costs and without forgoing economic development if it had pursued an alternative set of policies. They reject the old Tinbergen notion that the central bank can target only one variable per policy instrument. A simple inflation target would be unacceptable, for the central bank must also be concerned with the exchange rate and with unemployment. However, the main point they want to make is that adopting an inflation target can be a part of a monetary policy regime but an inflation target cannot be used to switch from one regime to another. In other words, Brazil should have first shifted to a monetary policy regime with low inflation and then adopted IT, rather than trying to use IT to achieve low inflation.

Bresser-Pereira and Gomes da Silva have long argued that Brazil's typically high inflation experience has more to do with what should be called fiscal policy than with monetary policy. In this chapter, they explain that indexation of public services was a major contributing factor. Thus, they propose that the government stop indexing public services as well as any other prices over which government has control – either as provider or regulator. Brazil's inflation is generated mostly on the supply side by pricing behavior and is not due to excessive aggregate demand. However, policy has wrongly focused on contracting demand to fight inflation, rather than tackling pricing directly. They would also eliminate indexing of government bonds, which keeps market interest rates and government debt service high. Given interest costs, the government must run a large primary surplus to keep the debt-to-GDP ratio from exploding. Bresser-Pereira and Gomes da Silva would lower interest rates and then reduce government spending as a signal that the government would not allow excessive demand to renew inflation. This would allow Brazil to escape from what the authors see as a high interest rate trap: the high rate encourages capital inflows that cause overvaluation of the currency. While this does help to lower inflation (by reducing import costs), the central bank is afraid to lower interest rates even as inflation comes down because this would reverse capital flows and generate pass-through inflation as the currency depreciates. Hence, achieving low inflation *first* by formulating an alternative monetary regime (rather than trying to achieve low inflation through high interest rates alone) would allow for a lower *level* of interest rates within which IT could operate.

12. Kelton: Social Security

Professor Kelton focuses on Albert Eisner's examination of the US social security system as an example of particularly clear thinking inspired by Keynes's insights. Like the story about money arising to reduce the transactions costs of barter, or the orthodox belief that supply and demand determine price, the claim that a trust fund finances social security benefits is a fairy tale. Eisner insisted that any projected shortfall of trust funds is just an accounting phenomenon with easy accounting fixes. The trust fund itself is just an accounting entity with no *ex ante* significance; payroll taxes do not 'go into' the trust fund and benefit payments do not 'come out of' it. Indeed, no tax revenue is used to make any federal government payments, for all payments are made by check or direct bank deposit. There is no possibility that a federal government program can go bankrupt or face any financing problem whatsoever. All benefit payments can be made when they come due, whether the trust fund is in surplus, balance, or deficit. Hence, there is no need to create private accounts, cut benefits, raise taxes, increase the retirement age, eliminate cost-of-living adjustments, or impose means tests to 'restore solvency' to the social security program. Unfortunately, Eisner's clear analysis is ignored even by supporters of the program, as Kelton demonstrates by exposing several fallacies promulgated by Paul Krugman, one of the most widely read economists involved in the social security debate in the US today.

PART V: MODERN DEVELOPMENT AND EXTENSIONS OF KEYNESIAN ECONOMICS

13. Cho: Finance

Bokhyun Cho's contribution investigates the impact of the evolution of financial structure on the formation of investor expectations and therefore investment. Cho's argument is that market liberalization and accompanying financial innovation have increased the instability of investment finance and decision making. This has created an environment of stagnating investment and sluggish economic growth. The policy implications of such a view call for the crafting of an alternative financial system and support macroeconomic stabilization policies. The chapter begins with a recounting of Keynes's and Post Keynesian views on these matters. As is well known, in *The General Theory*, investment is the independent variable determining the level of output, income, and employment in the economy. Cho argues that the financial sector can affect investment through two processes. The first is through the influence of the financial system on investor expectations, the second by way of the supply of credit. Some Post Keynesians, such as Moore and Asimakopulos have challenged some of Keynes's positions. However, Cho, following Wray, Kregel, and others, rejects these challenges and defends Keynes's original views. On the one hand, Cho rejects the extreme horizontalist view, instead combining endogenous money theory with a position that banks' liquidity preference can affect the supply of credit. On the other hand, Cho rejects Asimakopulos's claim that, under some circumstances, increased savings may be necessary to achieve a higher level of investment. Investment may be constrained by a shortage of credit but not by a shortage of savings.

Cho then turns to his analysis of the development of the financial sector and the implications for investment finance and expectations. He examines developing and industrialized economies since the mid-1970s and concludes that their financial sectors have been characterized by deregulation and market liberalization. Prior to that time, financial regulation provided some stability to the system. The period also has seen significant financial innovation. Cho argues that such financial liberalization and innovation have increased volatility of interest rates and stock prices, and they have shifted the financial sector's center of gravity from banks to capital markets. These developments have affected the liquidity preference of banks and individuals and altered banks' lending patterns. As a result, there has been greater instability of investment finance and a more uncertain environment under which investor expectations are formed. Cho concludes that these two developments have resulted in stagnating investment and sluggish growth. These factors have been further exacerbated by changes in both investment allocation and investor objectives brought on by the changed financial structure. Under the circumstances, Cho sees no alternatives to constructing a different financial system and supporting strong macroeconomic stabilization policies to promote economic prosperity.

14. Dickens: Probability, Investment Behavior, and Behavioral Finance

In his chapter, Edwin Dickens takes on a topic that has received significant attention: Keynes's writings on probability and their link to his theory of investment. Dickens draws on recent developments in the behavioral finance literature, including the winner's curse, betting quotients, preference reversals, and loss aversion, to argue that for any given investment project, the probability of the payoff, and therefore the expected profits, according to Keynes, will be lower than the estimates of orthodox economists. For Dickens, what is at issue is the orthodox versus Keynes's notion of risk. While the orthodox concept of risk is derived from viewing probability in terms of the principle of non-sufficient reason or the law of large numbers, Keynes's version of the concept is derived from viewing probability in terms of the logical relationship between propositions, which allows Keynes to introduce the idea of the weight of arguments.

Dickens begins by deriving the orthodox notion of risk from the definition of probability in terms of the principle of non-sufficient reason; he then uses the idea of the winner's curse from the behavioral finance literature to refute this version, as applied to investment decision making. The winner's curse states that anyone who makes a bid on an asset for what they think the asset is worth, will lose out. This implies, however, that no rational person would ever undertake investment. While Keynes may have believed that not very much investment would take place if it had to completely rely on cold calculation, he did not think that none would take place. Therefore, this version of the orthodox approach to probability and risk is rejected by Dickens. The author then turns to the orthodox definition of probability in terms of the law of large numbers, drawing on empirical data on betting quotients to invalidate this version (again, as applied to investment decision making). The law of large numbers applies to some types of gambling. For example, in the case of a coin toss, according to this approach, (rational) people should be willing to pay 50 cents for the opportunity to earn a payoff of $1 if a coin turns up heads and nothing if it turns up tails. But the empirical results of the betting quotient literature show that people are willing to pay not 50 cents but 40 cents. Dickens later argues that this result is consistent with the weight of argument approach, but it means that this second orthodox approach, too, is inapplicable to investment decision making. Finally, Dickens uses the definition of probability as a logical relationship between propositions to explain Keynes's notions of risk and the weight of an argument, drawing on the ideas of preference reversals and loss aversion from the behavioral finance literature to argue for their validity. Dickens concludes that Keynes's version of probability encompasses the orthodox version. Since Keynes recognizes the potential that investment decisions may operate in an environment of fundamental or radical uncertainty, it may not be possible to assign a numerical value to his estimate of the probability of the payoff from an investment project. Dickens argues, however, that it is still possible to demonstrate that Keynes's estimates of probability and expected profit are less optimistic than those of orthodox economists.

15. Gala: Real Exchange Rate Levels, Investment and Growth

Paolo Gala offers a Keynesian perspective on the relation of real exchange rate levels, investment, and economic growth, arguing that an undervalued currency can contribute to investment and capital accumulation. The chapter begins by examining two possible channels through which real exchange rates may affect growth in the long run: technological upgrading and capital accumulation. Drawing on Bhaduri and Marglin, Gala constructs a macro model in which investment depends on capacity utilization and profit margins and consumption depends on real wages. The real exchange rate is thus introduced, since, given productivity, it will define the level of real wages by setting the relative price of tradable to non-tradable goods in the worker consumption bundle. A relatively appreciated (undervalued) currency will mean lower (higher) tradable prices, higher (lower) real wages, lower (higher) profit margins, higher (lower) consumption, and lower (higher) investment. An undervalued currency may also lead to higher employment and investment by increasing capacity utilization through higher exports. Thus, investment-led growth would characterize the economy.

Alternatively, the technological argument is based on the idea that an undervalued currency may stimulate the nontraditional tradable sector of developing nations, which then could climb the technological ladder via learning by doing and cumulative technological change in the manufacturing sector. Such an argument, as is found in Williamson's 'development approach to exchange rates', is especially relevant for resource-rich countries. On the other hand, appreciated currencies would prevent the development of the manufacturing sector, with its associated economies of scale and technological spillovers.

Gala then turns to a discussion of East Asian experiences on the one hand, and African and Latin American experiences on the other, to support his theoretical argument. East and Southeast Asian growth strategies, which have been relatively successful, have been associated with undervalued currencies and investment-led growth. Most Latin American and African nations have suffered from balance-of-payments crises due to exchange rate overvaluation, and consumption- rather than investment-led growth cycles, as well as instability.

16. Huang: Liquidity Preference

Liquidity preference is the topic of the chapter by Wenge Huang, who seeks to reinterpret, remedy, and develop the concept as presented by Keynes in *The General Theory*. Huang reviews the debates regarding liquidity preference that followed the publication of *The General Theory*, and

Keynes's identification of the finance motive as an additional source of money demand. The author points out that the finance motive was soon forgotten – until its 'rediscovery' by Davidson in 1965 – and instead the IS–LM model became the most popular presentation of the Keynesian framework. But the IS–LM model has been criticized as misrepresenting Keynes and suffering from internal incoherence. Huang thinks the problem is due, at least in part, to the fact that the finance motive was not introduced in *The General Theory*, where the transactions motive was introduced first and emphasized. Subsequent presentations continued to introduce and emphasize the transactions motive and to ignore or de-emphasize the finance motive, a problem magnified by the fact that, in the investment–realization period – the time between when entrepreneurs make their investment decisions and when that investment is realized – the increase in the finance motive comes first and is of primary importance.

Huang argues that, if liquidity preference theory is reconstructed with the finance motive playing a stronger role than the transactions motive, it can be demonstrated that, in a capitalist economy with a modern banking system, the interest rate is determined by the supply of and demand for bank reserves rather than money supply and money demand.

The argument is simple and applies whether the interest rate is market determined or determined by the central bank – in other words, by whether it is a fixed or floating rate regime.

17. Keen: Revolving Fund of Finance

Steve Keen's chapter incorporates Keynes's notion of a revolving fund of finance into a circuit framework. Like Huang, Keen sees the finance motive as central to an understanding of Keynes's system. Investment must be financed, and so investment must be preceded by the demand for credit. If the loans are forthcoming, workers are hired and materials are purchased, causing incomes to rise. Some of the income is spent, but what is not is saved, and thus investment determines savings through changes in income. Savings does not determine investment, as finance is not savings. To confuse the two is – among other things – to confuse a stock and a flow. In addition, the finance–investment–income–savings process of Keynes is consistent with the endogenous view of the money supply. Keen argues that there are contradictions between this interpretation of Keynes and the circuit theory and that, where the two diverge, Keynes is correct and the circuit school is incorrect, due to the latter's confusion of stocks and flows, but that, nevertheless, the circuit approach is still indispensable to a full depiction of what Keynes in his lectures and early drafts of *The General Theory* called a 'monetary production economy'.

Beginning with what he calls the 'three canonical circuitist insights' (a commodity money-using economy is not a monetary economy; transactions in a monetary economy are three-sided, single-commodity exchanges; money is not defined in terms of different types of bank deposits), Keen argues that the circuit school derives the incorrect results that (i) a constant level of production requires an increasing stock of money; (ii) debts cannot be repaid in money; and (iii) aggregate money profits cannot be positive. He then shows that, from the same point of departure, a formal mathematical model can be erected that contradicts the circuit school and vindicates Keynes on all three of these results. In doing so, Keen not only draws on the circuit school, but he claims to reconcile horizontalist and structuralist approaches to endogenous money.

18. Le Heron: Monetary and Fiscal Policies

In his 'Monetary and fiscal policies in a Post Keynesian stock–flow consistent model', Edward le Heron seeks to reconcile liquidity preference and endogenous money approaches by simulating capitalist dynamics in a model now familiar to Post Keynesians, the stock–flow consistent macroeconomic model. The author builds a more 'realistic' version of the model (by taking into account, for example, Minsky's concepts of borrowers' and lenders' risks, and the amortization of circulating capital) and then uses it to examine the impact of contractionary monetary policy on banks and firms under three different (neutral, weak, and strong) counter-cyclical fiscal policy regimes.

In both the neutral and the weak counter-cyclical fiscal policy regimes, le Heron's simulations show that contractionary monetary policy (a rise of the central bank's short-term lending rate from 2 percent to 4 percent) results in marked economic contraction. This is explained by financial factors as the higher finance costs reduce cash flows and increase interest payments (increased borrowers' and lenders' risks), and credit rationing ensues. With strong counter-cyclical fiscal policy, however, bigger government budget deficits increase cash flows and, along with banks' unlimited willingness to lend to government, counter-balance the effects of contractionary monetary policy. While most Post Keynesians have viewed the money supply and the interest rate as a situation in which one variable is endogenous and the other exogenous, le Heron puts forward the idea that both may be endogenous if the liquidity preference of banks is considered.

19. Nevile and Kriesler: Expectations and Unemployment

J.W. Nevile and Peter Kriesler take on the topic of expectations and employment in their contribution, in which they argue – contra mainstream macroeconomics – that money, expectations, and macro policy can affect 'real' variables such as growth, output, and employment, even in the long run. When considered at all by conventional economics, expectations are confined to monetary phenomena and even to discussions of the Phillips curve. Ironically, this area where expectations sometimes are taken up by the mainstream is severely lacking, the authors contend, as there is no coherent story of the transmission mechanism linking expectations to inflation, and inflationary expectations may have no significant impact on actual rates of inflation. In Keynes, the most important area in which expectations play a role is investment determination, and therefore they can influence not only short-run but also long-run 'real' output and employment in the economy. Since money, expectations, and macro policy – on their own or in interaction – may affect investment, they may have a real, long-run impact.

In the case of macro policy, if government can effectively communicate that it is committed to using, for example, the fiscal and monetary policy tools at its disposal, to maintain high levels (or rates of growth) of demand in the economy, especially in the event of a downturn, this can ensure steady, higher rates of investment through stabilizing business expectations. Likewise, government failure to do so can just as well increase investor uncertainty, subjecting the economy to greater fluctuations in investment. In both cases, what Nevile and Kriesler rightly emphasize is that this is all the more urgent and important because investment determines employment and unemployment. If this is not the economics of Keynes, nothing is.

PART I

Keynes and heterodox economics

1. Heterodox macroeconomics: what, exactly, are we against?

John E. King*

INTRODUCTION

In his review of my *History of Post Keynesian Economics Since 1936* (King 2002), Bradley Bateman claims that I, and other heterodox macroeconomists, are attacking a straw man:

> [W]hy does he not ask hard questions, such as why behavioural macroeconomics and behavioural finance have flourished in the wake of the stock market's collapse, while post-Keynesians are largely ignored? . . . Apart from an occasional aside that mainstream economics has become ever more technical, there is little (or no) recognition that mainstream economics (whatever that hoary term might mean) is not today what it was forty years ago. (Bateman 2004, p. 582)

A similar charge is implicit in David Colander's extensive writings on 'Post Walrasian' (more recently, 'cutting-edge') economics, in which 'the old neoclassical orthodoxy, which we describe as an approach based on a holy trinity of rationality, greed, and equilibrium, is in the process of being replaced with a new orthodoxy, which can be described as an approach based on a holy trinity of purposeful behaviour, enlightened self-interest, and sustainability' (Colander et al. 2004, p. viii). Those who continue to attack neoclassical economics, on this account, are badly behind the times.

This argument needs to be taken seriously by all heterodox macroeconomists. Even if it proves to be entirely wrong it can do great damage, as a familiar historical example will confirm. In the early 1970s, Frank Hahn attempted to dismiss the importance of the Sraffa–Robinson critique of neoclassical capital theory by claiming that they, too, were attacking a

* I am grateful for comments on an earlier draft from Giuseppe Fontana, John Foster, John Henry, Mike Howard, Peter Kriesler and Mark Setterfield, together with participants at the December 2005 conference of the Society of Heterodox Economists, University of New South Wales; they are not responsible for errors of fact or opinion. I am especially grateful to John Henry for presenting an abbreviated version of this chapter at the UMKC conference, in my absence.

straw man, in this case the aggregate production function version of the theory that had already been discarded by the more perceptive neoclassical theorists in favour of a disaggregated, Walrasian general equilibrium version that was not subject to the Cambridge critique (Hahn 1975). It eventually became clear that Hahn's argument was false in all essentials: the neoclassicals did not and probably could not dispense with the aggregate version of marginal productivity theory, and Walrasian economics itself was soon abandoned (see Harcourt 1976 on the first point, and Lavoie 1992, pp. 37–41 on the second). But Hahn did manage to throw a great deal of dust in the faces of several generations of students, and the straw man accusation was an important factor in the long-term mainstream neglect of the capital controversies (Cohen and Harcourt 2003).

Before I turn to the Bateman–Colander critique, I need to define 'heterodox macroeconomics'. In a recent review of my *Elgar Companion to Post Keynesian Economics* (King 2003), Michelle Baddeley complains that the book should have been called *The Elgar Companion to Heterodox Economics*: 'The label Post Keynesian is generally used far too loosely as a catch-all term for anything that is not mainstream economics' (Baddeley 2005, pp. 350–51). In this chapter I am open to the opposite charge, as in my opinion almost *all* short-period macroeconomic theory is Post Keynesian, of one sort or another (fundamentalist Keynesian, Kaleckian or Minskyan), since it relies on the principle of effective demand. This is obviously not true of long-period theory, where neo-Schumpeterian or evolutionary growth theory, and a variety of class-driven classical-Marxian models of capital accumulation, compete with Post Keynesian, demand-driven, models. Almost the only non-Post Keynesian short-period model worthy of consideration is the Goodwin trade cycle model, which hinges on fluctuations in the reserve army of the unemployed and consequent swings in the share of profits, and does not emphasise – though it is not inconsistent with – the existence of demand constraints on output and employment (Goodwin 1967). This model is ignored here, for reasons of space, as is the neo-Schumpeterian approach to short-period macroeconomics (Foster 1987, ch. 8).

As for other heterodox schools, outside the classical-Marxian ('radical', Sraffian) wing(s), their macroeconomics is largely an empty set. This is true of the *institutionalists*, who take their macroeconomic theory almost entirely from the Post Keynesians. It is also true of *green economists*, who are in some trouble as a result, since they have no convincing reply to the popular objection that a steady-state economy would be a depressed economy, with high and rising unemployment. There is as yet no distinctively *feminist* macroeconomics, despite some interesting work on the gender impact of differing macroeconomic policies – an interesting and important question, but not directly relevant for my present purposes. Finally, *Austrian* macroeconomics is either oxymoronic or pre-Keynesian (see Dow 1996).

On my interpretation, Post Keynesian macroeconomics arose in the course of the critique of Old Keynesian theory, often known as the 'neoclassical synthesis'. Old Keynesian theory had three crucial elements: the IS–LM model of real output and the rate of interest, and the Phillips curve model of wage inflation, which both relate to the short period; and the Solow growth model, which deals with the long period. (At this point I should stress that in this chapter, but not alas in King (2002), I use the Cambridge terms 'short period' and 'long period', *not* the mainstream terms 'short run' and 'long run'. This is not pedantry; there are good methodological reasons for it, as will be seen in the third section). The Post Keynesian critique of the neoclassical synthesis was subsequently extended to monetarism and new classical macroeconomics, and, as already noted, is generally adopted by other heterodox schools when they turn to macroeconomic questions. In my view it remains valid, necessary and important.

According to Bateman all this might have been true 40 years ago, but it is no longer the case. To support his 'straw man' accusation, Bateman cites only one source, George Akerlof's (2002) Nobel Prize acceptance speech, published under the title 'Behavioral macroeconomics and macroeconomic behavior'. Some of the 'macroeconomic problems' that Akerlof discusses are not macroeconomic at all, and arguably not problems either ('the prevalence of undersaving for retirement' and 'the stubborn persistence of a self-destructive [black] underclass'). For the rest, he focuses on the causes of price and wage stickiness, with the implication that without such stickiness there would *be* no macroeconomic problems. Akerlof's explanation of involuntary unemployment centres on efficiency wage theory, and in particular his 'favourite version' of it, insider–outsider theory. Now there is one sense (a microeconomic sense) in which efficiency wage theory is undeniably true: it has been known at least since Adam Smith that high wages can cause high productivity, and the English railway-building magnate Thomas Brassey wrote a book on the 'efficiency of high wages', as it was then known, well over a century ago (Brassey 1874). But this is not a replacement for the Keynesian principle of effective demand, and it does not seem to have any obvious implications for macroeconomic policy. The insider–outsider variant of efficiency wage theory does have policy implications, however, and they are objectionable: 'empowerment of outsiders' by means of union-bashing and labour market deregulation (Lindbeck and Snower 1988). This has nothing to do with macroeconomics, behavioural or otherwise. And it is not clear from his Nobel speech that Akerlof has a coherent macroeconomics of any description. Where is his theory of investment expenditure, to take one (very important) example?

If there is little evidence in Akerlof's article of an emerging school of 'behavioural macroeconomics', perhaps such evidence can be located in the work of David Colander, from his initial writings on 'Post Walrasian' economics (Colander 1996) or his more recent advocacy of 'cutting-edge' economics? I shall come back to 'Post Walrasian' economics in the third section, since it raises an important methodological issue. As for the 2004 book of interviews with economists at the 'cutting edge', there is really very little on macroeconomics. The very detailed 24-page index has no references to 'accumulation', 'capital', 'growth' or 'inflation', and the one reference to unemployment is a brief mention (by Deirdre McCloskey) of the pernicious effects of minimum wages – a quintessentially microeconomic question. McCloskey and Kenneth Arrow express their 'bemusement' at the very idea of macroeconomics (McCloskey 2004, p. 28) or simple incomprehension (Arrow 2004, p. 301: 'I've never understood macro'!); the remaining interviewees simply ignore it. There is one very interesting exception: Duncan Foley, who would be claimed by many heterodox economists as one of their own, admits to rather liking the 'Keynesian cross' diagram (Foley 2004, p. 183) and writes at some length on the need to combine post-classical analysis with chaos theory. Foley, too, will feature in the third section. But the overall impression from these interviews is the absence of any emerging school of 'behavioural macroeconomics'.

In the remainder of this chapter I begin with the short period, setting out the 'new consensus' macroeconomic model that has dominated mainstream thinking since the mid-1990s, and suggest that this is merely a somewhat improved version of the Old Keynesian theory of the 1950s and 1960s. Next I discuss two important methodological issues, the role of 'microfoundations' and the way in which the short period is distinguished from the long period; in both respects, I argue, mainstream theorists have if anything gone backwards, not forwards, in recent decades. I then turn to long-period analysis, contrasting the supply-driven mainstream models of so-called 'new growth theory' with two types of heterodox analysis, the demand-driven Post Keynesian models and the class-driven classical-Marxian models of capital accumulation; my conclusion is that current mainstream theory does not constitute a great advance over the neoclassical growth theory of the 1950s and 1960s. Following this there is a brief discussion of macroeconomic policy and of (post-) Washington Consensus development policy, which again show little sign of 'behavioural' influences. I conclude that the accusation that heterodox critics have been attacking a 'straw man' is false.

THE 'NEW CONSENSUS' ABOUT THE SHORT PERIOD

There is unlikely to be too much disagreement about the 'new consensus' model of the short period. My exposition draws heavily on the excellent keynote address by Charles Goodhart at the 2004 Treviso conference of the European Society for the History of Economic Thought (Goodhart 2004), supplemented by a 1996 American Economic Association symposium on the 'core of usable macroeconomics' (Blanchard 1997; Solow 1997; Taylor 1997). I have also drawn selectively from Michael Woodford's monumental (785-page) *Interest and Prices* (2003), which is likely to prove canonical; it has recently been awarded the honour of a 14-page review in the *Journal of Economic Literature* (Green 2005) and a symposium in the *Journal of the History of Economic Thought* (June 2006, pp. 139–98).

The 'new consensus' model has just three equations. The first is an aggregate demand curve making real output a negative function of the rate of interest; this is the old IS curve slightly reconfigured. The second is a downward-sloping short-run Phillips curve, making the inflation rate a negative function of the output gap (itself closely and positively related to the unemployment rate). The novelty lies with the third equation, which replaces the LM curve and makes the real short-run interest rate a positive function of the (expected) inflation rate; this is the 'Taylor rule' for monetary policy. Heterodox economists may not much like the first two equations, but will perhaps admit that the alternatives are worse (would you prefer a vertical aggregate demand curve, with output always at the full employment level? Or a vertical short-run Phillips curve, with the actual and 'natural' unemployment rates always equal?). This does not preclude them from pointing out that neither function is likely to be stable over space or time, with uncertainty (in the first case) and social conflict (in the second) being neglected in the mainstream account. Heterodox theorists can take some pleasure from the third equation, which incorporates the Post Keynesian claims that money is endogenous and that the monetary authorities can at best control interest rates, not the stock of money (Kaldor 1970), and also acknowledges the important methodological principle that macroeconomic theory must be historically and socially specific (Hodgson 2001) – the Taylor rule would have been unthinkable before central bankers abandoned their monetarist illusions, and reasserted their 'independence', in the late 1980s. Subject to this (considerable) improvement, the 'new consensus' model is very similar to the 'neoclassical synthesis' that dominated mainstream macroeconomics in the 1950s and 1960s, and does not appear to be 'behavioural' in any important way.

These conclusions can be confirmed by reference to Woodford, whose avowed intention is to produce 'a new "neoclassical synthesis"' (Woodford 2003, p. 6; this is the heading of section 1.1 of the book). Unlike the old one, Woodford's neoclassical synthesis is explicitly derived from an intertemporal general equilibrium model with rational expectations. He is duly respectful to new classical macroeconomics, and even has kind things to say about 'real business cycle' theory (ibid., p. 8; it was a real struggle for me to decide where to put the inverted commas around this expression). Price and wage stickiness is fundamental to Woodford's analysis, for without it his conclusions would be entirely new classical. He takes this stickiness for granted ('an institutional fact, just like the available production technology') and makes no attempt to provide a 'behavioural' explanation for it (ibid., p. 6). Woodford endorses the marginal productivity theory of distribution, and his book is replete with references to Knut Wicksell and the 'natural rate of interest', but without Wicksell's well-known reservations about neoclassical capital theory and without any effort being made to deal with the paradoxes of reswitching and capital reversal. His own 'unobtrusive postulate' (compare Pasinetti 1969, pp. 519–22) is the assumption of 'complete financial markets', which sneaks in almost without comment (p. 64). As Charles Goodhart explains, what Woodford is assuming here is that every conceivable future state of the world is already known, probabilistically, and has been priced; there can be no genuine surprises, now or until the end of time. In particular, there can be no question of default. 'In such a system it is not clear why either money, or banks, or other financial intermediaries should exist' (Goodhart 2004, p. 8).

This last assumption is by itself enough to discredit the 'new consensus' in the eyes of heterodox economists of all persuasions, and to dispel any doubts about the autistic (rather than 'behavioural') nature of mainstream theory. There are many other objections. First, it is ironic that neoclassical microeconomists have pretty well abandoned general equilibrium theory while their macroeconomic cousins continue to rely upon it (I shall make more of this point in the next section). Second, price and wage stickiness is not the fundamental problem; is probably to be welcomed, since deflation brings a crop of macroeconomic difficulties with it and has to be seen as part of the problem rather than as the solution; and at any rate needs to be explained rather than being taken for granted. (In this respect, at least, Akerlof is on the right side.) Third, this cannot be done without serious consideration of uncertainty and the institutions that have been created in order to deal with it, and without allowing for the existence of surprise (Shackle 1955). Fourth, the marginal productivity theory of distribution was shown by the Cambridge controversies of the 1960s to be irreparably damaged, and needs to be replaced by one or more of the heterodox alternatives (class conflict; differential savings propensities and the rate of capital accumulation; the degree of monopoly; the money rate of interest). Fifth, there is nothing 'natural' about the rate of interest. And so on, and so on.

My conclusion is that in substance the 'new consensus' short-period model is not greatly different from the old-fashioned neoclassical synthesis; it is better in some respects and worse in others, and certainly not at all 'behavioural'. In terms of methodology, however, it is appreciably worse, as will now be demonstrated.

A METHODOLOGICAL INTERLUDE

This is intended to be a rather humble, low-key section. It contains no attack on 'positivism', 'ergodicity' or the logical basis of econometrics, and no endorsement (or rejection) of critical realism. All I want to do here is to identify two problems with mainstream macroeconomic methodology. The first is the relentless search for 'microfoundations', and the second is the basis of the distinction between short- and long-run analysis.

As far as the quest for microfoundations is concerned, there has been a significant shift in mainstream thinking since the 1970s, when it was a *project* (see Harcourt 1977 for the proceedings of the S'Agora conference, where this is made very clear). Now it is a *dogma*, which dominates theory-construction and overrides common sense: 'After gathering strength for some decades, the micro-economists ventured forth to reclaim the entire subject . . . Macroeconomics has practically been swallowed up. Even the term has been surplused in some circles, and sold second-hand to a sub-discipline concerned with statistical analysis of econometric time series' (Galbraith 2005, pp. 1–2). I offer three pieces of evidence in support of this interpretation, all drawn from recent sources. First, in his Schumpeter lectures Duncan Foley interrupts a very interesting discussion of classical theories of accumulation to *apologise* for not having provided microfoundations (Foley 2003, p. 30; the paragraph is headed 'caveat lector'). Second, Michel de Vroey seems, to one careful reviewer, to deny the existence of involuntary unemployment on the grounds that it is inconsistent with rational choice theory: money would be left on the table if someone were willing to work at or below the existing real wage but was unable to find a job (De Vroey 2004; Lodewijks 2005). Finally, while the first two-thirds of Olivier Blanchard's new analysis of European unemployment is macroeconomic and almost Post Keynesian in spirit, linking low unemployment to successful wage-fixing arrangements that preserve the rate and share of corporate profits in a way that John Cornwall might admire, the final third is entirely microeconomic, focusing on mismatch between unemployed workers and (non-existent) job vacancies and ignoring aggregate demand altogether (Blanchard 2005). If reality and mainstream theory are in conflict, it is better to deny the reality lest the theory come into question!

On this issue, Akerlof's 'behavioural macroeconomics' does indeed represent an improvement. David Colander, however, has gone backwards since 1996, when he argued (admittedly in rather vague terms) for the 'macrofoundations of microeconomics': 'The Post Walrasian perspective maintains that before there is any hope of undertaking meaningful micro analysis, *one must first determine the macro context within which that micro decision is made*' (Colander 1996, p. 61; original stress). Money, in particular, 'is part of the macrofoundational structure of the economic system, and must be modelled as such' (ibid., p. 62). Thus the Post Walrasian approach 'encompasses the Keynesian perspective' (ibid., p. 57). There is not much left of this in the 2004 book, where one of the 'cutting-edge' interviewees, Robert Axtell suggests that macroeconomics will become 'the main casualty' of the new agent-based analysis, 'as we can stuff the machine full of agents who are behaving in some boundedly rational way, behaviourally richer way' (Axtell 2004, p. 285). For Axtell, this is 'a new way to do macroeconomics'; to me, it seems more like the euthanasia of the discipline.

The microfoundations dogma provides a very good case study in the pitfalls of reductionism in the philosophy of science. It eliminates macroeconomics altogether by denying the 'fallacy of composition' or 'emergent properties' principles upon which any serious macroeconomic theory relies. (To take one example: Kalecki's statement that 'workers spend what they get, while capitalists get what they spend' is *only* true in the aggregate; any capitalist who behaves as if it applies to him will soon suffer the fate of the late Robert Maxwell, or Conrad Black.) Reductionism is a dangerous strategy for mainstream economists, since there is absolutely no reason why one should stop at the level of the (human) individual. Why not go back even further, to the gene (Dawkins 1991) or the subatomic particle (Wilson 1998)? David Colander was surely right in 1996: we need macrofoundations for microeconomics much more than we need the converse. Perhaps we should abandon architectural metaphors as unhelpful and misleading, and simply accept that while consistency between micro and macro explanations would be pleasing it is not always attainable; successful theorising, like happy marriage, calls for compromise (Chick 2002).

The second methodological question is a little more subtle. Cambridge Post Keynesians like Joan Robinson, Richard Kahn and Geoff Harcourt usually distinguish the 'long period' from the 'short period', rather than using the mainstream terminology that contrasts the 'long run' with the 'short run'. I'm not sure that they do this consistently, and they tend not to explain why they bother. I used to think that this was a trivial question for linguistic pedants, but I now realise that I was wrong. In the Cambridge tradition, which goes back through Keynes to Alfred Marshall, the short period is that in which capacity is fixed. In the long period, by contrast, capacity is variable but (since 1936, at least) there is no presumption that it is fully utilised. Thus both short- and long-period output and employment can be, and probably are, demand-constrained. Keynes's analysis in *The General Theory* was deliberately restricted to the short period, but this was done purely as a simplifying assumption; establishing the savings–investment relationship was difficult enough, without having also to deal with capital accumulation. He was criticised for this by both opponents and allies, Pigou (1936) for example complaining that it was inconsistent to have positive net investment and a constant capital stock and Michal Kalecki (1939) making a famous reference to the 'tragedy of investment', which had been neglected by Keynes. Joan Robinson (1956) intended her *Accumulation of Capital* as 'a generalisation of the *General Theory*' to meet these objections. The crucial point is that none of the Cambridge Keynesians (with the occasional exception of Nicholas Kaldor) maintained that the effective demand problems that characterised the short period were absent in the long period; they simply had to be analysed in a more general and therefore more satisfactory way.

But this is precisely what mainstream macroeconomists do contend: unlike the short run, where aggregate demand fluctuates, and may be important, the long run is a sort of magic kingdom in which all markets clear and there is full employment (of labour and capital), the Phillips curve is vertical at the 'natural rate' of unemployment, output and employment are always supply-constrained, and there is no problem of effective demand. There is no indication of a new, improved 'behavioural macroeconomics' here. Taking a long view, there is on the contrary clear evidence of theoretical retrogression. The magic kingdom view of the long run really begins with the 1956 Solow growth model; before then, the Harrod–Domar theory of capital accumulation allowed for the possibility that the warranted rate of growth might fall short of the natural rate of growth, and the actual growth rate might be lower than either. Only in what Robinson called, with deliberate irony, a 'golden age' would everything be for the best in the best of all possible worlds. As with the question of microfoundations, so with the treatment of the long period: mainstream macroeconomics has gone backwards in recent decades, and there is no sign whatever of a 'behavioural' correction.

To repeat: these are *methodological* questions, not empirical ones. They *precede* theory construction, and determine the ways in which evidence is collected and assessed. This is (almost) obvious with the issue of microfoundations. It is less obvious, but equally true – and even more important – with the short-period/long-period versus short-run/long-run dichotomy, as will be demonstrated in the next section.

THE LONG PERIOD: 'NEW GROWTH THEORY'

It is helpful to begin with a short excursion into the history of economic thought. The Solow growth model was devised as a solution to the problem of 'knife-edge' instability in the Harrod–Domar model: stability (and full employment) is restored by capital–labour substitution in response to changes in the relative prices of labour and capital, given a well-behaved aggregate production function. Solow introduced into the analysis the neoclassical principle of diminishing returns, which was missing from Harrod–Domar. In both models, though, technical change is exogenous, determining what Harrod unwisely termed the 'natural' rate of growth, and shifting the production function upwards in Solow's analysis.

Nicholas Kaldor, convinced of the truth of the Cambridge capital critique, tried to eliminate 'capital' altogether from his growth model, replacing the neoclassical production function with a 'technical progress function' linking the rate of growth of labour productivity to the rate of growth of investment. This had the effect of endogenizing technical change. Kaldor subsequently discovered Verdoorn's law, linking the rate of growth of productivity to the rate of growth of output, which he interpreted, in the spirit of his old teacher Allyn Young, as evidence of dynamic increasing returns that contradicted the neoclassical insistence on diminishing returns. All this reinforced his scepticism concerning the relevance of equilibrium theorising, and his sympathy for Gunnar Myrdal's principle of cumulative causation. It seemed, to Kaldor, to have important implications for economic policy, both for the treatment of backward regions within the rich countries and for the global relations between North and South (on all this, see King 1994).

No single, coherent theory of growth emerged from Kaldor's rich but very unsystematic writings, and he was largely ignored by more orthodox economists. Indeed, there was a 20-year interlude between (roughly) 1965 and 1985 when growth theory all but vanished as a subject from the mainstream literature. It is ironic that, when interest in the subject revived, the Kaldorian themes of endogenous technical change and dynamic increasing returns were prominent – though Kaldor's contribution was rarely acknowledged. 'New' growth theory did, however, retain some of the weakest features of the Solow model, including the aggregate production function and the neoclassical theory of distribution. Crucially, 'it shares with its Solovian predecessor an unrelenting focus on the supply side as the wellspring of growth', with the role of demand being purely 'peripheral' (Setterfield 2003, p. 24). But

> The question of whether the natural growth rate is exogenous or endogenous *to demand*, and whether it is input growth that causes output growth or vice versa, lies at the heart of the debate between neoclassical growth economists on the one hand, who treat the rate of growth of the labour force and labour productivity as exogenous to the actual rate of growth, and economists in the Keynesian/post-Keynesian tradition, who maintain that growth is primarily demand-driven because labour force growth and productivity growth respond to demand growth, both foreign and domestic. (León-Ledesma and Thirlwall 2002, pp. 441–2) emphasis added.

Heterodox growth theorists are inclined to think in terms of 'Say's law in reverse', with demand creating its own supply. It follows that 'there is no such thing as an exogenously determined production frontier. The production frontier moves with each movement of the actual growth rate' (ibid., p. 452; see Dutt 2006 for some reservations on this point). There is a rich variety of Kaldorian, Kaleckian and other Post Keynesian models of economic growth (Setterfield 2002), together with Marxian, classical and Sraffian models that emphasise class conflict rather than effective demand but are not necessarily inconsistent with a demand-driven approach to the theory of capital accumulation and growth (see, for example, Pasinetti 1993; Kurz and Salvadori 1995; Laibman 1997). All these models are macroeconomic; none of them has any need for microfoundations, of either a new classical or a New Keynesian kind. These important long-period issues are not addressed by Akerlof, and it is far from clear that 'behavioural macroeconomics' has anything at all to add to this body of theory.

MACROECONOMIC POLICY

This will be a relatively brief section, since a full treatment of policy issues would require a much longer chapter. In addition, and with the exception of some discussion of development questions, international macroeconomics will be largely ignored.

On *monetary policy* I cannot detect, either in mainstream analysis of monetary policy or in the actual conduct of policy itself, any indication of a 'behavioural' turn. In the post-monetarist or 'monetarism Mark II' era, theory and policy are very closely aligned. There is one target (the inflation rate) and one instrument (the rate of interest). Heterodox macroeconomists have worries about both (Kriesler and Lavoie 2007). Quite apart from the case for output or employment targeting, there are concerns that asset price inflation is neglected and financial fragility overlooked, so that stock market and housing bubbles, and household and corporate debt, are not regarded as serious problems that need policy solutions. Taking a single-instrument approach to these problems is rather like trying to mend a watch with a sledgehammer: you will hit the part that you are aiming at, but there will also be considerable collateral damage. Alternative instruments are not difficult to identify, ranging from the (re-)introduction of direct controls and (non-prudential?) regulation of various types to more market-friendly measures like the differential asset-based reserve requirements suggested by Tom Palley (2004) as a means of preventing asset price bubbles. Where does 'behavioural macroeconomics' fit into this picture? A good question! One might expect some recognition of the fact that human behaviour is complex, especially where money is concerned, so that monetary policy needs to be quite complex too. I cannot see any sign of any such recognition to date.

The situation is even worse with respect to mainstream thinking on *fiscal policy*, where the Old Keynesian principle of 'functional finance' (Lerner 1943) has given way to the pre-Keynesian principle of 'sound finance', which is invariably interpreted as requiring balanced budgets in the short run and fiscal consolidation in the long run. The most amazing nonsense is presented in defence of 'fiscal sustainability' (see Burger 2003 for a telling but excessively restrained critique), and the fiscal implications of population ageing (for example) stand in urgent need of a systematic heterodox analysis (Doughney and King 2006). There is no evidence of successful 'behavioural macroeconomics' here.

One entire area of macroeconomic policy has disappeared completely from the mainstream agenda: *prices and incomes policy* is no longer taken seriously as an anti-inflationary instrument, and indeed is rarely discussed. It is probably too early for anyone to be sure whether this is a permanent phenomenon. Perhaps a serious revival of the inflation dragon would restore interest in non-deflationary alternatives to monetary policy as a means of slaying it. Alternatively, the continuing atrophy of trade unionism in many OECD countries may now provide a sufficient reason for neglecting wage bargaining as a macroeconomic problem, at least in the Anglo-Saxon countries. The Post Keynesian corporatism of the 1960s and 1970s seems rather dated now, but it did have the advantage of taking social conflict seriously; 'behavioural macroeconomics' does not.

On *development policy* there is, of course, a huge heterodox literature, attacking the Washington Consensus as the form in which neoliberalism has been applied to developing economies and questioning the so-called Post-Washington Consensus as a refined and somewhat softened version of the original, with an increased focus on poverty reduction and (supposedly) allowing for account to be taken of market imperfections (Fine and Jomo 2005). This raises two obvious questions: in what analytical sense is the Post-Washington Consensus an improvement? Was it the child of 'behavioural macroeconomics'? A further, slightly less obvious, question also arises. To what extent is the Post-Washington Consensus better than the original as *macroeconomics* (as distinct from the critically important, but essentially microeconomic, issues of income distribution and poverty reduction)? Priewe and Herr (2005) answer this question in the negative, stressing the neglect in the mainstream literature of demand and finance; they also identify and criticise an Alternative Washington Consensus, which displays similar weaknesses. They come to some rather orthodox conclusions concerning the need for fiscal and monetary probity in developing countries, and the importance of avoiding balance-of-payments deficits. But they do so for quite different reasons, emphasising demand instead of supply (investment and exports must not be crowded out, for they are the principal engines of economic growth), and advocate some distinctly heterodox policies (capital controls and – modest – levels of protection). Clearly another chapter could and should be written on these questions, and yet another on the international dimensions of macroeconomic policy more generally. It seems safe to conclude, however, that there is nothing really 'behavioural' about the macroeconomics – such as it is – of the Washington, Post-Washington or Alternative Washington Consensus.

On balance, there is little to show that either mainstream thinking on macroeconomic policy, or the policy itself, has changed for the better in recent years. If anything, the reverse is true. And there is little or no evidence that these changes have been the result of 'behavioural' macroeconomic theory.

CONCLUSION

I conclude that Bateman is wrong. Mainstream macroeconomics has not progressed very much in recent years, and where it has advanced it has been towards positions already established by heterodox (read: Post Keynesian) theorists. This is most obviously true in the case of endogenous money and the abandonment of the LM curve, but the (rather hesitant) incorporation of social conflict in the analysis of the unemployment–inflation nexus might also be considered a moral victory for the heterodox. In some important dimensions, however, mainstream theory has gone backwards, for example with the microfoundations dogma, the incredible assumption of complete financial markets, and the fiscal policy ineffectiveness doctrine.

Heterodox economists can therefore still profitably oppose:

1. the aggregate demand curve in the 'new consensus' model of the short period, for the reasons summarised in the second section;
2. the microfoundations dogma, as explained in the third section;
3. the mainstream treatment of the long period, as demonstrated in the third and fourth sections; and
4. many aspects of mainstream macroeconomic policy, as argued in the fifth section.

Some of these criticisms are new. Others were correctly made against the mainstream macroeconomics of the neoclassical synthesis, 40 years ago.

Thus the 'straw man' argument can be rejected. However, two problems continue to worry me. First, heterodox economists have yet to get to grips with the Stiglitz variant of mainstream macroeconomic theory, which is evidently different from, and almost certainly superior to, the Blanchard–Solow–Taylor–Woodford variety, and perhaps incorporates some of the useful insights of Akerlof's 'behavioural macroeconomics'. A good place for heterodox critics to start would be Stiglitz and Greenwald (2003). Second, there is always difficulty in working out what is moving ahead as 'cutting-edge' theory and what is heading straight for a dead end – 'revolutionary science' versus 'aberrant normal science', in Kuhnian terms. Perhaps, as both Kuhn and Joan Robinson believed, only the young are really capable of discerning the intellectual future (King and Millmow 2003; compare Kuhn 1962). On one point I am quite certain. If 'behavioural macroeconomics' is to succeed it will need a methodological revolution. Until then, it reminds me of what Mahatma Gandhi is supposed to have said about Western civilization: 'That sounds like a very interesting idea!'.

REFERENCES

Akerlof, G.A. (2002), 'Behavioral macroeconomics and macroeconomic behavior', *American Economic Review*, **92**(3), June, 411–33.

Arrow, K.J. (2004), 'Kenneth Arrow', in D. Colander et al. (eds) pp. 291–308.

Axtell, R. (2004), 'Robert Axtell and H. Peyton Young', in D. Colander et al. (eds), *The Changing Face of Economics*, Ann Arbor, MI: University of Michigan Press, pp. 251–90.

Baddeley, M. (2005), 'Review of King (2003)', *Journal of the History of Economic Thought*, **27**(3), September, 348–51.

Bateman, B.W. (2004), 'Review of King (2002)', *History of Political Economy*, **36**(3), Fall, 581–3.

Blanchard, O. (1997), 'Is there a core of usable macroeconomics?', *American Economic Review*, **87**(2), May, papers and proceedings, 244–6.
Blanchard, O. (2005), 'European unemployment: the evolution of facts and ideas', paper presented at the Australian Conference of Economists 2005 Conference, University of Melbourne, September.
Brassey, T. (1874), *Work and Wages*, London: G. Bell.
Burger, P. (2003), *Sustainable Fiscal Policy and Economic Stability: Theory and Practice*, Cheltenham, UK and Northampton, MA, USA: Edward Elgar.
Chick, V. (2002), 'Keynes's theory of investment and necessary compromise', in S.C. Dow and J.V. Hillard (eds), *Keynes, Uncertainty and the Global Economy: Beyond Keynes*, Vol. II, Cheltenham, UK and Northampton, MA, USA: Edward Elgar, pp. 55–67.
Cohen, A.J. and Harcourt, G.C. (2003), 'Retrospectives: whatever happened to the Cambridge capital controversies?', *Journal of Economic Perspectives*, **17**(1), Winter, 197–212.
Colander, D. (1996), 'The macrofoundations of micro', in Colander (ed.), *Beyond Microfoundations: Post Walrasian Macroeconomics*, Cambridge: Cambridge University Press, pp. 57–68.
Colander, D., Holt, R.P.F. and Rosser, J.B. Jr (eds) (2004), *The Changing Face of Economics: Conversations With Cutting Edge Economists*, Ann Arbor, MI: University of Michigan Press.
Dawkins, R. (1991), *The Blind Watchmaker*, London: Penguin.
De Vroey, M. (2004), *Involuntary Unemployment: The Elusive Quest for a Theory*, London: Routledge.
Doughney, J. and King, J.E. (2006), 'Crisis? What crisis? Myth and reality in the debate on an ageing Australia', *People & Place*, **14**(1), 65–74.
Dow, S.C. (1996), *The Methodology of Macroeconomic Thought: A Conceptual Analysis of Schools of Thought in Economics*, Cheltenham, UK and Brookfield, USA: Edward Elgar.
Dutt, A.K. (2006), 'Aggregate demand, aggregate supply and economic growth', *International Review of Applied Economics*, **20**(3), July, 319–36.
Fine, B. and Jomo, K.S. (eds) (2005), *The New Development Economics: Post Washington Consensus Neoliberal Thinking*, London: Zed.
Foley, D. (2003), *Unholy Trinity: Labor, Capital, and Land in the New Economy*, London: Routledge.
Foley, D. (2004), 'Duncan K. Foley', in D. Colander et al. (eds), pp. 183–214.
Foster, J. (1987), *Evolutionary Macroeconomics*, London: Allen & Unwin.
Galbraith, James K. (2005), 'Global inequality and global macroeconomics', paper presented at the Australian Conference of Economists 2005 Conference, University of Melbourne, September.
Goodhart, C.A.E. (2004), 'Money and social relationships', paper presented at the Conference of the European Society for the History of Economic Thought, Treviso, Italy, February.
Goodwin, R.M. (1967), 'A growth cycle', in C. Feinstein (ed.), *Socialism, Capitalism and Growth: Essays Presented to Maurice Dobb*, Cambridge: Cambridge University Press, pp. 54–8.
Green, E.J. (2005), 'A review of *Interest and Prices: Foundations of a Theory of Monetary Policy* by Michael Woodford', *Journal of Economic Literature*, **43**(1), March, 121–34.

Hahn, F.H. (1975), 'Revival of political economy: the wrong issues and the wrong argument', *Economic Record*, **51**(135), September, 360–64.
Harcourt, G.C. (1976), 'The Cambridge controversies: old ways and new horizons – or dead end?', *Oxford Economic Papers*, **28**(1), March, 25–65.
Harcourt, G.C. (ed.) (1977), *The Microeconomic Foundations of Macroeconomics: Proceedings of a Conference Held by the International Economic Association, at S'Agora, Spain*, Boulder, CO: Westview Press.
Hodgson, G.M. (2001), *How Economics Forgot History: The Problem of Historical Specificity in Social Science*, London: Routledge.
Kaldor, N. (1970), 'The new monetarism', *Lloyds Bank Review*, **97**, July, 1–18.
Kalecki, M. (1939), *Essays in the Theory of Economic Fluctuations*, London: Allen & Unwin.
King, J.E. (ed.) (1994), *Economic Growth in Theory and Practice: A Kaldorian Perspective*, Aldershot, UK and Brookfield, US: Edward Elgar.
King, J.E. (2002), *A History of Post Keynesian Economics Since 1936*, Cheltenham, UK and Northampton, MA, USA: Edward Elgar.
King, J.E. (ed.) (2003), *The Elgar Companion to Post Keynesian Economics*, Cheltenham, UK and Northampton, MA, USA: Edward Elgar.
King, J.E. and Millmow, A. (2003), 'Death of a revolutionary textbook', *History of Political Economy*, **35**(1), Spring, 105–34.
Kriesler, P. and Lavoie, M. (2007), 'The new view on monetary policy: the new consensus and its Post-Keynesian critique', *Review of Political Economy*, **19**(3), July, 387–404.
Kuhn, T.S. (1962), *The Structure of Scientific Revolutions*, Chicago, IL: University of Chicago Press.
Kurz, H.D. and Salvadori, N. (1995), *Theory of Production*, Cambridge: Cambridge University Press.
Laibman, D. (1997), *Capitalist Macrodynamics: A Systematic Introduction*, Basingstoke: Macmillan.
Lavoie, M. (1992), *Foundations of Post-Keynesian Economic Analysis*, Aldershot, UK and Brookfield, US: Edward Elgar.
León-Ledesma, M.A. and Thirlwall, A.P. (2002), 'The endogeneity of the natural rate of growth', *Cambridge Journal of Economics*, **26**(4), July, 441–59.
Lerner, A.P. (1943), 'Functional finance and the federal debt', *Social Research*, **10**(1), February, 38–51.
Lindbeck, A. and Snower, D.S. (1988), *The Insider–Outsider Theory of Employment and Unemployment*, Cambridge, MA: MIT Press.
Lodewijks, J. (2005), 'Review of De Vroey (2004)', *History of Economics Review*, **42**, Summer, 123–5.
McCloskey, D. (2004), 'Deirdre McCloskey', in D. Colander et al. (eds), pp. 27–48.
Palley, T.J. (2004), 'Asset-based reserve requirements: reasserting domestic monetary control in an era of financial innovation and instability', *Review of Political Economy*, **16**(1), January, 43–58.
Pasinetti, L.L. (1969), 'Switches of technique and the "rate of return" in capital theory', *Economic Journal*, **79**(315), September, 508–31.
Pasinetti, L.L. (1993), *Structural Economic Dynamics: A Theory of the Economic Consequences of Human Learning*, Cambridge: Cambridge University Press.
Pigou, A.C. (1936), 'Mr. J.M. Keynes's general theory of employment, interest and money', *Economica* n.s., **3**(10), May, 115–32.

Priewe, J. and Herr, H. (2005), *The Macroeconomics of Development and Poverty Reduction: Strategies Beyond the Washington Consensus*, Baden-Baden: Nomos.
Robinson, Joan (1956), *The Accumulation of Capital*, London: MacMillan, p. 69.
Setterfield, M. (ed.) (2002), *The Economics of Demand-led Growth: Challenging the Supply-side Vision of the Long Run*, Cheltenham, UK and Northampton, MA, USA: Edward Elgar.
Setterfield, M. (2003), 'Supply *and* demand in the theory of long-run growth: introduction to a symposium on demand-led growth', *Review of Political Economy*, **15**(1), January, 23–32.
Shackle, G.L.S. (ed.) (1955), 'The logic of surprise', in *Uncertainty in Economics and Other Reflections*, Cambridge: Cambridge University Press, pp. 56–62.
Solow, R.M. (1997), 'Is there a core of usable macroeconomics we should all believe in?', *American Economic Review*, **87**(2), May, papers and proceedings, 230–32.
Stiglitz, J. and Greenwald, B. (2003), *Towards a New Paradigm in Monetary Economics*, Cambridge: Cambridge University Press.
Taylor, J.B. (1997), 'A core of practical macroeconomics', *American Economic Review*, **87**(2), May, papers and proceedings, 233–5.
Wilson, E.O. (1998), *Consilience: The Unity of Knowledge*, New York: Knopf.
Woodford, M. (2003), *Interest and Prices: Foundations of a Theory of Monetary Policy*, Princeton, NJ: Princeton University Press.

2. Keynes the Keynesian: a Lakatosian insight into Keynes's 'probable' theoretical contributions to macroeconomics after 1937

Jesús Muñoz and Joel Bonales

INTRODUCTION

The purpose of this chapter is to identify the main issues arising from the legacy of Keynes after 1936 by analysing which directions he would have taken if he had continued generating economic science. Directions in this context mean the paths that would have been followed by Keynes for widening the theoretical constructs, and the predictive power of his theory after his initial vision as expressed in his work *The General Theory of Employment, Interest and Money*. The economic conditions of the main societies were rapidly changing in the aftermath of the Second World War and Keynes would have been aware of this fact.

It is necessary, thus, to classify these directions in terms of their priority and field, by assessing both their likely occurrence and their continuity, since the theoretical work of Keynes was almost sidelined after 1936. A perspective related to the philosophy of science may be taken for the purpose at hand. Imre Lakatos (1978) suggests the use of scientific research programs (SRPs) for classifying scientific structures in terms of clusters of theories. This method is convenient, since it entails a demarcation criterion which stresses both continuity in science and the role of falsification for distinguishing between scientific and non-scientific assessments or theories. SRPs also allow the discovery of the predictive power of the theories to be analysed, based on the detailed contents of those theories.

After the main Lakatosian concepts are described, in ensuing sections the core insights of Keynes's SRP that are expressed in *The General Theory of Employment, Interest and Money* (hereafter TGT) are identified. TGT is the last and most important work of Keynes as it is the first complete and comprehensive theory of income and employment determination by using a theory of monetary production and his vision of uncertainty in economic activity. In TGT, Keynes constructed the fundamental relationships behind macroeconomics. The purpose of this chapter is to investigate whether those directions would have changed his legacy after TGT by linking philosophical and economic issues.

This is a compilation chapter in the field of the history of economic thought from a methodological perspective. The next section on philosophy of science and methodology can be skipped by the specialised reader. The ensuing section describes the background of Keynes's writings to 1936. The next two sections are complementary and represent the focus of this chapter. The first identifies the 'probable' economic directions that Keynes would have followed after 1936, divided into three categories: (i) main directions – outstanding among them the concepts of uncertainty and economic equilibrium as a special case, (ii) other – secondary – paths and (iii) rejection of standard paths. The second is a Lakatosian-type interpretation of the scientific relevance of these 'probable' directions. The last section is an overall economic conclusion of the 'likely' widening of the work of Keynes after 1936 as proposed in this study.

METHODOLOGICAL INTRODUCTION

Science is clear, objective, rational, real, systematic and communicable knowledge about a field, which must be empirically tested *vis-à-vis* reality, and therefore possesses a dynamic character.

The goals of science are both explanation and prediction (Machlup, 1978). Both apriorism and ultraempiricism are epistemological extreme strands. According to apriorism, the abstraction of processes is the most relevant constituent of knowledge. According to ultraempiricism, both hypotheses and problem identification depart from observation. The distinction between these two approaches will allow the methodological assessment of the perspectives from which hypothesis formulation arises in the case of Keynes's macroeconomics.

Methodology is the 'study of logical principles useful for determining if certain proposals are accepted or rejected as valid constituents of the structure of scientific knowledge' (ibid., p. 490).

Karl Popper is an advocate of falsificationism, according to which a theory must be continuously tested, and discarded – at least partially – in the event of not being able to stand refutations. Hence, falsificationism may be the main determinant of progress in science.

Lakatos and Scientific Research Programmes

The underlying organising principle of theories is the interrelation of systems. For this purpose, the epistemological theories of two successors of Popper are mentioned. Thomas Kuhn proposes the methodology of paradigms (Kuhn, 1970), whereas Lakatos suggests that of scientific research programs (Lakatos, 1978).

Paradigms are dramatically different, organising world views or approaches to scientific thought in terms of problems and their solutions. In contrast, SRPs analyse theories in terms of their gradual advance. The Lakatosian methodology is hereby chosen since continuity in the Keynesian SRP is assessed. SRPs are also an explicit criterion for the detailed comparison of theories.

The first constituent of SRPs is the core, which is not subject to falsificationism by methodological principle. The second constituent is positive or negative heuristics or guidelines for the application of theories to be used throughout the research. The third constituent is the protective belt, which comprises the auxiliary assumptions of theories, which vary with respect to either time or place and are often expressed as parameters.

SRPs are either progressive or degenerative according to the success of replacement of its constituents, particularly of the core. Thus SRPs must be chosen if their new contributions contain either new theoretical or empirical prescriptions. In turn, replacement of some heuristics means that the essence of that theory has not been modified at all. Finally, the replacement of a protective belt only widens the extent of application of that theory, sometimes in an artificial manner.

The internal history of science is the rational reconstruction of the meaning of an SRP. The external history of science is the description of empirical facts within a field of research. Both consistency and refutation are the main criteria for accepting an SRP (Blaug, 1980).

If differences between two schools arise only from their cores, both schools are independent SRPs. If the differentiation arises only from specific parts of their cores, both schools are independents sub-SRPs. If deviations from an original SRP on the part of any school do not stem from their cores, these schools are just scientific movements away from the original SRP.

The next step is to describe Keynes's SRP for identifying its relation with his 'probable' macroeconomics after 1937.

BACKGROUND: KEYNES'S ISSUES UNTIL 1936

The Keynesian SRP is described in this section in Lakatosian terms. Keynes's research was based on the consideration of aggregate variables. In TGT, Keynes explained the determination of aggregate output and, as a consequence, of employment, which was his main scientific and practical concern. The novelty was that aggregate demand is the determining factor of national income.

Keynes also had a different view of money as a store of value and used this view to link the real sector with the monetary sector. Other related revolutionary concepts initiated by Keynes were: a demand-determined equilibrium wherein involuntary unemployment was possible; the ineffectiveness of price flexibility to cure unemployment; a theory of money based on liquidity preference; the introduction of uncertainty and expectations; the potential inequality between savings and investment; the downward rigidity of wages; the marginal efficiency of investment, which breaks Say's law (reversing the savings–investment classical causation); and the replacing of the quantity theory of money with the liquidity preference approach. His most relevant practical contribution refers to the possibility of using fiscal and monetary policy to increase output and employment. These concepts are the basis of the lack of sufficient self-regulation mechanisms on the part of the system to achieve full employment.

Keynes's issues can thus be classified into theoretical, empirical and policy related. They are divided into the constituents of an SRP in Table 2.1.

The most remarkable concept of TGT is that the system lacks a self-adjustment mechanism for returning to full employment after a shock. Moreover, the system can be in equilibrium without attaining full employment of resources. Either flexibility or rigidity of prices guarantees no equilibria.

'PROBABLE' DIRECTIONS OF KEYNES AFTER 1936

Table 2. 2 is a compilation of the most easily discussed issues of a hypothetical research programme for Keynes after 1936, alongside possible new directions not included in Keynes's TGT SRP, such as income distribution. These likely salient paths that Keynes would have followed are analysed in Table 2.2.

Analysis of 'Probable' Keynes Directions

There are more than 1000 interpretations of the message of TGT (Gerrard, 1991). It is widely acknowledged, however, that Keynes's vision lies in

Table 2.1 Keynes's actual SRP

Core		Positive heuristics		Protective belt
A different concept of behaviour. Men are not always rational. 'Animal spirits' exist	Intuition and conjectures are important	Use the principle of effective demand (demand > supply). An unstable demand exists	Study involuntary unemployment, alongside voluntary and frictional unemployment	A high and relatively constant propensity to consume
Market-clearing equilibrium is a special case, sub equilibria are permanent	Piecemeal arrangements	Consider the pivotal role of investment in the fluctuations of aggregate demand	Consider that saving and investment result from different behaviours, thus, could be unequal	Intermediate conditions prevail in economic life
Verificationist, positive and static method. Assumptions are relevant	Irreversibility exists alongside a unique nonergotic world (non repetitious)	Analyse the consumption function in aggregate terms	Analyse: $C = f(Y)$ $I = f(r)$ $M^D = f(Y)$ M^S = given, where: $Y = C+I+G+X–IM$ $M^D = M^S$ $L^D = L^S$	The quantity theory of $ is a special case of reality. M^S is given
Uncertainty and irrationality, imperfect information	Macroeconomics studies the determination of income and employment at aggregate level	Consider the 'finance motive'	Consider that uncertainty has a large impact on investment via expectations	Refutation of Say's law (supply generates its own demand)
Money is not a veil, is non-neutral	Dynamic role of the public sector	Emphasise the quantification of aggregate variables	Study decision-making processes under uncertainty	Idle economies (operating below full capacity)
Observation of facts	The fallacy of composition exists	Emphasise quantity adjustments		Sticky wages
The present is relevant	Both the actual and the virtual world matter	Study liquidity preference		Liquidity trap
		Divide the economy into markets: product, labour and money		Fixed exchange rates ($\hat{e}$)
				No auctioneer exists

Table 2.2 *Keynes's 'Probable' directions after TGT*

		Core	
Equilibrium and subequilibrium (self-adjustment properties)	Endogenous and interactive money	Uncertainty and expectations	Method: departing from diagnosis, arriving at solutions within the current framework
		Positive heuristics	
Short-term emphasis	The 'finance' motive	Involuntary unemployment	Growth
Risk	Savings ≠ Investment	Sticky wages	Cycles
Emphasis on the goods market	Open economy macroeconomics	Aggregate supply	Financial crises
Inflation	Interest rate	Distribution	
Emphasis on quantities	Investment		
		Protective belt	
Consumption	Assumptions on money demand	Role of government and institutions	Push–cost inflation
Marginal efficiency of investment	Labour market stickiness	Extensions to the roles of exports, imports and exchange rates	Assumptions on money supply

expectations and his method is a consequence of this 'vision'. There is no certainty in the system and equilibrium is a special case of the system. Accordingly, the most important 'probable' paths are the self-regulating properties of the economic system, uncertainty and expectations, inflation and the 'finance motive'.

This Lakatosian analysis suggests that Keynes would not have changed his stance in terms of the self-regulating properties of the system, as this issue is at the heart of his revolution. Otherwise he would have accepted the classical results and macroeconomics would have not been born, as this science is an insight into the 'fallacy of composition' as opposed to microeconomics, which assumes in an aprioristic manner that full employment is the rule. For him the theory of effective demand would always be the theory for output as a whole.

Short term → speculators → money demand (M^d)

Short term → producers → effective demand

Long term → entrepreneurs → investment

Figure 2.1 Impact of uncertainty and expectations

The focus of Keynes on uncertainty and expectations is ubiquitous in TGT and is expressly addressed in Keynes (1937b). In his analysis outlined in the chapter 'The Heresies of John Maynard Keynes' of his book *The Worldly Philosophers*, Heilbroner states that '[u]ncertainty, not assurance, lays at the very core of capitalism' (1951 [1980], p. 275). For authors such as O'Donnell and Skidelsky this is the main feature of the Keynesian revolution. If uncertainty exists in both investment and the money market, it encourages savings (especially in liquid form) and therefore generates depressions according to standard Keynesian theory. Therefore, Keynes would have improved and quantified his treatment of expectations, where uncertainty is a non-measurable risk (Figure 2.1).

Inflation, a path initially researched by Keynes in his 1937 article in the *Quarterly Journal of Economics*, but anticipated in TGT, has proven to be as dangerous as depression in modern economies and especially in emerging economies. Keynes would have widened his exploration of that direction. Although he preferred to focus on depressions, he 'surely' would have balanced his position in view of the new inflationary situation, and his ability to be ahead of his time. According to Skidelsky (1992, p. 116), 'Keynes himself would have said – in fact he did say – that at full employment any exogenous injection of demand leads to inflation'. By researching inflation, Keynes would also have provided a more complete theory of prices.

The key role of the 'finance motive' (TGT) is justified by the fact that new financial institutions and instruments exist, as borrowers are different from lenders. This issue is related to money demand (the fourth motive for holding money) and investment. Whereas investment has psychological roots, saving is a consequence of investment and has monetary roots, but it is determined by income. Investment is as volatile as human nature, and it certainly determines both income and employment. This path has been followed by both Davidson and Minsky (in his fragility hypothesis) as surely would have been followed by Keynes.

Other Paths

Modern finance theory is based on risk. The main impact of risk is on investors both in the industrial and in the financial sectors. Keynes would also have conducted research on equity finance. This is a consequence of the acknowledgement of the existence of 'animal spirits', or, for example, speculators in either forward or futures markets, whose existence was envisaged by Keynes before 1936.

Failures in capital markets bring about failures in the overall economy. This is a consequence of the reality of unstable investment (the hypotheses of financial transparency and the 'original sin' – of inherited external debt – in collapsing emerging economies). The analysis in Chapter 12 of TGT allows us to infer that a reduction of investment due to either 'bubbles' in financial markets or pessimistic expectations is at the heart of recessions. So a 'probable' direction would have been research on financial crises. The emphasis of Keynes after the Second World War would have been on the financial sector, most surely with a wider conception of money and its substitutes. Investment is also of course at the heart of the performance of domestic economies and especially of that of employment. Investment is the key for industrialisation and only industrialised economies – or regions or sectors – have solved the problem of unemployment in capitalist economies (before capitalism, unemployment was unknown). Hence the insight on the necessary 'socialisation' of investment would have been deepened by Keynes.

On the key role of investment in the stabilisation of economies, according to Skidelsky, '[t]he point is that the effects of a Keynesian policy depend on expectations' (1992, p. 555). And if investment depends on uncertainty and expectations, 'the instability of investment demand emerges as a crucial factor in economic fluctuations' (ibid.). Controlling investors leads to controlling recessions. If interest rates are to be raised by means of a tightening monetary policy, investment (and consequently aggregate demand) must increase rather than the demand for money. This is not clear here. Tighter money should increase r and lead to a decrease on money demand and a decrease in investment according to conventional interpretation.

Neither his dichotomy between savers and investors, nor his theory of the interest rate, would have been modified by Keynes after 1936, because, in his words, 'the rate of interest' is 'the inducement not to hoard' (Keynes, 1937a, p. 110), rather than the incentive for saving as it was considered to be in the classical SRP. Keynes was (perhaps) an exogenous money person, but he would have become an endogenous money person. He was taking money as given in TGT, but this consideration was part of his protective belt.

For some economists, Chapter 19 of TGT (related to changes in money wages) is the apex of TGT. Keynes thought that unlike in the classical system, downward wage stickiness was necessary to ensure that money retained its special characteristics and not to solvable institutional arrangements. Actually, Keynes said that nominal wage increases differ from real wage increases, so that if Keynes had analysed inflation after 1936 he would have produced further insights about the labour market. His heuristics was based on the goods markets as his main concern at that time was depressions. In addition, money wage flexibility does not solve the problem of depression as stated in TGT. These paths would have been continued by Keynes.

On the other hand, Keynes would probably have widened both his consumption and his preference for liquidity functions, because of the 'finance motive'. Larger industrial societies are more linked to finance. No preconceptions would have been held by Keynes about the types of unemployment in industrial societies, but he would always have acknowledged the concept of involuntary unemployment.

Rejection of Standard Paths

The story of other paths such as income distribution, growth, aggregate supply, microfoundations and open economy macroeconomics seems to 'have been' rather different. Distribution is superficially mentioned in the last chapter of TGT, and this direction was followed by Nicholas Kaldor, Joan Robinson, and Michal Kalecki. Keynes assumed that it was constant just as was the marginal propensity to consume, but he would have extended his theory to other economies, a path which might be difficult to believe, given his interest in Western Europe and the United States. Distribution is clearly worse in depressed economies. Keynes would have changed his interests to include pure development (growth and income distribution). Hints of this direction appear in the last chapter of TGT. An unfair distribution for him was linked to the savings structures and the interest rate.

Concerning growth and aggregate supply, we paraphrase Skidelsky, 'Keynesian growth policy seemed to be what was left when plentiful supply, protectionism and obsolete ideologies were removed from the picture' (Skidelsky, 1997, p. 115). Keynes would have realised that no gulf would have existed between dynamic and static macroeconomics. He was concerned by the latter issue as this was at the heart of economic ills, and sufficient for his demonstration of unemployment equilibrium.

The path of microfoundations would not have been chosen by Keynes as it contradicts his message in TGT. He would probably, however, have made contributions to microeconomics. Nor had he been interested in imperfect competition. His interest in markets would have continued to be restricted to their impact on macroeconomic problems. The benign times prevailing in the 19th century were already past. Further, he had a clear idea of the formation of policies for fighting depressions. As Milton Friedman said, the only proof of relevance of microfoundations to macroeconomics is their empirical test.

Open economy macroeconomics is the most extensive field for research, especially since 1945. Keynes would have been interested in the trade balance, widening his analysis of income determination. Nevertheless he would have shifted from fixed exchange rates to flexible rates, just as he advocated flexible rates rather than the blind adherence to the gold standard. This is due to both the evolution of international finance and his speed of thought. Keynes would have become an innovator in international finance, as Skidelsky states, 'Keynes was the first to realize and state clearly that an overvalued currency would be a weak, not a strong currency' (1987, p. 26).

Keynes is a great monetary economist, and 'even his substantial contributions to international economics, dealt largely with the financial and monetary aspects' (Minsky, 1975, p. 1). Several economists before Keynes and some of his contemporaries are generally considered to have made major pioneering contributions to this area, for example, Wicksell and Knut Fisher. Keynes is a great monetary economist in the sense that he linked the real and the monetary sectors, which in Walras, were for instance, separate entities as money was a veil. Keynes linked the monetary and the real sectors, via the role of interest rates which after being determined by the money market – rather than in the capital market – negatively affect investment, thereby generating uncertainty and modifying the equilibrium in the products market. For Keynes, liquidity preference affects overall equilibrium.

Finally, the work of Mundell on the inclusion of the *BP* line into the IS–LM scheme and his consideration of the uses of policies is strictly Keynesian, so that Keynes would have accepted Mundell's theoretical addition to John Hicks's framework.

RELEVANCE OF 'PROBABLE' DIRECTIONS: A LAKATOSIAN ANALYSIS

The issue is whether the Keynesian SRP would have changed as the original one (until 1936) would have not been able to predict novel facts. In Kuhn's terms, we could investigate whether the paradigm represented by TGT could be superseded by a new paradigm.

Keynes would have not created a new paradigm when analysing these directions along the lines taken by the neoclassical synthesis, for instance.

The explanation of the functioning of the macroeconomy by Hicks recognises TGT only as a special case, destroying Keynes's vision of a general theory. Likewise the main message of the neoclassical synthesis takes many points of the classical economists and attempts to provide microfoundations for macroeconomics.

Keynes would not have changed his core after 1936, as it was outlined in TGT. According to the discussions above, the main constituent of his core is the lack of self-regulating properties on the part of the system. In addition, in Keynes's core, time was considered in a historic rather than a logical perspective. His picture of human nature was accurate in the sense that men were considered by him as not always behaving rationally, and money – the main institution in economics – was non-neutral in terms of its effect on real sector developments. These views actually determined his discovery of macroeconomics. Furthermore, Keynes would have not modified his core after 1936 as it defined his method for conducting action, since it enhanced quantitative – refined – research on the part of both policy makers and theorists.

Keynes would have 'stuck' to his theories, which explained new observations as well as the functioning of newly expanding aggregate markets. The most outstanding example of a growing market is the financial market, a subject in which Keynes was a continuous innovator.

Although he was focused on international finance at the end of his life, he would have paid attention to domestic finance developments, especially in developed countries. After all, the acknowledgement of heterogeneity and instability in modern financial systems – the core of globalisation – is a proof of Keynes's vision.

Keynes would only have strengthened his original message, providing new heuristics and changing his protective belt, thereby creating a scientific movement away from the views expressed in TGT. This statement is based on the acceptance of his core novelties. His legacy has been accepted by posterity, and he would not have challenged this intellectual capital.

It can also be said by following the history of Keynes's macroeconomics after February 1936 that Keynes's SRP is able to stand refutations at least on most core issues. Therefore macroeconomics is a formal science, as it allows both internal history reconstruction and external history refutations. Whereas reconstruction has accepted Keynes as its benchmark, refutations to Keynes's theory have always been to either heuristic or protective belt-related issues. *The General Theory* has withstood refutations since 1936.

A caveat to the former reasoning on the soundness of the 'probable' Keynes SRPs after TGT is that geniuses sometimes return to the path followed in their youth. There is no corroborating evidence to support this hypothesis, but Keynes's mind was unpredictable as well as improving and consistent. Speed of thought is not the opposite of either consistency or accuracy. The details of a comprehensive work are irrelevant, although they appear in the short term as changes in cores. This is true for the work of Keynes. Another caveat is that Keynes was a weak verificationist (Skidelsky, 2001), but he would have changed in this sense, too.

CONCLUSIONS

Keynes's legacy can be assessed from the analytical (including policies), quantitative and political perspectives. These classifications help us to understand his essential issues and to infer conclusions about their evolution.

Intellectuals often have a vision, which not only illuminates the present or the past, but anticipates the future. Keynes is among the latter. According to the editorial introduction to Volume VII, *CW* (1973a), which is an edition of TGT, it is impossible to predict the state of the revisions of TGT if Keynes had enjoyed good health, but we can be certain that he would have revised TGT.

According to the three sections above, Keynes would not have changed his core after 1936. The roots of his revolution were already sown. We also have methodological support for this statement. However, Keynes would have widened his positive heuristic with new assumptions or would have launched new hypotheses. No new Keynesian revolution would have arisen. However, alternative methodological analyses are necessary to confirm this statement. SRPs are a useful methodological device. Nevertheless, SRPs are not unique, nor are they exhaustive or perfect. The use of analyses in the field of the history of economic thought for analysing the probable Keynesian paths discussed in this chapter is required to complement this study. In fact, this is a theme in the history of economic thought, where the past can illuminate our insights into the future.

The alternative pattern is that he would have become a conservative since he was a dissident in 1936 and a conservative before the publication of TGT. In this second scenario, however, his ideas would finally have become part of the orthodoxy. Moreover, the world after the Second World War was certainly different, just as the times of TGT were different from those of the *Treatise*. It can be said that the study of interrelations among aggregates would have become the main components of Keynes's scheme after 1936–37. Finally, there are (compromise) views. For example, according to Pasinetti, '[a] Keynesian "revolution", in the strict sense of the word, might as yet remain unaccomplished' (Pasinetti, 1997, p. 13). This may be a highly general statement. It can be argued that most of Keynes's issues were demonstrated once and for all in 1936.

Keynes would have ended up creating new 'visions' but in other fields of economics – probably in finance – not necessarily in terms of additions to his macroeconomics of 1936. Alternatively, he would have widened his original vision of TGT. A change of vision is accepted forever. He would never have returned to the 'classical' world. The economic situation prevailing in the 19th century was a special case in the history of humankind, just as equilibrium is a special case of theory.

Keynes presented a novel view of the economic system. Keynes's vision enhanced empirical research in economics. The three main aggregate markets envisaged by Keynes face uncertainty. These issues would never have returned to their original form. The pre-eminent role of finance in the economies of the 21st century validates this conclusion. According to this discussion, Keynes was far ahead of his time in his forward 'vision' in 1936.

The novelty of this chapter lies in that whereas authors such as Blaug (1978) use the methodology of SRPs, they do not analyse the future or 'probable' Keynesian SRP after 1937. On the other hand, other authors such as Thirlwall (1999) or Harcourt (2001) have analysed 'probable' contributions by Keynes under different scenarios, but not from methodological (Lakatosian or otherwise) perspectives. The use of the Lakatosian perspective was also undertaken here in order to avoid undertaking either historical or plain speculative analyses on the future of the Keynesian SRP. In addition, the philosophical perspective used in this chapter adds an interdisciplinary scope to the assessment of the legacy of Keynes. With regard to new directions of research in these terms, it would also be interesting to analyse in methodological terms how the work of those who identified themselves as Keynesians immediately after the publication of TGT differed from the work of Keynes in 1936, or the cores of the actual successors of Keynes.

REFERENCES

Blaug, M. (1978), *Economic Theory in Retrospect*, 3rd edn, Cambridge: Cambridge University Press.

Blaug, M. (1980), *The Methodology of Economics, or How Economists Explain*, Cambridge: Cambridge University Press.

Gerrard, B. (1991), 'Keynes's General Theory. Interpreting the interpretations', *Economic Journal*, **101**, 272–87.

Harcourt, G.C. (2001), *50 Years a Keynesian and Other Essays*, Basingstoke: Palgrave.

Heilbroner, R.L. (1951 [1980]), *The Worldly Philosophers*, 5th edn, New York: Simon & Schuster.

Hicks, J.R. (1937), 'Mr. Keynes and the "classics", a suggested interpretation', *Econometrica*, **5**, 147–59.

Hicks, J.R. (1974), *The Crisis in Keynesian Economics*, Oxford: Blackwell.
Kalecki, M. (1936), 'Some remarks on Keynes's *General Theory*', *Ekonomista*, **3**, 18–26.
Keynes, J.M. (1923), *A Tract on Monetary Reform*, in *Collected Writings of J.M. Keynes (CW)*, Vol. 4, London: Macmillan.
Keynes, J.M. (1931), *Essays in Persuasion*. New York: Harcourt Brace.
Keynes, J.M. (1937a), 'Alternative theories of the rate of interest', *Economic Journal*, **47**, 241–52.
Keynes, J.M. (1937b), 'The General Theory of Employment', *Quarterly Journal of Economics*, **51**, 209–23; *CW*., Vol. XIV (1973), pp. 109–23.
Keynes, J.M (1973a), *The General Theory of Employment, Interest and Money*, in *CW*, Vol. VII, edition of the Royal Economic Society, London: Macmillan.
Keynes, J.M. (1973b), *The General Theory and After: Part II, Defence and Development*, in *CW*, Vol. XIV, London: Macmillan.
Keynes, M. (ed.) (1975), *Essays on John Maynard Keynes*, Cambridge: Cambridge University Press.
Krugman, P. (2001), 'Are we all Keynesians now?', http://web.mit.edu/krugman/ www/.
Kuhn, T.S. (1970), *The Structure of Scientific Revolutions*, Chicago, IL: Chicago University Press.
Lakatos, I. (1978), *The Methodology of Scientific Research Programmes*, Cambridge: Cambridge University Press.
Machlup, F. (1978), *Methodology of Economics and Other Social Sciences*, New York: Academic Press.
Minsky, H.P. (1975), *John Maynard Keynes*, New York: Columbia University Press.
Moggridge, D.E. (1992), *Maynard Keynes: An Economist's Biography*, London: Routledge.
Nevile, J.W. (2000), 'What would Keynes have thought of the development of IS–LM', in W. Young and B. Zilberfarb (eds), *IS–LM and Modern Macroeconomics*, Boston, MA: Kluwer Academic.
O'Donnell, R.M. (1991), *Keynes as Philosopher-Economist*, proceedings of the Ninth Keynes Seminar held at the University of Kent, London: Macmillan.
Pasinetti, L. (1997), 'J.M. Keynes "revolution" – the major event of twentieth-century economics?', in L. Pasnetti (ed.), *The Impact of Keynes in the Twentieth Century*, Cheltenham, UK and Lyme, USA Edward Elgar, pp. 3–15.
Popper, K. (1959), *The Logic of Scientific Discovery*, London: Hutchinson.
Skidelsky, R. (1992), *John Maynard Keynes. Volume II. The Economist as Saviour 1920–1937*, London: Macmillan.
Skidelsky. R (1996), *Keynes*, Past Masters, Oxford: Oxford University Press.
Skidelsky. R (1997), 'The conditions for the reinstatement of Keynesian policy', in L. Pasinetti (ed.), *The Impact of Keynes in the Twentieth Century*, Cheltenham, UK and Lyme, USA Edward Elgar, pp. 36–51.
Skidelsky, R. (2000), *John Maynard Keynes. Volume III. Fighting for Britain 1937–1946*, London: Macmillan.
Thirlwall, A.P. (ed.) (1978), 'Keynes and Laissez Faire', 3rd Keynes Seminar, University of Kent at Canterbury.
Thirlwall, A.P. (writing as J.M. Keynes) (1999), 'A "Second Edition" of Keynes' *General Theory*', *Journal of Post Keynesian Economics*, **21**, 367–86.
Vercelli, A. (1991), *Methodological Foundations of Macroeconomics*, Cambridge: Cambridge University Press.

PART II

Founding fathers of Post Keynesian economics

3. Minsky and Keynes on investment volatility: was there an overstatement?

André Lourenço*

INTRODUCTION

The subject of this chapter is the financial theory of investment developed by Hyman Minsky, taking into special account his books *John Maynard Keynes* (1975) and *Stabilizing an Unstable Economy* (1986). Following the 'two-price model' of investment determination developed there, the pace of this fundamental macroeconomic variable would be directly linked with the ratio between the price of capital assets in secondary markets and the flow-supply price of these goods.

The problem identified in this subject is, from our perspective, that such a theory overstates in a significant way the volatility[1] of investment[2] in capitalist economies. As we shall argue, perhaps the main reason for this is the direct link postulated between investment determination and the price of capital goods in secondary markets (usually represented by an index of share prices).

Explicitly aiming to render compatible the relative empirical stability of investment with the degree of volatility foreseen in his theory, Minsky (1982) proposed that the twin operation of 'big government' as a fiscal thwarting device of effective demand fluctuations (and hence profits), and of 'big banks' (monetary authorities) as lenders of last resort, reduces empirical volatility as compared to the theoretical one, for example, the one that would exist if government and/or monetary authorities refused to operate as such dampeners – in other words, if *laissez-faire* were predominant. However, institutional changes and financial innovations that have taken place since the Bretton Woods' breakdown, as well as the shift in the

* The author would like to thank Prof. Dr Fernando Cardim de Carvalho, for his valuable comments as well as acknowledge the support received from the Foundation for Research Support of Rio de Janeiro State (FAPERJ). All remaining errors are the exclusive responsibility of the author.

emphasis of economic policy from full employment to price stability targets, have reshaped those scenarios, making them propitious to the reappearance of the Minskyan crises all over the world, although the growth of the world economy has declined significantly since then. And, even though such crises have damaged several economies, there still seems to be evidence that the capitalist system, even in its contemporary phase, is less prone to financial crises than presumed in the Minskyan investment theory.

Throughout this chapter, we shall assume that some of the main reasons for this volatility overstatement in Minsky's investment theory can be comprehended through a comparative reading of this author and of Keynes's investment theory as outlined in Chapters 11 and 12 of *The General Theory*.[3] Hence, the methodology proposed here includes a comparative reading of the distinct investment theories proposed by Minsky (1975, Chs 4–7) and Keynes (1936, Chs 11–12), in order to identify divergences between both. After this comparison, we investigate the theoretical elements responsible for the overstatement of the excessively volatile character of the pace of private investment in the two-price Minskyan model.

THE CHOICE OF THE REPRESENTATIVE FIRM

When comparing Minsky's and Keynes's investment theories, the first notable aspect is the difference concerning the characteristics of the firms considered representative in the capital goods sector by each of these authors.

In Keynes's view, a representative firm presents (i) diminishing marginal product, and (ii) finite demand price elasticity, so that saturation can be caused on the demand side.[4] For Minsky, a representative firm produces in an oligopolistic environment. Consequently, its supply curve under the constant marginal product is horizontal, and the sales price is obtained through a mark-up over unitary variable costs. However, as in perfect competition models, the demand side that corresponds to the capital goods sector is represented by an infinitely price-elastic curve. As a consequence, this odd combination generates a situation of non-existence of equilibrium, similar to that already pointed out by Piero Sraffa in the 1920s: the firm's supply and demand curves, remaining parallel, do not intersect.

What are the impacts of these different choices of representative firms over investment determination? The diagram proposed by Minsky (1975: 108) can be used to assess this point more carefully. In Figure 3.1, *Pk* is the demand price and *Pi* is the supply price of investment goods; *QiQi* is the

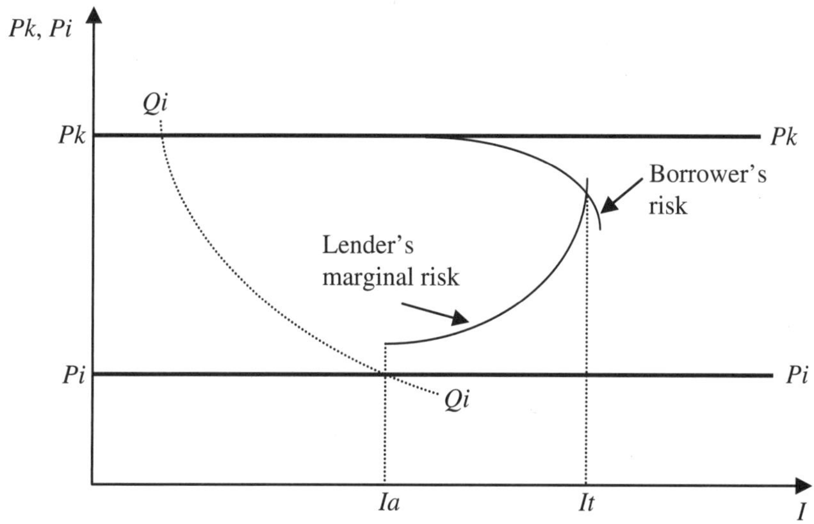

Figure 3.1 The two-price model with a Minskyan representative firm

function representing the amount of internal resources available to finance the purchase of investment goods at different prices; *Ia* is self-financed investment amount; and *It* is the total investment amount.

The indeterminacy in the model is avoided by the operation of the so-called 'principle of increasing risk', which, beyond a certain point, causes the demand curve to bend downward as a response to the decreasing liquidity in the borrower's portfolio. Simultaneously, the exhaustion of the firm's own resources imposes the search for new sources of (external) financing. Due to the principle of increasing risk working on the lender's side, these external resources will be available only at increasingly scarce terms, and also at increasing costs.[5] As a result, the intersection of the *Pk* and *Pi* curves occurs in the segments that were bent by the risks of the borrower and the lender.

The peculiar configuration of the representative firm in Minsky renders the investment pace too dependent on risk assessment, which is highly subjective and volatile.[6] Thus, we arrive at the first volatility aspect of investment level in Minsky's theory.

In Keynes, however, the adopted representative firm experiences different results. The presence of diminishing marginal product, combined with market saturation in the capital goods sector, imposes significant limitations on the effect of risk assessment over the pace of investment, as shown in Figure 3.2.

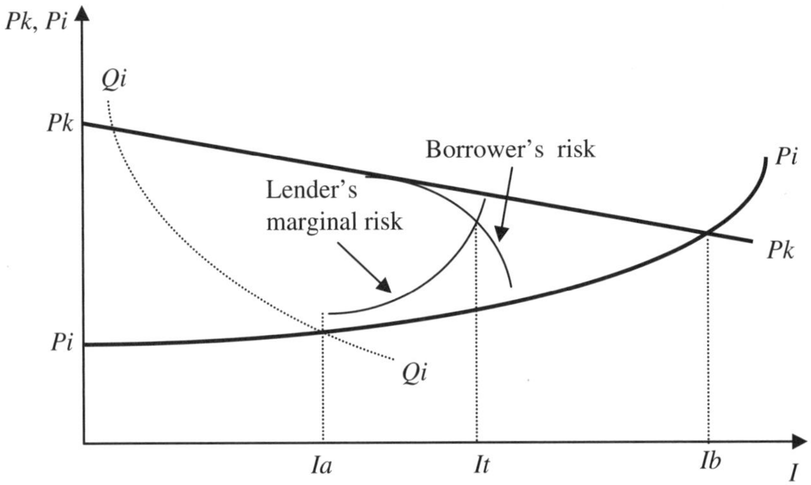

Figure 3.2 The two-price model with a representative firm according to Keynes

The risk assessment of the borrower and the lender still affects total investment, *It*, making it smaller than what would take place in the absence of constraints generated by increasing risk – the amount represented by *Ib* in the figure.[7] Nevertheless, the inclination of *Pk* and *Pi* functions reduces significantly the possibility of transferring risk assessment volatility to the investment determination. Such a possibility becomes less likely in proportion to the acuity of the inclination of both curves.

Another aspect that could circumscribe even further the transmission of this volatility is the existence of meaningful technical indivisibilities regarding certain categories of investment goods. These indivisibilities prevent investment from happening – both in Keynes and in Minsky – unless the intersection between *Pk* and *Pi* occurs at a point located far enough to the right of the axis of abscissae in Figures 3.1 and 3.2 as to contemplate the whole (indivisible) investment project. This means that variations in risk assessment, as long as they remain restricted to certain values, could have no effect over investment.

We can therefore conclude that the very peculiar configuration of supply and demand curves for the Minskyan representative firm is the most favorable one to transmit the volatility inherent in risk assessment to the investment determination. On the other hand, the characteristics of representative firm according to Keynes are the least favorable for such a transmission. This may be helpful in understanding the reasons why the volatility originated in the borrower's and the lender's risk occupies such a secondary role in *The General Theory* when compared with Minsky's works: 'This duplication of allowance for a portion of the risk has not hitherto been emphasized, so far as I am aware; *but it may be important in certain circumstance*' (Keynes, 1936: 122; emphasis added).

It is possible to classify such diverse configurations of the representative firm according to their potential to transmit credit risk volatility to investment determination. One could conclude that the 'pure' models of oligopoly and perfect competition would be intermediary cases, while Minsky and Keynes would be the extreme situations of the greatest and the smallest transmission potential, respectively.

FINANCE AND INVESTMENT: THE 'REAL' AND THE 'MONETARY' FACTORS

Another reason for an overstatement of investment volatility in Minsky's theory can be traced back to the link between real and financial phenomena that occurs through the *Pk* curve. This function represents two different concepts simultaneously, the demand price of investment goods and the market price of capital assets. For Minsky, however, both concepts seem not only interchangeable, but even virtually indistinguishable: 'It is assumed that the market price for capital assets is the demand price for investment output' (Minsky, 1982: 134).

This link is illustrated in Figure 3.3. The curve *Pk* (*M*, *Q*) represents the liquidity preference scale and determines the *Pk* price (understood as the price of capital assets) for a given money supply[8] and also for a given asset supply. This determined price of capital assets – Pk_0 in the figure – works like a ceiling on the demand function for investment goods, $Pk_{/B}$. This function bends downward as a consequence of the borrower's increasing risk, where total investment level is determined by its interception with the *Pi* curve. The $Pi_{/L}$ curve represents the supply of investment goods, a function that includes the lender's risk.

However, the *Pk* (*M*, *Q*) curve is extremely volatile. It reflects changes in the decisions of the agents' portfolio allocation (and so their liquidity preference), in a context where the confidence regarding the state of long-term expectations that provide the basis for those decisions is fragile. These changes have a direct impact on the investment level, because they have the potential to shift the entire $P_{K/B}$ curve, which is very important to investment determination. More importantly, the changing state of long-term expectations shifts the *Pk*, $P_{K/B}$, and $Pi_{/L,}$ curve simultaneously.

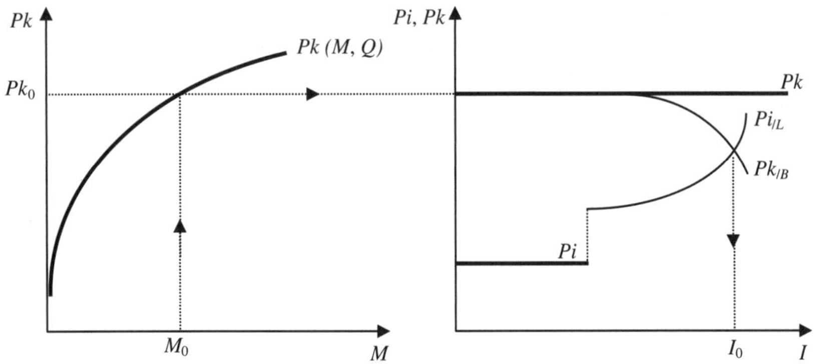

Source: Based on Minsky (1975: 113, diagram 5.6). We omit some elements in order to obtain a simpler approach.

Figure 3.3 Demand price of investment goods and market price of capital goods

Therefore, volatility has a still greater impact on the determination of the pace of investment because, besides subjective credit risk and volatile assessment, there is also the volatility that emerges from the pricing of capital assets.

Nevertheless, in *The General Theory* there are some differences in the link between investment determination and financial aspects. On the one hand, there is the so-called 'marginal efficiency of capital' schedule and, on the other, the mechanics of the determination of the rate of interest in the monetary market.

The marginal efficiency of capital schedule is the result of a process that involves two stages:

1. For each investment good, a scale is made, showing the relation between variations in their quantity and in their marginal efficiency.
2. The scales for different kinds of investment goods are aggregated, so as to determine the relation between the amount of aggregate investment and the corresponding marginal efficiency of capital, in general, that the investment will establish.

The rate of interest determination, on the other hand, is discussed in Chapters 13, 15, and 17 (Minsky's approach) of *The General Theory*. The final result is that the rate of interest depends on the so-called, 'liquidity preference scale' – through several psychological and entrepreneurial 'motives' to demand liquidity – and an exogenous monetary supply.

The LPS (liquidity preference scale) and the MgEK (marginal efficiency of capital) curves are 'unstable' in the Minskyan sense. The Keynesian LPS curve, as well as Minsky's *Pk* (*M*, *Q*) curve, derives its volatility from portfolio allocation decisions regarding the rule of money in a world of non-probabilistic risks ('strong' uncertainty or uncertainty in the Knight–Keynes sense). At another level, LPS volatility is also influenced by expectations regarding future rate of interest, while MgEK also fluctuates because of volatility expectations regarding future quasi-rents from investment (*Q*s).

The variable that integrates investment determination with monetary mechanisms in *The General Theory* is 'the' rate of interest. Wealth holders, acting as profit maximizers, equalize this rate of interest with the marginal efficiency of capital as an *ex ante* decision criterion. So, given money supply and the elements that determine the position of the LPS and the MgEK curves, it is possible to determine investment amount I_0 – Chapter 17 is better as it provides the own rate analysis.

The LPS and MgEK curves, however, are not independent. As shown by Davidson (1972: 160–70), the finance motive to demand liquidity forces the LPS curve to include also the parameters of the MgEK curve. Thus, variations in expected quasi-rents, for instance, would change both in opposite directions. But, for our purposes, this interdependence has an interesting stabilizing effect on the investment level, because it provokes an anti-cyclical behavior in the rate of interest – at least where this specific motive to demand liquidity is concerned.

Keynes also provided an alternative presentation of his model through demand and supply prices of investment goods, considering it equivalent to the device presented in Figure 3.3. Minsky disagrees with and criticizes such equivalence. For him, the building of an MgEK curve with a downward inclination would lead to the conclusion that there are no meaningful differences between this and the (neo)classical demand for capital function. Thus, it would contradict the very existence of 'attenuating factors' interposed between investment and capital productivity: the variability of prospective quasi-rents and the relation between the (subjective) discount rate of an asset's yield and 'the' market rate of interest.

Minsky's criticism seems misguided here.[9] Concerning the first aspect, Keynes insisted on the variability of quasi-rents and that these were a result of scarcity, not productivity, of capital (Keynes, 1936: Ch. 16). The differences between conventional formulations and *The General Theory* become quite clear when Keynes points out, as the major problem in (neo)classical conception, the failure to distinguish between Q_1 and the whole series, $Q_1, Q_2, \ldots, Q_n$, of quasi-rents, which 'involves the whole question of the place of expectation in economic theory' (Keynes, 1936: 117). Obviously, it is not something to be belittled. In particular, it seems that the problem has nothing to do with the presentation of the model in terms of the rate of interest and the marginal efficiency of capital or in terms of supply and demand prices.

Regarding the second aspect, the existence of variability in the relation to the discount rate of an asset's yield and rate of interest, Minsky seems to have a point in theoretical terms. Indeed, there is a difference between a subjective (and agent-specific) rate of discount and the current rate of interest. Nevertheless, in a similar manner, this fact does not seem to have any relation with the way the model is presented. The fact that Keynes had not fulfilled the definition of this capitalization rate in his presentation does not make it *per se* superior to the alternative, which can also be slightly modified to insert this element. Moreover, as Minsky himself recognized (Minsky, 1975: 102–3), the relation between both rates depends on the state of confidence that was implicitly built in to the LPS curve; therefore, the meaning of this issue was probably overstated as well.

In our view, one relevant difference between Keynes's and Minsky's investment models is that, while the first postulates the equalization of two 'own rates of interest', the monetary rate of interest and the marginal efficiency of capital, the second proposes the equalization of two price levels, the demand price for investment goods and the market price of capital assets (shares as proxies). The crucial point is that, while Keynes is very careful to demonstrate that the rate of interest and the marginal efficiency of capital are different concepts whose equalization occurs only in (*ex ante*) equilibrium, in Minsky the demand price for investment goods and the market price for shares are hardly distinguishable.

In Chapter 12 of *The General Theory*, Keynes discussed the relation between investment and the market for shares in the following terms: 'a high quotation for existing equities involves an increase in the marginal efficiency of the corresponding type of capital and therefore has the same effect (since investment depends on a comparison between the marginal efficiency of capital and the rate of interest) as a fall in the rate of interest' (Keynes, 1936: 126, footnote).

Here there seems to be an anticipation of Chapter 17: the own rate of interest of shares rises, being equalized in equilibrium to the marginal efficiency of capital – and to the market rate of interest, too. As a consequence, an autonomous fall in the own rate of interest of shares is prone to increase the level of investment. But there is a specific aspect in this case: if there are expectations regarding an increase in the quasi-rents of investment goods – the '*q*' attribute – for a given expected dividends policy of one firm, then there will be a simultaneous increase in the expected flow of dividends, in the own rates of interest, and therefore in the prices of shares as well.

The equalization of the own rate of interest of shares and the marginal efficiency of capital implies that Minsky's equalization of shares and demand for capital prices does not seem to have any plausible economic justification to this point of view,[10] once it claims simultaneously the equalization of expected quasi-rents, capital gains and liquidity premia for both assets.

Such observations, however, do not exhaust the discussion of relations between the level of share prices and the pace of investment, because:

> [T]he daily revaluations of the Stock Exchange, though they are primarily made to facilitate transfers of old investments between one individual and another, inevitably exert a decisive influence on the rate of current investment. For there is no sense in building up a new enterprise at a cost greater than that at which a similar existing enterprise can be purchased; whilst there is an inducement to spend on a new project what may seem an extravagant sum, if it can be floated off on the Stock Exchange at an immediate profit. (Keynes, 1936: 126)

In this assertion, Keynes seems to draw attention to the fact that shares do not constitute only a kind of debt whose service is conditioned to the existence of the profits and the dividend policy of the firm. The shares also represent property and managerial rights over the firm, in proportion to the participation of each shareholder in the so-called 'voting capital'. But such a phenomenon creates a special link between the market for shares and the market for investment goods. This situation is clarified in the second sentence of the quotation above, which seems to establish a relation between the necessary sum to acquire control of a firm in the stock market and the necessary amount to build up a new firm in the same sector. This line of thought could promote the same kind of arbitrage proposed by Minsky between shares and physical assets. However, there are some essential differences:

1. In Minsky, arbitrage occurs among shares and, in principle, any investment good; in Keynes, the firm is not divisible: arbitrage occurs between a certain volume of shares and the whole firm.
2. In Minsky, arbitrage occurs between the demand prices of investment goods and the market prices for shares; in Keynes, it occurs between two amounts: (i) the quantity represented by a critical volume of shares – that is, the quantity of shares that is equivalent, under conditions established by the laws of the country where the operation is undertaken, to acquire control over a firm – times the value of this collection of shares; and (ii) the amount equivalent to the quantity of investment goods needed to build productive capacity equivalent to the firm that has shares for sale in stock markets and whose purchase is being considered, times the supply price of a unit of these goods.

3. Finally, in Minsky, perfect arbitrage is assumed; in Keynes, on the other hand, arbitrage is quite imperfect and asymmetrical and does not necessarily establish equalization between the two values, due in great part to the predominance of speculation in stock markets.[11]

Another financial aspect that emerges when comparing these approaches is that, in Minsky, the representative firm has saleable shares in stock markets. If we admit that quite a significant number of firms do not have such shares, a significant amount of investment is decided without any direct link with the prices of assets in secondary markets. So, the acceptance of a greater diversification regarding this issue can also be seen as a factor that reduces the volatility of investment decisions.[12] After such observations, it is possible to conclude that, in Keynes, the links that associate investment decisions with the behavior of the financial market seem weaker than in Minsky, especially as a result of the greater diversification of behavior shown in Keynes. Hence, the Minskyan investment theory, with more homogeneous behavior, seems to present a greater degree of volatility than the Keynesian one.

ENDOGENOUS EXPECTATIONS AND THE STATE OF CONFIDENCE

For Minsky, one of the most important aspects of volatility in investment decisions is that, under certain circumstances, the validation of past decisions of investment and indebtedness feeds a process of increasing fragility in financial relations, which acquires a characteristic cumulative indebtedness. Behind this movement, one is able to find not only a process of increasingly optimistic expectations validation but also the sharing of a 'general state of confidence in business', which renders all economic systems vulnerable to outbreaks of optimism and pessimism.

In Keynes, investment decisions depend fundamentally on expectations of quasi-rents. He observed that these expectations are referred to as both 'existing facts which we can assume to be known more or less for certain', and 'future events which can only be forecasted with more or less confidence' (Keynes, 1936: 123) – embodied in the state of long-term expectations.

Short-term expectations are the object of a gradual and continuous revision process, linked in great part to past results. Therefore, expected and obtained results are intertwined, and the recent performance becomes predominant in determining these expectations (Keynes, 1936: Ch. 5). Long-term expectations, however, which are the relevant ones in investment decisions, cannot be substituted for obtained results and still remain exogenous in great proportion (Carvalho, 1992: 68).

Notwithstanding this, in Minsky, there is evidence that long-term expectations are, to a certain degree, more endogenous than in Keynes, having a repetition framework closer to short-term expectations. Financial margins of safety, for instance, decrease as past expectations validate former margins, and so on, successively. This may seem a paradox, as the spirit of his contribution would be more inclined to demonstrate the autonomy of the financial sphere in relation to a productive one and its ability to generate cycles which requires more of an active and independent role for expectations.

The consequence is that the Minskyan model, besides being more mechanistic in this aspect, still fails to render the business cycle completely endogenous.[13] In this model, cyclical reversions remain basically inexplicable except by shocks – which is not surprising, given the known resistance of the long-term state of expectations to analytical treatment. However, it seems that the excessive dependence of these long-term expectations on past results – especially the excessive sharing of the 'general state of confidence in business' – contributes to an overstatement of volatility in the behavior of some economic variables, mainly during debt deflation and/or investment *boom* periods. Keynes had already warned that liquidity and financial market stability benefited from the heterogeneity of expectations. Minsky composes a scenario in which agents are difficult to distinguish from one another on institutional grounds – it is enough to remember his remarkable assertion that 'all agents are banks' – and where expectations depend on a generalized state of confidence, shared by the financial and the productive sectors. Therefore, the inevitable result of such a scenario is an overstatement of the volatility of capitalist economies, both in the ascending and the descending phases of the business cycle.

CONCLUSION

This chapter tried to show the several reasons why the Minskyan model of investment determination considerably overstates the degree of instability in capitalist economies. Among the issues mentioned as responsible for this phenomenon, we highlighted the choice of a quite peculiar representative firm, which removed all non-financial barriers from the investment determination process. Such a choice may indeed be legitimate on methodological grounds, as long as it can emphasize certain issues of the capitalist economy. However, before looking for new proxies to reality – for instance, economic policy propositions – it would be sensible to reinsert the limits that were removed, in order to decrease the risk of excessive loss of realism.

The chapter also showed that, even when considering that Minsky's model chose as representative a firm with saleable shares in the stock market, the aspects related to the pricing of financial assets assumed a disproportionate role in the investment determination process. The choice for greater institutional diverseness and the consideration of certain microeconomic characteristics of stock markets (such as the agency–principal problem, takeover risks, and so on) could perhaps avoid certain characteristics of Minskyan investment theory that make it so vulnerable to criticism of an overstatement of volatility.

Another issue related to institutional diverseness points out the need to work with long-term expectations that are less attached to past results and have greater heterogeneity in their formation, with agents whose utility function takes non-economic elements as part of life, and, ultimately, even with a less substantive way of describing rationality (perhaps more like Herbert Simon).

The common element to all these issues is the excessive homogeneity of agents, expectations, and firms in the Minskyan theory. As Keynes observed, given strong or non-probabilistic uncertainty, the very existence of diversity of opinion concerning the future is fundamental to keeping the volatility of financial markets under control. Hence, it is not surprising that, when Minsky excessively stylized certain crucial aspects of the investment decision in capitalist economies, he overstated their degree of volatility.

NOTES

1. Minsky deals with volatility and instability as similar concepts. In Minsky (1975: 95), instability is defined *en passant*: 'The other functions, which directly embody present views about the future, are not stable, i.e., they are prone to shift'. Recently, a somewhat different view has been suggested (Ferri and Minsky, 1991: 4): 'We define dynamic instability in a rather informal way. Essentially, we mean the irregular pattern and the persistence in time of the most common macroeconomic diseases, such as unemployment and inflation. This instability can give rise to runaway situations such as deep depressions or hyperinflation phenomena'. In this chapter, we prefer to use the concept of volatility in the situations above referred to by Minsky, in contrast to the concepts of dynamic and structural instability proposed by Vercelli (1991).
2. One of the most critical views concerning this overstatement about instability is that of Lerner (1978: 118–19): 'Yet Joan Robinson and Hy Minsky and an apparently increasing number of younger economists see an "intractable instability" in the capitalist economy whereby any expansion leads to further expansion and any contraction leads to further contraction'. But: 'nothing can cure optimism as much as finding that the product is not selling, and nothing is as good a medicine for pessimism as finding that sales and profits are high'.
3. The relevant comparison is with Chapters 11 and 12 of this book, because, in general equilibrium, the relevant comparison would be with Chapter 17, where a somewhat different theory is put forward.

4. The combination of such hypotheses is not compatible with the operation of the firm in perfect competition, as Chick (1983) observed. In her opinion, the implicit hypothesis in theoretical treatment of supply conditions in Keynes's *General Theory* is the 'polipoly' one.
5. Not only in terms of costs, but also by increasing contractual demands by the lenders.
6. In this regard, one must acknowledge the fragility of the knowledge basis to calculate the expected profitability of investment, already pointed out by Keynes in Chapter 12 of the *General Theory*. This fragility implies the possibility of great magnitude shifts of the whole *Pk* curve.
7. On the other hand, if there were no lenders' or borrowers' risks in the Minskyan model, and if *Pk* were greater than *Pi*, then the investment level would be infinite.
8. The way to make a 'given' money supply compatible with the endogenous money theory is to restrain it to a sufficiently restricted definition – for instance, monetary base – and assume that the preference for liquidity of the commercial banking system is also embodied in the $Pk = f(M, Q)$ curve.
9. He probably would have achieved finer results if he had questioned the somewhat careless aggregation procedure used to build the MgEK curve.
10. In addition, in the case of the second restriction, equalizing the *Q*s of both assets implies that all profits are distributed as dividends to shareholders. There is also an asymmetry: *Qk* may fall below zero, but *Qa* may not.
11. Ultimately, it is possible to question the own 'pure' concept of arbitrage, because, if there is an inescapable time gap between observation and decision taking and making, decisions will always have to be based upon expected, not effective, values. Therefore it should consider the own rates of interest instead of merely making an arbitrage between 'given' prices – conceptually, even if the time gap involved in the decision is very short.
12. This is not a benefit in itself, because 'the liquidity of investment markets often facilitates, though it sometimes impedes, the course of new investment' (Keynes, 1936: 132). As Crotty (1990) pointed out, however, it is possible that, even concerning the management of a firm which has shares for sale in stock exchanges, the predominance of financial aspects in investment decisions could have been exaggerated, because the principal–agent problem – the conflicting objectives between managerial body and owners – was neglected. Under such conditions, even in such enterprises, managers would have the power to make at least some of their objectives predominant over those of the owners. The consequence would be a less rigid connection between financial markets and investment decision than those proposed by Minsky or even by Keynes.
13. Unless one considers some relations of the model as non-linear.

REFERENCES

Carvalho, F.C. (1992), *Mr. Keynes and the Post Keynesians*, Aldershot, UK and Brookfield, USA: Edward Elgar.

Chick, V. (1983), *Macroeconomics After Keynes*, Cambridge, MA: MIT Press.

Crotty, J. (1990), 'Owner–manager conflict and financial theories of investment stability: a critical assessment of Keynes, Tobin and Minsky', *Journal of Post Keynesian Economics*, **12** (4), summer, 519–42.

Davidson, P. (1972 [1978]), *Money and the Real World*, 2nd edn, Basingstoke: Macmillan.

Ferri, P. and Minsky, H.P. (1991), 'Market processes and thwarting systems', Jerome Levy Economics Institute working paper no. 64, Annandale-on-Hudson, NY.

Keynes, J.M. (1936), *The General Theory of Employment, Interest and Money*, London: Macmillan.

Lerner, A.P. (1978), 'The scramble for Keynes' mantle', *Journal of Post Keynesian Economics*, **1** (1) 115–23.
Minsky, H.P. (1975), *John Maynard Keynes*, New York: Columbia University Press.
Minsky, H.P. (1982), *Can 'It' Happen Again? Essays on Instability and Finance*, New York: M.E. Sharpe.
Minsky, H.P. (1986), *Stabilizing an Unstable Economy*, New Haven, CT: Yale University Press.
Vercelli, A. (1991), *Methodological Foundations of Macroeconomics: Keynes and Lucas*, Cambridge: Cambridge University Press.

4. Two founding fathers of the Post Keynesian critical appraisal of self-balancing mechanisms?

Lino Sau*

INTRODUCTION

The Post Keynesian literature has often scrutinised the similarities and differences between the theoretical work of John Maynard Keynes and Michał Kalecki. On the one hand, Davidson (2000) has emphasised that the principle of effective demand elaborated by Keynes is more general and, to some extent, superior to that independently discovered and elaborated by Kalecki. On the other hand, Kriesler (2002) and Lopez (2002) have argued that Kalecki's theory of price, distribution, investment, money and finance is, in many respects, superior to Keynes's *General Theory*.

There are certainly many differences between the contributions of these two economists; nevertheless, in this chapter we try to 'compound' Keynes's and Kalecki's critical analysis of the 'classical' assumption that flexibility of wages and prices is always able to ensure full employment equilibrium. In fact, both Keynes (1923, 1931, 1936) and Kalecki (1937, 1944, 1966) denied the existence of *self-balancing* endogenous mechanisms able to stabilise the economic system, and opened the way to Post Keynesian approaches seeking to demonstrate that wage and price flexibility can be *destabilising*. In 'A Tract on Monetary Reform' (1923), in a set of writings from 1931 to 1933 and in *The General Theory* (1936: Ch. XIX), Keynes questioned the viability of flexible wages and prices to restore full employment. In a comment on Pigou (1944) and in *Studies in the Theory of Business Cycles* (1966), Kalecki argued that falling prices will not necessarily stimulate an increase in aggregate demand when firms and households have extensive nominal payments.

The chapter is organised as follows: in the next two sections we analyse the contributions by Keynes and Kalecki, respectively, on the destabilising

* This is a more extensive and modified version of a former paper published in Studi Economici 2006/1, Franco Angeli ed., Naples. I thank Franco Angeli for the authorisation.

role of wage and price flexibility and we try to emphasise the similarities between them; in the fourth section, we look at the mainstream approach where the income and stabilising function works above all through Pigou's 'real balance effect'; in the fifth section we try to show how the Post Keynesians' critical appraisal of the mainstream arguments is, in many aspects, based on *both* Keynes's *and* Kalecki's perspectives; in the final section, we set out our conclusions.

KEYNES'S VIEW

In Chapter XIX of *The General Theory* entitled 'Changes in money wages', Keynes observed: 'For the classical theory has been accustomed to rest the supposedly self-adjusting character of the economic system on an assumed fluidity of money-wages; and, when there is rigidity, to lay on this rigidity the blame of maladjustment' (Keynes, 1936: 257). As is well known, his decisive blow against the 'classical' approach was to the idea that the capitalistic economic system is always capable of self-balancing and reaching full employment equilibrium.

According to Keynes, the 'classical' economists were mistaken in holding that a reduction in money wages necessarily leads to an increase in employment since such would be the case if, and only if, the reduction were accompanied by unvaried aggregate effective demand:

> [W]hilst no one would wish to deny the proposition that a reduction in money-wages *accompanied by the same aggregate effective demand as before* will be associated with an increase in employment, the precise question at issue is whether the reduction in money-wages will or will not be accompanied by the same aggregate effective demand as before measured in money, or, at any rate, by an aggregate effective demand which is not reduced in full proportion to the reduction in money-wages . . . (Keynes, 1936: 259–60)

Keynes shows, on the contrary, that wage and price deflation leads to a *decline* in effective demand and thus to a fall in income and employment. As for the effects on the propensity to consume, he remarks:

> A reduction of money-wages will somewhat reduce prices. It will, therefore, involve some redistribution of real income (a) from wage-earners to other factors entering into marginal prime cost whose remuneration has not been reduced, and (b) from entrepreneurs to rentiers to whom a certain income fixed in terms of money has been guaranteed. What will be the effect of this redistribution on the propensity to consume for the community as a whole? The transfer from wage-earners to other factors is likely to diminish the propensity to consume. The effect of the transfer from entrepreneurs to rentiers is more open

> to doubt. But if rentiers represent on the whole the richer section of the community and those whose standard of life is least flexible, then the effect of this also will be unfavourable. What the net result will be on a balance of considerations, we can only guess. Probably it is more likely to be adverse than favourable. (Ibid.: 262)

The problem of redistributive effects associated with variations in the value of money is, as we know, one of the issues already addressed by Keynes in 'A Tract on Monetary Reform' (1923). Here, in the chapter entitled 'The Consequences to Society of Changes in the Value of Money', he remarks: 'Thus a change in prices and rewards, as measured in money, generally affects different classes unequally, transfers wealth from one to another, bestows affluence here and embarrassment there, and redistributes Fortune's favour so as to frustrate design and disappoint expectation' (Keynes, 1923: 1). According to Keynes, while on the one hand the fall in price level favours the class of rentiers (as creditors), on the other hand it penalises the entrepreneurs (as debtors), and it is on their decisions that the levels both of current production and of investment depend.

With regard to the former aspect, Keynes observes that 'a fall in prices, effects redistribution of real wealth from those who make the decisions which set production into motion to those who are inactive once they have lent their money' (ibid.: 30). In 'A Tract on Monetary Reform', moreover, Keynes makes it clear that, as he sees it, the expectation of a fall in the level of prices can entail a drastic cut in production:

> During the lengthy process of production the business world is incurring outgoings in terms of *money* – paying out in money for wages and other expenses of production – in the expectation of recouping this outlay by disposing of the product for *money* at a later date.[1]
>
> That is to say, the business world as a whole must always be in a position where it stands to gain by a rise of price and to lose by a fall of price. . . . Now it follows from this, not merely that the *actual occurrence* of prices changes profits some classes and injures others . . . but that a *general fear* of falling prices may inhibit the productive process altogether . . . For if prices are expected to fall . . . entrepreneurs will be reluctant to embark on lengthy productive processes involving a money outlay long in advance of money recoupment – whence unemployment. The *fact* of falling prices injures entrepreneurs; consequently the *fear* of falling prices causes them to protect themselves by curtailing their operations. (Ibid.: 33–4)

As for the effects produced by a decline in wages and prices on aggregate investment, Keynes makes a distinction between the fall in current wages and the expectation of further reductions in them in the future:

> If the reduction of money-wages is expected to be a *reduction relatively to money-wages in the future*, the change will be favourable to investment . . . If, on the other hand, the reduction leads to the expectation, or even to the serious possibility, of a further wage-reduction in prospect, it will have precisely the opposite effect. For it will diminish the marginal efficiency of capital and will lead to the postponement both of investment and of consumption. (Keynes, 1936: 263; see also Keynes, 1925)

Keynes thus paid particular attention to the effects produced by a cumulative process in expectations of a fall in prices, and thus to the effects of wage and price flexibility in a dynamic context.

However, it is above all when we consider the effect that the deflationary process has on the debt burden, in the case of agents who have borrowed money, that we find particularly good reason for a substantial critique of Pigou's 'real balance effect' and its alleged stabilising role. In this connection Keynes observes:

> [T]he depressing influence on entrepreneurs of their greater burden of debt may partly offset any cheerful reactions from the reduction of wages. Indeed if the fall of wages and prices goes far, the embarrassment of those entrepreneurs who are heavily indebted may soon reach the point of insolvency, – with severely adverse effects on investment. Moreover the effect of the lower price-level on the real burden of the national debt and hence on taxation is likely to prove very adverse to business confidence. (Keynes, 1936: 264).

Should the debt burden be such as to produce a state of widespread insolvency, then entrepreneurs faced with increasing liabilities may well be tempted to sell the assets. This would lead to a fall in the price of the assets,[2] with negative repercussions on the stability of the general financial structure. In fact, in 'The Consequences to the Banks of the Collapse of Money Values' (1931), Keynes notes how a sharp fall in the value of equitable assets can also mean greater financial fragility for the banks since they would see a drastic reduction in their 'margin of safety';[3] indeed, he wrote (Keynes, 1931: 156):

> It is for this reason that a decline in money values so severe as that which we are now experiencing threatens the solidarity of the whole financial structure. Banks and bankers are by nature blind. They have not seen what was coming. . . . In the United States some of them employ so-called 'economists' who tell us even today that *our troubles are due to the fact that the prices of some commodities and some services have not yet fallen enough*, regardless of what should be the obvious fact that their cure, if it could be realised, would be a menace to their institution.

The deterioration in the 'state of credit'[4] would ensue, again with a negative impact on investment, income and employment.

KALECKI'S VIEW AND THE SIMILARITIES WITH KEYNES

Kalecki (1944) arrives at considerations remarkably close to those formulated by Keynes in *The General Theory* and in various other contributions mentioned above. Referring to the increase in wealth in real terms brought about by deflation in prices, he observes:

> The increase in the real value of the stock of money does not mean a rise in the total real value of possessions if all the money (cash and deposits) is 'backed' by credits to persons and firms, i.e. if all the assets of the banking system consist of such credits. For in this case, to the gain of money holders there corresponds an equal loss of the bank debtors. . . . The adjustment required would increase catastrophically the real value of debts, and would consequently lead to wholesale bankruptcy and a 'confidence crisis'. (Kalecki, 1944: 132)

Keynes had had the opportunity to read Kalecki's critical comment on Pigou as early as the first months of 1944. In a letter of 22 February addressed to Kalecki (Kalecki, *Collected Works*, vol. 1, 1990, p. 567) he expresses his agreement with him, while also offering some suggestions:

> Looking through your note on Pigou again, the following point occurs to me. Is there anything in it? I offer to you, for what it is worth, as a possible addition. On Pigou's assumption, the *real* rate of interest in Irving Fisher's sense would be constantly rising. This would have two effects: a) people would save more, and not less, as Pigou assumes. b) if the real value of money is constantly increasing, there will be a strong pressure to repay debts. Thus, at the limit, it would become impossible for the banks to keep the stocks of money constant except in so far as it was backed by gold. Thus, in effect, Pigou is assuming two contradictory hypotheses.[5]

Kalecki returned to the problem of the rising debt burden consequent upon wage and price deflation in Chapter V of his *Studies in the Theory of Business Cycles* (1966) entitled 'Money and Real Wages'. In analysing the indirect effects of a change in the general level of wages and prices on employment, Kalecki observes:

> A general reduction of prices increases the burden of indebtedness, since money incomes diminish while the 'old' debts do not. This causes difficulties in servicing the debts, ending frequently in failures. As a result confidence in the solvency of firms is undermined which may lead to an increase in the long-term rate of interest even though the short-term rate declines. (1966: 49)

As for the redistribution of wealth occurring subsequent to a fall in wages and prices, Kalecki (ibid.: 49–50, n. 2) – like Keynes (compare Chapter 1 of

'A Tract on Monetary Reform' – sees it having unfavourable effects on production and employment. Kalecki states: 'when prices decline in the same proportion as wages, this will also be true of profits. But the money income of rentiers consisting of the interest on "old" debts does not change and therefore, their relative share in profits increases'. Thus the shift in distribution occurs at the expense of the entrepreneurs and to the advantage of the rentiers. All this adds up to the fact that

> If the entrepreneurs are 'poorer' than the rentiers, this kind of shift will result rather in a decrease of total capitalists' consumption. In the contrary case the result would be an increase. The first pattern applies usually to societies where the concentration in industry is not too far advanced; the second to developed capitalist economies. But the final outcome is by no means certain even in this case, because quite a number of firms are in a precarious financial position, as a result of the decline in income while their 'old' debts remain unchanged, and this discourages any investment activity on their part. (Ibid.: 50, n. 2)

In Kalecki's analysis, therefore, 'the fluctuations in production and profits depend on the fluctuations in capitalists' consumption and investment' (ibid.: 46) and 'since the workers spend on consumption goods as much as they receive in wages, the remainder of the national income, being the share of capitalists, is just equal to their expenditure on consumption and investment goods. Therefore the capitalists as a class determine by their expenditure their profits and in consequences the aggregate production' (ibid.: 44–5).

We find the fall in aggregate demand ensuing upon a decline in wages and prices further reflected in Kalecki's work if we consider the 'principle of increasing risk' formulated in 1937. Here, he argues that the level of investment depends negatively on the degree of indebtedness (given by the ratio between debt and internal sources of financing). An increase in the debt burden brought about by plunging prices would have the effect of reducing the internal net worth[6] of the firms, increasing the risk involved in indebtedness (debtor's risk) and leading to a decline in investment and so in income and employment, producing effects in sharp contrast with the results expected according to the mainstream approach.

SELF-BALANCING ENDOGENOUS MECHANISM AND THE AUTOMATICITY OF FULL EMPLOYMENT

Nevertheless, despite the reservations stressed by Keynes and Kalecki, as is well known, the mainstream macroeconomic approach continues to accept, implicitly or explicitly, the assumption that flexibility in wages and prices is always able to ensure full employment equilibrium. The argument goes that, should a fall in aggregate demand lead to involuntary unemployment, the more rapidly wages and prices fall, the faster will be the adjustment towards full employment.

In terms of the traditional aggregate demand – aggregate supply (AD-AS) model, if the economic system as a whole were to meet with involuntary unemployment, caused by a fall in aggregate demand, then wage and price flexibility would bring about adjustments both on the supply side (downward shift in AS) and on the aggregate demand side (movement along AD). The stabilising role that deflation plays on aggregate demand is accomplished essentially through two channels: (i) the so-called 'Keynes effect' and (ii) the 'Pigou effect' or 'real balance effect'. In the former case, the fall in the general level of prices produces an increase in the supply of money in real terms and so leads to a fall in the interest rate, which in turn should favour an increase in investment and the generation of expansive effects. However, there is also a 'liquidity trap' at work, which could compromise the regular functioning of this adjustment mechanism. Thus, as we well know, the stabilisation process makes use of the 'real balance effect' by virtue of which price deflation, generating an increase in wealth in real terms, favours the expansion of aggregate consumption, and thus of income and employment.

As to the theoretical background, the emphasis placed on the 'Pigou effect' as relevant to macroeconomic analysis is due above all to Don Patinkin. In fact, in an article under the 'unequivocal' title of 'Price flexibility and full employment' (1948), making a critical comparison between Keynes's analysis (1936) and Pigou's contribution (1943), Patinkin identifies precisely in the absence of the real balance effect from the consumption function the factor that had led the author of *The General Theory* to suppose, erroneously, that there were no automatic mechanisms that could favour the attainment of full employment (compare Patinkin, 1948: 555). By contrast, according to Patinkin, Pigou's analysis 'has demonstrated the *automaticity* of full employment within the framework of the classical *static* model – the main mechanism by which this is brought about being the effect of a price decline on cash balances' (ibid.: 555). As this quotation shows, however, Patinkin makes a point of limiting the validity of Pigou's conclusions to the *static* context. That is, only in the case that the fall in wages and prices be not such as to generate expectations of further reductions. It is, in fact, only in this case that: 'there always exists a sufficiently low price level such that, *if expected to continue indefinitely*, it will generate full employment' (Patinkin, ibid.: 557).[7] Indeed, he warns that on proceeding from static to dynamic analysis, it immediately becomes crucial to consider the role of expectations *vis-à-vis* future prices, for '[i]t is quite possible that the original price decline will lead to the expectation of further declines. Then purchasing decisions will be postponed, aggregate demand will fall off, and the amount of unemployment increased still more' (ibid.: 557–8). Patinkin returned to these points and elaborated upon them further in the 1950s, as a result growing somewhat sceptical about the effective functioning of the 'Pigou effect', to the extent that he concluded: 'only further investigation will tell us whether a price decline does indeed have a positive net effect on total expenditure' (Patinkin, 1951: 263).

Even after Patinkin's scrutiny (1948, 1951), both the authors of the subsequent 'neoclassical Keynesian synthesis' (Hicks, 1957, 1974) and many exponents of the more recent current of New Keynesians[8] (Mankiw, 1986, 1992; Romer, 1993) have continued to argue that only the presence of 'rigidity' or 'stickiness' in wages and/or prices can effectively prevent the 'Pigou effect' from fully exercising its function as an endogenous self-balancing mechanism. Keynes's and Kalecki's theories would thus prove to remain, to some extent, even today an interesting and useful 'special case', valid only in as much as there are institutional factors or the imperfections of the real world that *curb* the regular functioning of market forces.

TWO FOUNDING FATHERS FOR THE POST KEYNESIANS' CRITICAL APPRAISAL TO MAINSTREAM?

The critical and sympathetic observations that Keynes and Kalecki had to make on the alleged stabilising role performed by wage and price flexibility were subsequently taken up and further formulated by various authors working on Keynesian lines, thus giving rise to a stimulating new current in research (King, 1994; Arestis, 1996) that is in sharp contrast with the mainstream approach. Suffice it here, as illustrations of the point with a few representative examples, to cite the contributions by Tobin (1975, 1980, 1993), Minsky (1975, 1982, 1984)[9] and, more recently, Caskey and Fazzari (1987, 1989, 1992).[10] As is well known, in the chapter entitled 'Real balance effects reconsidered', Tobin (1980) demonstrated that if the marginal propensity to spend of debtors' (represented mainly by entrepreneurs) is, as one may reasonably suppose, greater than that of creditors, then the effect that wage and price deflation has on the debt burden (that is, the 'Fisher' or 'debt deflation' effect) can predominate and force out Pigou's real balance effect, with destabilising consequences. To this we must add that if the fall in the general level of prices should trigger expectations of further falls, then the resulting increase in the real interest rate can induce a further decline in investment, income and employment (Tobin, 1975), and possible states of insolvency for the debtors: the creditors, for their part, would experience a dramatic loss of confidence (see also Keynes, 1931), facing the heavy costs of credit recovery.

In this connection, Minsky (1975, 1982, 1984) applied the principle of increasing risk formulated by Kalecki (1937); (see the third section, above) to demonstrate that the decline in internal net worth brought about by wage and price deflation has the effect of increasing not only the 'lender's risk' but also the 'borrower's risk',[11] entailing a rise in the cost of financing and so a further decline in investment, income and employment. As we know, the theory of financial instability formulated by Minsky seeks to yoke various aspects of Kalecki's analysis to the theory of Keynes and finds consistency precisely in abandonment of the 'Pigou effect' as the means of automatic adjustment. Remarking critically on the 'neoclassical Keynesian synthesis', he observes (Minsky, 1975: 54): 'Falling wages, prices and cash-flows to enterprises will make the burden of debt to potential bank borrowers increase over the life of the loan. A decline in wages and prices will tend to set off a money-decreasing debt deflation process, which will exacerbate the initial deficit of demand of labor – that is wage and price-level flexibility is disequilibrating'. Moreover, as Minsky goes on to point out, the revolutionary scope of Keynes's thought also extends to the crucial role played by money and credit in the process of financing production and investment.[12] As Keynes inverted the causal relation between saving and investment, this means that investment decisions are not financed by saving but with the money created by banks: the diffusion of bank money makes transparent the Keynesian theory's casual relationship between investment and saving (see Rochon, 1999; Bertocco, 2005). Debt and credit positions are therefore a consequence of the spreading of a fiat money made up of bank money.

In virtue of the fact that a monetary capitalistic economy moves along the lines of the M - C - C′ - M′ process (with C′> C and M′ > M), it follows that the change in the debt burden brought about by the variation in the level of prices has fundamental repercussions on the stability of the economic system. As soon as fiat money is taken into account, income fluctuations caused by a lack of effective demand, become more frequent. Minsky (1982) argued that the latter can be properly described as a monetary phenomenon. In fact, the alternation of phases of boom and bust is due to changes in banks' criteria in appraising firms' investment projects.

The analysis proposed by Tobin and Minsky has in turn given rise to particularly relevant results from the macroeconomic point of view (see Caskey and Fazzari, 1987, 1989, 1992). They have, in fact, led to a substantial modification of the traditional AD–AS model, above all with respect to aggregate demand. Indeed, should the Fisher effect successfully oust the Pigou effect, then the AD curve would no longer be negative in relation to prices, with the consequence that, were the economy to be in a depressive phase, wage and price deflation could cause a further decline in income and employment,[13] with destabilising effects.

CONCLUSIONS

In the light of the considerations presented in the previous sections, it appears fairly evident that, reading anew both the contributions by Keynes and those by Kalecki, the role of the self-balancing mechanism which mainstream macroeconomics attributes to Pigou's 'real balance effect' needs a radical reappraisal: in a depressive phase, wage and price flexibility is more likely to produce destabilising rather than stabilising effects.

As we have seen, the first point of departure was Keynes himself (1923 and 1936 ch. 19) as he noted that falling money wages and price levels will lead to redistributions of income first from wage earners to non-wage earners, the net effect of which would be the reduction in the economy-wide average and marginal propensity to consume. The income redistribution effect was taken up by Kalecki: if profit earners have a lower propensity to consume than wage earners, then the average and the marginal propensity to consume in the economy declines and thus aggregate demand declines. Thus, far from being stabilising, the reduction in money wages, in a situation of unemployment can lead to reductions in aggregate demand and thus more unemployment.

The second point had already been expressed by Keynes (1923, 1931), by Irving Fisher (1933) and by Kalecki (1944) in a comment on Pigou. It is known as the 'debt deflation effect': as financing contracts are established in nominal terms, then the redistribution of wealth between debtors and creditors, following wage and price deflation, can bring about a further decline in income and employment. Moreover, if the decline in prices is such as to generate expectations of yet more declines, then the resulting rise in the *real* interest rate will, once again, trigger destabilising effects. These well-known aspects were given a central role in Keynesian approaches such as those by Minsky (1975), Tobin (1980) and Caskey and Fazzari (1987, 1992).

The review of the contributions on the destabilising effects of flexibility by Keynes and Kalecki certainly shows the existence of several, important similarities between them on this topic: far from being competitive their analyses should be seen as complementary (see also. Kriesler, 2002; Lopez, 2002). Therefore, the answer to the 'core' question of the chapter concerning the existence of two founding fathers for Post Keynesians' critical appraisal to self-balancing mechanisms is positive!

NOTES

1. Thus it is already clear in 'A Tract' that Keynes accepts the M-C-M, process as underlying a monetary economy. As we know, this is a point that goes back to Marx's analysis contained in the first book of *Capital* (compare chapters IV and VII: M-C-C′-M′ with C′> C and M′> M) and was to occupy a central position in 'A Monetary Theory of Production' of 1933a,b. This aspect will be discussed further in the last section.
2. The fall in the cost price of capital goods has two causes: there exists no 'perfect' secondary market for the sale of these goods, and at the same time they are *firm specific*.
3. Capital goods often constitute collateral, and thus a guarantee to the creditor against debtor insolvency. These aspects have come under the attention of the so-called 'debt deflation school', which we consider in the last section.
4. Keynes refers to the, 'confidence' which the financial institutions place in loan applicants.
5. Keynes had also asked for Pigou's answer to Kalecki's criticisms, but to no avail.
6. Given by the difference between financial assets and liabilities.
7. In the 1951 book these considerations are further clarified and developed (see Simonazzi and Vianello, 2004). Moreover, Patinkin was also convinced that a policy of wage and price deflation would be difficult to implement from the practical viewpoint, and the adjustment due to the *real balance effect* would actually be a very long-term process.
8. Here, however, distinction must be made between the so-called New Keynesians who took nominal rigidities into consideration (for example, Mankiw, 1986, 1992 and Romer, 1993), and the New Keynesians who analysed the effects of asymmetric information on the financial market (for example, Greenwald and Stiglitz, 1993). In fact, while the former do not deny that wage and price flexibility can play a stabilising role, the latter, by contrast, see pro-cyclic flexibility as destabilising. On this point, see Messori (1999).
9. Minsky is often counted among the supporters of the so-called 'debt deflation school' which grew up mainly in the United States thanks to Fisher's (1933) contribution.
10. This listing of significant contributions is by no means exhaustive. On the issue of destabilising flexibilities, see also: Davidson (1972); Delong and Summers (1986); Hahn and Solow (1986); Greenwald and Stiglitz (1993); and, more recently, Simonazzi and Vianello (2004).
11. See Minsky (1975 p. 145). We find explicit references to the question of 'lender's risk' and 'borrower's risk' in Keynes's *General Theory* (Keynes, 1936: 284).
12. These aspects were central both in 'A Monetary Theory of Production' (1933a) and in 'The distinction between a co-operative economy and an entrepreneur economy' (1933b). Unfortunately they were overlooked in *The General Theory* where particular emphasis is put on the concept of money demand as store of wealth but not as means of payment (see Minsky, 1975; Palley 2002, Bertocco, 2005). The more recent monetary circuit approach (Graziani, 1996) has emphasised this point of Keynes's analysis.
13. On this question, see Greenwald and Stiglitz (1993), Tobin's chapter in Harcourt and Riach (1997) and D'Orlando and Nisticò (1998).

REFERENCES

Arestis, P. (1996), 'Kalecki's role in Post Keynesian economics: an overview', in J. King (ed.), *An Alternative Macroeconomic Theory: The Kaleckian Model and Post-Keynesian Economics*, Norwell, MA: Kluwer, pp. 11–34.

Bertocco, G. (2005), 'The role of credit in a Keynesian monetary theory', *Review of Political Economy*, **3**, 25–37.

Caskey, J. and S. Fazzari (1987), 'Aggregate demand contractions with nominal debt commitments: is wage flexibility stabilizing?', *Economic Inquiry*, **25**: 583–97.

Caskey, J. and S. Fazzari (1989), 'Debt commitments and aggregate demand: a critique of the neoclassical synthesis and policy', in W. Semmler (ed.), *Financial Dynamics and Business Cycles*, New York: M.E. Sharpe, pp. 188–202.

Caskey, J. and S. Fazzari (1992), 'Debt, price flexibility, and aggregate stability', *Revue Économie Politique*, **102** (4), 4–27.

Davidson, P. (ed.) (1972), *Money and the Real World*, New York: John Wiley & Sons.

Davidson, P. (ed.) (2000), 'There are major differences between Kalecki's theory of employment and Keynes's general theory of employment interest and money', *Journal of Post Keynesian Economics*, **23** (1), 3–25.

D'Orlando, F. and S. Nisticò (1998), 'Some questions for new Keynesians', in R. Rotheim (ed.), pp. 221–8.

DeLong, J.B. and L. Summers (1986), 'Is increased price flexibility stabilizing?', *American Economic Review*, **6**, 1931–44.

Fisher, I. (1933), 'The debt-deflation theory of great depressions', *Econometrica*, **1**, 337–57.

Graziani, A. (1996), 'Money as purchasing power and money as a stock of wealth in Keynesian economic thought', in G. Deleplace and E. Nell (eds), *Money in Motion*, London: Macmillan 111–18.

Greenwald, B.C. and J. Stiglitz (1993), 'Financial market imperfections and business cycles', *Quarterly Journal of Economics*, **5**, 77–112.

Hahn, F. and R. Solow (1986), 'Is wage flexibility a good thing?', in W. Beckerman (ed.), *Wage Rigidity and Unemployment*, London: Gerald Duckworth pp. 111–18.

Harcourt, G.C. and P.A. Riach (1997), *A 'Second Edition' of The General Theory*, Vol. 2, London: Routledge.

Hicks, J.R. (1957), 'A rehabilitation of "classical" economics', *Economic Journal*, **67** (266) (March), 147–59.

Hicks, J.R. (1974), *The Crisis in Keynesian Economics*, Oxford: Basil Blackwell.

Kalecki, M. (1937), 'The principle of increasing risk', *Economica*, **4**, 440–47.

Kalecki, M. (1944), 'Professor Pigou on "The Classical Stationary State": A Comment', *Economic Journal*, **6**, 131–2.

Kalecki, M. (1966 [1972]), *Studies in the Theory of Business Cycles, 1933–39*, Oxford: Basil Blackwell; translated from *Salari monetari e salari reali. In Studi sulla teoria dei cicli economici 1933–39*, Milan: Il Saggiatore.

Kalecki, M. (1990), 'Capitalism: business cycles and full employment', in J. Osiatynski (ed.), *Collected Works*, Oxford: Clarendon Press.

Keynes, J.M. (1923), 'A tract on monetary reform', in D. Moggridge (ed.), *Collected Writings*, Vol. IV, London: Macmillan.

Keynes, J.M. (1925), 'The economic consequences of Mr. Churchill', in D. Moggridge (ed.), *Collected Writings*, Vol. IX, London: Macmillan.

Keynes, J.M. (1931), The consequences to the banks of the collapse of money values', in D. Moggridge (ed.), *Collected Writings*, Vol. IX, London: Macmillan.

Keynes, J.M. (1933a), 'A monetary theory of production', in D. Moggridge (ed.), *Collected Writings*, Vol. XIII, London: Macmillan.

Keynes, J.M (1933b), 'The distinction between a co-operative economy and an entrepreneur economy', in D. Moggridge (ed.), *Collected Writings*, Vol. XXIX, London: Macmillan.

Keynes, J.M. (1936), *The General Theory of Employment, Interest and Money*, London: Macmillan.

King, M. (1994), 'Debt deflation: theory and evidence', *European Economic Review*, **9**, 419–45.
Kriesler, P. (2002), 'Was Kalecki an "imperfectionist"? Davidson on Kalecki', *Journal of Post Keynesian Economics*, **24** (4), 623–30.
Lopez, J. (2002), 'Two versions of the principle of effective demand: Kalecki and Keynes', *Journal of Post Keynesian Economics*, **24** (4), 37–58.
Mankiw, G. (1986), 'Issues in Keynesian macroeconomics: a review essay', *Journal of Monetary Economics*, **7**, 125–35.
Mankiw, G. (1992), 'The reincarnation of Keynesian economics', *European Economic Review*, **12** (April), 67–72.
Messori, M. (1999), *Financial Constraints and Market Failures*, Cheltenham, UK and Northampton, MA, USA: Edward Elgar.
Minsky, H. (1975), *John Maynard Keynes*, New York: Columbia University Press.
Minsky, H. (1982), 'Debt deflation processes in today's institutional environment', *Banca Nazionale del Lavoro Quarterly Review*, 375–93.
Minsky, H.P. (1984), *Potrebbe ripetersi? Instabilità e finanza dopo la crisi del 29* [Can If Happen Again? Instability and Finance After the Great Depression], Turin: Einaudi.
Palley, T. (2002), 'Endogenous money: what it is and why it matters', *Metroeconomica*, **2**, 152–80.
Patinkin, D. (1948), 'Price flexibility and full employment', *American Economic Review*, **38**, 543–64.
Patinkin, D. (1951), 'Price flexibility and full employment', revised edn, American Economic Association (eds), *Readings in Monetary Theory*, Boston, MA: Allen & Unwin, pp. 260–71.
Pigou, A.C. (1943), 'The classical stationary state', *Economic Journal*, **53**, 313–51.
Rochon, L. (1999), *Credit, Money and Production*, Cheltenham, UK and Northampton, MA, USA: Edward Elgar.
Romer, D. (1993), 'The new Keynesian synthesis', *Journal of Economic Perspectives*, **9** (Winter), 58–69.
Rotheim, R. (1998), *New Keynesian Economics/Post Keynesian Alternatives*, London: Routledge.
Simonazzi, A. and F. Vianello (2004), 'Deflation. The happy short life of unconventional thinking', Università di Roma 'La Sapienza', working paper series.
Tobin, J. (1975), 'Keynesian models of recession and depression', *American Economic Review, papers and proceedings*, **55**, 195–202.
Tobin, J. (1980), *Asset Accumulation and Economic Activity*, Oxford: Blackwell.
Tobin, J. (1993), 'Price flexibility and output stability: an old Keynesian view', *Journal of Economic Perspectives*, **7** (1), Winter, 45–65.

5. The contributions of Tom Asimakopulos to Post Keynesian economics

G.C. Harcourt*

INTRODUCTION

Tom and I knew one another for 35 years. Our close friendship dates from the late 1960s, after Tom had made a major shift in his approach to economics. This followed his year at MIT in 1965–66 where, listening to Bob Solow's lectures, the significance of Joan Robinson's critique of neoclassical theory and method fell into place (see Harcourt, 1991, 42, and Abe Tarasofsky's moving account of this episode quoted in the Preface of Harcourt et al. (eds), 1994, xii). Tom immediately took up the implications of the critique and started to spell them out in his own work. This was a courageous decision. It removed him from being regarded as one of the most promising young theorists in mainstream economics in Canada to an unpopular maverick position for which there was little understanding and even less tolerance among his peers.

When Tom and I were research students at King's College in the 1950s, he worked with Harry Johnson. My supervisors were Nicky Kaldor and then Ronald Henderson, but I was very much influenced by Joan Robinson, especially by *The Accumulation of Capital* (1956). I read her *magnum opus* in my second year as a research student, having been to her lectures on it the year before with Tom and our mutual friend and my former teacher at Melbourne University, Keith Frearson. Tom and Keith worked carefully through their lecture notes and the book itself when it was published. Tom was puzzled and irritated by her arguments, and by her criticisms of the orthodox theories of value and distribution and neoclassical methodology on which he had been brought up. I did not have many talks with Tom

* In writing this chapter, I have drawn heavily on my chapters in Harcourt et al. (eds) (1994) and Arestis and Sawyer (eds) (1992 [2000]). I acknowledge the criticisms on a draft of this chapter by an anonymous referee who is not responsible for my response or lack of response to them.

about economics but I did observe with awe the worksheets for his PhD dissertation in the (old) Marshall Library; they were an appropriate index of his systematic thoroughness and command of technique. His research topic was a three-commodity, three-country study in international trade theory entitled 'Productivity Changes, the Trade Balance and the Terms of Trade'. It required painstaking, voluminous calculations in calculus.

His first mentor was Jack Weldon, and Murray Kemp was also an important influence (see Harcourt, 1991, 42, n. 2). I imagine (but I don't know) that Tom was taught Keynes from *A Treatise on Money* and *The General Theory* and Marshall from the *Principles* by Jack, together with Joan Robinson and Edward Chamberlin (1933) from the originals and Piero Sraffa from the 1926 *Economic Journal* article, just as I was in Melbourne. I expect that he came to know J.R. Hicks from *Value and Capital* (and the *Trade Cycle?*), Roy Harrod from his 1939 article and 1948 book, Paul Samuelson from the *Foundations* (1947) and his published articles, and, I also imagine, some original D.H. Robertson. Reading Jack Weldon's superb chapter on the classical theory of distribution in Tom's book on income distribution (1988a), in retrospect I am not surprised that Tom came to the later views that he did, for the crucial seeds were sown early on by Jack. Nevertheless, in the 1950s and early 1960s, his overall structure of analysis differed from what it was to become, now reflected in the volume of selected papers (Asimakopulos, 1988b), the introduction to and his chapter in the edited book on income distribution, his microeconomics text (1978a), and his last book (1991). These, the views he had developed over the years in teaching Keynes, Harrod and Joan Robinson to his students, were set out lucidly and in full for posterity.

Tom's published writings show more than any other scholar's work I know well[1] the great value of developing books and articles from teaching material, which is how the bulk of Tom's published work originated. The need to explain explicitly and clearly the assumptions of the analysis, to understand other authors' views, the need to present a perspective and to explain the origins and relevance of concepts – all the demands on a good teacher were supplied in Tom's writings. They were built up from years of experience of lecturing on the issues, often at different levels. So, in speaking of Tom the economist I must also speak on Tom the man; the two were inseparable.

His attitudes to teaching and research reflected his philosophy of life in general. The most admirable aspect of his economics was that teaching was the top priority. He loved teaching the microeconomics course to the Honors students at McGill University. Even though he had a teaching assistant for the course, he made sure that from time to time he gave tutorials himself. A particularly poignant instance is that during his last illness he gave tutorials in the hospital amphitheatre a few weeks before his death. I have rarely known a teacher so thorough in the preparation of background notes in which the assumptions and arguments would be laid out clearly, simply and with great force. Tom's careful scholarship unobtrusively shone through in appropriate quotes, citations and sensible reading lists.

Another characteristic of Tom's work was his ability to retain the essential message and thrust of great authors, and to pass their message on, fully and fairly. At the same time he ironed out mistakes, inconsistencies, muddles and the blurred vision which inevitably must characterize the work of innovative original thinkers, charting new and/or unfamiliar territories. Because Tom did this for the great authors whose work he read, analyzed and taught, the structure of his own thought is a model of coherence, clarity and logical consistency.

Tom wrote to me on 26 April 1984, soon after the death of Joan Robinson, that he had written 'a "critical" review [of her contributions (Asimakopulos, 1984), because she was] too important an economist to be treated any other way, but the basis for [all his] criticism [came] from her own critical writings'. Joan was as hard on herself as she was on others, that is to say, very hard indeed. Tom too had exacting standards. The more he liked and respected a person, especially a student, the harder he would be. I am sure he would wish the same attitudes to be present in evaluations of his contributions. It is more difficult to fault him by these standards than it was Joan Robinson. I attribute this partly to differences in temperament, especially as Joan grew older, but mainly to Tom's conscientious attention to detail in classes, where he would often be teaching less gifted pupils than those whom Joan taught for most of her life.

TOM'S APPROACH IN TEACHING AND WRITING

Tom insisted that all discussions of economic issues be grounded in the nitty-gritty of reality, of a recognizable economy with its specific history, institutions and 'rules of the game', as Joan Robinson used to put it. This was true not only of his discussions of employment and growth theories but also of his microeconomic lectures and the textbook (1978a) that grew out of them. The chapters are full of real-world examples; the theory is assessed by how well it illuminates them. Tom deplored the habit in modern macroeconomics of ceasing to distinguish, in models which are supposed to relate to capitalist economies, between the capital goods sector and the consumption goods sector, with the different motives and financial power of the decision makers in, and the purchasers of the products of, each sector. This failure meant that the differential impacts of their behavior as a group or class on economic processes were missed out. He was critical of Martin Weitzman's influential article in 1982 on increasing returns and involuntary unemployment, just because the model in the article was not recognizable as one of a capitalist economy because these essential features were missing in its specification. (Nicky Kaldor loved it – or, at least, he loved its conclusions.) Tom wrote: 'There is no investment in this model . . . and it thus cannot even begin to analyze the question of the determinants of the levels of, and fluctuations in, output and employment in modern economies' (Asimakopulos, 1985, 352). 'The model does not contain workers or capitalists, but only units of a single "composite" factor of production, and there can thus be no wages or profits, even though the terms are used' (352). The production units are referred to by Weitzman 'as "firms or plants" (795), but they are no more . . . than a combination of factor units come together to produce goods . . . There is [therefore] no factor unit doing the "hiring" with the others being "hired" . . . Weitzman ignores the specification of his model and uses the verb "to hire" ' (788) (Asimakopulos, 1985, 352–3). Tom points out that Weitzman attributes 'persistent involuntary under-utilization of the major factors of production' to insufficient overall demand, itself traceable in turn to the unemployed lacking 'the means to communicate or make effective their potential demands' (Weitzman, 1982, 787). But for Keynes, such communication was not sufficient 'for an increase in employment to be self-sustaining, because the value of the increased output contains a profit component. Investment, as well as consumption, must increase in order to establish a higher equilibrium level of output and employment' (Asimakopulos, 1985, 353–4). Tom concludes: 'Weitzman is unable to deal with Keynes's approach, or to examine its micro-foundations because there is no investment in Weitzman's model' (354).

Again, when Tom (1978b) contrasted the model(s) of the firm implied in Kinut Wicksell's and Alfred Marshall's writings, he much preferred Marshall's model because its essential features were more recognizably those of actual firms in a historically real, capitalist economy. One of Wicksell's specifications, by contrast, was much more abstract and idealized and so did not give rise to categories of income and classes of persons to be found in actual firms, or to results which were legitimately comparable with those from Marshall's model. The setting for Tom's critique was the discussion in the modern literature 'concerning the appropriate criterion for firms to use in choosing the optimal technique for investment . . . maximization of the internal rate of return on the amount invested and maximization of the present value of the investment' (Asimakopulos, 1978b, 51). Tom points out: 'The decision-makers in each of these models have different roles [and so] each . . . refers to a different reality' (51). He adds: 'the failure to appreciate this difference is due to the absence in much of current economic theory of specifications of the institutional settings for the analyses . . . A necessary element in a theoretical model, if it is to be used to gain insights into the operation of actual economies, is the specification of the social relations of production which pertain to those economies' (51–2).

Tom argued that Marshall included two important features of modern economies in his model: first, the concept of ownership of the means of production by a minority (the 'capitalists') which allowed them to organize and control production and purchase the labor power of the majority (the 'workers'); second, two types of capitalists, entrepreneurs who use their own as well as borrowed capital to organize production, and rentiers who lend their capital but are otherwise passive as far as production is concerned. Wicksell had only one, or sometimes, none of these features in his model.

TOM'S LATER APPROACH

In his later approach Tom took a stance which reflected those of his first mentor, Jack Weldon, and his second major mentor, Joan Robinson and, through her, Kalecki. In his chapter on the classical theory of distribution (Weldon, 1988), Jack stresses that there were recognizable macroeconomic processes in classical thought to which was linked the crucial organizing concept of the surplus, its creation, extraction, distribution and use. This became central to Tom's thought, too, though he was most interested in what was happening in the sphere of distribution and exchange. There he traced the interrelationships between the theory of effective demand, especially of investment, and employment and distribution, their links back to underlying pricing mechanisms, and also (with John Burbidge) how a theory of tax incidence could be developed within this framework.

The crucial change in Tom's structure of analysis occurred when he fully comprehended Joan Robinson's distinction between logical time and historical time. This was associated with her methodological critique of neoclassical theory as she saw it, the illegitimacy of applying propositions drawn from a comparison of differences to an analysis of processes involving actual changes occurring. (She eventually summed this up in the graphic phrase 'History versus Equilibrium'.) Joan wrote about all this in an intuitive manner, criticizing those economists who argued for a tendency towards equilibrium, whereas, she argued, either an economy (or a market or an industry or a firm) is *in* equilibrium and has been for a long time, logically since the expulsion from the Garden of Eden, *or* it is not. In the latter case, economists observe a specific situation with a particular history, structure and set of expectations. Their role is to analyze what happens next when a change is imposed on the existing situation. Joan often used the analogy of a pendulum, the ultimate resting place of which is independent of whether it is given a slight nudge or arbitrarily lifted high and let go. In physics it ends up at the same place but in any economic system the analogy does not apply. Even in the first case it might not be true that an economy (et al.) would return after a slight nudge, unless the traders responsible for making the market and setting the prices had had such a long time to experience the realization of equilibrium prices that they did not panic when the (small) nudge occurred. But if the economy had never reached an equilibrium position in the past, how could it be argued that people will ever have the experience to know that they will reach one in the future? Analytically, Joan Robinson (and Kaldor) were talking about path-dependent equilibria – where an economy ends up depends on the path taken on the way. In Joan Robinson's case, she thought that it was often unlikely that it would *ever* end up in an equilibrium position though it might remain in a tranquil position for a while, one which superficially seemed to have equilibrium characteristics.

These insights underlay much of Tom's later work. An early example is Tom's article, 'Keynes, Patinkin, historical time and equilibrium analysis' (1973, 47–76). Here he contrasts the economic model examined in Patinkin's 1956 book (which acknowledged an 'obvious dependence . . . on the . . . concepts and techniques [of *The General Theory*])' with the model underlying *The General Theory*. This difference is reflected in the treatment of historical time, expectations, and the forces leading to positions of full-employment equilibrium.

> Keynes' model is . . . a causal model . . . deals with a particular situation at a particular period of time. Given . . . the . . . features of the particular situation examined, . . . the model works out what will happen next . . . may not be one of full employment . . . expectations may be disappointed with repercussions on behavior in future periods. Patinkin's model . . . is an equilibrium model. Attention is concentrated on equilibrium relations . . . embodies the assumption that forces will move the system to equilibrium if the position examined [is] one of disequilibrium. (Asimakopulos, 1973, 179)

Keynes's 'essentially static' analysis is nevertheless 'concerned with a segment of actual, historical time . . . The *memory* of past states and previous transaction prices affect present attitudes . . . Patinkin's model . . . deals with a very different "world" . . . more readily described in terms of simple equations' (180, emphasis in original). In particular, expectations continue to be held with certainty, even though they may be disappointed and 'the basis on which expectations are formed' is seen to be responsible. 'Patinkin's model is . . . essentially "timeless", with the economy's history having no role in [its] development . . . [it] does not provide a useful theoretical basis for understanding the workings of the economies for which Keynes' model was developed' (181).

These arguments are reflected in Tom's discussion of local and global stability in his microeconomics textbook (1978a). He gives a clear account (82–7) of the differences between Marshallian and Walrasian stability in a competitive market. He then points out the limited nature of the concepts – local and global, Marshallian or Walrasian, or any combination of these. For *always*, the equilibrium sits there waiting to be found while the stability analysis does its thing, whereas the essence of the Robinsonian critique is that the very act of seeking the equilibrium position changes the equilibrium position itself. In the section 'limitations of standard stability analysis', Tom writes:

> The standard methods . . . are mechanical. Expectations and the passage of time are ignored . . . the experience of non-equilibrium situations does not affect the positions of the demand and supply curves . . . the experience of changing prices does not change the expectations about future conditions . . . There is no time . . . other than a representation of demand and supply conditions for [a] particular slice of time. They cannot be used to trace a movement over a series of such slices, or during this particular period . . . if the initial price is not an equilibrium price, without additional assumptions concerning . . . the foundation of expectations, the holding of stocks, and possible changes over time in the values of the parameters. (Asimakopulos, 1978a, 86–7)

In terms of Jan Kregel's classic paper (1976) on the various models in *The General Theory*, as well as the papers after it, the shifting equilibrium method emerges as the dominant one. In Keynes's theory, not only were short-term expectations not immediately fulfilled, but also their very non-fulfillment was allowed to feed back into the formation of long-term expectations and so change the implied equilibrium (rest state) position associated with the point of effective demand itself. Grappling with this issue led to some of Tom's most incisive work, such as his critique of Keynes's theory of investment and the two-sided relationships between accumulation and profits which he put in its place (scrupulously acknowledging the influence of Kalecki and Joan Robinson on his 1971 paper); his exposition of Kalecki's theory of investment (1977), where, by the time the chain of reasoning had been gone through, he had returned again to the arbitrary position from which, for convenience, he had started the analysis and had explicitly handled any problems raised by his discussion at each point on the way, so making sure that the analysis *was* set in historical time. Again, in Asimakopulos and Burbidge on tax incidence (1974; Asimakopulos, 1988b), all these issues are faced fairly – and dealt with. The conclusion is a model of clarity and modesty.

We have obtained results on the incidence of taxation by concentrating on situations of short-period equilibrium. This is appropriate for comparisons with the neoclassical models because they deal only with equilibrium positions and it is in line with Kalecki's work in this area. It is only a first step, however, and a fuller treatment of the subject would require the tracing of the effects of tax changes over time. A change in tax at the beginning of a short period, even if we assume that it does not affect current investment, would probably work itself out over more than one short period. The resulting changes in output, prices, profits etc. will affect investment decisions and these will lead to further changes. In order to assess the longer-term effects of tax changes the analysis must be carried out within the context of a fully articulated growth model that permits the effects of the changes to be traced out over time (Asimakopulos and Burbidge, 1974; Asimakopulos, 1988b, 70).

Finally, in his 1983 paper for the Joan Robinson Memorial issue of the *Cambridge Journal of Economics*, which precipitated one of the most prolonged controversies of the 1980s in Post Keynesian theory, Tom discussed the deficiencies of Keynes's and Kalecki's modes of attack on the interrelationship between finance, saving and investment. In Keynes's 1937 articles on the rate of interest (*CW*, vol. XIV, 1973) in which he discussed his neglect in *The General Theory* of the finance motive as an additional reason for demanding money, he reached the startling conclusion that: 'the investment market can become congested through shortage of cash [but] never . . . through shortage of saving . . . the most fundamental of my conclusions within this field' (*CW*, vol. XIV, 1973, 22). Tom re-examined Keynes's arguments and also Kalecki's, for he discerned a similarity between Keynes's concept of a 'revolving fund' of finance and Kalecki's 'image' of the circle of finance which closes itself (Kalecki, 1935, 343). Tom wished to show that their models were not general but rather assumed a situation of considerable unemployment and undercapacity utilization of existing plant, with ample unused finance in the banking system, so that output and prices (perhaps) could be changed without pressure on interest rates. Moreover, it would be legitimate to proceed as if income had risen to give the new desired saving equal to the new desired investment immediately. That is to say, it was allowable to slide over the distinction between the existence of a short-period rest state (with unemployment) and the process by which it was attained, a procedure which was not generalizable to all situations of the economy. In a sense Tom was to side with Ralph

Hawtrey and, later, Hicks (in *The Crisis in Keynesian Economics*, 1976), in their reluctance to accept Keynes's short-cut method whereby the short-period rest state point could be used to 'explain' critical observations on the economy (see Harcourt, 1981, 250–64).

Tom insisted that, for Post Keynesian analysis to be operational, it must be done in terms of periodic analysis. He criticized Joan Robinson's later views in which she changed the definition of the short period so that it became 'not a length of time but a state of affairs'. She argued that the expressions, 'short period' and 'long period', should be used 'as adjectives, not as substantives' (Joan Robinson, 1971, 17–18). Tom objected to this approach because it took away 'the setting for Keynes's theory since there is no time available to permit variations in the utilization of productive capacity in response to changing short-term expectations' (Asimakopulos, 1988b, 196). (The simplification then required for Keynes's theory, which he himself shied away from, is to suppose that most production and gestation periods in the economy are of much the same length and that decisions about production, and about investment, are synchronized.) Joan Robinson's views are, I think, connected to the insights contained in Hugh Townshend's 1937 paper in the *Economic Journal*, 'Liquidity-premium and the theory of value' and to those in Nicky Kaldor's 1939 paper, 'Speculation and economic stability'. The arguments of both of these papers, together with those of Keynes himself in his 1937 papers, lie behind, for example, Snippe's 1985 critique of Tom's article. Victoria Chick, in her entry on Townshend in the *New Palgrave*, has put the essence of the position very well indeed:

> Townshend's note takes issue with Hicks's [subsequent] attempt to transform the theory of liquidity preference into a mirror image of the loanable funds theory by Walras's Law. Townshend saw that this was an attempt to retain the link between prices and flow concepts of cost and demand . . . [He argued] that it was in the nature of Keynes's . . . theory that expectations of the future could change the value of assets overnight and be reflected in the market prices of those assets even in the absence of actual trading. Thus current prices could be determined by subjective as well as objective fact and future prices were indeterminate. (1987, 662)

This leads into Kaldor's analysis in which he discusses, in effect, the characteristics of those markets where stocks dominate flows, and expectations dominate tangible economic factors, in the determination of prices, so that the analysis must concentrate on a moment in time before being extended to illuminate periods of time. Tom drew on Kaldor's analysis in order precisely to define those conditions which must hold in the financial sectors in order that the simple multiplier story of Keynes and Kalecki went through.

It involves taking a view of what is the typical way in which an investment project is financed over its lifetime; that is, to get it off the ground in the first place and, then, to build the financial aspect of it into the liability side of the firm's balance sheet in a permanent form. For the economy as a whole, this requires consideration of both how banks behave in aggregate and how new saving from newly created income associated with new investment expenditure and secondary rounds of consumption expenditure is held. This requires, in turn, a consideration of the term structure of interest rates (and, increasingly, the factors which lie behind the holding of equities and the issue of new ones). Kaldor postulated a group of speculators who needed to take a view on the long-term rate of interest (and presumably the prices of equities) in order that they could 'do their thing' and so keep the long-term rate of interest at levels it would have attained anyway, had there not been a rise in aggregate expenditure in the first place.

Tom was very careful to distinguish between the identity, $S = I$. and the equilibrium condition, $S = I$, something which neither Keynes nor Kalecki ever had really clear in their own minds. But there was a faint blur in Tom's discussion of saving which literally is a decision not to spend, not a provision of finance as such. Kregel points this out in his comment in the *Journal of Post Keynesian Economics* (1986); he argues that what Tom identified as temporary or undesired savings are in fact cash balances arising from decisions to hold or to disgorge (96; see also Kregel's essay in Harcourt et al., 1994 (eds)). This pushes the argument back to the crucial role of the banks in allowing the new investment process to go through in its entirety, that is, to Keynes's original position.

To help settle the arguments, may I ask whether the following statement can be given a rigorous precise meaning within the context of these exchanges? 'Yesterday's' saving may influence 'today's' investment, and 'today's' saving may influence 'tomorrow's' investment, but it is 'today's' investment which is responsible for 'today's' saving. This both reveals a deep Keynesian insight and is *not* precise, for the distinction between 'desired' and 'actual' remains blurred. In sorting this out Tom's approach was invaluable, even if he lost sight of some of the elements in the argument whereby a 'moment' of time really was the proper vantage point from which to begin the analysis.

TOM ON KEYNES, HARROD AND JOAN ROBINSON

In his last book (Asimakopulos, 1991), Tom dealt with the contributions of Keynes, Harrod and Joan Robinson. He examined the work of the last two scholars because both of them, in their own distinctive ways, were attempting to 'generalize *The General Theory* to the long period'. In Tom's reading, both conceded, in the end, that they failed. While it could plausibly be argued that the analysis of *The General Theory* is directly applicable to actual economies in the here and now[2] even when simplified to rest state analysis, Tom nevertheless agreed with Keynes's judgment: 'I should, I think, be prepared to argue that, in a world ruled by uncertainty with an uncertain future linked to an actual present, a final position of equilibrium, such as one deals with in static economics, does not properly exist' (*CW*, vol. XXIX, 1979, 222). From this standpoint, both Harrod's warranted rate of growth and Joan Robinson's Golden Ages were *not* the operational counterparts in growth theory of the aggregate demand and supply schedules (and their intersection) of *The General Theory*. Kalecki's (1968) (and R.M. Goodwin's) cyclical growth models, in which long- and short-period factors impinge *simultaneously* on the economic decisions of the here and now to create activity, employment and distribution, were, I conjecture, Tom's favored way forward.

Because of this, Tom was impatient with, and skeptical of the neo-Ricardian long-period method (outside the domain of doctrinal debates, where even Joan Robinson would allow its use if it exposed lack of logic in her opponents' propositions). Far from accepting that general theory could only be done using the long-period method, whereby general propositions could be made about the interrelationships between persistent forces at work in economies, Tom denied that, in general, there could be either convergence on or fluctuations around such centers of gravitation. He thus rejected the Milgate–Eatwell–Garegnani interpretation of *The General Theory* (1983) as a long-period theory (only to be labeled an imperfectionist for doing so!). By doing so, he also rejected Marshall's view that short-period normal equilibrium positions could be regarded as stations on the way to the central long-period normal equilibrium cross.

TOM'S RELATIONSHIP WITH PIERO SRAFFA

What then of Tom's relationship to the work of our mutual pastor of Cambridge research students from the 1950s, Piero Sraffa? I have deliberately separated this from his attitudes to the approach of the neo-Ricardians for, while they explicitly claim kinship with Sraffa, they have moved on in directions which are not obviously associated with Sraffa himself. Sraffa's writings are relevant for Tom's approach in two ways. First, Tom took on board the technical aspects of Sraffa's 1926 article in the *Economic Journal*; that is, the conditions which have to be satisfied in the real world for Marshall's partial equilibrium procedure to be applied legitimately. As a result, Tom is one of the few economists who have tackled successfully the aggregation problems in *The General Theory*, by making explicit the conditions which have to be satisfied before both the aggregate demand schedule and the aggregate supply schedule may be regarded as coherent concepts. In doing this, Tom expunged the confusions in Keynes's presentation of aggregate demand in *The General Theory* – the two different concepts, only one of which survives as coherent (see Asimakopulos, 1991, 20–23), as well as explaining how the aggregate supply curve could be constructed without running foul of, among other things, the Sraffa critique (see, in particular, Asimakopulos, 1988b, 104–13).

Tom thus carefully absorbed the technical critique but he did not go the whole way with Sraffa in the latter's conceptual critique of supply and demand theory. This is clear in Tom's 1988b chapter on Sraffa and Keynes. Tom comments (129) that, in the system of *Production of Commodities by Means of Commodities* (1960), Sraffa had left 'formally open' the question whether demand could affect the prices of production in a complete economic system 'even though the general thrust of Sraffa's work implied that demand is not important in this context or, at least, that its influence on price is "not comparable" with those of labor and material inputs'. In a footnote (n.3, 142), Tom amplifies this and reports Sraffa's response:

> I had written to Sraffa in 1971 and had observed that his theoretical framework did not permit any conclusions about the effects of demand on prices unless the assumption of constant returns to scale were added. He responded in a letter dated 11 July 1971: 'You say "I don't see how demand can be said to have no influence on prices, unless constant returns . . ." I take it that the drama is enacted on Marshall's stage where the claimants for influence are utility and cost of production. Now utility had made little progress (since the 1870s) towards acquiring a tangible existence and survives in textbooks at the purely subjective level. On the other had, cost of production has successfully survived Marshall's attempt to reduce it to an equally evanescent nature under the name of "disutility", and is still kicking in the form of hours of labor, tons of raw materials, etc. This, rather than the relative slope of the two curves, is why it seems to me that the "influence" of the two things on price is not comparable.'

Tom was probably too sympathetic to the approaches of Marshall and Keynes completely to agree with Sraffa, even though, in Tom's later writings, agreement with Marx and Kalecki on other matters was evident.[3] This *may* mean that Tom would have agreed with Joan Robinson's (nearly final) statement on the connection between Sraffa's approach and those of Marx in 'Accumulation and exploitation: an analysis in the tradition of Marx, Sraffa and Kalecki' (Bhaduri and Joan Robinson, 1980). They argued that Sraffa's target (in his prelude to a critique) was not 'current neoclassical teaching rooted in general equilibrium and "scarce means with alternative uses" [but] the amorphous moralizing of Marshallian theory of "factors of production" receiving "rewards" consonant with their respective productivities'. They claimed that Sraffa showed 'that the influence upon distribution in capitalist industry must be divided into two separate elements. On the one side are the technical factors . . . [on the other] the share of wages in net output (and therefore the potential ratio of profit on capital) [which] depends upon commercial, social and political influences and the class war' (111). Production potential and actual output coincide or diverge according to the state of effective demand, itself affected by the distribution of income. Sraffa's particular contribution was to establish that 'In principle, a given technical situation is compatible with any proportion of relative shares [thus ruling] out the notion of earnings determined by productivity' (111). In Joan Robinson's view, the second half of the story is easily released into historical time. It is the challenge of the 'first half of the story – the influence of changes in technology on demand for labor, on accumulation and on effective demand – [which needs to be taken up afresh]' (111). Those scholars who respond to this challenge will be continuing in a tradition to which not only Tom's two mentors contributed so much but also Tom himself.

CONCLUSION

To sum up: Tom has left a fine legacy in print. As interpretations of Keynes, Kalecki, Harrod and Joan Robinson and (to a lesser extent) Sraffa, his books and papers will continue to be invaluable. Tom stands fair and square with these scholars as an economist who deeply understood the economic and political processes at work in capitalism and how they may best be modeled. His outstanding papers included the path-breaking work on short-period tax incidence (written with John Burbidge: Asimakopulos and Burbidge 1974; Asimakopulos, 1988b), his critical analysis of Keynes's investment theory (1971), his stalwart defense of Keynes's contributions as set in a short-period context (1984, 1985, 1989), and his paper on saving, investment and finance in Keynes and Kalecki in the 1983 Joan Robinson Memorial issue of the *Cambridge Journal of Economics* (1983, 1988b).

His writings on pensions will also continue to instill common sense and provide relevance. Along with Weldon, Tom stressed that public pension schemes involve redistribution through taxes, and thus command over resources, from the working to the retired (or ill or widowed) in the here and now. They are not associated with a process of saving now for dissaving later on. Moreover, because any ongoing scheme of necessity must exist in an environment of uncertainty about the future, analysis should not be based on models which assume away uncertainty, as virtually all the well-known models in the literature do.

It would be wrong to end here for the most important thing in Tom's life was his family. Tom was strict but he doted on 'his girls' – all three, Marika, Anna and Julia. Their friends noted what a united, supportive, loving, happy family they were, no more so than in the last years of Tom's life. After Tom died (Cambridge University Press accepted his 1991 book in the last week of his life), Marika saw through its preparation just as she had been the ever-present helpmate with his earlier books.

NOTES

1. The one possible exception is Eric Russell, but I can assure you that that is praise indeed!
2. We have seen that there is a dispute as to whether we mean a moment or a stretch of actual time.
3. For another view on these issues, see the essay by Neri Salvadori in Harcourt et al. (1994).

REFERENCES

Arestis, P. and M. Sawyer (eds) (1992 [2000]), *A Biographical Dictionary of Dissenting Economists*, Cheltenham, UK and Northampton, MA, USA: Edward Elgar.

Asimakopulos, A. (1971), 'The determination of investment in Keynes' model', *Canadian Journal of Economics*, **4**, 382–8.

Asimakopulos, A. (1973), 'Keynes, Patinkin, historical time, and equilibrium analysis', *Canadian Journal of Economics*, **6**, 179–88.

Asimakopulos, A. (1977), 'Profits and investment: a Kaleckian approach', in G.C. Harcourt (ed.), *The Microeconomic Foundations of Macroeconomics*, London: Macmillan, pp. 328–42.

Asimakopulos, A. (1978a), *An Introduction to Economic Theory: Microeconomics*, Oxford: Oxford University Press.

Asimakopulos, A. (1978b), 'The non-comparability of criteria for the choice of optimal technique', *Australian Economic Papers*, **17**, 51–62.

Asimakopulos, A. (1983), 'Kalecki and Keynes on finance, investment and saving', *Cambridge Journal of Economics*, **7**, 221–33.

Asimakopulos, A. (1984), 'Joan Robinson and economic theory', *Banca Nazionale Del Lavoro Quarterly Review*, December, 381–409.

Asimakopulos, A. (1985), 'The foundations of unemployment theory: a comment', *Journal of Post Keynesian Economics*, **7**, 352–62.

Asimakopulos, A. (ed.) (1988a), *Theories of Income Distribution*, Boston, MA: Kluwer Academic.

Asimakopulos, A. (1988b), *Investment, Employment and Income Distribution*, Oxford: Polity Press.

Asimakopulos, A. (1989), 'The nature and role of equilibrium in Keynes's *General Theory*', *Australian Economic Papers*, **28**, 16–28.

Asimakopulos, A. (1991), *Keynes's General Theory and Accumulation*, Cambridge: Cambridge University Press.

Asimakopulos, A. and J.B. Burbidge (1974), 'The short-period incidence of taxation', *Economic Journal*, **84**, 267–88, reprinted in Asimakopulos (1988b).

Bhaduri, A. and J. Robinson (1980), 'Accumulation and exploitation: an analysis in the tradition of Marx, Sraffa and Kalecki', *Cambridge Journal of Economics*, **4**, 103–15.

Chamberlin, E.H. (1933), *The Theory of Monopolistic Competition*, Cambridge, MA: Harvard University Press.

Chick, V. (1987), 'Townshend, Hugh (1890–1974)', in John Eatwell, Murray Milgate and Peter Newman (eds), *The New Palgrave. A Dictionary of Economics*, vol. IV, London: Macmillan, p. 662.

Eatwell, John and Murray Milgate (eds) (1983), *Keynes's Economics and the Theory of Value and Distribution*, London: Duckworth.

Goodwin, R.M. (1967), 'A growth cycle', in C.H. Feinstein (ed.), *Socialism, Capitalism and Economic Growth: Essays Presented to Maurice Dobb*, Cambridge: Cambridge University Press.

Harcourt, G.C. (1981), 'Marshall, Sraffa and Keynes: incompatible bedfellows?', *Eastern Economic Journal*, **7**, 39–50, reprinted in Sardoni (ed.) (1992), pp. 250–64.

Harcourt, G.C. (1991), 'Athanasios (Tom) Asimakopulos 1930–1990: A Memoir', *Journal of Post Keynesian Economics*, **14**, 39–48.

Harcourt, G.C., A. Roncaglia and R. Rowley (eds) (1994), *Income and Employment in Theory and Practice. Essays in Memory of Athanasios Asimakopulos*, Basingstoke: Macmillan.

Harrod, R.F. (1939), 'An essay in dynamic theory', *Economic Journal*, **49**, 14–33.

Harrod, R.F. (1948), *Towards a Dynamic Economics*, London: Macmillan.

Hicks, J.R. (1939), *Value and Capital*, Oxford: Clarendon Press.

Hicks, J.R. (1950), *A Contribution to the Theory of the Trade Cycle*, Oxford: Clarendon Press.

Hicks, J. (1976), *The Crisis in Keynesian Economics*, Oxford: Clarendon Press.

Kaldor, N. (1939), 'Speculation and economic stability', *Review of Economic Studies*, **7**, 1–27.

Kalecki, M. (1935), 'A macrodynamic theory of business cycles', *Econometricia*, **3**, 327–44.

Kalecki, M. (1968), 'Trend and business cycle reconsidered', *Economic Journal*, **78**, 263–76.

Keynes, J.M. (1930), *A Treatise on Money*, 2 vols, London: Macmillan.

Keynes, J.M. (1936), *The General Theory of Employment, Interest and Money*, London: Macmillan.

Keynes, J.M. (1937a, 1937b, 1973), *Collected Writings*, vol. XIV, London: Macmillan.

Keynes, J.M. (1979), *Collected Writings*, vol. XXIX, London: Macmillan.

Kregel, J.A. (1976), 'Economic methodology in the face of uncertainty: the modelling methods of Keynes and the Post Keynesians', *Economic Journal*, **86**, 209–25.

Kregel, J.A. (1986), 'A note on finance, liquidity, saving and investment', *Journal of Post Keynesian Economics*, **9**, 91–100.

Patinkin, D. (1956), *Money, Interest and Prices*, New York: Row Peterson.

Robinson, J. (1933), *The Economics of Imperfect Competition*, London: Macmillan.
Robinson, J. (1956), *The Accumulation of Capital*, London: Macmillan.
Robinson, J. (1971), *Economic Heresies: Some Old-fashioned Questions in Economic Theory*, Basingstoke: Macmillan.
Samuelson, P.A. (1947), *Foundations of Economic Analysis*, Cambridge, MA: Harvard University Press.
Sardoni, C. (ed.) (1992), *On Political Economists and Modern Political Economy. Selected Essays of G.C. Harcourt*, London: Routledge.
Snippe, J. (1985), 'Finance, savings and investment in Keynes's economics', *Cambridge Journal of Economics*, **9**, 257–69.
Sraffa, P. (1926), 'The laws of returns under competitive conditions', *Economic Journal*, **36**, 535–50.
Sraffa, P. (1960), *Production of Commodities by Means of Commodities. Prelude to a Critique of Economic Theory*, Cambridge: Cambridge University Press.
Townshend, H. (1937), 'Liquidity-premium and the theory of value', *Economic Journal*, **47**, 157–69.
Weitzman, M.L. (1982), 'Increasing returns and the foundations of unemployment theory', *Economic Journal*, **92**, 787–804.
Weldon, J.C. (1988), 'The classical theory of distribution', in A. Asimakopulos (ed.) (1988a), pp. 15–47.

6. Asimakopulos's criticism of Keynes's short-period equilibrium: a reformulation

Abdelkader Slifi*

INTRODUCTION

In *The General Theory of Employment, Interest and Money (1936)*, it seems that Keynes's method is 'only half in time and half in equilibrium'. On the one hand, he rejects the classical method, which consists of establishing long-term tendencies of economic variables towards long-period equilibrium. By taking into account uncertainty, he seems to favour a method with a historical treatment of time. In this way, he justifies the instability of the long-period equilibrium by the volatility of long-term expectations:

> Keynes was looking at the actual situation and trying to understand how an actual economy operates; he brought the argument down from timeless stationary states into the present, here and now, when the past cannot be changed and the future cannot be known. (Robinson, 1971: ix)

On the other hand, in order to demonstrate the principle of effective demand on the basis of the existence of an equilibrium level of unemployment, Keynes defines the concept of short-period equilibrium and uses it within the framework of a comparative static method in order to study the determination of the volume of employment. In this way, he obtains the identity between saving and investment by overlooking the time required for the multiplier effect to be worked out and by assuming a stable position of the short-period equilibrium volume of employment.

According to Asimakopulos, 'there is a constant tension in Keynes's theory between his desire to deal with a capitalist economy moving through historical time and the use of short-period equilibrium' (1987: 17). Nevertheless, the contradiction can be overstepped and both methods made compatible in a coherent framework, by putting the issue in the

* I am grateful for constructive suggestions by the anonymous referee.

perspective of the transition of Keynes's thought from the *Treatise on Money* to the *General Theory*. Keynes's wish to demonstrate the existence of an equilibrium level of unemployment made him adopt Kahn's (1931) saving function and identity between saving and investment. Indeed, the identity between saving and investment is not a necessary condition for conceiving variations in the output and employment levels: it is sufficient to take away the underlying hypothesis of full employment behind the *Treatise*'s fundamental equations. Actually the difference between the *Treatise on Money* and the *General Theory* is not so much the possibility of conceiving variations in the output and employment levels which rests primarily on the hypothesis of full employment, but the possibility of conceiving dynamic processes in disequilibrium positions. This possibility disappears in the *General Theory* since short-term expectations are assumed to be fulfilled. Keynes himself thought that a chapter showing the effects of allowing mistaken expectations should be provided (1973b, *CWJMK* XIV:[1] 182).

Our purpose is to follow Keynes's suggestion by specifying the treatment of short-term expectations. Our aim is to show that: (i) the conception of the relation between saving and investment which is inherited from Kahn's (1931) criticism of the lack of a saving function in the *Treatise on Money*, implies the multiplier effect is realised at any time; and (ii) the proposition that the effects of allowing mistaken expectations can be neglected, is justified by two special features of Keynes's model: the definition of the period and the assumption of the stability of the short-period equilibrium.

First, we define the short-period equilibrium in the light of the transition from the *Treatise on Money* to the *General Theory*. By specifying the role of short-term expectations in the determination of effective demand, we argue that the peculiar definition of the period confines Keynes's *General Theory* to an analysis in terms of equilibrium. Then, we specify the conditions of the stability of the short-period equilibrium, by studying the effect of considering disappointed short-term expectations.

THE DETERMINATION OF THE SHORT-PERIOD EQUILIBRIUM IN THE LIGHT OF THE TREATISE'S FUNDAMENTAL EQUATIONS

Keynes thought that the method used in the *General Theory* was consistent with the one used in the *Treatise*:[2]

> The significance of both my present and my former argument lies in their attempt to show that the volume of employment is determined by the estimates

> of effective demand made by entrepreneurs, an expected increase of investment relatively to saving as defined in the *Treatise* being a criterion of an increase in effective demand. (1936: 78)

The novelty brought by Keynes's *General Theory* is neither the effective demand principle which was already underlying the *Treatise*, nor the allowance for changes in the output level which rests on the assumed elasticity of supply.[3] The novelty rests on the peculiar definition of the period so that income is spent in the same period in which it is received.

In Chapter seven of the *General Theory* 'The meaning of saving and investment: further considered', Keynes compares his two works and tries to delete the difference between definitions:

> In my *Treatise on Money* the concept of changes in the excess of investment over saving, as there defined, was a way of handling changes in profit, though I did not in that book distinguish clearly between expected and realised results. I there argued that change in the excess of investment over saving was the motive force of governing changes in the volume of output. Thus the new argument, though (as I now think) much more accurate and instructive, is essentially a development of the old. Expressed in the language of my *Treatise on Money*, it would run: the expectations of an increased excess of investment over saving, given the former volume of employment and output, will induce entrepreneurs to increase the volume of employment and output. (1936: 77–8)

The *Treatise's* Fundamental Equations

Following the *Treatise*'s fundamental equations, the monetary equilibrium of entrepreneurs, which does not necessarily correspond to the equilibrium of the goods market, is thus defined:

$$I^e = S$$

$$Q^e = I^e - S = 0$$

$$P^e = P^*$$

$$r^e = r^*,$$

where I^e is the expected amount of investment, S is the current amount of saving, Q^e is the expected windfall profits (or losses), P^* is the normal price level, P^e is the expected price level, r^* is the normal rate of profit and r^e is the expected rate of profit. The most significant notion is the normal rate of profit which is defined as 'that rate of remuneration which if they were open to make new bargains with all the factors of production at the currently prevailing rates of earnings, would leave them under no motive either to increase or to decrease their scale of operations' (1930: 124–5). Given the definition of the normal rate of profit, we can consider that the Marshallian notion of normality of the rate of profit corresponds to transposition of the Ricardian notion of uniformity of the rate of profit to an aggregate model:

> [I]t is by altering the rate of profits in particular directions that entrepreneurs can be induced to produce this rather than that, and it is by altering the rate of profits in general that they can be induced to modify the average of their offers of remuneration to the factors of production. (Ibid. 141)

Now, assuming an excess of expected investment over current saving, we can define the monetary disequilibrium of entrepreneurs:[4] $I^e > S$; $Q^e > 0$; $P^e > P^*$; $r^e > r$. Following the *Treatise*'s fundamental equations, income is thus defined:[5]

$$Y = P^* O,$$

where P^* is the normal price level of goods and O the current output level.

Anticipating windfall profits, entrepreneurs will be induced to increase employment in order to change the scale of production, N being the volume of employment:

$$Q^e = \Delta(wN).$$

In the general case, the levels of output and price will both rise, in consequence of expected windfall profits, according to the elasticity of the labour supply, which depends on the gap between the current volume of employment and the volume of full employment. So, it is the degree of elasticity of labour supply which will determine to what extent the excess of demand will be absorbed by price inflation and to what extent it will be absorbed by change in output.[6]

By approximating on a logarithmic basis:

$$\frac{\Delta(PO)}{PO} = \frac{\Delta P}{P} + \frac{\Delta O}{O}.$$

If we assume full employment, wage inflation will absorb the excess demand in the goods markets, such that it will bring about a price-level inflation (ΔP):

$$\Delta P = Q^e = I^e - S.$$

If we postulate infinite elasticity of the labour supply so that wage is constant, change in output will absorb the excess of demand. So, by taking away the assumption of full employment which prevents the change in the output level, we can define a utilisation function, expressing the relation of the volume of employment to the level of effective demand and study the consequential variation of the volume of employment to a disequilibrium situation which generates expected windfall profits:

$$\Delta Y = \Delta(P^* O) = P^* \Delta O.$$

In a given short period, with fixed capital stock, given the propensity to consume and the long-term forecast, which is characteristic of the *General Theory*, the variations in income, resulting from the windfall profits will be carried out in several waves. The first corresponds to the response to investment expenditures; the second corresponds to the response to the demand for consumer goods emanating from the recently hired workers and will depend on the rise of the wage bill ($w\Delta N$) and the marginal propensity to consume (c). But this demand for consumer goods cannot be satisfied unless the employment and the production levels in the sector of the consumer goods rise. The two first waves thus initiate the multiplier effect, by causing successive excesses of demand in the consumer goods market:

$$\Delta Y = Q^e + cQ^e + c^2 Q^e \ldots + c^{\infty} Q^e.$$

As we define $Q^e = I^e - S = \Delta I^e$, we obtain the multiplier effect:

$$\Delta Y = \frac{\Delta I^e}{1 - c}.$$

So, the novelty brought by the *General Theory* rests primarily on the modification of the definition of the period. Since income is supposed to be spent during the same period in which it is received, the subsequent increases to the mobilisation of windfall profits are included because changes in output are allowed, so that windfall profits no longer exist as such. When expectations on the current rate of profit are not fulfilled, entrepreneurs have time to modify these decisions until their expectations are fulfilled. It seems that, while the *Treatise* took place before the realisation of the quantity adjustment, the *General Theory* is concerned with the equilibrium positions with a normal rate of profit, so that the possibility of carrying out windfall profits is saturated and there is no more inducement to change the scale of production. Actually, the specific feature in the *Treatise* which excluded them from the former definition was due, not only to the specific definitions of income and saving, but to the fact that their holders had not planned the corresponding expenditures.

In the *General Theory*, the definition of the period, which assumes the interval of time necessary for the windfall profits to be engaged in the change in the scale of production, implies a definition of income, which uses (so to speak) windfall profits. This definition overlooks the disequilibrium positions and focuses on the relation *ex post* between saving and investment, that is, after the mobilisation of windfall profits have generated the variation in income and saving necessary to restore equilibrium *ex post* when the relation *ex ante* was in disequilibrium. But this overlooking is only valid because Keynes assumed fulfilled short-term expectations.

However, if expectations concerning prices and windfall profits are not fulfilled, entrepreneurs will modify their decisions concerning employment after having noticed the possibility of realising windfall profits or losses. The excess of expected investment over saving must be considered as an order of investment goods, which is paid in advance but is not satisfied immediately by a supply of investment goods, because time is required for the rise in employment, production and income to take place. Actually, prices and the rate of profit remain at their normal levels in the whole course of the process, because of the absence of transactions in disequilibrium positions: 'I am not so much interested myself in the brief intermediate period during which higgling of the market is discovering the facts' (Keynes, letter to Hawtrey, 1973b, *CWJMK*, XIV: 27).

The Identity between Saving and Investment and the Definition of the Period

We can specify the implicit saving function, s being the propensity to save out of income:

$$S = sY.$$

Kahn's (1931) criticism of the *Treatise on Money* justifies the introduction of the propensity to save out of windfall profits (s) – should this be (s'):

$$S' = sY + s'Q^e.$$

In his demonstration, Kahn distinguishes between Q_1 and Q_2, respectively, the windfall profits of the sector producing investment goods and of the sector producing consumer goods, I' being the cost of production and I the market price of the investment goods:

$$Q_1 = I' - S + (1 - s')Q$$

$$Q_2 = I - I + s'Q$$

$$Q = Q_1 + Q_2.$$

Then:

$$Q = I' - S + I - I' + (1 - s')Q + s'Q$$

$$Q = I - S + Q.$$

Thus, we obtain the identity:

$$I \equiv S.$$

Similar to Kahn's identity between saving and investment, Keynes will focus on the situations in which the full multiplier effect is realised. This demonstration does not mean that: 'If we define income to include profits, and saving as being the excess of income thus defined over expenditure on consumption, then saving and the value of investment are identically the same thing' (Keynes, 1973a, *CWJMK*, XIII: 251). This conception of the identity between saving an investment is only a definitional one. But Kahn's demonstration is even valid when income is defined so that it does not include windfall profits. The definition of the period is such that prices and the rate of profit have time to reach their normal levels. At the end of the period, the multiplier is realised, so the short-period variables of the economic system have reached their equilibrium values.

One of the main novelties of the *General Theory* compared to the *Treatise* is the concept of the propensity to consume. Kahn considers the multiplier relation to be the saving function that the *Treatise on Money* missed. The concept of the propensity to consume allows Keynes to build a saving function, according to which saving becomes an increasing function of income. Following this principle, the income level is the adjusting variable which allows equality between saving and investment. According to Keynes (1936: 111), the influence of the interest rate on propensity to consume can be neglected within the framework of the short period. This conception leads to the definition of the short-period equilibrium through the multiplier principle, where the causation takes place from investment to saving via the variations of income. The causation's direction implies that investment is an autonomous component of demand. As investment depends on the interest rate, the interest rate must be independent of the goods market equilibrium, and particularly independent of saving. In fact, the monetary interest rate is determined in the money market, which is upstream from the goods market within the recursive model of the *General Theory*.

Therefore, Keynes considered the equality between saving and investment as an identity, that is, always equal. To a certain extent, that is a good approximation of the relation between saving and investment, because these two variables are equal whatever the level of the rate of interest. Keynes seems to be right by concluding: 'In the previous chapter saving and investment have been so defined that they are necessarily equal in amount, being, for the community as a whole, merely different aspects of the same thing' (1936: 74). Keynes even ventures some hazardous definitions, the identity becoming transformed into confusion: 'the propensity to save is a curve which relates the amount of investment to the amount of income' (Keynes, 1973a, *CWJMK*, XIV: 551–2).

Kahn himself tried to moderate Keynes: 'I do not like you saying that saving and investment are "different names for the same thing". They are different things (that is the whole point) – they are certainly different acts – but they are equal in magnitude' (ibid.: 637). Nevertheless, an identity is an always-checked equality, a truism that does not explain anything about the logical and historical advance of the realisation of the equality. This conception is based on two assumptions: the definition of period and income, which we have highlighted with a comparative approach between the *Treatise* and the *General Theory*; the stability of the short-period equilibrium according to which the convergence of the current values of the variables towards their equilibrium values can be considered as instantaneous, prices remaining at their normal level. In the shadow of those two assumptions, there is ambivalence over the role of expectations in the *General Theory*. While long-term expectations are affected by uncertainty there is no place for unfulfilled short-term expectations.

THE STABILITY OF THE SHORT-PERIOD EQUILIBRIUM

Keynes emphasises the importance of uncertainty, which affects entrepreneurs' decisions and prevents us from considering a state of fulfilled expectations as the general case. The equilibrium positions for which all the forces put into action by the modifications of the decisions, consequential to unfulfilled expectations, are at rest. Keynes favours the historical treatment of time, in opposition to the static treatment which is based on the analogy with the treatment of space (one can move from one point to another while keeping the possibility of coming back), because if the forecasts are erroneous they can be immediately corrected and decisions consequently modified, so the passage from one position to another is instantaneous.

Nevertheless, Asimakopulos (1982, 1983 and 1987) reproaches Keynes for using comparative statics and for overlooking the time required for the full multiplier effect to be worked out:

> With his concentration on short-period equilibrium values, and his use of comparative statics to evaluate the effects of a change in investment or in the propensity to consume, Keynes tended to overlook the time required for the full multiplier effect of a change in autonomous expenditures to work themselves out. (Asimakopulos, 1987: 20)

According to Asimakopulos, Keynes failed in his attempt to show what determines the volume of employment 'at any time' because he concentrates on its equilibrium levels. The main subject of the criticism is to be found in Keynes's conception of finance as a revolving fund (Asimakopulos, 1983). We reformulate this criticism regardless of finance by focusing on Keynes's treatment of short-term expectations in the determination of the short-period equilibrium.

In Chapter three of *The General Theory*, Keynes defines effective demand as the point of intersection between the aggregate demand and aggregate supply functions. The former shows the expected aggregate proceeds for a given volume of employment, and the latter links the decisions of employment with given expected aggregate proceeds (1936: 25). In Chapter five, Keynes specifies this process of decision:

> Thus the behaviour of each individual firm in deciding its daily output will be determined by its short-term expectations – expectations as to the cost of output on various possible scales and expectations as to the sale-proceeds of this output . . . it is upon these various expectations that the amount of employment which the firms offer will depend. (1936: 46)

According to Hawtrey, while expected price must be considered as independent of the volume of employment for each individual demand curve, that is no longer possible with the aggregate demand curve: 'Each employer's expectation is presumably confined to his own product, and I do not see how you are going to aggregate these particular expectations into a total consumption and total investment' (1973b, *CWJMK*, XIV: 597). Asimakopulos (1982) concludes that Keynes's definition of the effective demand must be restated because of the lack of microfoundations of the aggregate functions.[7] Then, he argues that Robertson (1955) has noticed the existence of a second version of the aggregate demand function: the multiplier principle.

The multiplier can be defined as a process of adjustment between saving and investment. Indeed, even if income is thus defined not to include windfall profits, it varies in response to the excess of investment over saving (or the contrary). The interest rate is not the adjusting variable but an independent variable which is determined in the money market upstream of the general model. Variation in the interest rate (or of the marginal efficiency of capital (MEK) is generally considered as the origin of the disequilibrium by causing the variation of the investment expenditures which brings about the process of adjustment of saving via the variations of income.

This means that there is a level of income which ensures the equality between saving and investment whatever the interest rate is: it is the equilibrium level of income which corresponds to the point of effective demand. Saving would thus be identical to the investment from the point of view of the interest rate because investment is equal to saving whatever the interest rate is. But a relation can be called an identity only relatively to the adjusting variable. Here, the adjusting variable is not the interest rate but income, the interest rate being an independent variable. However, it is not exact to say that $I = S$ whatever the value of Y. Under these conditions, asserting that saving and investment are identical is improper if not logically erroneous.

The Multiplier Principle in Historical Time

Following Keynes's method, the short period must be sufficiently long that short-term expectations are fulfilled and short-period variables reach their equilibrium values and that the multiplier effect is completely carried out. Thus, while being placed within the framework of the short period, Keynes neglects 'the time required for the value of dependent variables (in particular employment and income) to reach short-period equilibrium when there is a change in say, investment' (Asimakopulos, 1991: 5). This conception does not allow us to distinguish between *ex ante* and *ex post* relations between saving and investment. It rests on presupposing that the short-period equilibrium exerts such a strong attraction force over the current values of the variables that it is legitimate to neglect the dynamical process which allows their convergence towards this equilibrium.

Let us start with an equilibrium situation, assuming a decrease in the interest rate, so that entrepreneurs will desire an increase in the investment expenditures. A dynamic analysis requires specifying the temporal process which leads from one equilibrium to another. It means studying the stability of the equilibrium system.

Keynes argues that the stability of the short-period equilibrium lies on the assumption of a marginal propensity to consume lower than one (Keynes, 1936: 30). Indeed, if marginal propensity to consume was equal to one, the variation of investment would generate only an equivalent amount of income and no saving. But this justification is insufficient to prove the stability of the short-period equilibrium. Keynes is aware that the adjusting process of employment towards his equilibrium level is not instantaneous, but he asserts in an ambiguous way: 'in every interval of time the theory of the multiplier holds good in the sense that the increment of aggregate demand is equal to the product of the increment of aggregate investment and the multiplier as determined by the marginal propensity to consume' (1936: 123).

The concept of marginal propensity to consume and his treatment of variations rather than amounts makes Keynes's analysis a dynamic one. Nevertheless, he assumes no difference between short-term expectations and realised results:

> I began . . . by regarding this difference as important. But eventually I felt it to be of secondary importance, emphasis on it obscuring the real argument. For the theory of effective demand is substantially the same if we assume that short-period expectations are always fulfilled . . . The main point is to distinguish the forces determining the position of equilibrium from the technique of trial and error by means of which the entrepreneur discovers where the position is. (1973b, *CWJMK*, XIV: 181)

For example, pessimistic short-term expectations concerning effective demand would be unimportant in so far as they would lead to new expectations and a new process of production providing a higher level of aggregate demand nearer the effective demand. Keynes's assertion is coherent, but it requires specifying the implicit assumptions under which it will be valid. Keynes himself thought that a study considering the consequences for his model of allowing disappointed short-term expectations would be a useful complement to the *General Theory*.

Let us put the dynamic equation of equilibrium, according to the thesis that investment generates saving, the t date being defined as the date where expected proceeds are formulated in $t+1$, these expectations being corrected if not fulfilled:

$$Z_{t+n} = D_t$$

$$Y_{t+n} = C_t + I_t$$

$$S_{t+n} = I_t.$$

There is dynamic equilibrium if a given variation in investment generates an equivalent amount of saving at the end of n series of expectations. For example, if we start from an *ex ante* disequilibrium, such as $S_t < I_t$, we must describe the adjusting process as:

$$\Delta S = S_{t+n} - S_t = I_t - S_t.$$

Let us assume that a first set of expectations at the t date:

$$Y_0 = 1000,\ C_0 = 800,\ S_0 = 200,\ \text{and}\ I_0 = 300.$$

A first set of corrections takes the non-expected part of the investment expenditures:

$$Y_1 = C_0 + I_0 = 1100.$$

The difference between I and S implies expected windfall profits which lead entrepreneurs to change the scale of production. The distribution of wages causes a new series of expectations which take into account the first effect of the multiplier on the demand for consumer goods:

$$Y_2 = C_1 + I_0 = c\ Y_1 + I_0 = 1180.$$

We notice a shift between income to which propensity to consume is applied and income that the consumer expenditure helps to generate. In a similar way:

$$Y_3 = C_2 + I_0 = c\ Y_2 + I_0 = 1244$$

$$Y_4 = C_3 + I_0 = c\ Y_3 + I_0 = 1295.2.$$

By generalising:

$$Y_n = C_{n-1} + I_0 = c\ Y_{n-1} + I_0.$$

When n is infinite, Y_n tends towards Y_{n-1}, so:

$$Y_n = \frac{I_0}{1-c} = 1500$$

$$S_n = I_0 = 300$$

The dynamical equilibrium condition is:

$$S_{t+n} = I_t.$$

Now, let us specify the assumptions that we have implicitly retained in this demonstration of the stability of the multiplier principle.

The Conditions of the Stability of the Short-period Equilibrium

1. c is lower than one;
2. c is not affected by the progressive rise of effective demand;
3. c is independent of the rate of interest;
4. the state of the long-term forecasts is given, and particularly independent of the short-term forecasts;
5. the rate of interest is not affected by the progressive rise of the effective demand; and
6. the elasticity of the labour supply is infinite, so that the relation between expected windfall profit and employment decisions brings about the full realisation of the multiplier effect without allowing a change in prices.

Therefore, during the realisation of the multiplier process, investment expenditures which initiate the process as well as the successive flows of expenditures in consumer goods do not affect the initial conditions, that is, the parameters which are the state of the long-term forecast, the rate of interest, the marginal propensity to consume and the stock of capital.

Assumption 1 was considered by Keynes as the essential justification of the stability of the short-period equilibrium, but it is clear that this assumption is not the most important one. Assumption 2 is consistent with the normal psychological law according to which marginal propensity to consume decreases when income grows. If expectations are not fulfilled, it should be considered that marginal propensity to consume decreases with income. Assumptions 3, 4 and 5, which rest on independence between short- and long-term expectations must ensure that investment is independent of erroneous short-term anticipations so that the process does not become unstable. Assumption 5 is essential, because without this assumption, interest rate loses its status as an independent variable and investment loses its status as an autonomous variable. Following the last assumption, Hicks argues that in *The General Theory*,

> [Keynes] had to abandon the *Treatise* simplification, the study of the price-changes without quantity-changes . . . Quantity-changes had to be allowed for. He wanted to study them in the same way as price-changes had been studied; so the natural way to begin was to seek to construct a model in which quantities changed with no effect on prices. (1985: 57)

In the general case, an excess demand for investment goods involves an adjustment of saving to investment either thanks to variation in the price of the investment goods or to variation in the volume of the output of investment goods. Assuming underutilisation of the equipment and elasticity of labour supply, variation in the output level is allowed, but in so far as entrepreneurs will be induced to increase output and their promptness in doing it will leave no place for a variation in prices. However, the condition that the entrepreneurs are induced to change the scale of production is that they anticipate a rate of profit higher than the normal rate of profit in their industry, that is, expected prices are higher than normal prices. In Keynes's view, these expectations, although they are necessary to stimulate the increase in employment, are not carried out since a variation of output must substitute for the variation of price. The price level is constant, not because of imperfect competition but because the equilibrium condition is satisfied.

Concerning assumption 4, in Chapter 5 of *The General Theory*, Keynes establishes a clear distinction between short- and long-term expectations, but he does not clearly justify the dichotomy and the independence of the latter from the former: 'Nevertheless, we must not forgot that, in the case of durable goods, the producer's short-term expectations are based on the current long-term expectations of the investor; and it is of the nature of long-term expectations that they cannot be checked at short intervals in the light of realized results' (1936: 51). Moreover, the problem arising from the distinction of the prices of each good is that expected prices, and particularly the price of the investment goods, must be based on long-term expectations of the other entrepreneurs, which are affected by uncertainty. Finally, there is a possibility that transactions will be realised in disequilibrium, so the short-period equilibrium is no longer independent of the adjusting process from which it results. Therefore, the multiplier effect is then inevitably affected by the temporal sequence of its realisation, so the short-period equilibrium must change as entrepreneurs must correct their erroneous expectations. There is no longer a guarantee that equilibrium is reached at a given time.

But this way of describing the adjusting mechanism of income to its equilibrium level is not in conformity with Keynes's approach in terms of equilibrium, although he seems to have considered this possibility: 'I certainly agree that the volume of output depends on the anticipated price, not on the actual price' (1973b, *CW* XIV: 144). Nevertheless, the way in which these prices are expected is arguable:

> Entrepreneurs have to endeavour to forecast demand. They do not, as a rule, make widely wrong forecasts of the equilibrium position. But, as the matter is very complex, they do not get it just right; and they endeavour to approximate to the truth position by a method of trial and error. (1973, *CWJMK*, XIV: 182)

CONCLUSIONS

Keynes thus claims to reconcile an approach in terms of disequilibrium within the framework of the long period with an approach in terms of equilibrium within the framework of the short-period. Following Keynes, 'the fact that our knowledge of the future is fluctuating, vague and uncertain renders wealth a peculiarly unsuitable subject for the methods of the classical economic theory'. So the notion of getting into equilibrium is 'a metaphor based on space to explain a process which takes place in time' (ibid.: 112). Robinson concludes: 'In space, it is possible to go to and from and correct misdirections, but time goes only one way' and 'this is why equilibrium cannot be achieved by a process of trial and error' (1978: 12).

But, the argument which justifies the rejection of the concept of long-period equilibrium as a realisable and *a fortiori* stable state should be applicable to the concept of short-period equilibrium. Whereas Keynes uses the multiplier within the framework of a comparative static method which implies that its effects are carried out constantly so that the variables of the short period instantaneously reach their equilibrium values, Asimakopulos's criticism has suggested that we consider the multiplier as a temporal adjusting process of saving to investment via the variations of income rather than an instantaneous mechanism. By taking disappointed expectations into account, a historical treatment of time in the Keynesian theory of employment allows us to restate the statute of the relation between saving and investment. Keynes is right when he says:

> In maintaining the equality of saving and investment, I am, therefore, returning to an old-fashioned orthodoxy. The novelty in my treatment of saving and investment consists, not in my maintaining their necessary aggregate equality, but in the proposition that it is, not the rate of interest, but the level of incomes which (in conjunction with certain other factors) ensures this equality. (1973b, *CWJMK*, XIV: 211)

NOTES

1. *Collected Writings of John Maynard Keynes*, volume XIV.
2. Regarding the consistency between the two books, see, for example, Shackle (1974) and Amadeo (1989).
3. In response to Joan Robinson's comments on the *Treatise*, Keynes wrote: 'I think that you are a little hard on me as regards the assumption of constant output. It is quite true that I have not followed out the consequences of change of output in the earlier theoretical part . . . [but] it is only at a particular point in the preliminary theoretical argument that I assume constant output' (Keynes, 1973b, *CWJMK*, XIV: 270).
4. The other alternative disequilibrium situation can be defined as an excess of current saving over expected investment.

5. This equation is deduced from the fourth fundamental equation (1930: 123) as follows:

$$(PO = Y + I - S$$

$$(P - P^*)O + P^*O = Y + I - S$$

$$Q + P^*O = Y + Q.$$

6. This idea was first established by Lindahl (1930).
7. See Weintraub (1957), Parinello (1980) and Casarosa (1981).

REFERENCES

Amadeo, E.J. (1989), *Keynes's Principle of Effective Demand*, Aldershot, UK and Brookfield, US: Edward Elgar.

Asimakopulos, A. (1982), 'Keynes's theory of effective demand revisited', *Australian Economic Papers*, **21**, June, 18–36.

Asimakopulos, A. (1983), 'Kalecki and Keynes on finance, investment and saving', *Cambridge Journal of Economics*, **7** (3–4), September–December, 221–33.

Asimakopulos, A. (1987), 'The nature and the role of equilibrium in Keynes's *General Theory*', *Australian Economic Papers*, June, 16–28.

Asimakopulos, A. (1991), *Keynes's General Theory and Accumulation*, Cambridge: Cambridge University Press.

Casarosa, C. (1981), 'The microfoundations of Keynes's aggregate supply and aggregate demand analysis', *Economic Journal*, **91** (361), 188–94.

Hicks, J.R. (1967), *Critical Essays in Monetary Theory*, Oxford: Oxford University Press.

Hicks, J.R. (1985), *Methods of Dynamic Economics*, Oxford: Clarendon Press.

Kahn, R.H. (1984), *The Making of Keynes' General Theory*, Cambridge: Cambridge University Press.

Keynes, J.M. (1930), *A Treatise on Money, The Pure Theory of Money*, in *The Collected Writings of John Maynard Keynes,* Vol. V, 1971, London: Macmillan.

Keynes, J.M. (1936), *The General Theory of Employment, Interest and Money*, in *The Collected Writings of John Maynard Keynes,* Vol. VII, 1973, London: Macmillan.

Keynes, J.M. (1973a), *The General Theory and After. Part I: Preparation*, in *The Collected Writings of John Maynard Keynes*, Vol. XIII, London: Macmillan.

Keynes, J.M. (1973b), Letter from R.H. Kahn to Keynes in: *The General Theory and After. Part II: Defence and Development*, in *The Collected Writings of John Maynard Keynes*, Vol. XIV, London: Macmillan, p. 637.

Lindahl, E.R. (1930), 'The interest rate and the price level', in *Studies in the Theory of Money and Capital*, New York: Kelley, 1939.

Parinello, S. (1980), 'The price level in Keynes' effective demand', *Journal of Post Keynesian Economics*, **3** (1), 63–78.

Robertson, D.H. (1955), 'Keynes and supply functions', *Economic Journal*, **65** (263), 474–7.

Robinson, J. (1971), *Economic Heresies*, London: Macmillan.

Robinson, J. (1978), 'Keynes and Ricardo', *Journal of Post Keynesian Economics*, **1** (1), Fall, 12–18.

Shackle, G.L.S. (1974), *Keynesian Kaleidics: The Evolution of a General Political Economy*, Edinburgh: Edinburgh University Press.
Weintraub, S. (1957), 'The micro-foundations of aggregate demand and supply', *Economic Journal*, **67** (267), 455–70.

PART III

Keynesian models

7. Modeling Keynes with Kalecki

Colin Richardson and Jerry Courvisanos*

INTRODUCTION

The starting-point for *neoclassical* interpretations of Keynes's system is 'Modeling Keynes with Hicks'. Students are thereby misled into believing that Keynes analysed a general equilibrium exchange economy (summarized by the IS curve, with production merely an 'exchange with nature') in which the underlying barter transactions were obscured by a 'veil of money' (summarized by the LM curve). However, Keynes himself strongly emphasized that his analysis applied to a monetary production economy, one in which both aspects were well integrated.

By contrast, the starting-point for *Post Keynesian* interpretations of Keynes's system should be 'Modeling Keynes with Kalecki'. It is true that Keynes's *quaesitum* can be understood by a close reading of both volumes of his *Treatise on Money* and then the *General Theory*, but his analysis was lengthy and complex, with hardly any mathematics or graphs deployed. Keynes, in fact, criticized the use of mathematical models to understand complex reality: '[I]n ordinary discourse . . . we can keep "at the back of our heads" the necessary reserves and qualifications and the adjustments which we shall have to make later on, in a way in which we cannot keep complicated partial differentials "at the back" of several pages of algebra which assume they all vanish' (Keynes, 1936, pp. 297–8).[1] However, modern economics teaching practice demands mathematical models that track rigorous arguments in an erudite manner. Post Keynesian instructors need a mathematical modeling tool of comparable simplicity to Hicks's IS–LM framework to help students understand how a capitalist monetary production economy actually works, *sans* pure exchange and the veil of money.

Michał Kalecki was a Polish auto-didactic economist who used engineering-based mathematical tools to explain the modern capitalist monetary production economy. Kalecki's prior claim, and the depth he

* The authors wish to thank an anonymous referee for helpful suggestions, but remain responsible for the entire content.

added, to the Keynesian approach was first identified by Joan Robinson (1964). A more recent analysis (Chapple, 1991, 1995) delineates the relationship between Kalecki's theory of modern capitalism and Keynes's *General Theory*. These studies reinforce our position: the need for a simple mathematics-based model of Keynes's approach that cannot be hijacked by the mainstream, forming a basis for policy analysis and *praxis* that the heterodox economics community can use as a teaching method utilizing equations and spreadsheets.

This chapter section sets out first the intellectual foundations of using Kaleckian insights to provide a heterodox version of Keynes's model of capitalism and then expounds the 'in principle' argument for a simple modeling approach that can serve as a teaching aid. Second, the equations and identities of our dynamic Keynes–Kalecki (KK) model are listed, with exogenous growth rates for the supply of labor and its average productivity. This model is capable of tracking the real capital stock through simulated historical time as it physically depreciates and is renewed via real investment outlays.

The KK model is deployed to demonstrate Kalecki's vision of the long period being but a succession of short periods. Using this view of *historical time*, we demonstrate the effects of various policy recommendations in a capitalist economy facing a doubling of the growth rate of its labor supply, based on three different institutional settings: (i) the entrepreneurs' lower money-wage growth and work intensification policies; (ii) the trade unionists' higher money-wage growth and job-sharing policies; and (iii) Kalecki's planned market economy based on maintaining a viable profitability gap to ensure entrepreneurs grow investment at whatever rate is needed to maintain a near-zero unemployment steady state in the long term.

We go on to explain how a researcher could make this core macroeconomic model more realistic and worthy of being calibrated against statistical databases. Our conclusion is followed by the KK model's equations and identities in Appendix 7A1, together with time series plots of various policy outcomes in Appendices 7A2–4.

THE INTELLECTUAL CAPITAL UNDERLYING THE KEYNES–KALECKI MODEL

The simple thesis that this modeling exercise is built on is that Keynes alone will always be susceptible to being hijacked by neoclassical economists, due to the links that the mainstream inevitably will find among Keynes's tangled Marshallian roots. However, incorporating the major elements of Kalecki's approach into Keynes's system will provide a model impregnable to the 'bastardisation' that has happened (and will continue to happen) to Keynes's *General Theory* model on its own. The two elements of Kalecki's thought that need to be incorporated into Keynes's system are the dynamics of investment and profits and the distribution of income based on class.

The KK model is first expounded, then subjected to computer simulation experiments within three institutional settings, having 'Entrepreneurs', 'Trade Unionists' and 'Kaleckians' in charge of policy formation. This teaching model stands on the shoulders of a set of seminal works that have tackled this project of modeling Keynes with Kalecki over the last 30 years. All the previous contributions have been significant in furthering the model building and unlocking the secrets of how such a KK monetary production economy would operate.

Athanasios (Tom) Asimakopulos, inspired by the work of Joan Robinson, began this project by underpinning Keynes's effective demand analysis with both Kalecki's double-sided investment–profit relationship (Asimakopulos, 1977) and his class-based income distribution theory derived from mark-up pricing practices under monopoly capitalism. The determinants of income shares, 'given the propensities to save, are thus the mark-ups and capitalists' expenditures in real terms' (Asimakopulos, 1975, p. 330). Harris (1974) developed this idea further with Kalecki's 'degree of monopoly', showing how unemployment and excess capacity are the normal case under capitalism, with prices and profit margins being governed by the monopoly position of firms. Harcourt and Kenyon (1976) were able to link monopoly pricing and the investment decision into a coherent graphical representation in which 'a unique solution could be found for the size of the margin above 'normal' prime costs and the level of planned expenditure, given the firm's expectations about the future level of demand' (Harcourt, 1982, pp. 122–3).

The late 1970s and into the 1980s saw some Post Keynesians attempting to incorporate Kalecki into the Keynesian analysis through use of the *neoclassical* static 'equilibrium' concept. These essentially graphical expositions, with Kaleckian concepts integrated into Keynes's framework, are evident in Skouras (1979), Lianos (1983–84) and Reynolds (1987, pp. 97–107). Sawyer (1982, p. 150), in his Kaleckian alternative macroeconomic exposition, even uses the Hicksian IS–LM equilibrium model to show a decline in investment opportunities and unemployment.

These modeling attempts flew in the face of Kalecki's central message that a change in investment in 'no way results in a process leading towards equilibrium' (Kalecki, 1990, p. 231). Asimakopulos (1989, p. 17) argues that Keynes shared with Kalecki a 'temporary resting place' view of employment, given the volatile nature of investment. Thus arises the need to model Keynes explicitly with Kalecki's approach to the capitalist economy, rather than the other way around, as was attempted in the 1980s. This latter approach failed to be accepted in the mainstream; in fact, the mainstream moved *further* away, even to the extent of rejecting Keynes in textbook macroeconomics (see Mankiw, 1998).

Bhaduri (1986, p. ix) stated in his preface that the radical content of Keynesianism in his book came through what was learnt from Kalecki, whose analysis had Marxian origins. This ushered in a major shift in the Post Keynesian approach to modeling Keynes: the explicit incorporation of Kaleckian concepts as *foundations*, rather than 'add-ons'. Arestis (1992) spent half his book demolishing the grand neoclassical synthesis before advancing an alternative dynamic Post Keynesian model that placed Kalecki at the center, with income distribution and decision making (private and public) being determined through relative power. In the same year, Lavoie (1992, p. 422) stated that 'the economics of Kalecki provides better foundations for a post-Keynesian or post classical research programme than does the economics of Keynes'.

During the same period, the decision-making process in organizations within market capitalism was also questioned, with Davidson (1991) taking his cue from Chapter 12 of Keynes (1936) and developing the fundamentally uncertain (non-ergodic) nature of the future, hence very limited insights being provided by the past. Courvisanos (1996) shows how Kalecki's investment analysis provides a strong institutional foundation to the investment instability that arises out of this non-ergodocity. From this emerges the endogenous susceptibility cycle in long-term expectations, explaining the persistence of business cycle volatility. As a learning process, Kaleckian economics sees the chain of short-term decisions (taken in historical time) making up the long-term trend, a 'statistical artefact' having no independent existence.

Building on this in recent work on long-run Kaleckian models of growth by Lavoie (2002) and Cassetti (2003), Kaleckian economics is now about more than just filling in a lacuna in Keynes's economics, as suggested by Toporowski (2003, p. 229). In fact, Lavoie (2006, p. 105) argues cogently that heterodox authors draw upon the flexible Kaleckian model of growth as a tool of analysis. With the increased popularity of Kalecki's economics (see Blecker, 2002), it is time to provide a more fundamentally Kaleckian exposition of the Post Keynesian model, drawing on research by scholars of Kalecki's *oeuvre*.

The remainder of this section *explicitly* models Keynes upon a Kaleckian foundation. Our small part of the intellectual history of the KK model was developed in the 1990s. Keynes/Kalecki economics is presented in a simple mathematically-based model that is a robust and distinct alternative to the 'bastard Keynesian' approaches adopted by the mainstream.

METHODOLOGY

Much mathematics-based Post Keynesian modeling has employed econometric methods consistent with the neoclassical static equilibrium approach (Downward, 2003). This method is based on making specific assumptions to derive abstract theoretical models, then writing up 'results' based on speculation of outcomes from this exercise. There may also be some separate empirical testing, using regression techniques, aimed at providing a *post hoc* rationalization of the modeling results already obtained. All the econometric limitations of such an approach – including choosing assumptions, identifying and collecting data and manipulating these data to provide conclusions that show at least some partial regularities – raise serious questions about the suitability of such a methodology. Keynes's view regarding partial differentials that are assumed to vanish, should give warning to any Post Keynesian who attempts to model the economy. Recent Post Keynesian criticisms that embrace his warning have emerged. From an open system and non-ergodic perspective, the econometric approach is seen as a closed system based on an ergodic world view (see Dow, 2001). From a critical realist perspective, such a plurality of partial regularities from an unpredictable system ensures that '[e]conometric inferences are thus inherently problematic' (Downward, 2003, p. 97).

The mathematical methodology employed in this section is distinctly different; it is a variant of the system dynamics approach. 'Systems dynamics is well-suited to Post-Keynesian–institutionalist economic model building. It is a dynamic, disequilibrium approach to modeling complex systems that portrays human behavior and micro-level decision making as it actually is, rather than as it might be in an idealized state' (Radzicki, 2008, p. 162). In utilizing this approach, partial differentials are always in the picture and do not (in Keynes's sense) 'vanish'. System dynamics is thus a vital supplement to verbal reasoning, rather than the way standard econometrics has *replaced* verbal reasoning (see, for example, any issue of *the American Economic Review* since the early 1980s).

The integrated dynamic model developed by Kalecki is most appropriate for this KK modeling exercise. A system dynamics model uses computer simulation to identify patterns of behavior in the model based on certain circumstances. This is seen through changes in the variables (and in such ratios as the profit rate) over a long succession of simulated historical short periods that can be represented as separate columns on a spreadsheet.

A simple KK model is expounded with a very basic set of five behavioral relationships that are supported by the underlying intellectual capital. The rest of the model consists of identities, given parameters and an exogenous natural rate of growth.

The baseline case is the KK model in a constant 2 percent per period (2 percent pp) steady state of full-employment growth. This growth rate is maintained because there is a constant positive gap of 3 percent pp between the return on capital (8 percent pp rate of profit) and the cost of capital (5 percent pp rate of interest) that is exactly sufficient to keep entrepreneurs expecting *and realizing* that particular degree of excess profitability. When we simulated the passage of historical time, we observed a classic steady state with all time-series data plotting as 2 percent pp exponential growth paths over an indefinite future with full employment and zero price inflation.

With aggregate demand growth being equal to the economy's natural rate of growth (comprising 1percent pp increases in both workforce and labor productivity), we introduced a higher workforce growth rate of 2 percent pp. We then imagined the Entrepreneurs arguing with the Trade Unionists over the most efficient way to ensure these extra workers find employment, that is, how best to raise the rate of economic growth to 3 percent pp, in line with the new higher natural rate of growth. Only after the effects of their four suggested policies (two per side) are demonstrated by KK model runs can both classes potentially unite behind a fifth, Kaleckian, policy that it is demonstrated *will* achieve and maintain their agreed societal goal of steady economic growth at 3 percent pp, with profitability slightly higher at 9 percent pp and minimal rates of inflation and unemployment.

Three different institutional settings are examined: (A) Entrepreneurs' Ideal, where (A1) money-wage growth is moderated or (A2) work is intensified, leading to higher productivity; (B) Unions' Ideal, where (B1) money-wage growth is raised or (B2) job sharing is practised, leading to lower average productivity; and (C) Kalecki's Ideal, where (C1) investment planning raises the rate of real investment. In each case, the same KK model is used, with its cumulative causation explained by the positive (investment–profits–investment) and negative (price–excess capacity–price) circular feedback loops that impart the economic dynamics. The patterns that emerge from these five simulation exercises enable comparisons of outcomes, as well as providing a simple teaching system to convey the dynamics of an economy that, once set up with certain institutional settings, develops path dependence as historical time passes.

By far the most important aspect of our KK model is the macroeconomic feedback from investment to profits. In his *Treatise on Money*, Keynes called it 'the Widow's Cruse', while Kalecki's Dictum states that 'capitalists earn what they spend, and workers spend what they earn'

(Sawyer, 1985, p. 73).[2] This mechanism, which neoclassical economists ignore in their fruitless search for 'the micro foundations of macroeconomics', is the feedback loop that constitutes 'the macro foundations of microeconomics'. Specifically, this is the Post Keynesian microeconomics of a monetary production economy that should replace the discredited general equilibrium economy with its ergodicity, its fictional auctioneer, its *tâtonnement*, its barter exchange fixation, and its veil of money.

THE KK MODEL

Our KK model's algebra is set out in Appendix 7A1. The model has 22 main variables, one 'equilibrium' variable and nine other variables; making 32 in all. Only five of its 22 main variables are determined by behavioral equations based on Keynesian and Kaleckian insights. These five are the drivers of the economy. The remaining 27 variables are determined by identities: mathematical statements that are true *ex definitione*. Only 12 parameters are needed to govern the model's dynamic behavior.

There is one 'equilibrium' variable: the entrepreneurs' profitability gap $xr_t = [r_{t-1} - i_t]$ % pp. When xr_t is zero, for instance, this indicates that entrepreneurs are 'content' with their real investment [I^*_t units pa] and production [Q_t units pa] decisions, even though this generates a stationary state of zero growth in which new investment simply replaces their depreciated capital.

The five behavioral equations that drive this dynamic economy determine the following five variables:

1. Unit price: $P_t = P_{t-1} + \alpha(v_t - 1)$dollars per unit, where $v_t = Q_t/Q^*_t$ is the ratio of production to available capacity. This equation shows that the monetary production economy's all-purpose consumption/investment commodity has a money price that rises (falls) whenever production exceeds (falls short of) available capacity. This equation is not Kaleckian; it is our answer to the false neoclassical charge that Keynes's system needs 'sticky prices' or some form of market power to make it work. Our unit price is completely flexible and it is the one that would prevail if perfect competition between numerous small businesses really did exist, as in the *General Theory*. Our KK model results undermine the neoclassical claim that Keynesian involuntary unemployment cannot occur if prices are competitively set and highly flexible.
2. Money-wage rate: $w_t = w_{t-1}(1 + w_q gq_t + w_p gp_t)$ dollars per worker pp. This equation shows that the money wage is inflexible downwards, in

line with Keynes's teaching, and will rise with growth in labor productivity and/or price inflation. This formulation is widely accepted by economists, some of whose versions *also* allow for higher rates of unemployment to depress the level to which money wages otherwise rise. Econometric testing has failed to disconfirm this near-universal labor market hypothesis.

3. Real consumption: $C^*_t = W_t/P_t$ units pp, which utilises Kalecki's classical assumptions that entrepreneurs do all the saving, while wage earners (including entrepreneur directors and managers to the extent that they pay themselves salaries for organizational and decision-making skills) do all the consuming.
4. Real investment: $I^*_t = (1 + \beta xr_t)dK^*_t$ units pp, which means that if the profitability gap is zero, entrepreneurs merely replace that fraction (d = 6 percent) of their opening real capital stock (K^*_t units) which will depreciate away during the current short period. Over time, this ensures the maintenance of a classical stationary state, that is, the no-growth economy is in dynamic 'equilibrium' or, as Post Keynesians put it, is 'fully adjusted'. However, if xr_t percent pp is above (below) zero, this results in positive (negative) *net* investment to the extent of the profitability gap times the 'animal spirits' reaction coefficient (β), which also is based on the 'susceptibility' of investment influencing the entrepreneurs (see Courvisanos, 1997). So, if $\beta = 11.13$ and the profitability gap is +3 percent, entrepreneurs will lift gross real investment by 33.4 percent more than the dK^*_t units needed to simply replace their depreciating capital stock.
5. Production: $Q_t = C^*_t + I^*_t$ units pp, which means that production is undertaken in response to (and is equal to) the sum of real consumption and real investment expenditures, in this one-commodity world with no inventory investment. The equation reflects Keynes's teaching that entrepreneurs always can 'find the point of aggregate demand' in the short period and fix their levels of production accordingly.

The five behavioral equations above constitute the very heart of our KK model. They are the *only* targets available for critics of Post Keynesianism to aim at, since all other relationships in the model are 'bulletproof' identities. Every other relationship is a definitional identity, which no economist, neoclassical or otherwise, can argue with.

There are 12 parameters in our 'BaseCase' KK model:

$\alpha =$ 0.5, a price adjustment coefficient on the production/capacity ratio (v_t);

$\beta =$ 11.13, an investment reaction coefficient on the profitability gap (xr_t);
$w_q =$ 1.0, indicating 100 percent passthrough of productivity growth into money wages;
$w_p =$ 1.0, indicating 100 percent passthrough of price inflation into money wages;
$i = 5$ percent pp, the interest rate set exogenously, for example, by a horizontalist central bank;
$d =$ 6 percent pp, the depreciation rate for capital goods, which lasts for 16.7 periods;
$q_0 =$ 100 units per employee pp, the initial average productivity of labor;
$gq =$ 1 percent pp, the growth rate of average labor productivity;
$N_0 =$ 3,203 potential employees, the initial size of the economy's workforce;
$gN =$ 1 percent pp, the growth rate of the economy's workforce;
$K^*_0 =$ 800,000 units, the entrepreneurs' initial stock of real capital; and
$z =$ 2.498 units of capital, needed to produce one unit of the single all-purpose good.

There are also nine other variables playing no part in the system, being merely various ratios and one difference, namely, the profit margin ($rm_t = P_t wc_t$ dollars per unit). None the less, they are of some interest, for example, the Keynesian multiplier ($k_t = Y_t/I_t$) is not derived from a consumption function and is not necessarily constant. Also, the mark-up ($m_t = rm_t/P_t$ %) can vary in a quite non-Kaleckian manner because we have assumed neoclassical flexible prices – though only to demonstrate their complete compatibility with involuntary unemployment in Keynes's *quaesitum*.

THE KK DYNAMIC MODEL: THREE INSTITUTIONAL SETTINGS WITH FIVE POLICIES

From a teaching perspective, this section outlines five simple experiments conducted within three different ideal institutional settings over an 'era' (here defined as 100 simulated short periods). As experimentalists, we want to observe what happens as this model capitalist monetary production economy develops through historical time. Each experiment represents a different policy applied within one of the institutional settings. In turn, Entrepreneurs, Trade Unionists and Kaleckians run the KK model to check out the efficacy of their favored policies for lifting the economy out of its 2 percent pp steady-state and onto a new 3 percent pp steady-state growth path. This is assumed to have been necessitated by an increase in the rate of workforce growth from the 'BaseCase' of $gN=1$ percent pp to the 'PerturbedCase' of $gN=2$ percent pp, with average labor productivity growth remaining unchanged at $gq=1$ pp. Appendix 7A2 shows that, after an era of simulated historical time, the 2 percent pp (3 percent pp) natural rate of growth economy maintains (rises to) an unemployment rate of zero (62.3 percent). Clearly something has to change, otherwise there will be 14 171 unemployed and starving citizens at the turn of the new era, with only 8577 workforce members still in employment.

Setting A is called the 'Entrepreneurs' Ideal', based on their notion that if only (A1) money-wage growth can be moderated, or else (A2) work intensity can be increased, everything will be fine. Policy A1 was achieved by decreasing the Productivity-Wage Passthrough from $w_q=1.0$ to 0.9, and Policy A2 achieved by raising the speed/duration of work so that Labor Productivity Growth increased from $gq=1$ percent pp to 1.1 percent pp. Unfortunately, Appendix 7A3 shows that the impact of Policy A1 will result in even *less* employment (6379 workers), a higher unemployment rate (72 percent) and an excess capacity rate of 25.6 percent. This is accompanied by a severe deflation of unit wage cost (wc_t falls from \$10 to \$3.78) and profit margin (rm_t down from \$2.50 to \$1.39), hence also price (P_t decreases from \$12.50 to \$5.17) over the era. Not shown are the only slightly less damaging effects of Policy A2.[3] There still is less employment after 100 periods ($L_{100}=7777$ workers and $u_{100}=65.8$ percent) but at least these figures are better than under the Entrepreneurs' alternative Policy A1. Also, the excess capacity rate of zero ensures no changes in initial wage cost, profit margin or price. Under all policies except the Kaleckian, the economy's initial 8 percent profit rate on capital stock remains constant for 100 periods (which is also true of both the BaseCase and the PerturbedCase).

Setting B is called the 'Trade Unionists' Ideal', based on (B1) raising money-wage rate growth to stimulate aggregate demand, or else (B2) job sharing, which reduces average labor productivity to 'spread the pain' of absorbing the extra workforce entrants. The first was achieved by increasing the Productivity-Wage Passthrough from $w_q=1.0$ to 1.1, and the second by lowering the duration of work so that Labor Productivity Growth decreased from $gq=1$ percent pp to 0.9 percent pp. Although not shown, by the turn of the era, Policy B1 delivers the best employment (13 784 workers) and unemployment (39.4 percent) outcomes of all four policies under institutional settings A and B. However, the associated negative excess capacity rate ($x_{100}=-60.7$ percent) precludes its implementation: realistically, physical production cannot exceed capacity by this percentage, even in wartime.[4] Severe price and wage cost inflation outpaced profit margin increases and, at the constant 8 percent profit rate, there simply was no incentive for entrepreneurs to invest in expanding their production capacity. Although not shown, Policy B2 maintains wage and price stability with zero excess capacity but delivers only 9461 jobs by the turn of the era, at which time the unemployment rate has climbed to 58.4 percent.

Setting C is called 'Kalecki's Ideal', based on harnessing the profit–investment–profit feedback loop to lift the constant profitability gap from its BaseCase value of 3 percent to 4 percent by (C1) a raft of Keynesian–Kaleckian planning policies designed to raise the growth rate of real investment from 2 percent to 3 percent pp, while simultaneously restricting the growth of money wages to minimize inflationary pressures. The profitability gap is the major explanator of investment behavior (Courvisanos and Richardson, 2006), so Kaleckian policies were focused on raising the β-coefficient which multiplies xr_t. Specifically, it was encouraged by non-coercive investment planning measures to rise from $\beta = 11.13$ to 12.55, partly as the result of an incomes policy deal with the trade unions. This moderated the passthrough of labor productivity growth into money-wage rises from $w_q = 1.0$ to 0.8 and helped lift the 'animal spirits' of entrepreneurs. Despite being a deeper cut than the $w_q = 0.9$ of Policy A1, this did not disadvantage the working class because the KK model shows (a) the real wage increasing from 80 to 290.9 units under C1 versus 197.6 units under A1 and (b) employment rising from 3203 to 22 508 wage earners under C1 versus 6379 wage earners under A1. Our final Appendix 7A4 displays excellent Policy C1 outcomes over 100 periods: as noted above, there was employment of 22 508 workers, but also an unemployment rate just over 1 percent and an excess capacity rate of a little under 1 percent, together with price and wage cost rising more slowly than profit margin, so that the inflation rate never tops $gp_t = 0.4$ percent pp.

As a result of these five simulations, two crucial observations can be made. The first is that both Entrepreneurs and Trade Unionists got it wrong because they ignored the influence of animal spirits and expected profitability on real investment, hence realized profit rate and profitability gap impacting subsequently via revision of expectations. Second, Kalecki's Ideal shows that by creative investment planning and adopting an incomes policy (thus harnessing the power of the gap between expected profitability and actual cost of capital), the four nightmare outcomes of the other two Ideals can be banished. The profitability gap and its β-coefficient (reflecting animal spirits and susceptibility) is the significant solver of the macroeconomic problem and leads to understanding better the microeconomics of the economy as well. Courvisanos and Richardson (2006) provide the theoretical and computer simulation experiments to support this proposition, now partly incorporated into Institutional Setting C for teaching purposes. The positive investment–profits–investment feedback loop engendering cumulative causation and path dependence stems from this Kaleckian rule of a constant and sufficiently wide profitability gap. Together with an incomes policy to dampen the endogenous growth of money wages, this Kaleckian policy approach can achieve and maintain the desired full-employment steady state growth trajectory throughout any stretch of simulated historical time.

POSSIBLE FURTHER DEVELOPMENTS OF THE KK MODEL

Our simple teaching model could be expanded into a realistic representation of a contemporary capitalist economy by incorporating standard treatments from the extant literature of imports, exports, international capital flows, taxation and government spending and so on and adding a central bank policy reaction function to alter the interest rate in response to changes in the inflation rate from time to time. This enhanced model also could be changed from an open economy macro engine into a similarly dynamic and realistic full-blown *microeconomic* system by disaggregating the labor and capital stocks, plus the flows of production, consumption, profits and so on, and computing vectors of money-wage rates, labor productivities, profit margins and prices. If this were to be achieved, one would be able to trace how the positive feedback mechanism of Kalecki's Dictum 'rules the roost' in terms of the 'macrofoundations of microeconomics'.

With investment determining profits (hence also the average profit rate, around which all single-industry profit rates cluster) the microeconomic analyst then would have a model worthy of estimation against statistical datasets.

In a previous Kaleckian computer simulation experiment conducted by the authors (Courvisanos and Richardson, 2006), the instability of the economy was demonstrated in a far more complex model. The system dynamics complexity in that particular model created business cycles with amplitudes that were *endogenously* confined within a 'corridor of viability'. The model allowed the system to cycle widely, but always within limits that ensured the capitalist economy did not fly off into chaos. This was a demonstration of how dynamic complex system models can produce unstable time paths with embodied technical progress, but with the endogenous fluctuations moderated by emergent limits to investment, borrowing and excess capacity.[5]

As part of our program to create a realistic representation of a typical contemporary mixed economy, we plan to combine our basic teaching KK model with the complexity elements of this other model. We then will be able to generate endogenous dynamic behavior that can cause fully adjusted stationary and steady states to emerge, as well as traverses to converging, diverging and cyclical growth paths. The level of complexity will make such a version more appropriate for upper-level undergraduate teaching and for masters degree coursework.[6]

CONCLUSION

The power of this KK model resides in its Kaleckian roots that anchor and feed Keynes's general theorizing about the dynamics of capitalist economies, now finally free of the fear of being hijacked by the mainstream. The model stands in stark contrast to the various interpretations of Keynes that have been proposed by the neoclassicals: John Hicks's IS–LM equilibrium, Paul Samuelson's synthesis, Milton Friedman's liquidity preference, Robert Lucas and Thomas Sargent's rational expectations, N. Gregory Mankiw's sticky markets, and so it goes on. Furthermore, the KK model is simple to understand because it is made up of only five behavioral equations, all steeped in the Post Keynesian tradition. All the remaining relationships are unexceptional definitional identities.

The results from our five experiments make strong intuitive sense to Post Keynesians, but the model generating them is sufficiently complex to show the level of interaction and cumulative causation that emerges. Under Kalecki's Ideal, there are the priceless benefits of a continuously fully employed economy with no excess capacity and effectively zero inflation, despite a doubling of the workforce growth rate. In all three institutional settings, technical change with incremental innovation is incorporated, so this element cannot be seen as differentiating the outcomes. Courvisanos (2005) shows how such innovation can be much more sustainable in a planned market economy than in the neoclassical 'free markets' version.

At the first level of abstraction, the results of these experiments are intuitively satisfactory as regards trend activity over an era of 100 short periods. Closer approaches to reality through opening the economy, modeling taxation and government expenditure, adding more sectors, and incorporating cyclical behavior can tell us more at the sacrifice of simplicity, but with the need for enhanced computer power and design ingenuity. Research points to the need to conquer these horizons while continuing to provide simple teaching tools that can be useful for communicating the policy alternatives available in a real-world economy.

NOTES

1. We are indebted to Claudio Sardoni (1995, p. 202 fn. 23) for reminding us of this excellent quote.
2. Professor Geoffrey Harcourt suggests that Kalecki's Dictum would be better phrased as 'wage-earners spend what they earn while profit-receivers receive what they spend' (Dalziel and Lavoie, 2003, p. 340 fn. 4). Although neoclassicals are content to believe one surprising truth about capitalist economies (that banks create money out of thin air), they cannot bring themselves to accept another: that it is entrepreneurs' own combined investment outlays that create the aggregate of profits they all partake of.
3. The figures of all experiments marked 'not shown' are available from c.richardson@imperial.ac.uk.
4. The model as presented is not a complete system dynamics model, in that phenomena like unrealistically large negative unemployment and excess capacity rates can occur. This was done to maximize transparency and minimize arbitrary choices of, for instance, floors and ceilings that restrict the free variation of the teaching model's variables. While it may prove necessary in a research model for estimation against statistical datasets, incorporating such limits in this teaching model would make it difficult for students to discriminate between outcomes that are purely equation driven and those that are (fully or partly) exogenously constrained.
5. This theoretical result suggests that the estimated parameter set of a more complex research model (in which free variation is permitted) could be such as to *endogenously* 'enforce' variation within realistic limits on such variables as the unemployment and excess capacity rates.
6. The KK model is built utilizing an Excel spreadsheet, whose advantage is that every student understands the basic concepts involved in replicating equations across the columns that represent short periods. The principal disadvantages are that these equations are hidden behind their numerical outcomes, auditing a spreadsheet is difficult, and only discrete time simulations can be modeled with relative ease.

REFERENCES

Arestis, P. (1992), *The Post-Keynesian Approach to Economics: An Alternative Analysis of Economic Theory and Policy*, Aldershot, UK and Brookfield, USA: Edward Elgar.

Asimakopulos, A. (1975), 'A Kaleckian theory of income distribution', *Canadian Journal of Economics*, **8** (3), 313–33.

Asimakopulos, A. (1977), 'Profits and investment: a Kaleckian approach', in G.C. Harcourt (ed.), *The Microeconomic Foundations of Macroeconomics*, Boulder, CO: Westview Press, pp. 328–42.

Asimakopulos, A. (1989), 'The nature and role of equilibrium in Keynes's *General Theory*', *Australian Economic Papers*, **28** (52), 16–28.

Bhaduri, A. (1986), *Macroeconomics: The Dynamics of Commodity Production*, London: Macmillan.

Blecker, R. (2002), 'Distribution, demand and growth in neo-Kaleckian macromodels', in M. Setterfield (ed.), *The Economics of Demand-Led Growth: Challenging the Supply-Side Vision of the Long Run*, Cheltenham, UK and Northampton, MA, USA: Edward Elgar, pp. 129–52.

Cassetti, M. (2003), 'Bargaining power, effective demand and technical progress: a Kaleckian model of growth', *Cambridge Journal of Economics*, **27** (3), 449-64.

Chapple, S. (1991), 'Did Kalecki get there first? The race for the *General Theory*', *History of Political Economy*, **23** (2), 243–61.
Chapple, S. (1995), 'The Kaleckian origins of the Keynesian model', *Oxford Economic Papers*, **47** (3), 525–37.
Courvisanos, J. (1996), *Investment Cycles in Capitalist Economies: A Kaleckian Behavioural Contribution*, Cheltenham, UK and Brookfield, USA: Edward Elgar.
Courvisanos, J. (1997), 'Keynes and the susceptibility of investment', in P. Davidson and J.A. Kregel (eds), *Improving the Global Economy*, Cheltenham, UK and Lyme, USA: Edward Elgar, pp. 79–92.
Courvisanos, J. (2005), 'A post-Keynesian innovation policy for sustainable development', *International Journal of Environment, Workplace and Employment*, **1** (2), 187–202.
Courvisanos, J. and C. Richardson (2006), 'Corridor of viability: complexity analysis for enterprise and investment', in M. Setterfield (ed.), *Complexity, Endogenous Money and Macroeconomic Theory: Essays in Honour of Basil J. Moore*, Cheltenham, UK and Northampton, MA, USA: Edward Elgar, pp. 125–51.
Dalziel, P. and M. Lavoie (2003), 'Teaching Keynes's principle of effective demand using the aggregate labor market diagram', *Journal of Economic Education*, **34** (4), 333–40.
Davidson, P. (1991), 'Is probability theory relevant for uncertainty? A Post-Keynesian perspective', *Journal of Economic Perspectives*, **5** (1), 129–43.
Dow, S. (2001), 'Post-Keynesian methodology', in R. Holt and S. Pressman (eds), *A New Guide to Post-Keynesian Economics*, New York: Routledge, pp. 11–20.
Downward, P. (2003), 'Econometrics', in J. King (ed.), *The Elgar Companion to Post Keynesian Economics*, Cheltenham, UK and Northampton, MA, USA: Edward Elgar, pp. 96–101.
Harcourt, G. (1982), *The Social Science Imperialists*, edited by Prue Kerr, London: Routledge & Kegan Paul.
Harcourt, G. and P. Kenyon (1976), 'Pricing and the investment decision', *Kyklos*, **29** (3), 449–77, reprinted in Harcourt (1982), pp. 104–26.
Harris, D. (1974), 'The price policy of firms, the level of employment and distribution of income in the short run', *Australian Economic Papers*, **13** (22), 144–51.
Kalecki, M. (1990), 'Some remarks on Keynes's theory', in J. Osiatyński (ed.), pp. 223–32; originally published in Polish by *Ekonomista*, 1936, pp. 18–26; English translation by B. Kinda-Hass (1982) in *Australian Economic Papers*, **21** (32), 245–53.
Keynes, J.M. (1936), *The General Theory of Employment, Interest and Money*, London: Macmillan.
Lavoie, M. (1992), *Foundations of Post-Keynesian Economic Analysis*, Aldershot, UK and Brookfield, USA: Edward Elgar.
Lavoie, M. (2002), 'The Kaleckian growth model with target return pricing and conflict inflation', in M. Setterfield (ed.), *The Economics of Demand-Led Growth: Challenging the Supply-Side Vision of the Long Run*, Cheltenham, UK and Northampton, MA, USA: Edward Elgar, pp. 172–88.
Lavoie, M. (2006), 'Do heterodox theories have anything in common? A Post-Keynesian point of view', *Intervention: Journal of Economics*, **3** (1), 87–112.
Lianos, T. (1983–84), 'A graphical exposition of a post Keynesian model', *Journal of Post Keynesian Economics*, **6** (2), 313–23.

Mankiw, N.G. (1998), *Principles of Economics*, 3rd edn 2004, Mason, OH: South-Western.

Osiatyński, J. (ed.) (1990), *Collected Works of Michał Kalecki, Volume I Capitalism: Business Cycles and Full Employment*, Oxford: Clarendon Press.

Radzicki, M. (2008), 'Institutional economics, Post-Keynesian economics, and system dynamics: three strands of heterodox braid', in J.T. Harvey, and R.F. Garnett Jr. (eds), *Future Directions for Heterdox Economics*, Ann Arbor, MI: University of Michigan Press, pp.156–89.

Reynolds, P. (1987), *Political Economy: A Synthesis of Kaleckian and Post Keynesian Economics*, Brighton: Wheatsheaf Books.

Robinson, J. (1964), 'Kalecki and Keynes', in *Problems of Economic Dynamics and Planning: Essays in Honour of Michał Kalecki*, Oxford: Pergamon Press and Warszawa: PWN – Polish Scientific Publishers, pp. 335–42; reprinted in J. Robinson (1965), *Collected Economic Papers*, vol. 3, Oxford: Basil Blackwell.

Sardoni, C. (1995), 'Interpretations of Kalecki', in G. Harcourt, A. Roncaglia and R. Rowley (eds), *Income and Employment in Theory and Practice: Essays in Memory of Athansios Asimakopulos*, New York: St. Martin's Press, pp. 185–204.

Sawyer, M. (1982), *Macroeconomics in Question: The Keynesian-Monetarist Orthodoxies and the Kaleckian Alternative*, Armonk, NY: M.E. Sharpe.

Sawyer, M. (1985), *The Economics of Michał Kalecki*, London: Macmillan.

Skouras, T. (1979), 'A "Post Keynesian" alternative to "Keynesian" macromodels', *Journal of Economic Studies*, **6** (5), 225–36.

Toporowski, J. (2003), 'Kaleckian economics', in J. King (ed.), *The Elgar Companion to Post Keynesian Economics*, Cheltenham, UK and Northampton, MA, USA, Edward Elgar, pp. 226–29.

APPENDIX 7.A1 KK MODEL EQUATIONS/IDENTITIES, WITH BASECASE INITIAL VALUES (PERIOD $t=0$) SHOWN

Main Variables

Expenditure	$Y_t = C_t + I_t$	\$4,003,441 pp
Employment	$L_t = Q_t/q_t$	3,203 workers pp
Employment Growth	$gL_t = (L_t - L_{t-1})/L_{t-1}$	1.0% pp
Unit Price	$P_t = P_{t-1} + \alpha(v_t - 1)$	\$12.50 per unit
Price Level	$p_t = 100P_t/P_0$	100.00
Inflation Rate	$gp_t = (P_t - P_{t-1})/P_{t-1}$	0.0% pp
Money Wage Rate	$w_t = w_{t-1}(1 + w_q gq_t + w_p gp_t)$	\$1,000 per worker pp
Wage Bill	$W_t = w_t L_t$	\$3,202,746 pp
Real Consumption	$C^*_t = W_t/P_t$	256,219 units pp
Consumption	$C_t = P_t C^*_t$	\$3,202,746 pp
Real Capital Stock	$K^*_t = (1 - d)K^*_{t-1} + I^*_t$	800,000 units
Capital Stock	$K_t = P_t K^*_t$	\$10,000,023
Real Investment	$I^*_t = (1 + \beta xr_t)dK^*_t$	64,056 units pp
Investment	$I_t = P_t I^*_t$	\$800,696 pp
Saving	$S_t = Y_t - C_t$	\$800,696 pp
Production	$Q_t = C^*_t + I^*_t$	320,275 units pp
Capacity	$Q^*_t = K^*_t/z$	320,256 units pp
Profits	$R_t = Y_t - W_t$	\$800,696 pp
Profit Rate	$r_t = R_t/K_t$	8.0% pp
Unemployment Rate	$u_t = (N_t - L_t)/N_t$	0.0%
Production/ Capacity Ratio	$v_t = Q_t/Q^*_t$	1.0
Excess Capacity Rate	$x_t = 1 - v_t$	0.0%

Profitability Gap

Profit Rate > Cost of Capital?	$xr_t = [r_{t-1} - i_t] > 0?$	3.0% pp

Parameters

Price Adjustment Coefficient	$\alpha = 0.5$	0.5
Investment Reaction Coefficient	$\beta = 11.13$	11.13

Productivity-Wage Passthrough	$w_q = 1.0$	1.0
Inflation-Wage Passthrough	$w_p = 1.0$	1.0
Interest Rate	$i = 0.05$	5.0% pp
Depreciation Rate	$d = 0.06$	6.0% pp
Initial Labour Productivity	$q_0 = 100$	100 units per worker pp
Labour Productivity Growth	$gq = 0.01$	1.0% pp
Initial Workforce	$N_0 = 3{,}203$	3,203 workers
Workforce Growth	$gN = 0.01$	1.0% pp
Initial Real Capital Stock	$K^*_0 = 800{,}000$	800,000 units
Capital–Capacity Ratio	$z = 2.498$	2.498

Other Variables

Propensity to Save	$s_t = S_t / Y_t$	20.0%
Propensity to Consume	$c_t = C_t / Y_t$	80.0%
Keynesian Multiplier	$k_t = Y_t / I_t$	5.0
Profit Share	$rs_t = R_t / Y_t$	20.0%
Wage Share	$ws_t = W_t / Y_t$	80.0%
Wage Cost	$wc_t = w_t / q_t$	$10.00 per unit
Profit Margin	$rm_t = P_t - wc_t$	$2.50 per unit
Mark-up	$m_t = rm_t / P_t$	20.0%
Real Wage Rate	$wr_t = w_t / p_t$	80 units per worker pp

APPENDIX 7.A2 KK MODEL (BASECASE AND PERTURBEDCASE WITH 2% pp WORKFORCE GROWTH)

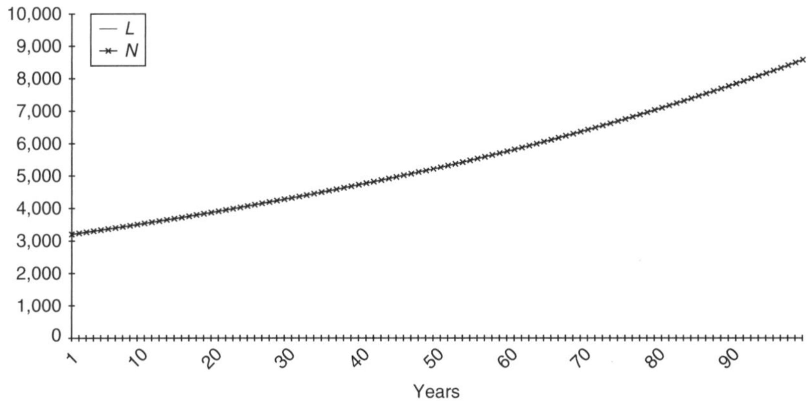

Figure 7.A2.1 *BaseCase $g^N = 1\%$ pa: workforce and employment growth coincide*

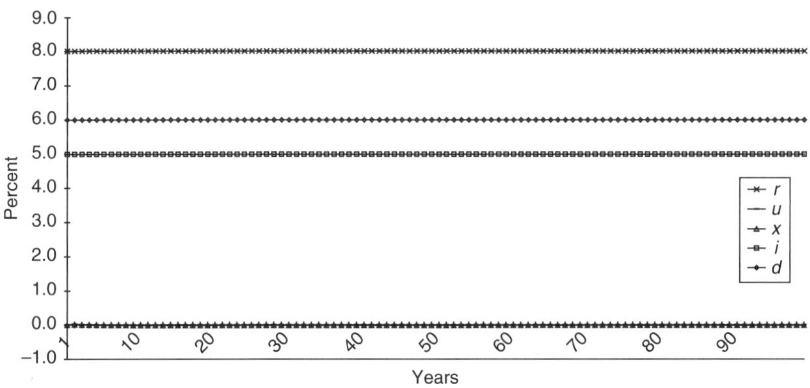

Figure 7.A2.2 *BaseCase $g^N = 1\%$ pa: rates of unemployment and excess capacity are zero*

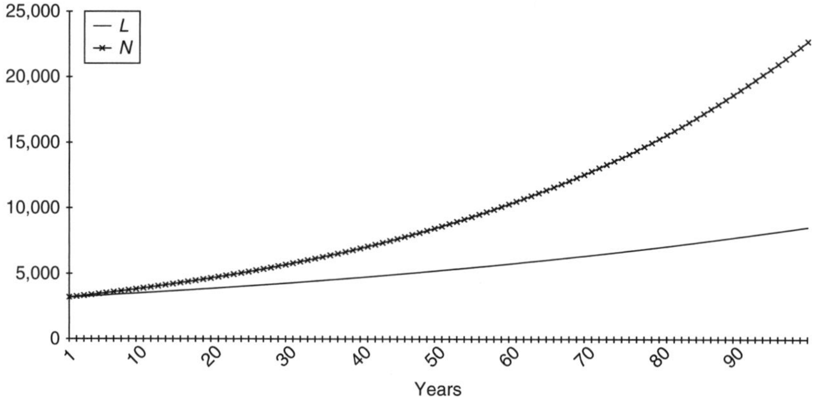

Figure 7.A2.3 *PerturbedCase* $g^N = 2\%$ *pa: workforce growth exceeds employment growth*

APPENDIX 7.A3 KK MODEL (SETTING A, POLICY A1)

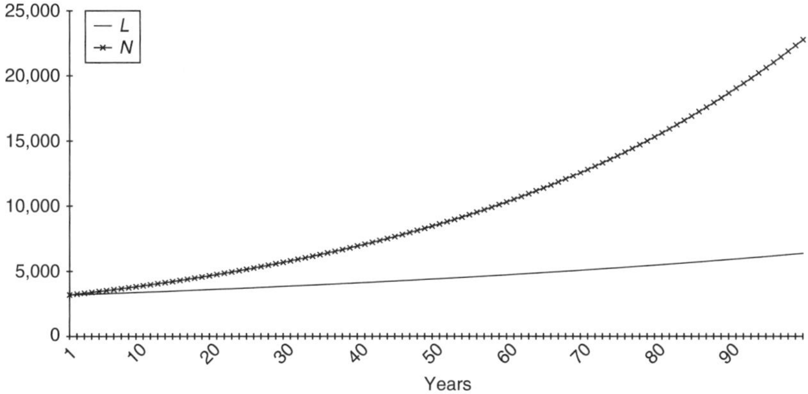

Figure 7.A3.1 *CaseA1: workforce growth far exceeds employment growth*

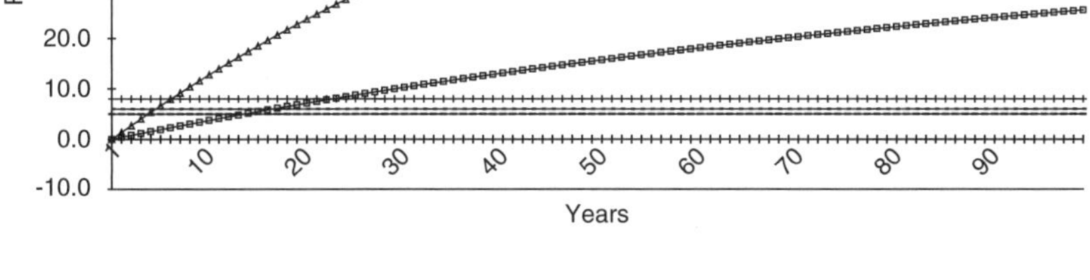

Figure 7.A3.2 *CaseA1:how unemployment and excess capacity rates build up*

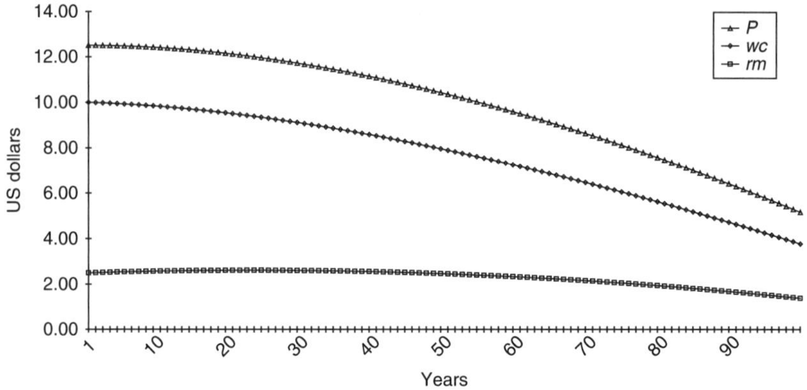

Figure 7.A3.3 CaseA1: how price, wage cost and profit margin fall

APPENDIX 7.A4 KK MODEL (SETTING C, POLICY C1)

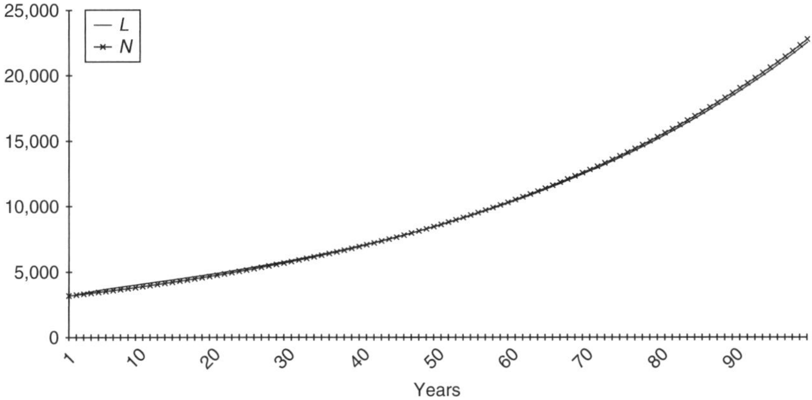

Figure 7.A4.1 *CaseC1: rough equality between workforce growth and employment growth*

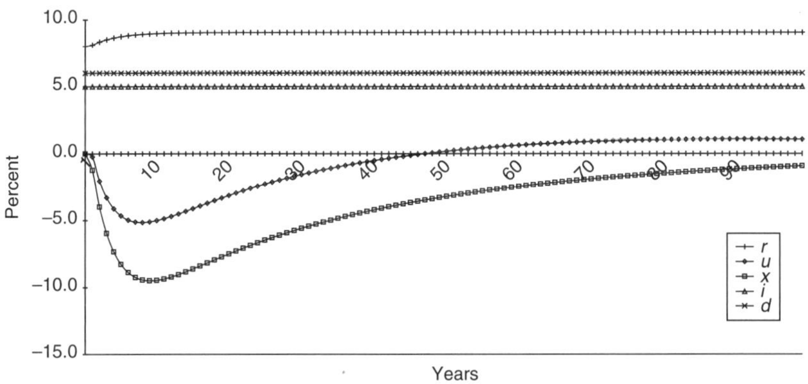

Figure 7.A4.2 *CaseC1: initial profit rate rise creates negative unemployment and excess capacity, which then stabilise*

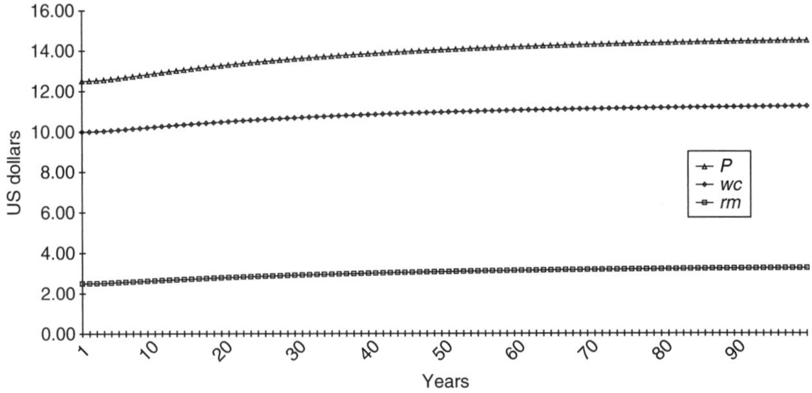

Figure 7.A4.3 *CaseC1: price and wage cost are rising slower than profit margin*

8. A Keynesian model for the 21st century

H. Sonmez Atesoglu*

INTRODUCTION

What kind of a Keynesian model can ensure that the fundamental Keynesian ideas will have staying power in the 21st century – ideas such as less than full-employment equilibrium level of output, monetary non-neutrality, an autonomous expenditures-driven economy, and others? In this chapter it will be argued that the well-known models such as the conventional Keynesian IS–LM model, the recently introduced Romer–Taylor model and the fundamentalist Keynesian Weintraub–Davidson aggregate demand and supply model are not suitable for this task.[1] In this chapter, an alternative Keynesian model for aggregate output and employment is presented. The model follows from the fundamental Keynesian taxonomy between expenditures that are dependent upon and independent of aggregate income. In addition, policy implications of the Keynesian model are discussed. Finally, a Keynesian model with a monetary sector is introduced and the monetary policy aspects and difficulties in the implementation of these policies with respect to the US economy are discussed. The Keynesian models presented, although relatively simple, prove to be useful for interpreting past events, yield illuminating predictions and are preferable to the well-known Keynesian-type models.

For many years after it was introduced by Hicks (1937), the IS–LM model was considered as the best rendition of the economics of Keynes by most economists. However, this model is fundamentally in contradiction with the Marshallian partial equilibrium approach of Keynes. The IS–LM model is a general equilibrium model (see for example, Friedman, 1974; Hoover, 1984; and Rogers, 1989). This methodological distinction matters because it has implications on causality among the key macroeconomic variables examined. For example, the long-term interest rate in Keynesian

* I benefited from the comments of Colin Rogers, Malcolm Sawyer, Mark Setterfield and John Smithin while writing this chapter; I would like to thank them. However, all views expressed and errors are my responsibility.

economics is determined primarily by the actions of the central bank, and changes in the long-term interest rate lead to changes in other macroeconomic variables. However, in the IS–LM model, the long-term interest rate is determined endogenously – passively adjusting to changes brought about by other macroeconomic variables.

Furthermore, in the IS–LM model the money supply is assumed to be an exogenous variable controlled by the Federal Reserve. But, in reality the Fed controls the federal funds rate and, thereby, interest rates and money supply are determined endogenously by developments in other macro variables. This problem is recognized by the Romer–Taylor model recently introduced by Romer (2000) and Taylor (2000, 2004) as a replacement for the IS–LM model. The Romer–Taylor model, while retaining the IS part of the model for explaining the commodity sector, has eliminated the demand and exogenously determined supply for money – the LM part – and introduces a central bank reaction function for describing interest rates and monetary policy. In the Romer–Taylor model, the central bank sets the federal funds rate, and thereby interest rates, in response to developments in the inflation rate and aggregate output. In the Romer–Taylor model, the central bank is assumed to be always successful in making the economy produce an output equal to its full-employment level, with the effective and precise conduct of monetary policy by controlling real interest rates. This new classical full-employment feature of the model is inconsistent with the economics of Keynes. The full-employment nature of the Romer–Taylor model is unrealistic and ignores the fact that, although the Fed can control nominal short-term rates, its control of the important long-term rates and real short- and long-term interest rates is difficult.

An alternative Keynesian model is the Weintraub and Davidson aggregate demand and supply model (see, for example, Weintraub, 1981–82; Davidson, 1994; and Atesoglu, 1999, 2000). This model provides an explanation of nominal aggregate income with nominal autonomous expenditures. It also explains aggregate employment with autonomous expenditures in wage-units. The Weintraub and Davidson model retains key ideas of Keynes, for example the possibility of less than full-employment equilibrium, monetary non-neutrality, and other ideas. But, although this model maps closely with the macroeconomic approach of the General Theory of Keynes (1936, 1969), it has not been popular for various reasons (see King, 1994). The neoclassical microeconomic foundations of this model are mentioned as a reason for its unpopularity by King. However, the economics of Keynes has a neoclassical foundation. The main reason for the Weintraub–Davidson model's unpopularity appears to be the cumbersome nature of the model and, in particular, the intuitively difficult-to-grasp unconventional aggregate supply and demand curves with which this model is usually depicted.

The Keynesian model of output and employment proposed in this chapter is presented in the following section. This model follows from the basic Keynesian taxonomy. There has been an ongoing debate over the years as to what constitutes the main innovations of Keynesian economics. Analytically, the basic taxonomy introduced by Keynes 70 years ago stands out. The Keynesian insight of dividing aggregate income into a part dependent on income and a part that is independent of income – autonomous – continues to be the foundation taxonomy for macroeconomics. The Keynesian classification scheme has proven to have staying power and is starting to be comparable to the classical equation of exchange. Various economists, such as Harrod (1951), Hansen (1953), Friedman (1974), and Davidson (1994), recognize the significance of the Keynesian taxonomy.

A KEYNESIAN MODEL OF OUTPUT AND EMPLOYMENT

The Keynesian model detailed below is a demand-driven model based on fundamental Keynesian taxonomy: $Q = C + I + G + NX$ where, Q is GDP, C is consumption spending, I is investment spending, G is government spending, and NX is net exports. All variables are in real terms. Formally, the model can be presented with the following equations:

$$Q = C + I + G + NX \quad \text{(output and expenditures)}, \tag{8.1}$$

$$C = C_o + c(Q - T) \quad \text{(consumption function)}, \tag{8.2}$$

$$T = T_o + tQ \quad \text{(tax function)}, \tag{8.3}$$

$$NX = NX_o - mQ \quad \text{(net export function)}, \tag{8.4}$$

where variables with the subscript $_0$ represent an autonomous component of an associated variable. Here I and G are assumed to be autonomous variables independent of income.

Equations (8.1–4) can be solved for Q to obtain a reduced form of the model for income:

$$Q = 1/1 - c(1 - t) + m\,(I + G + C_o - cT_o + NX_o) \quad \text{(reduced form for } Q\text{)}, \tag{8.5}$$

changes in Q, with respect to changes in variables in the brackets, yield multipliers for each autonomous variable: $\partial Q/\partial I = \partial Q/\partial G = \partial Q/\partial C_o = \partial Q/NX_o = 1/1 - c(1 - t) + m$, and $\partial Q/\partial T_o = -\,cT_o\,/1 - c(1 - t) + m$.

Assuming a simple production relation, where labor productivity, and aggregate employment, N, determine Q, an equation for determination employment can be written:

$$N = qQ \quad \text{(aggregate employment)}, \tag{8.6}$$

where q is the employment to output ratio, inverse of labor productivity. Substitution of equations (8.5) in (8.6) gives a reduced form of the model for employment:

$$N = q/1 - c(1-t) + m(I + G + C_o - cT_o + NX_o) \quad \text{(reduced from for } E\text{)} \tag{8.7}$$

Changes in N, with respect to a change in an autonomous variable, give multipliers for employment: $\partial N/\partial I = \partial N/\partial G = \partial N/\partial C_0 = \partial N/\partial T_0 = \partial Q/NX_0 = q/1 - c(1-t) + m$, and $\partial N/\partial T_0 = -qc/1 - c(1-t) + m$.

In this Keynesian model, Q and N are simultaneously determined. The model is depicted in Figure 8.1. AQ curve in Figure 8.1 represents reduced form equation (8.1), and its slope is the general multiplier term, $1/1 - c(1-t) + m$ and $A = I + G + C_0 - cT_0 + NX_0$ is the autonomous expenditures. The N curve in Figure 8.1 represents aggregate employment, equation (8.6), where q is the slope of the N curve.

In this figure, Q_e is the equilibrium level of income and N_e is the equilibrium level of employment. Equilibrium levels Q and N are consistent with those determined by equations (8.5) and (8.7), respectively. In Figure 8.1, note that when there is a change in an autonomous variable there will be a change in the equilibrium levels of Q and N, as described by the multipliers detailed above.

Recently, a Keynesian model, similar to the one discussed above, was empirically applied to the US economy by Atesoglu (2005–06), for assessing the effects of a rise in defense spending after the September 11, 2001 terrorist attacks on the US. The empirical results presented are supportive of the Keynesian model. The model is also able to provide a quantitatively plausible explanation of Q and N and other variables, and yields illuminating quantitative predictions for assessing the effects of a rise in defense spending.

KEYNESIAN AND CLASSICAL MODELS

In the Keynesian model, with respect to output and employment the emphasis is on the commodity sector of the economy, with the main drivers

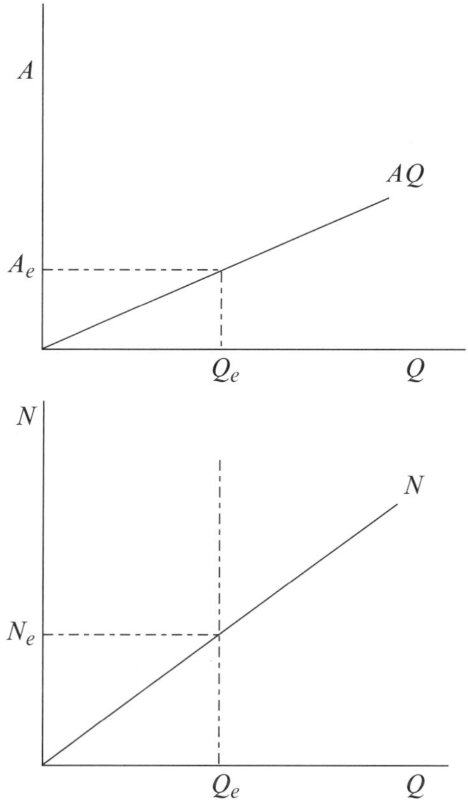

Figure 8.1 *Keynesian model of output and employment*

of the economy being autonomous expenditures, such as I and G. This contrasts with the old and the new classical models, such as the real business cycle model (see, for example, O'Sullivan and Sheffrin, 2003) where emphasis is on the labor market. In classical models, N is determined by real wages, and N determines Q, consistent with a neoclassical production function for the economy. According to the real business cycle model, technological shocks are the primary driver of the economy. In the old and new classical models, adjustments in real wages ensure that the economy produces Q almost always equal to the full-employment level of income, Q_f.

In the Keynesian model, there is no guarantee that Q_e is equal to Q_f, and N_e is equal to N_f. There is no inherent mechanism that forces the economy to produce Q_f that would result in N_f. In the Keynesian model, as seen in Figure 8.2, given the values of autonomous expenditures, the final level of autonomous expenditures, A, depends on interest rates through the effects

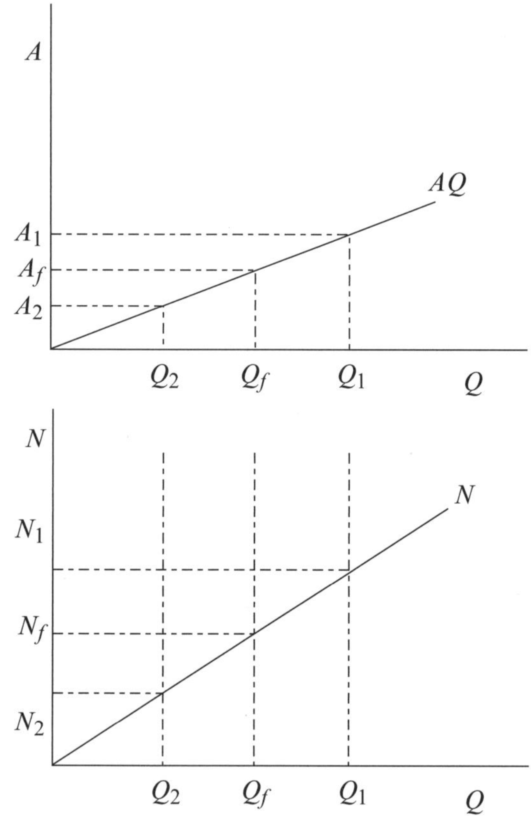

Figure 8.2 Full employment in the Keynesian model of output and employment

of interest rates on *C*, *I* and *NX*. Interest rates, in particular long-term rates, can be high and place *A* in a position that results in $Q_e < Q_f$ and $N_e < N_f$. This less-than-full-employment equilibrium situation can be persistent, since in the Keynesian model when the economy is in equilibrium the long-term interest rate (cost of capital) is equal to return on capital. Therefore, firms would not make profits by increasing output and investment (see Rogers, 1989: 176–9;, and Chick, 1983: 71).

In new classical macroeconomics $Q_e < Q_f$ and $N_e < N_f$ are considered temporary and short-run disequilibrium positions of the economy. In the long run, a fall in wages and costs in general would induce firms to raise output to Q_f and employment to N_f (see Friedman, 1997). But, in the Keynesian model, in the long run, a fall in wages and costs in general would be accompanied by a fall in prices and thereby revenues, and there would be no incentive for firms to expand output and investment. In the Keynesian model, a fall in wages and costs would not result in an upward rise in A that would lead to $Q_e = Q_f$ and $N_e = N_f$.

In the Keynesian model $Q_e < Q_f$ and $N_e < N_f$ for long periods of time. This is consistent with the experience of the US economy during the Great Depression years, 1929 to 1941. For 12 straight years the US economy was producing output below its full-employment level (see Gordon, 2000). The substandard performance of the Japanese economy during the 1990s and early 2000s is also consistent with the Keynesian model. The ongoing unemployment rate was about 2 percent in 1990, increased to 4.1 percent in 1999 and continued to increase to 5 percent by 2004 (see Blanchard, 2006).

FISCAL POLICY IMPLICATION

In the Keynesian model, depending on the values of parameters and autonomous variables, the economy can be at $Q_e < Q_f$, $Q_e = Q_f$ or $Q_e > Q_f$. In Figure 8.2, Q_1 and N_1 represent a situation of $Q_e > Q_f$, and Q_2 and N_2 represent a situation of $Q_e < Q_f$. These non-full-employment positions indicate an opportunity for employing fiscal and monetary policy for achieving Q_e equal to Q_f and N_e equal to N_f.

When Q_e is not equal to Q_f, a clear implication of the Keynesian model is to engineer adjustments in G and T_o and raise A to achieve an equilibrium level of income equal to Q_f. A well-known episode of discretionary fiscal policy in the US is the 1964 tax cut. Aggregate output was below its full-employment level in the early 1960s. The tax cut was an expansionary fiscal policy designed to raise aggregate output. In Figure 8.2, the 1964 tax cut can be described as an effort to raise output from Q_2 to Q_f. Arestis and Sawyer (2003) make a strong case for discretionary fiscal policy. But, the active stabilization of the economy by fiscal policy, although practiced vigorously in the 1960s, is no longer popular with policy makers in the US, due to persistent budget deficits and political difficulties of restrictive fiscal policies.

The Keynesian model discussed above also suggests the possibility of improving the stability of the economy by increasing the size of the relatively more stable autonomous variables, such as government spending. The model also suggests the possibility of improving the stability of the economy by increasing the stability of private investment spending. It is well known that investment is the most volatile component of the Keynesian model.

The idea of stabilizing and encouraging investment by 'socializing investment' was originated by Keynes (see Rogers, 1989). In this view, the government should account for a relatively larger portion of investment, and government investment should be undertaken with the objective of increasing the rate of return of private sector investment. The relatively larger portion of investment owned by the government should reduce the volatility of investment, since government-owned investment would be less responsive to changes in interest rates and rates of return.

Apart from the ideological objections that some economists may have against these ideas, due to ongoing budget deficits, the idea of increasing the size of government spending or 'socializing investment' would not be considered as a feasible policy option by policy makers. However, it should be observed that such a socialization of investment has already taken place since the publication of the *General Theory*. Fiscal policy in the form of socialization of investment, such as investment in the interstate highway system, nuclear energy, the aero-space industry, and the internet to name a few, has increased the return on private investment and improved its stability, and allows the contemporary US economy to perform closer to its full-employment level.

MONETARY POLICY IMPLICATIONS

In the Keynesian model, monetary policy, through interest rates, along with autonomous variables, such as government spending, determine the level of A and there by Q_e and N_e. Effects of monetary policy are reflected as changes in A. Monetary policy engineered changes in the interest rate can lead to changes in the components of C, I and NX as they are interest rate sensitive. For example, in Figure 8.2, real income can fall from Q_f to Q_2 and N_f to N_2 due to a shortage of liquidity in the economy. This unfavorable situation can develop due to an increase in the demand for money brought about by an increase in uncertainty. Davidson (2002) emphasizes the role of uncertainty as a determinant for liquidity – the demand for money. Uncertainty may develop due to an unexpected event, for example, an international security threat, which can lead to a rise in interest rates and lower A_f to A_2. A diligent central bank may be able to resolve this problem by lowering the interest rates by increasing the reserves and the money supply with an effective expansionary monetary policy. The Federal Reserve's action of sharply increasing liquidity available to the financial system after the September 11, 2001 terrorist attacks is a recent example of a successful preemptive expansionary monetary policy (Davidson, 2002; Mishkin, 2006).

Although inflation targeting remains a controversial monetary policy strategy (see, for example, Atesoglu and Smithin, 2006), inflation targeting is the primary goal of monetary policy for an increasing number of central banks. The Taylor rule of monetary policy (Taylor, 1993, 1999), which encompasses inflation targeting, is able to provide a fairly accurate description of the stance of monetary policy under Chairman Alan Greenspan in the US (see Mishkin, 2006).

The workings of an inflation-targeting strategy can be discussed with reference to Figure 8.2. Initially, consider the economy to be producing Q_f level of output and there is an ongoing inflation inherited from the past, which is equal to the target level of the central bank inflation rate. For example, due to a war a significant rise in defense spending may increase aggregate output from Q_f to Q_1 and N_f to N_1. Along with this expansion in the economy, the inflation rate is likely to rise above the central bank target. There is a large body of evidence, for example a study by Atesoglu (1997), suggesting that an expansion of output would lead to a rise in the inflation rate in the US.

In response to a rise in inflation, an inflation-targeting central bank will react by raising the interest rates. The rise in the interest rates will lower A_1 down towards to A_f, and along with this, the inflation rate will fall. The inflation-targeting central bank will ideally continue to raise interest rates until A_1 falls to A_f, and inflation is equal to the central bank target. The expansion induced by a rise in defense spending in the US after September 11, 2001 and following the Iraq war, and the Federal Reserve reaction of engineering consecutive increases in the federal funds rate discussed by Atesoglu (2005–6), is a recent example of inflation targeting by the Federal Reserve in the US.

A KEYNESIAN MODEL WITH A MONETARY SECTOR

A widely accepted formal theoretical extension of a Keynesian model that can explain monetary sector and monetary policy as it is currently practiced remains to be developed. In Figure 8.3, a tentative Keynesian model, consistent with monetary policy cases discussed above, is presented. Formally, this model can be derived by retaining equations (8.1–4) and (8.6) of the Keynesian model above, while specifying I as a negative function of the long-term interest rate, r.

In Figure 8.3, the two figures on the left are the same as in Figure 8.1 except for a change in the top-left figure. Here the vertical axis is measuring r rather than A. This reflects the fact that some parts of A and in particular I may depend on r. The intercept of this 'IS' curve measured on the horizontal axis represents the autonomous spending independent of r.

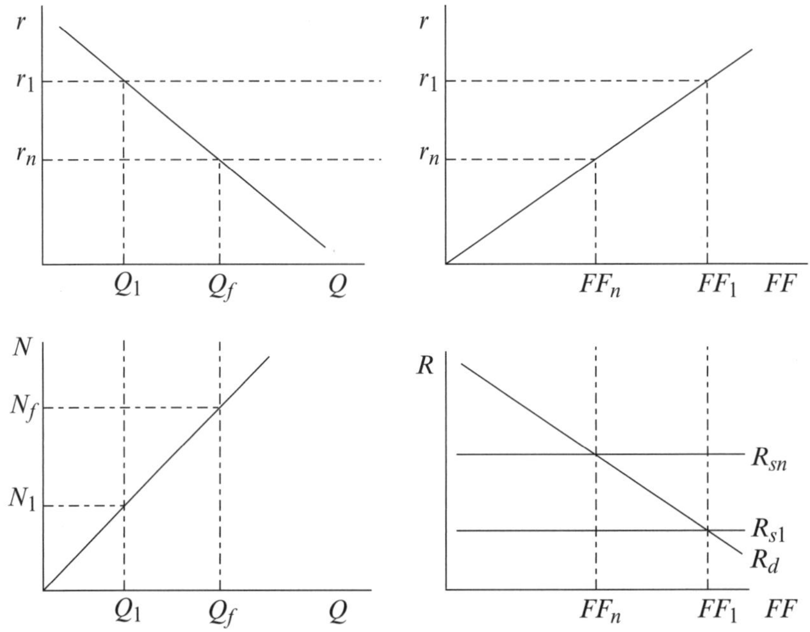

Figure 8.3 Keynesian model with a monetary sector

The top-right figure is the relation between r and FF. In this expanded model, r is assumed to be a linear positive function of FF, the federal funds rate. This relation can be explained with reference to the Keynesian liquidity preference model for supply and demand for money, or in accordance with the term structure theory of interest rates, or, alternatively, following the loanable funds model. There appears to be no widely accepted consensus for the preferred explanation.

Currently FF is the operating monetary policy target used by the Federal Reserve. FF is determined in the market for bank reserves, R, the bottom-right figure. In this market R_s, the supply of reserves, is assumed to be a variable under the control of the Federal Reserve. The demand for reserves, R_d, is assumed to be a linear negative function of FF. The rationale for the negative relation is the fact that FF represents the opportunity cost of holding non-interest-bearing reserves for the depository institutions. The Federal Reserve selects the target level of FF, and given the demand for reserves, adjusts supply of reserves consistent with the target level of FF.[2]

In Figure 8.3, when the federal funds rate is set at FF_1 the long-term interest rate will be r_1 and corresponding to this, the equilibrium output will be Q_1 and employment N_1. Note that causality runs from FF and r, and from these interest rates, to Q and N, in other words, from the monetary sector to the commodity sector of the economy. This causal sequence, emphasized among others by Chick (1983) and Rogers (1989), is consistent with the Keynesian emphasis on the crucial role of long-term interest rates in determining other macroeconomic variables, like Q and N. The causal sequence is also consistent with the current conduct of monetary policy in the US – the determination and control of interest rates by the Federal Reserve.

The causal sequence described here follows the Marshallian–Keynesian partial equilibrium approach, allowing interdependence among markets by considering one market at a time. First, FF is determined in the reserve market. Second, given FF, r is determined in the market for interest rates. And, third, given r, Q and N are determined in the commodity and labor markets. The Keynesian partial equilibrium causal sequence contrasts with that of the general equilibrium IS–LM model where r is determined by the simultaneous interaction of the commodity and monetary sectors, indicating a bi-directional causality between interest rates and Q and N.

In Figure 8.3, when the economy is at less than its full-employment position, Q_1 and N_1, the Federal Reserve can lower the federal funds rate to FF_n with an open market purchase of government securities and shift R_{s1} to R_{sn}, and increase the reserves of the banking system. FF_n will lead to a lower long-term interest rate, r_n, and a lower long-term interest rate will result, Q_f and N_f. The long-term interest rate, r_n, which is consistent with the full-employment of the economy, is identified as the neutral interest rate by Keynes in the *General Theory* (p. 243).

A neutral interest rate rule for monetary policy can be considered as an alternative to the Taylor rule reportedly employed by the Federal Reserve. Although there may be disagreements as to what constitutes the full-employment level of Q and N, as long as inflation is due to a rise in Q relative to Q_f, a neutral interest rate policy is likely to stabilize the economy. However, if inflation is due to a struggle for larger income shares or is due to price shocks, such as a rise in the price of crude oil, then another instrument of policy is required to complement the neutral interest rate rule. This instrument may be a type of incomes policy. In recent years, an incomes policy was proposed as an additional instrument of policy, for example by Weintraub (1978) and Davidson (1994, 2006). The alternative to incomes policy for coping with price and wage shocks is a restrictive monetary policy which would clash with the interest rate rule and lead to high levels of unemployment.

DIFFICULTIES IN MONETARY POLICY

In the US, the central bank, the Federal Reserve, can effectively control short-term interest rates such as the federal funds rate and prime rate. But, the Federal Reserve's control over long-term rates, as illustrated in Figure 8.3, is, in practice, difficult. Recent empirical evidence by Atesoglu (2003–04, 2005) is revealing. The evidence shows that there is a very close, and almost immediate, statistically reliable relation between the federal funds rate controlled by the Federal Reserve and the prime rate charged by commercial banks. However, the relation between the federal funds rate and long-term rates, while statistically reliable, indicates very long lags in the effect of federal funds rates on long-term rates – lags of about two and a half years for a substantial effect. The presence of long lags in the effect of the federal funds rate on long-term interest rates raises doubts concerning the effective and timely conduct of monetary policy.

Furthermore, if investment, and thereby A, is sensitive to real, rather than nominal, interest rates (see Mankiw, 2003; Taylor, 2004; Mishkin, 2006), the Federal Reserve conduct of monetary policy becomes more complicated. This is due to the fact that it is difficult to measure expected inflation, and thereby real interest rates, and these variables are not normally under the control of the Federal Reserve. Because of the difficulties discussed above, a straightforward implementation of monetary policies that were described above with the help of Figures 8.2 and 8.3, is in reality much more challenging.

CONCLUSION

There is a strong possibility that among the models considered, the Keynesian model of output and employment presented above, following the basic macroeconomic taxonomy introduced by Keynes 70 years ago, will survive the test of time and remain an important part of the macroeconomic theory in the 21st century. There seems to be a wide support for this macroeconomic model and the theoretical explanation it provides for the functioning of the commodity sector. The Keynesian model of output and employment, although relatively simple, has proven to be useful for interpreting past events and yields illuminating predictions.

Although a more complete Keynesian model with a monetary sector was introduced, it can only be considered as a tentative alternative. There are disagreements among economists about the modeling of the monetary sector and its interaction with the commodity sector of the economy. Although there is no longer widespread disagreement concerning the endogenous nature of the money supply, there is no consensus concerning how long-term interest rates are determined and whether nominal or real interest rates should be emphasized for explaining the effects of monetary policy. A widely accepted and realistic formal theoretical extension of the Keynesian model of output and employment that can explain monetary sector and monetary policy as it is currently practiced remains to be developed.

NOTES

1. Another influential interpretation of Keynes was by Minsky (1975).
2. See Moore (1988) for a discussion of the Federal Reserve administration of the *FF* and other short-term rates.

REFERENCES

Arestis, P. and M. Sawyer (2003), 'Reinventing fiscal policy', *Journal of Post Keynesian Economics*, **26**, Fall, 1–25.
Atesoglu, H.S. (1997), 'A Post Keynesian explanation of United States inflation', *Journal of Post Keynesian Economics*, **19**, 639–49.
Atesoglu, H.S. (1999), 'A Post Keynesian explanation of employment in the United States', *Journal of Post Keynesian Economics*, **21**, 603–10.
Atesoglu, H.S. (2000), 'Income, employment, inflation, and money in the United States', *Journal of Post Keynesian Economics*, **22**, 639–46.
Atesoglu, H.S. (2003–04), 'Monetary transmission–federal funds rate and prime rate', *Journal of Post Keynesian Economics*, **26**, Winter, 357–62.
Atesoglu, H.S. (2005), 'Monetary policy and long-term interest rates', *Journal of Post Keynesian Economics*, **27**, 533–9.
Atesoglu, H.S. (2005–06), 'Economic consequences of a rise in defense spending after September 11, 2001', *Journal of Post Keynesian Economics*, **28**(2), 181–90.
Atesoglu, H.S. and J. Smithin (2006), 'Inflation targeting in a simple macroeconomic model', *Journal of Post Keynesian Economics*, **28**(4), 673–88.
Blanchard, O. (2006), *Macroeconomics*, Upper Saddle River, NJ: Pearson Education.
Chick, V. (1983), *Macro Economics after Keynes*, Cambridge, MA: MIT Press.
Davidson, P. (1994), *Post Keynesian Macroeconomic Theory*, Aldershot, UK and Brookfield, USA: Edward Elgar.
Davidson, P. (2002), *Financial Markets, Money and the Real World*, Cheltenham, UK and Northampton, MA, USA: Edward Elgar.
Davidson, P. (2006), 'Can, or should, a central bank inflation target?', *Journal of Post Keynesian Economics*, **28**, 689–703.
Friedman, M. (1974), 'A theoretical framework for monetary analysis', in R.J. Gordon (ed.), *Milton Friedman's Monetary Framework*, Chicago, IL: University of Chicago Press, 1–62.
Friedman, M. (1997), 'John Maynard Keynes', *Economic Quarterly*, **83**(2), 1–23.

Gordon, R.J. (2000), *Macroeconomics*, 8th edn, Reading, MA: Addison-Wesley-Longman.
Hansen, A.H. (1953), *A Guide to Keynes*, New York: McGraw-Hill.
Harrod, R.F. (1951), *The Life of John Maynard Keynes*, London: Macmillan.
Hicks, J. (1937), 'Mr. Keynes and the Classics', *Econometrica*, **5**, 147–59.
Hoover, K.D. (1984), 'Two types of monetarism', *Journal of Economic Literature*, **22**, March, 58–76.
Keynes, J.M. (1936), *The General Theory of Employment, Interest and Money*, London: Macmillan.
Keynes, J.M. (1969), 'The General Theory of Employment: Fundamental Concepts and Ideas', in *Money*, edited by R.W. Clower, Harmondsworth, UK: Penguin Books, 215–25.
King, J.A. (1994), 'Aggregate supply and demand analysis since Keynes', *Journal of Post Keynesian Economics*, **17**, Fall, 3–31.
Mankiw, N.G. (2003), *Macroeconomics*, New York: Worth.
Minsky, H.P. (1975), *John Maynard Keynes*, New York: Columbia University Press.
Mishkin, F.S. (2006), *The Economics of Money, Banking and Financial Markets*, Boston, MA: Pearson–Addison-Wesley.
Moore, B.J. (1988), *Horizontalists and Verticalists*, Cambridge: Cambridge University Press.
O'Sullivan, A. and S.M. Sheffrin (2003), *Macroeconomics Principles and Tools*, Upper Saddle River, NJ: Prentice-Hall.
Rogers, C. (1989), *Money, Interest and Capital*, Cambridge: Cambridge University Press.
Romer, D. (2000), 'Keynesian macroeconomics without the LM curve', *Journal of Economic Perspectives*, **14**(2), Spring, 149–70.
Taylor, J.B. (1993), 'Discretion versus policy rules in practice', *Carnegie-Rochester Conference Series on Public Policy*, **39**, 195–214.
Taylor, J.B. (ed.) (1999), 'A historical analysis of monetary policy rules', in *Monetary Policy Rules*, Chicago, IL: University of Chicago Press, 319–41.
Taylor, J.B. (2000), 'Teaching modern macroeconomics at the principles level', *American Economic Review*, **90**, 90–94.
Taylor, J.B. (2004), *Principles of Macroeconomics*, 4th edn, Boston, MA: Houghton Mifflin.
Weintraub, S. (1978), *Capitalism's Inflation and Unemployment Crises*, Reading, MA: Addison-Wesley.
Weintraub, S. (1981–82), 'Keynesian demand serendipity in supply-side economics', *Journal of Post Keynesian Economics*, **4**, 181–91.

9. Capital accumulation, income distribution, technical progress and endogenous money in a Post Keynesian macrodynamic model

Luciano Dias Carvalho and José Luís Oreiro

INTRODUCTION

The objective of this chapter is to analyze the dynamic path of some macroeconomic variables – in particular, the profit rate, the interest rate and the degree capacity utilization – in a Post Keynesian macrodynamic model of capital accumulation, income distribution and technological progress. In order to do that, we shall present the basic structure of a Post Keynesian macroeconomic dynamic model of the third generation[1] whose main features – which distinguish it from other Post Keynesian models – are the great importance given to the technological progress for the determination of long-term dynamics of the economy and its effects over the banking mark-up and interest rates.

In fact, banking mark-up is supposed here as dependent on the rate of technological progress. The explanation for this uncommon specification to the Post Keynesian models is the assumption that banking mark-up is determined by banks' liquidity preference, in accordance to the so-called structuralist view of money supply endogenity (see Pollin, 1991). Changes in a bank's liquidity position, in turn, are a consequence of a growing demand for finance due to an increasing level of investment expenditures. Since increasing investment is a direct consequence of technological progress, we can use the rate of technological progress as a proxy of the rate at which investment is increasing over time. Thus, when the rate of technological progress receives a positive shock, commercial banks increase the mark-up over the short-term interest rate which is controlled by the central bank. The short-term interest rate is used by the central bank as the only instrument of monetary policy, whose main goal is supposed to be inflation control.

After presenting the basic structure of the macrodynamic model, it will be simulated in order to determine the dynamic paths of some economic variables. We shall then calibrate the parameters of structural equations in order to get a set of trajectories and equilibrium values that are as close as possible to the stylized dynamics of capitalist economies. We shall use 'true' numerical values for the parameters whenever reliable estimates of these values exist.

This chapter has five sections, including the introduction. In the next section we present the basic structure of the model that will be used for the computer simulation. In the third section we describe the qualitative behavior of the model in the short- and long-period equilibrium. In the fourth section we present the calibration method of the model at hand and define its standard dynamics. In the final section, we present some concluding remarks.

THE BASIC BUILDING BLOCKS OF THE MODEL

The present model is an attempt to integrate the theoretical structure of growth and distribution models of the Cambridge school with the Post Keynesian monetary theory, based on the concept of monetary production economy.[2] The integration proposed is made by means of connecting the pace of technological progress with the banking mark-ups and and interest rates.

Previous attempts to integrate the real and monetary aspects of Post Keynesian economics were made by Jarsulic (1989), Dutt (1989, 1992), Dutt and Amadeo (1993), You (1994), Watanabe (1997) and Lima and Meirelles (2003). The major difference between our contribution and theirs is the link between banking mark-ups and technological progress.

The present model offers an original contribution to Post Keynesian literature since it incorporates the Schumpeterian vision of the importance of bank credit for the introduction of technological innovations. The model also incorporates other Post Keynesian ideas such as inflation resulting from class conflict between capitalists and workers, mark-up pricing and technological progress generated by a defensive behavior of firms against the increase of labor costs.

Block 1 Prices and Production[3]

Suppose a closed economy without governmental activities, where oligopolistic firms produce, by means of a Leontief technology, a homogeneous output usable for consumption and investment. Real output is given by:

$$Q = \min\,[Ku_k;\ L/q], \tag{9.1}$$

where Q is the level of output, K is the stock of capital, u_k is the ratio between 'full-capacity' output and capital, L is the level of employment and q is the labor–output ratio.

There is no 'labor hoarding', so firms use only the required labor for producing the 'planned' level of output. The employment level is determined by:

$$L = qQ. \tag{9.2}$$

Due to an oligopolistic market structure, firms have market power to set the prices of their output. Prices are set by means of a mark-up over unitary direct costs. However, in the short run, the mark-up rate desired by firms may differ from the effective rate of the mark-up. Deviations of effective from desired rate of mark-up may result as firms may increase their market share at the expense of profit margins. In the long run, the mark-up rate must be high enough to generate a 'normal' or 'conventional' rate of profit. So, a situation where the effective rate of the mark-up is less than the desired rate will induce firms to increase prices in order to adjust the former to the latter. Since the wage share is an inverse function of the mark-up rate, we can determine price inflation by the difference between effective wage share and the wage share 'desired' by capitalists; that is, the wage share compatible with the desired rate of mark-up. Formally, we have:

$$\hat{P} = \rho[S - S_f], \tag{9.3}$$

where $\hat{P}$ is the proportional rate of variation in prices, $(dP/dt)(1/P)$; ρ is a parameter of sensitivity $(0 < \rho < 1)$ and S_f is the wage share determined by the desired rate of mark-up. Based on Kalecki (1971), the price charged by firms is determined by a mark-up rate, Z_f, over primary costs of production. Mathematically we have:

$$P = (1 + Z_f)W \cdot q, \tag{9.4}$$

where W is the nominal wage rate.

The wage share desired by capitalists, S_f, depends inversely on the degree of capacity utilization, expressing Kaldor's idea that firms react to an increase in the demand for their products by an increase in profit margins:

$$S_f = \theta - \varphi u, \tag{9.5}$$

where Z_f is the desired rate of mark-up,θ and φ are positive parameters.

Block 2 Income Distribution

Income is generated in the production process so that only productive activities are capable of producing income. In this setting, aggregate income is the sum of wages and profits. Interest payments are seen as a deduction of profits that accrue to productive capitalists. So we have:

$$Q = VL + rK, \tag{9.6}$$

where $V \equiv W/P$ is the real wage rate, W is the nominal wage, P is the level of prices and r is the profit rate defined as the monetary flow of profits divided by the nominal value of capital stock.

Using equations (9.2) and (9.6), we find the following expression for the wage share:

$$S = V \cdot q. \tag{9.7}$$

The wage share assumes values between 0 and 1, more precisely, $0 < S < 1$; so the profit share, m, can be written as:

$$m = 1 - S. \tag{9.8}$$

The profit rate can be written as a function of the profit share and the degree of capacity utilization. So that:

$$r = m \cdot u, \tag{9.9}$$

where u is the degree of capacity utilization, $u = Q/Q^*$; $Q^* = u_k K$ is the 'full capacity' output.

Block 3 Labor Market

The proportional rate of variation of nominal wage grows in accordance with the gap between the wage share desired by workers, S_w, and the effective value of the wage share. The speed of increase in wage inflation is determined by a positive parameter λ, as demonstrated by the following equation:

$$\hat{W} = \lambda[S_W - S]. \tag{9.10}$$

The wage share desired by workers is a direct function of the bargaining power of unions in comparison with that of capitalists. We assume that this bargaining power will always increase with the employment rate.[4] Formally we have:

$$S_W = \varepsilon E, \tag{9.11}$$

where ϵ is a positive parameter, and E is the employment rate, understood as the ratio between the employment level and the labor force (L/N). The employment rate is related to the degree of capacity utilization as we can see in the following equation:

$$E = u \cdot k, \tag{9.12}$$

where k is the capital-to-efficiency-labor ratio defined as the ratio between the capital stock, K, and supply of labor in efficiency units, N/q, as shown by:

$$k = K/(N/q). \tag{9.13}$$

Labor force is assumed to grow at a constant rate η:

$$\hat{N} = \eta \tag{9.14}$$

Block 4 Banking Behavior and Monetary Policy

The short-term interest rate, i^B, set by the central bank, is the only instrument of monetary policy, whose main or sole goal is inflation control. We suppose that the central bank increases the nominal short-term interest rate as a reaction to any increase in the rate of inflation.[5] The central bank follows an interest rate rule given by:

$$i^B = \phi \cdot \hat{P}, \tag{9.15}$$

where ϕ is a positive parameter that reflects the sensitivity of the nominal short-term interest rate to changes in the inflation rate.

Commercial banks also have market power, so the lending rate of interest is determined by means of a mark-up, Z_B, over the nominal short-term interest rate, i^B, which is the opportunity cost for bank lending. So we have:

$$i = Z_B i^B. \tag{9.16}$$

Banking mark-up here is modeled as being a function of the rate of technological innovation. Banking mark-up is supposed to be a direct function of a bank's degree of liquidity preference in accordance to the so-called structuralist view of money and finance (see Pollin, 1991). Following Keynes's finance motive for holding money (see Keynes, 1973, p. 209; Davidson, 2002, pp. 97–100), we assume that increases in the degree of liquidity preference occurs when the economy is carried out of the stationary state by means of an increasing level of investment in capital assets. Increasing investment, in turn, is a direct consequence of technological progress, so the rate of technological progress can be thought of as a proxy to the rate at which investment is increasing over time. In formal terms we have:

$$Z_B = \mu \cdot \hat{\Gamma}, \tag{9.17}$$

where μ is a positive parameter, and $\hat{\Gamma}$ is the sensitivity of capital accumulation to the rate of technological innovation.

Block 5 Capital Accumulation and Technological Progress

The rate by which firms desire to increase their capital stock is described by the following equation:[6]

$$\frac{I^d}{K} = \alpha + \beta(r - i) + \tau \cdot \hat{\Gamma}, \tag{9.18}$$

where I^d/K is the desired investment by firms as a ratio to capital stock, α is a positive parameter representing the autonomous component of capital accumulation, β and τ are, respectively, positive parameters that measure the sensitivity of investment to the difference between the profit rate, r, and the banking rate of interest, i, and the sensitivity of capital accumulation to the rate of technological innovation, $\hat{\Gamma}$.

The rate of technological innovation, in turn, is defined as being determined by the wage share in income, as we can see below:

$$\hat{\Gamma} = \psi \cdot S, \tag{9.19}$$

where ψ is a positive parameter that measures the sensitivity of the rate of technological innovation to the wage share.

Technological progress is of the labor-saving type, so its occurrence is associated with a reduction in the labor–output ratio, q. The link between wage share and the rate of technological innovation is due to the fact that one of the main reasons for firms to innovate is to pressure over profitability that came from wage increases. The rate of decrease in the labor–output ratio is determined by the following equation:

$$\hat{q} = \psi \cdot S, \tag{9.20}$$

where $\hat{q}$ is the rate of change of the labor–output ratio.

As firms operate with excess capacity, they will adjust the level of capacity utilization to the level of effective demand. This means that the rate of profit will be determined by the condition of equalizing the desired rate of capital accumulation to savings as a ratio of capital stock. Assuming that workers spend all they get, and capitalists save a constant share of their profit income, we get the following equation:

$$\frac{I}{K} = sr, \tag{9.21}$$

where I/K is the growth rate of the capital stock, and s is the capitalists' propensity to save.

THE QUALITATIVE BEHAVIOR OF THE MODEL IN THE SHORT AND LONG RUNS

In the short run, wage share and the capital-to-efficiency-labor ratio are kept constant. All other dependent variables are determined within the limits of the short run. Output level and capacity utilization are determined in order to ensure equalization between the growth rate of capital stock desired by firms and the saving rate of the economy; that is, $I/K = I^d/K$.

Using equations (9.3), (9.5), (9.8), (9.9), (9.15), (9.16), (9.17), (9.18), (9.19) and (9.21), we can determine the short-run equilibrium value for the degree of capacity utilization, u^*, as follows:

$$u^* = \frac{-A{\cdot}S^2 + B{\cdot}S + \alpha}{(s-\beta)(1-S) + C{\cdot}S}, \tag{9.22}$$

where $A \equiv \beta\mu\phi\psi\rho$, $B \equiv \beta\mu\phi\psi\rho\theta + \tau\psi$ and $C \equiv \beta\mu\phi\psi\rho\psi$. Assuming the usual Keynesian hypothesis that the propensity to save is greater than the propensity to invest, then $C > 0$ and we can guarantee that the denominator of this expression is positive. From (9.22) we can see that the equilibrium level of capacity utilization is a non-linear function of the wage share. The effect of a change in the wage share over the equilibrium level of capacity utilization is given by:

$$\frac{\partial u^*}{\partial S} = \frac{D{\cdot}S^2 - F{\cdot}S + G}{[(s-\beta)(1-S) + C{\cdot}S]^2}, \tag{9.23}$$

where $D \equiv A(s-\beta) - A{\cdot}C$; $F \equiv 2A(s-\beta)$; $G \equiv (B+\alpha)(s-\beta)\alpha{\cdot}C$.

As can be seen, the denominator of this expression is always positive for any value of the wage share. In turn, the numerator has ambiguous signs for the numerical values of D and G. F is always positive since it is assumed that the propensity to save is bigger than the propensity to invest ($s > \beta$). We suppose that $D > 0$ and $G > 0$. The assumption of $D > 0$ implies that the financial sector has a smaller influence over investment decision of firms than the difference between the propensities to save and to invest. So the equilibrium level of capacity utilization will increase with the wage share for lower values; and it will decrease with wage share for higher values of this variable, describing an inverted-U curve in the space $< u, S >$.

The banking interest rate suffers a joint influence from the rate of technological progress and the nominal short-term interest rate. This last, in turn, is influenced by the rate of inflation, which also depends on the degree of capacity utilization. Thus, the interest rate charged by banks is determined by:

$$i = (\mu\phi\psi\rho)\cdot S^2 - (\mu\phi\psi\rho\theta)\cdot S + (\mu\phi\psi\rho\psi)u\cdot S. \tag{9.24}$$

Substituting the equilibrium level of capacity utilization, given in equation (9.22), in equation (9.24), we determine the short-run equilibrium value for banking interest rate, as can be seen in equation (9.25):

$$i^* = \frac{\Psi\cdot S^3 + \chi\cdot S^2 + \pi\cdot S}{(s-\beta)(1-S) + C\cdot S}, \tag{9.25}$$

where

$$\Psi \equiv C(\mu\phi\psi\rho) - (\mu\phi\psi\rho)(s-\beta) - A(\mu\phi\psi\rho\varphi) < 0,$$
$$\chi \equiv (\mu\phi\psi\rho\theta)(s-\beta) + B(\mu\phi\psi\rho\varphi) - C(\mu\phi\psi\rho\theta) > 0,$$
$$\pi \equiv (\alpha\mu\phi\psi\rho\psi) - (\mu\phi\psi\rho\theta)(s-\beta) > 0.$$

The equilibrium growth rate of capital stock, I^*/K, can be found after using equations (9.8), (9.9), (9.21) and (9.22):

$$\frac{I^*}{K} = \frac{sAS^3 - HS^2 + MS + s\alpha}{(s-\beta)(1-S) + CS}, \tag{9.26}$$

where $H \equiv s(A+B)$ and $M \equiv s(B-\alpha)$. When $A > 0$ and $0 < \alpha < B$, then the parameters H and M are positive, that is, $H > 0$ and $M > 0$.

The equilibrium value for the rate of profit is determined after substituting equations (9.8) and (9.22) in (9.9). So, we arrive at the following expression:

$$r^* = \frac{AS^3 - (A+B)S^2 + (B-\alpha)S + \alpha}{(s-\beta)(1-S) + CS}. \qquad (9.27)$$

In the long run, capital stock, labor force, labor–output ratio, wage share and capital-to-efficiency-labor ratio are no longer constants, but change through time. For the long-run equilibrium analysis, we suppose that the degree of capacity utilization, the growth rate of capital stock and banking interest rates are always at their short-run equilibrium values.

From the definitions of the wage share, SVq and the capital-to-efficiency-labor ratio, $k \equiv K/(N/q)$, the long-run behavior of the system can be analyzed by means of the following differential equations:

$$\hat{S} = \hat{W} - \hat{P} + \hat{q}, \qquad (9.28)$$

$$\hat{k} = \hat{K} + \hat{q} - \hat{N}, \qquad (9.29)$$

where $\hat{S} = \partial S/S$; $\hat{k} = \partial k/k$; and so on.

Substituting the equations (9.3), (9.5), (9.10), (9.11), (9.12) and (9.20) in equation (9.28), we can present the proportional variation rate of the wage share as a function of the capital-to-efficiency-labor ratio, K, and of the equilibrium value of the degree of capacity utilization, u^*, which in turn depends solely on the wage share, S. We have that:

$$\hat{S} = u^*[(\lambda\varepsilon)k - \rho\varphi] - (\lambda + \psi + \rho)S + \rho\theta. \qquad (9.30)$$

Equalizing the proportional growth rate of the wage share to zero and applying the total derivative to the resultant of this expression, it is possible to determine the slope of *locus* $\hat{S} = 0$, through the following equation:

$$\frac{\partial k}{\partial S} = \frac{[\rho\varphi - (\lambda\varepsilon)k](\partial u^*/S) + (\lambda + \psi + \rho)}{u^*\lambda\varepsilon}. \qquad (9.31)$$

The denominator of this expression is always positive for any value of the wage share, that is, $u^* > 0, \forall\, 0 < S < 1$. The derivative of the equilibrium level of capacity utilization to wage share, $\partial u^*/\partial S$, is a non-linear function of S as determined by equation (9.22). If we suppose that prices adjust more quickly than nominal wages, then we have $[\rho\varphi - (\lambda\varepsilon)k] > 0$. If we also suppose that $[\rho\varphi - (\lambda\varepsilon)k](\partial u^*/\partial S) > \lambda + \psi + \rho$, then the slope of locus $\hat{S} = 0$ will be negative, $\partial k/\partial S, < 0$, for low values of the wage share $(0 < S < S^*)$ and positive, $\partial k/\partial S > 0$, for high values of the wage share $(S^* < S < 1)$. Moreover, since $\partial u^*/\partial S$ is a quadratic function of wage share, there can be two real roots that satisfy equation $\hat{S} = 0$.

We know that

$$I \equiv \frac{\partial K}{\partial t} \Rightarrow \frac{I}{K} \equiv \hat{K} \equiv sr = s(1 - S)u.$$

When substituting this equation together with equations (9.14) and (9.20) in equation (9.29); we can show the proportional variation rate of capital-to-efficiency-labor ratio, $\hat{k}$, as a function of the wage share, S, as we can see in equation (9.32):

$$\hat{k} = \frac{sA \cdot S^3 + \Omega \cdot S^2 + \Sigma \cdot S + \Lambda}{(s - \beta)(1 - S) + C \cdot S}, \tag{9.32}$$

where $\Omega \equiv C\psi - H - \psi(s - \beta) < 0$; $\Sigma \equiv J + \eta C + \psi(s - \beta) - \eta(s - \beta) > 0$; $\Lambda \equiv s\alpha + \eta(s - \beta) > 0$; and η is the exogenous growth rate of the labor force.[7]

Given these restrictions to the values of the parameters, it is possible to divide the distributive domain into two regions that we call PL (profit-led regime) and WL (wage-led regime). In region PL, defined in the interval $0 < S < S^*$, an increase in wage share will result in a decrease in the level of capacity utilization and profit rate. The decrease in u and r more than offsets the decrease in the banking interest rate, so that the rate of capital accumulation rate decreases as a result of an increase in S. On the other hand, in region WL, defined in the interval $S^* < S < 1$, an increase in wage share will result in an increase in the level of capacity utilization and profit rate, since the increase in the level of capacity utilization more than offsets the reduction in the profit share. As a result of these changes, the rate of capital accumulation increases with S.

The Jacobian matrix of the system composed by equations (9.30) and (9.32) is given by:

$$J_{11} \equiv \partial\hat{S}/\partial S = (\partial u^*/\partial S)(\lambda\varepsilon \cdot k - \rho\varphi) - (\lambda + \psi + \rho), \tag{9.33}$$

$$J_{12} \equiv \partial\hat{S}/\partial k = \lambda\varepsilon \cdot u^* > \text{o}, \tag{9.34}$$

$$J_{21} \equiv \partial\hat{k}/\partial S = [\partial(I^*/K)/\partial S] + \psi, \tag{9.35}$$

$$J_{22} \equiv \partial\hat{k}/\partial k = 0. \tag{9.36}$$

Due to the existence of non-linearities in the model and to the fact that the analysis that we aim to do in this section is merely qualitative, there are diverse possible long-run equilibrium configurations in the space $(K - S)$. We choose to analyze just one of these possible long-equilibrium configurations, more precisely, the one that has an unstable equilibrium of saddle-path type in region PL and stable equilibrium in the region WL.

Since we are supposing that prices adjust more quickly than nominal wages and remembering that in region PL, $\partial u^{*}/\partial S < 0$, $J_{12} > 0$ and $J_{22} = 0$, the nature of the equilibrium in this region will depend on the signal of J_{11}. The analysis of this region shows us that if $(\partial u^{*}/\partial S)\cdot[(\lambda\varepsilon)k - \rho\psi] > (\lambda + \psi + \rho)$, the trace of the Jacobian matrix will be positive, $Tr|J| > 0$. As $\partial(I^{*}/K)/\partial S > 0$, which makes $J_{21} > 0$ for all values of the wage share in the interval between 0 and 1, then $Det|J| < 0$. In this case, the dynamic system will have an unstable equilibrium of saddlepath type. However, if $(\partial u^{*}/\partial S)\cdot[(\lambda\varepsilon)k - \rho\varphi] < (\lambda + \psi + \rho)$, then the trace of the Jacobian matrix will be negative, $Tr|J| < 0$, and since the determinant of the Jacobian matrix continues to be negative, $Det|J| < 0$, then the system will not have an equilibrium.

In analyzing region WL we see that $\partial u^{*}/S > 0$, the proportional variation of the wage share with regard to itself will be negative, $J_{11} < 0$; and since $J_{22} = 0$, the trace of the Jacobian matrix will also be negative, $Tr|J| < 0$. Since $J_{12} > 0$, $\forall 0 < S < 1$, the nature of the equilibrium in this region will depend on the signal of J_{21}. We assume that $\partial(I^{*}/K)/\partial S < 0$, for the values of the wage share that lie in this region; if $\partial(I^{*}/K)/\partial S > \psi$ then $J_{21} < 0$ the determinant of the Jacobian matrix will be greater than zero, $Det|J| > 0$ and the system will have a stable equilibrium. However, if $\partial(I^{*}/K)/\partial S < \psi$ then $J_{21} > 0$, the determinant of the Jacobian matrix will be negative, $Det|J| < 0$, and the system will have no equilibrium at all.

Given that, then diverse combinations exist in the space $(k - S)$ that generate some type of equilibrium. Among these combinations, Figure 9.1 shows us one example where there is an unstable equilibrium of saddlepath type in region PL, and a stable equilibrium in region WL. Since throughout the distributive domain we have $J_{12} > 0$ and $J_{22} = 0$, the determination of this configuration will depend on the signals of J_{11} and J_{21} which, in turn, depend on the relative bargaining power of capitalists and workers; the 'flexibility' of prices and nominal wages; the relative importance of the difference between the propensity to save and the propensity to invest *vis-à-vis* the financial variables; and the strength of technological innovation, among other factors.

We assume that in region PL, $J_{11} > 0$, therefore we consider the sensitivity of prices to be greater than that of nominal wages and that the influence of the product between the degree of capacity utilization and the parameters that define the real wage rate is bigger than the sum of the parameters of the equations of the rate of technological innovation, the level of prices and the nominal wages. Moreover, we assume that $J_{21} > 0$, that is, that the difference between the propensity to save and to invest is bigger than that of the product of all parameters of the banking interest rate equation.

For region WL we establish that $J_{11} < 0$ and $J_{21} < 0$. The negative signal of the first element of the Jacobian matrix, J_{11}, can easily be checked. It is

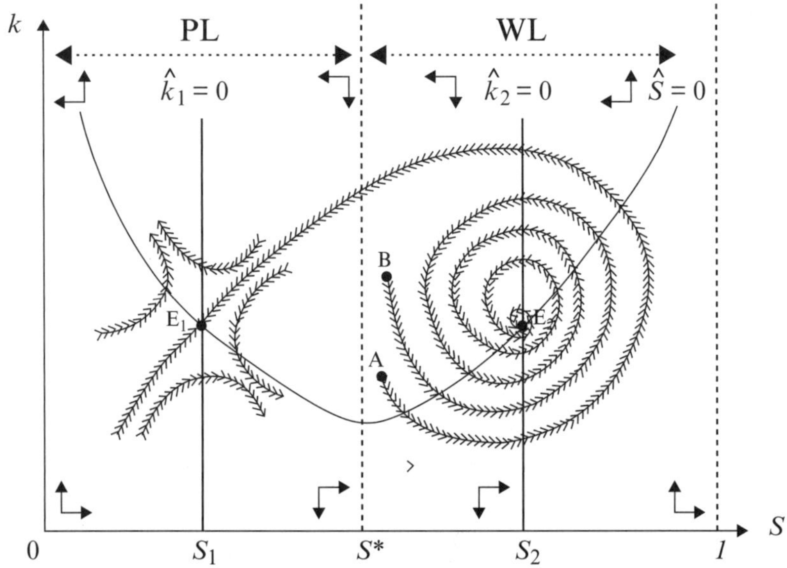

Figure 9.1 A possible long-run equilibrium configuration

enough to remember that in this region $\partial u^*/\partial S > 0$. The negative signal of the second element requires that we establish, in the first place, that the difference between the propensity to save and to invest is bigger than the product of all the parameters of the banking interest rate equation. In the second place, it is necessary to assume that the sensitivity of the accumulation rate to changes in the wage share is greater than the sensitivity of the technological innovation rate to changes in this variable.

Analyzing the dynamic behavior of the system in the space $(k - S)$, we see that there is subregion inside region WL where state variables will exhibit dampened fluctuations around equilibrium point E_2, as can be observed by the trajectory that leaves point B.

This zone, whose dynamics is characterized by dampened fluctuations, we shall call the zone of stability and its complement will be called the instability zone. In the event that the economy is moving inside the instability zone, its behavior will be explosive except if it starts just on point A. If this happens to be the case, the economy will converge to the equilibrium point E_1, in region PL.

The saddlepath trajectory separates the zone of stability from the zone of instability. In fact, any trajectory that begins above the one represented by the saddlepath will converge to the equilibrium point in the WL region; and any trajectory that begins below that one will generate an explosive dynamics.

DEFINING THE STANDARD DYNAMIC TRAJECTORY[8]

The staring-point of the analysis of comparative dynamics is the definition of the standard dynamic trajectory against which other trajectories will be compared. To do that, we have to define the initial values for all the parameters of the model, trying to set values that are 'founded' in empirical evidence about the magnitude of these parameters in the real world. Table 9.1

Table 9.1 Parameters and values in standard dynamic trajectory

Parameter	Value	Description
α	0.01	Autonomous propensity to invest or 'animal spirits' of investors
s	0.80	Propensity to save of capitalists
β	0.75	Coefficient that measures the sensitivity of desired investment to the difference between the profit rate and the banking interest rate
τ	0.25	Coefficient that measure the sensitivity of desired investment to variations in the rate of technological progress
ψ	0.03	Coefficient that measures the sensitivity of the rate of technological progress with regard to variations in the wage share
ρ	1.10	Coefficient that measures the sensitivity of price inflation with relation to the difference between the effective wage share and the one determined by the desired mark-up rate of the firms
θ	0.40	Parameter that measures the autonomous component of the desired wage share by firms
ϕ	0.70	Coefficient that measures the influence of the degree of capacity utilization over the wage share desired by firms
λ	0.50	Coefficient that measures the sensitivity of wage inflation to the difference between the wage share desired by workers and the effective wage share
ε	0.025	Coefficient that measures the sensitivity of the wage share desired by workers to the employment rate
η	0.01	Population growth rate
ϕ	1.50	Coefficient that measures the sensitivity of the nominal short-term interest basic rate to the changes in the rate of inflation
μ	1.15	Coefficient that measures the influence of the rate of technological progress over banking interest rate

presents the parameters with their respective value and the function that they play in the model.

Based on Kaldor (1993), the propensity to save of the capitalists, s, was assumed to be 0.8.[9] We assume that this economy presents a population growth rate, η, to the order of 1 percent (or 0.01) per year. We also assumed that the sensitivity of the short-term interest rate with the rate of inflation, ϕ, is 1.50, an estimation based on econometric evidence for the Brazilian economy (Blanchard, 1999, p. 359).

However, many parameters of the model have no numerical values founded on empirical evidence, therefore they are free parameters. However, it is possible to infer reasonable (in economic terms) values for these parameters. To do that is enough to isolate its effects by means of the assumption that the other parameters of the equation being analyzed assume a zero value.

For example, we are assuming a value for the autonomous part of the investment function of $\alpha = 0.01$. The choice of this value can be justified by the fact that when we set the values of parameters β and τ equal to zero, equation (9.18), which determines the desired rate of capital accumulation, shows that firms desire a growth rate of capital stock of 1 percent per period, a very reasonable number.

Following this same procedure, we determine the values for the other parameters. In fact, for the parameter that describes the sensitivity of the rate of technological progress with relation to the wage share, ψ, we assume a maximum limit of growth rate of labor productivity of 3 percent per period. Assuming a 10 percent difference between the wage share desired by workers and the effective value of the wage share ($S_W - S = 0.1$), then wage inflation will be 5 percent, which suggests the value $\lambda = 0.5$.

Once we have set the parameter values that produce a satisfactory equilibrium, and defining the initial conditions of the system as follows: $k[0] = 0.5$ and $S[0] = 0.75$, it is possible to analyze the behavior of some macroeconomic variables. For this, we analyze the time behavior of the level of capacity utilization, u; the rate of capital accumulation, $I/K \equiv dK/K$; the profit rate, r; and finally, the banking interest rate, i.

Figure 9.2 shows the time path of the degree of capacity utilization and the rate of capital accumulation. We can see that the degree of capacity utilization starts at a value of 37.96 percent and increases during the next 20 periods, reaching a maximum value of 94 percent. Then it decreases to its steady-state value of 71.98 percent. It is important to note that the level of capacity utilization never reaches 100 percent, so that firms always operate with excess capacity. The rate of capital accumulation, in turn, starts at a value of 2.53 percent and increases during the next 45 periods, reaching its steady-state value of 17.73 percent per period.

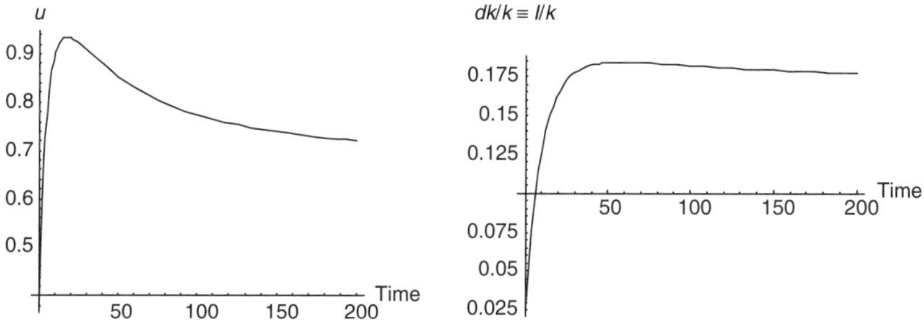

(a) Capacity utilization (*u*)

(b) Capital accumulation (*dk/k* ≡ *I/k*)

Figure 9.2 Standard dynamics for u *and* dK/K

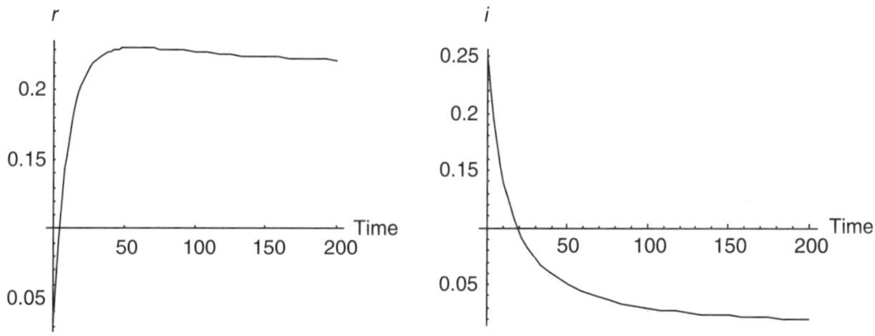

(a) Profit rate (*r*)

(b) Banking interest rate (*i*)

Figure 9.3 The standard dynamics for r *and* i

The trajectories for the profit rate and the banking interest rate are shown in Figure 9.3. As we can see, the profit rate, starting at a 3.16 percent value, grows at decreasing rates until reaching its steady value of 22.16 percent in period 46. The banking interest rate starts at an initial value of 24.96 percent, decreasing during the entire simulation period, until it reaches its steady-state value of 1.93 percent.

FINAL REMARKS

The objective of the this chapter was to analyze the long-run features of a Post Keynesian macroeconomic dynamic model by means of a numerical analysis carried out through computational simulation. For this, we first show the structure of a third-generation macro-dynamic model that incorporates some elements of Post Keynesian monetary theory, especially the interdependence between the real and monetary factors for the determination of the long-run dynamics of the system.

The central element that differentiates the present model from other Post Keynesian models is the way that money exerts its influence over the macro-economic variables in the study. This influence is given through the link between the rate of technological progress and the banking rate of interest. We supposed that an increase in the rate of technological progress increases the banking interest rate as a result of the increase in the bank's liquidity preference. Monetary policy is also important for the results of the model. We assumed that the central bank conducts monetary policy in order to reach a target for the real rate of interest, so that money supply is endogenous.

NOTES

1. Post Keynesian models of growth and distribution can be grouped into three generations of models. The first generation is composed of the balanced growth models such as those of Kaldor (1957) and Pasinetti (1962). The main theoretical issue of this generation of models is to determine what conditions must be met in order to produce a full-employment growth path for real output; that is, the conditions required for equalization between *warranted* and *natural* growth rates in Harrod (1939) terms. The second generation of models is not concerned with balanced growth paths. This generation of models considers growth and capital accumulation as an open process, determined by institutions (for example, union power) and 'animal spirits' of capitalists. Growth is determined by the firms' desired rate of capital accumulation and real output is demand determined. One example of this class of models is Rowthorn (1981). The first and second generations of models have in common the fact that both deal with non-monetary economies within a linear structure of dynamic equations. The third generation of models – which may be inspired by Kregel (1985), critic of the Cambridge theory of growth and distribution – tried to integrate the real and monetary sides of Post Keynesian theory within a dynamic framework characterized mainly by non-linearities. Some examples of this class of models are Jarsulic (1988) and Watanabe (1997). For more details, see Carvalho (2005).
2. For more details on the concept of the monetary economy of production, see Davidson (1978) and Carvalho (1992).
3. The first, second and third blocks follow Lima (1999).
4. Or to a decrease in the unemployment rate. For more details, see Blanchard (1999, p. 305).
5. This is the equivalent of saying that the central bank has a real interest rate target.
6. By means of this equation, we differentiate, among others, between Lima (1999) and Rowthorn (1981). Moreover, the rationale for this investment function can also be found in the work of Dutt (1994), based on the ideas of Schumpeter (1912 [1934]), Kalecki (1971) and Nelson and Winter (1982).
7. Because equation (9.32) is cubical, there can be three real roots that solve equation $\hat{k} = 0$. However, only two of these roots assume positive values in the space $(k-S)$. In addition, applying the total derivative to locus $\hat{k} = 0$, we can also verify that k is insensitive to variations in S; so locus $\hat{k} = 0$ will be represented by means of two vertical straight lines.

8. The software used in the simulation was the program Mathematica 4.1.
9. For Kaldor (1993), the US and the UK had a propensity to save of around 0.7. While Germany would present a propensity to save of 0.8.

REFERENCES

Blanchard, O. (1999), *Macroeconomia: Teoria e Política*, Rio de Janeiro: Campus.

Carvalho, F.C. (1992), *Mr. Keynes and the Post Keynesians: Principles of Macroeconomics for a Monetary Production Economy*, Aldershot, UK and Brookfield, USA: Edward Elgar.

Carvalho, L.D. (2005), 'Endogeneidade Monetária, Crescimento Econômico e Distribuição de Renda: uma Integração Teórica da Macro-dinâmica Pós-keynesiana', Master's dissertation, Federal University of Paraná, Curitiba, Brazil.

Davidson, P. (1978), *Money and the Real World*, 2nd edn, London: Macmillan.

Davidson, P. (2002), *Financial Markets, Money and the Real World*, Cheltenham, UK and Northampton, MA, USA: Edward Elgar.

Dutt, A.K. (1989), 'Accumulation, distribution and inflation in a Marxian/Post Keynesian model with a rentier class', *Review of Radical Political Economics*, **21** (3), 18–26.

Dutt, A.K. (1992), 'Expectations and equilibrium: implications for Keynes, the Neo-Ricardian Keynesians, and the Post-Keynesians', *Journal of Post Keynesian Economics*, **14** (2), 145–70.

Dutt, A.K. (ed.) (1994), 'On the long-run stability of capitalist economies: implications of a model of growth and distribution', in *New Directions in Analytical Political Economy*, Aldershot, UK and Brookfield, USA: Edward Elgar.

Dutt, A.K. and E.J.A. Amadeo (1993), 'Post-Keynesian theory of growth, interest and money', M. Barazini and G.C. Harcourt (eds), in *The Dynamics of the Wealth of Nations: Growth, Distribution and Structural Change*, New York: St. Martins's Press, pp. 224–50.

Harrod, R. (1939), 'An essay in dynamic theory', *Economic Journal*, **49**, March, 14–33.

Jarsulic, M. (1989), 'Endogenous credit and endogenous business cycle', *Journal of Post Keynesian Economics*, **12** (1), 35–47.

Kaldor, N. (1957), 'A model of economic growth', *Economic Journal*, **67**, 591–624.

Kaldor, N. (1993), 'Marginal productivity and the macroeconomic theories of distribution', in C. Panico and N. Salvadori (eds), *Post Keynesian Theory of Growth and Distribution*, Cambridge: Cambridge University Press.

Kalecki, M. (1971), *Selected Essays on the Dynamics of the Capitalist Economy*, Cambridge: Cambridge University Press.

Keynes, J.M. (1973), 'Alternative theories of the rate of interest', in *The Collected Writings of John Maynard Keynes*, vol. XIV, London: Macmillan.

Kregel, J.A. (1985), 'Hamlet without the prince: Cambridge macroeconomics without money', *American Economic Review*, **75** (2), 133–9.

Lima, G.T. (1999), 'Progresso Tecnológico Endógeno, Crescimento Econômico e Distribuição de Renda', in G.T. Lima J. Sicsú and L.F. Paula (eds), *Macroeconomia Moderna: Keynes e a Economia Contemporânea*, Rio de Janeiro: Campus, 78–99.

Lima, G.T. and A.J. Meirelles (2003), 'Mark-up Bancário, Conflito Distributivo e

Utilização da Capacidade Produtiva: Uma Macrodinâmica Pós-Keynesiana', *Revista Brasileira de Economia*, January–March, 245–65.

Nelson, R. and S. Winter (1982), *An Evolutionary Theory of Economic Change*, Cambridge, MA: Harvard University Press.

Pasinetti, L. (1962), 'Rate of profit and income distribution in relation to the rate of economic growth', *Review of Economic Studies*, **29**, 262–79.

Pollin, R. (1991), 'Two theories of money supply endogenity: some empirical evidence', *Journal of Post Keynesian Economics*, **13** (2), Spring, 366–96.

Rowthorn, R. (1981), 'Demand, real wages and economic growth', *Thames Papers in Political Economy*, Fall, 2–53.

Schumpeter, J. (1912 [1934]), *The Theory of Economic Development*, 2nd edn, New York: Harper.

Watanabe, K.-I. (1997), 'An endogenous growth model with endogenous money supply: integration of Post-Keynesian growth models', *Banca Nazionale Del Lavoro Quarterly Review*, **200**, March, 191–223.

You, Jong-Il (1994), 'Macroeconomic structure, endogenous technical change and growth', *Cambridge Journal of Economics*, **18**, 121–47.

PART IV

Keynesian policy

10. Keynes on the control of the money supply and the interest rates

Carlo Panico

INTRODUCTION

This chapter examines Keynes's views on the ability of the monetary authorities to control the money supply and the interest rates. Its aim is to evaluate whether Keynes could agree on the horizontal slope of the money supply function, whether his position can be located in any one of the sides of the recent debates on the ability of the central bank to control the money supply, and whether it is this part of his contributions that makes his work depart from the traditional neoclassical approach.

Keynesian economists emphasise that monetary policy tends to stabilise the interest rate at a specific level by letting the money supply accommodate the requirement of the economy. This idea was dominant at the time of the Radcliffe Report and during the two following decades.[1]

During the 1980s, the analysis of the money supply was at the centre of a large debate among Keynesian authors, some of whom have made the idea of the Radcliffe Report more stringent. Following the contributions of Moore, they have stated that in a credit money economy the central bank has no technical ability to control the monetary issue. The horizontal slope of the money supply thus has a necessary character, since variations in bank loans only depend on the decisions of bank borrowers, not of banks themselves (Moore, 1983, pp. 543–5), while the central bank is bound to perform a fully accommodating role of lender of last resort. These positions have been considered 'extreme' by other authors.[2] They have denied that the money supply function must be necessarily horizontal and have claimed instead that the monetary policy may not be fully accommodating so that the horizontal slope of the money supply function, though a valid assumption in macroeconomic models, must be considered a *simplifying* analytical device to describe the behaviour of the monetary authorities.

The idea that monetary policy tends to stabilise the interest rate at a specific level is also shared by a large number of economists outside the Keynesian school.[3] Yet, the attention drawn by the more stringent position held by some Keynesians on the horizontal slope of the money supply function reduces the possibility of consensus over this point. Some years ago, for instance, Tobin (1983, pp. 35–6) wrote that he was close to Nicholas Kaldor in the controversy with the monetarist school. Yet, in the face of the views subsequently expressed by some Keynesians on the lack of technical ability of the central bank to control the money supply, Tobin stated that if Kaldor's position had to be interpreted along the lines presented by these authors, he found it difficult to agree with it:

> If the message of the endogenous money movement is meant to be that macroeconomic outcomes are beyond the control of the monetary authorities, it is refuted by recent history in the United States and elsewhere. Central banks have repeatedly falsified predictions that the innovations and ingenuities of financial markets would render them impotent. What is endogenous and what is exogenous continues to depend on the policy rules and operating procedures of monetary authorities. (Tobin, 1991, p. 224)[4]

Keynes's views on this subject are examined by considering the content of his *Collected Writings*. Among them, *A Treatise on Money* is the most detailed on the technical working of the monetary system. A large part of the treatment of these technicalities is concerned with the ability of the banking system as a whole (that is, the central bank and the other banks) to control the money supply and the interest rate. The answers he gave to these questions underline the complexity of the problem and the need to take into account the institutional arrangements that historically prevail. Keynes (1930a, vol. I, pp. 14–19) noticed that the conditions prevailing in the first part of the 19th century, or after the introduction of the Peel Act of 1844, were different from those prevailing after the First World War, when the Bank of England began to make a systematic use of open market operations (Keynes, 1930a, vol. II, pp. 206–7).

This pragmatic approach makes Keynes's position open to different interpretations. It will be argued that although it shared with them some common points, Keynes's position is opposed to that of those authors who consider that the horizontal slope of the supply of money function reflects the technical inability of the monetary authorities to control the monetary issue. Yet, it is not in conflict with the idea that the money supply function should be assumed horizontal because the monetary authorities, although able to control the amount of money in circulation, decide to stabilise the interest rate at a specific level, by making the money supply accommodate the requirements of the economy and counteract the effects of financial speculation. Furthermore, it will be argued that what really matters in defining Keynes's position in a specific school of thought is whether the level of the interest rate that the monetary authorities want to stabilise is determined by the traditional forces of productivity and thrift, as supposed by the contemporary neoclassical school, or by a 'conventional' theory that underlines the relevance of some other historically prevailing factors.

The chapter is organised as follows. The next section reconstructs Keynes's position on the technical control of the money supply up to the early 1930s, dealing mainly with *A Treatise on Money*. The third section examines his position at that time on the authorities' ability to control the structure of the interest rates. In the fourth section we consider Keynes's views on the previous points at the time of *The General Theory*. The fifth section examines the evidence available on these points after the publication of *The General Theory*. The final section draws some conclusions.

CONTROL OF THE MONEY SUPPLY

To reconstruct Keynes's position on the technical control of the money supply, let us consider how he dealt with the different sources of base money creation, that is, the re-funding of the banking sector, the funding of the government sector, and the role of the foreign sector. *A Treatise on Money* presents the most detailed analysis of this subject in Keynes's writings.

The central points of the analysis of the re-financing of the banking sector are the ability of the member banks to 'actively creat[e] deposits by lending' (Keynes, 1930a, vol. I, pp. 21–2), and the power of the central bank to control the aggregate of reserve resources that determine the 'pace' which is common to the banking system as a whole (ibid., vol. I, p. 25).

Keynes's views on these problems are in some respects close to those considering that the monetary authorities have no technical ability to control the money supply. In Volume II of *A Treatise* he claimed that the supply of base money issued through this channel is *necessarily* horizontal:

> The banking system has no direct control over the prices of individual commodities or even the rates of money earnings of the factors of production. Nor has it, in reality, any *direct* control over the quantity of money; for it is characteristic of modern systems that the central bank is ready to buy for money at a stipulated rate of discount any quantity of securities of certain approved types. Thus, in spite of the qualifications which we shall have to introduce later in respect of the so-called 'open-market' operations of central banks – it is broadly true to say that the governor of the whole system is the rate of discount. For this is the only factor which is directly subject to the will and *fiat* of the central authority, so that it is from this that induced changes in all other factors must flow. (Ibid., vol. II, p. 189)

Keynes's view on the lack of technical ability of the monetary authorities to control the money supply is, however, trimmed down, as the previous quotation shows, by the qualifications relative to the so-called 'open market' operations. These qualifications clarify why the views expressed by Keynes in other parts of his writings cannot be considered in line with the previous one:

> Assuming the central bank is also the note-issuing authority, the aggregate reserve resources of the member banks will be under the control of the central bank, provided the latter can control the aggregate of its note issue and its deposits. In this case the central bank is the conductor of the orchestra and sets the tempo. (Ibid., vol. I, p. 26)

The role of open market operations can be examined in the context of the issue of base money through the channel related to the funding of the government sector. The Bank of England started to use them systematically after the First World War. The main objective of these activities was to regulate the amount of reserves of the member banks (ibid., vol. II, p. 206) and, through the control of banks' reserves, to regulate the amount of bank loans:

> [If the latter can be regulated] in such a way that the market rate of interest is equal to the natural rate, then the value of investment will be equal to the volume of saving, total profits will be zero, the price of output, as a whole, will be at an equilibrium level, and there will be a motive moving productive resources between the production of consumption goods and the production of capital goods unless or until the purchasing power of money is also at an equilibrium level. (Ibid., vol. I, p. 142)

The use of open market operations was considered by Keynes (1930a, vol. II, p. 208) the best device hitherto evolved for the control of the creation of bank money by the member banks. According to him, it was also relevant for the operation of the bank rate policy. The Bank of England sets the bank rate, but has 'no despotism in the matter' (ibid., vol. I, p. 170), since it cannot determine the market conditions to which this rate is related.

Bank rate policy and open market policy cannot be carried on along different lines (ibid., vol. II, p. 225). Yet, within the complex operation of monetary policy they can serve different purposes. Changes in the bank rate affect the short-term rate, while open market operations can also be used to produce a direct influence on the long-term interest rates, which are those relevant for investment decisions.

With respect to the control of the money supply, open market operations are the most effective. Keynes states:

> Changes in bank rate may, amongst other things, affect the volume of central bank 'advances'; but they do much else besides, and their influence on central bank advances is an uncertain, incidental result of a much wider complex of

> consequences which a change in bank rate sets up. Open-market operations, on the other hand, produce a direct effect on the reserves of the member banks and hence on the volume of deposits and of credit generally, by their immediate consequences and apart from their indirect reactions. (Ibid., vol. II, p. 225)

The power of the central bank is thus greatly enhanced by the use of these operations.

The working of the external channel for the issue of base money depends on the international agreements entered into by the country. When the British economy adhered to the gold standard, the central bank had no control over the domestic interest rate, which depends on the conditions prevailing in the international financial markets. Moreover, although it has the tools to control the money supply, the central bank has to accommodate the amount of money in circulation to the demand for it coming from the economy at the interest rate fixed by the international markets. This participation can create two kinds of problems:

> If the country adheres to an international standard and that standard is itself unstable, it is, of course, impossible to preserve the stability of the domestic price level in the face of this. But even if the international standard is itself stable, it may still be impossible to keep the domestic price level stable if the changes in the demand schedule for capital in terms of the rate of interest are different at home from what they are abroad. (Ibid., vol. II, pp. 314–15)

In 'Can Lloyd George do it?', Keynes examined the problem in more detail. He tried to consider the possibility of an easier credit policy by the Bank of England, which might not lead to a loss of gold that the Bank cannot afford. His answer to this question had a prudent and pragmatic character:

> Now if the Bank were to try to increase the volume of credit at a time when, on account of the depression of home enterprise, no reliance could be placed on the additional credit being absorbed at home at the existing rate of interest, this might quite well be true. Since market rates of interest would fall, a considerable part of the new credit might find its way to foreign borrowers, with the result of a drain of gold of the Bank. Thus it is not safe for the Bank to expand credit unless it is certain beforehand that there are *home* borrowers standing ready to absorb it at the existing rates of interest. (Keynes, 1929, p. 118)

To reduce the risk of gold losses in the presence of an expansionary credit policy it is 'essential that the Bank of England should loyally co-operate with the government's programme of capital development and do its best to make it a success' (ibid., p. 118). Moreover, it is essential that there is an intense cooperation between the central bank and the other banks. This second point was stressed in the Addendum I to the Report of the Committee on Finance and Industry, dated 29 May 1931:

> The risk of expanding credit would be much diminished if the Bank of England would take the clearing banks more into its confidence, in the way in which it has traditionally confided in the leading accepting houses, and invite their co-operation. We desire to state this conclusion with some emphasis. While the quantity of money is controlled by the Bank of England, the way in which additional supplies are used can be largely directed by the clearing banks, and co-operation between these banks and the Bank of England is essential. The Committee as a whole have recommended in para. 372 that this should be done. If this recommendation is acted upon so that the clearing banks on their side can make it clear when they are in a position to direct additional credit into the domestic channel and when they are not, and the Bank of England on its side can tell the clearing banks when an expansion or contraction of credit is intended to have its natural repercussions on the foreign short-term loan position and when it is not, it will be much easier than it is now to ensure that domestic enterprise and investment of whatever kind shall never be starved of the accommodation which it requires. (Keynes, 1931a, pp. 284–5).[5]

Thus, Keynes's analysis of the external channel for the creation of base money also confirms that at the end of the 1920s and the beginning of the 1930s he held the view that the central bank has a technical ability to regulate the money supply. Yet, this ability may not lead the central bank to fix in an autonomous and rigid way the amount of money in circulation. Monetary policy may accommodate the money supply to the demand for it coming at a rate of interest fixed by other national or international objectives.

CONTROL OF THE INTEREST RATE

In many parts of *A Treatise*, Keynes (1930a, vol. II, pp. 325 and 332–3) put on one side the limits set by international complications in order to examine whether the monetary authorities have the power to set the rate of interest at a level that would allow full employment and price stability. To achieve this result, the authorities have to be able (i) to identify the natural interest rate, that is, the level of this rate that brings about equilibrium conditions, whose determination in *A Treatise* was still in line with the traditional neoclassical approach; and (ii) to stabilise the market interest rate at that level.

Keynes argued that the monetary authorities have the power to identify the natural interest rate. He recognised that there could be some difficulties, particularly during periods of economic crisis, and, after the slump of 1929, he became more open to making concessions to the doubts expressed by the central bankers:

> I have more sympathy today than I had a few years ago with some of the doubts and hesitations such as were expressed in 1927 by Governor Strong and other

> witnesses before the Committee of the United States Congress on Stabilisation. (Ibid., vol. II, p. 305)

Yet, after reporting this evidence, he concluded that the authorities tend to underestimate their technical ability on this subject:

> [H]ow far are we prepared to attribute to a central bank a greater degree of influence on the price level than these authorities believed it to have? I think that in one fundamental respect they have mistaken the character of the problem and have underestimated the possibility of control. (Ibid., vol. II, p. 310)

As to the stabilisation of the market interest rate at the natural level, Keynes (ibid., vol. I, pp. 227–30) again gave a positive answer and claimed that the monetary authorities tend to operate by counteracting the effects of the bullish and bearish sentiments in order to maintain the market rate of interest at the equilibrium level. However, he recognised that there can be some problems and limitations, particularly because the authorities, in order to achieve their objectives, have to keep under control not only the short-term rate, but also the whole structure of the rates of interest.

> It may be convenient to summarise forthwith my final conclusions as to the limitations, which must be ultimately conceded, on the actual power of the banking system to control the price level:
>
> a) It is much easier to preserve stability than to restore it quickly after a serious state of disequilibrium has been allowed to set in . . .
> b) Granted all reasonable intelligence and foresight on the part of the managers of the monetary system, non-monetary causes of instability may sometimes arise so suddenly that it is impossible to counteract them in time. In this event it may be inevitable that an interval should elapse before stability can be restored.
> c) If there are strong social and political forces causing spontaneous changes in the money rates of efficiency wages, the control of the price level may pass beyond the power of the banking system . . .
> d) If the country adheres to an international standard and that standard is itself unstable, it is, of course, impossible to preserve the stability of the domestic price level in the face of this. . . .
> e) Even if the banking system is strong enough to preserve the *stability* of the price level, it does not follow that it is strong enough both to *alter* the price level and to establish equilibrium at the new level without long delays and frictions.
>
> In short, I should attribute to the banking system much greater power to *preserve* investment equilibrium than to force the prevailing rate of money incomes away from the existing level or from the level produced by spontaneous changes, to a new and changed level imposed by conditions abroad or by arbitrary decree at home. (Ibid., vol. II, pp. 314–15)

The monetary authorities tend to have their main, direct influence on the short-term rate even if, to control the economy, they must regulate the long-term interest rate, which is the relevant variable for investment decisions. Fortunately, Keynes said, the influence of the short-term on the long-term rate 'is much greater than anyone . . . would have expected' (ibid., vol. II, p. 316). Yet, there are some forces preventing policy interventions on the short-term rate from producing similar movements in the long-term rate.

In *A Treatise*, Keynes mentioned two forces preventing a reduction of the long-term rate. First, when the economy is heavily depressed and future perspectives highly uncertain, 'lenders are most exigent and least inclined to embark their resources on long term unless it be on the most exceptionable security' (ibid., vol. II, p. 334). As will be seen in the next section, this element, referred to as 'lender risk', was examined in detail in subsequent work. Second, there may be some resistance to the fall in the long-term rate because, after a long period of high interest rates, lenders might have become accustomed to them and tend to foresee the future trends of financial markets accordingly (ibid., vol. II, p. 344).

In two other writings, subsequent to *A Treatise*, Keynes referred to another element that can prevent the reduction of the long-term interest rates. In the presence of decreasing short-term rates, banks may find it difficult to reduce the rate on their loans, owing to the high and rigid costs of intermediation that they have to pay.

Epstein (1995) recalls one of these two writings, the one published in the *Economic Journal* in 1932. His 'illiquidity trap' refers to the fact that, owing to the costs of intermediation and the need to recover at least the general rate of profits on its own capital, the banking sector may resist a reduction of the interest rate on its loans. The salaries paid to employees and the existence of agreements with depositors impose some rigid constraints on banks' costs, establishing a high rate of remuneration of their loans:

> The position of the banks (the Big Five) presents a difficult practical problem. Since the War they have incurred expenses partly through generosity to their employees, partly through ostentation and partly through excessive competition for new business, which assume the permanence of relatively dear money. It is said that their expenses now amount to somewhere in the neighbourhood of 2 per cent of their total deposits. Moreover, there are many old-standing arrangements for allowing 2½ per cent on deposits which they are loth to disturb and which it might be unfair to disturb in view of the depositors having accepted this rate all through the dear money period. Thus with Treasury bills yielding ½ per cent and loans to their money market round 1 per cent, the banks are dependent on earning high rates on their advances if they want to cover their expenses. The practical result is that, by obstinately maintaining their charges on advances at 5 per cent except to strong or favoured customers or those who threaten to go

> elsewhere, the banks are something of an obstruction to a decline in the rate of interest to certain types of borrowers; and it is difficult to see the way out. In the same way in the United States the fear of the Member Banks lest they should be unable to cover their expenses is an obstacle to the adoption of a whole hearted cheap money policy. (Keynes, 1932, p. 122)

Keynes had expounded similar arguments in greater detail during the Harris Foundation Institute Round Tables in 1931 where he states:

> There is a particular reason why the discount rate method, I think, is of limited applicability, and that is this: the discount rate represents the pure rate of interest. The number of borrowers who are entitled to the pure rate of interest is very few. The average borrower has to pay some premium over and above the pure rate of interest, partly to cover risk. The business of collecting deposits and lending them out again is an expensive business. Banks must necessarily charge their borrowing clients more than the pure rate of interest to cover expenses. When banks are charging their customers 6 per cent it may be that 3 per cent is the pure rate of interest, 1 per cent is protection against risk, and 2 per cent is expenses. Well, that 1 per cent and 2 per cent do not go down with the pure rate of interest, so even if you reduce the pure rate of interest to naught, it might still be reasonable for banks to be charging their customers three per cent. Therefore the amount of reduction to the average discount rate is limited, and it may still be paying a fairly high rate even when the pure rate of interest has reached almost the vanishing point. (Keynes, 1931b, p. 535)

The existence of rigid costs of intermediation leads banks to be in opposition to the introduction of cheap money policies. Keynes, however, considered that this position of the banks was not well worked out:

> There has been a surprising amount of opposition, so far as I can gather, on the part of prominent bankers to a very easy money policy on the part of the Federal Reserve. Various plausible and implausible economic reasons are adduced for that opposition, but I cannot help coming, the more and more I have heard it argued, to the opinion that these plausible and implausible arguments are really vamped up, and that the most important thing at the bottom of it is that very cheap money doesn't suit the banks. It makes it more and more difficult for them to earn their expenses. They are short-sighted about it. They don't realise that enlarging the basis of credit and getting things right is to their advantage more than earning interest. They don't want to see rates of interest too low, for it means their earning power is going to be seriously impaired. That is partly due to the fact that their expenses are so large a proportion of total receipts, but I think it is also due to the fact that for competitive reasons they have got into the habit of paying so much too much on their deposits. If the banks could be persuaded to agree on some common action which would bring down deposit rates very greatly, I am inclined to believe that that would mitigate their opposition to cheap money policies. It would not be such a desperate business for them to have cheap money if their expenses were being kept down on the other side to a somewhat proportional extent. (Ibid., pp. 537–8)

To sum up, at the time of *A Treatise*, Keynes was confident that the monetary authorities were able to identify the natural interest rate. When, after 1929, the economic crisis became more dramatic, he acknowledged that the authorities could have some difficulty in identifying this rate, but concluded that the ability of the central banks should not be underestimated. As a consequence, according to Keynes, the monetary authorities can stabilise the market rate of interest at the equilibrium level: as a matter of fact, they tend to work along these lines. To do that, they try to affect the whole structure of the interest rates by operating mainly and directly on the short-term rates. In general they are able in this way to influence the long-term rates. In some cases, however, the authorities may not succeed in achieving this result. This failure may occur when the banking sector feels highly uncertain as to the possibility of recovering its long-term loans owing to a negative perspective of the economy; when it has been long accustomed to high long-term rates; and when it finds it difficult to cut the rates on its loans, owing to the rigidity of some costs of intermediation (high salaries, high deposits' remunerations and perception of a high risk of lending).

KEYNES'S POSITION AT THE TIME OF *THE GENERAL THEORY*

In 1932, with the introduction of the notion of a 'monetary theory of production', Keynes parted with the neoclassical tradition and began his journey towards the publication of *The General Theory*. The notion of a 'monetary theory of production' implied the rejection of the separation between a 'real' and a 'monetary' department of economics, the consequent abandonment of the concept of 'natural rate of interest' and the development of a new 'conventional' theory of the rate of interest.

This rejection by Keynes of the positions of the neoclassical schools of thought did not bring about a similar change in the analysis of the technical working of the monetary system and of the technicalities regarding the ability of the monetary authorities to control the money supply and the interest rate. As a matter of fact, in *The General Theory* the analysis of these technicalities was the same as that described in *A Treatise*. The monetary authorities still have the ability to control the amount of banks' reserves and of money in circulation. Yet, this ability does not lead the central bank to fix in a rigid way the amount of money in circulation. On the contrary, monetary policy tends to accommodate the supply of money to the demand for it coming at a rate of interest fixed by other national or international objectives.

In *The General Theory*, the level at which monetary policy tends to stabilise the market interest rate depends on the current policy of the monetary authorities and on the market expectations concerning its future policy. The policy decisions, however, are not constrained by the attempt to identify a natural rate of interest determined by the traditional forces of productivity and thrift. Along the lines of his new 'conventional' theory of the rate of interest, which underlines the relevance of other historically prevailing factors, Keynes pointed out that the authorities can stabilise the market rate of interest at any level that they consider durable and appropriate for the economy.

The credibility of the monetary authorities plays a relevant role here. In order to be successful, the policy proposed must be considered credible by the representative opinion:

> Thus a monetary policy which strikes public opinion as being experimental in character or easily liable to change may fail in its objective of greatly reducing the long-term rate of interest, because M2 may tend to increase almost without limit in response to a reduction of *r* below a certain figure. The same policy, on the other hand, may prove easily successful if it appeals to public opinion as being reasonable and practicable and in the public interest, rooted in strong conviction, and promoted by an authority unlikely to be superseded. (Keynes, 1936a, p. 202)

An important role in limiting the power of the monetary authorities is attributed again in *The General Theory* to the international agreements, which are entered into by a country. And again, international complications apart, Keynes argued that the ability of the authorities to establish specific financial market conditions may be limited by the need to control not only the short-term rate, but also the whole structure of the interest rates.

He also referred to the problems that can arise when the authorities deal only with short-term securities: 'There are those limitations which arise out of the monetary authority's own practices in limiting its willingness to deal to debts of a particular type' (ibid., pp. 207–8; see also pp. 197 and 206).

Moreover, he mentioned the possibility that the expectation of a rise in the interest rate makes the demand for money infinitely elastic. The occurrence of what the subsequent literature named the 'liquidity trap' was, however, considered a theoretical possibility rather than a practical case:

> There is the possibility, for the reasons discussed above, that, after the rate of interest has fallen to a certain level, liquidity-preference may become virtually absolute in the sense that almost everyone prefers cash to holding a debt which yields so low a rate of interest. In this event the monetary authority would have lost control over the rate of interest. But whilst this limiting case might become practically important in the future, I know of no example of it hitherto. (Ibid., pp. 207–8; see also pp. 201–2)

This flattening out of the liquidity function may also come about in what he considered very abnormal circumstances, when the financial system has reached such a level of disruption as to make it difficult for any lender to part with liquidity:

> The most striking examples of a complete breakdown of stability in the rate of interest, due to the liquidity function flattening out in one direction or the other, have occurred in very abnormal circumstances. In Russia and Central Europe after the war . . . whilst in the United States at certain dates in 1932 there was a crisis of the opposite kind – a financial crisis or crisis of liquidation, when scarcely anyone could be induced to part with holdings of money on any reasonable terms. (Ibid., p. 207)[6]

Finally, Keynes referred again to the resistance of the banking sector to reduce the interest rate on their loans, owing to the rigidity of some costs of intermediation. With respect to the writings of 1931 and 1932, recalled in the previous section, *The General Theory* focused on another element of cost that introduces rigidity. He referred to the lenders' risk, which had been already mentioned in *A Treatise* and which is due to the moral hazard (that is, voluntary defaults or other means of escape, possibly lawfully, from the fulfilment of an obligation) or to involuntary defaults because of the disappointment of the expectations of the borrower (ibid., pp. 145–6):

> There is, finally, the difficulty discussed in section iv of chapter 11, p. 144, in the way of bringing the effective rate of interest below a certain figure, which may prove important in an era of low interest rates; namely the intermediate costs of bringing the borrower and the ultimate lender together, and the allowance of risk, especially for moral risk, which the lender requires over and above the pure rate of interest. As the pure rate of interest declines it does not follow that the allowances for expense and risk decline *pari passu*. Thus the rate of interest which the typical borrower has to pay may decline more slowly than the pure rate of interest, and may be incapable of being brought, by the methods of the existing banking and financial organisation, below a certain minimum figure. This is particularly important if the estimation of moral risk is appreciable. For where the risk is due to doubt in the mind of the lender concerning the honesty of the borrower, there is nothing in the mind of a borrower who does not intend to be dishonest to offset the resulting high charge. It is also important in the case of short-term loans (e.g. bank loans) where the expenses are heavy; – a bank may have to charge its customers 1½ to 2 per cent, even if the pure rate of interest to the lender is nil. (Ibid., pp. 207–8)

To sum up, in *The General Theory*, in spite of the change that occurred in Keynes's position in the neoclassical school of thought, the analysis of the technicalities regarding the ability of the monetary authorities to control the supply of money and the interest rate remained the same as that of *A Treatise*. The monetary authorities still have the ability to control the amount of banks' reserves and of money in circulation. Yet, this ability does not lead the central bank to fix in a rigid way the amount of money in circulation. On the contrary, monetary policy tends to accommodate the supply of money to the demand for it, coming at a rate of interest fixed by other national or international objectives.

The difference between the two main works of the Cambridge economists can thus be found in the theory of the rate of interest and in the fact that the natural rate of interest, determined by the traditional forces of productivity and thrift, represented in *A Treatise* the level at which the market rate of interest had to be stabilised by the monetary authorities, while in *The General Theory*, as underlined by the new 'conventional' theory of the rate of interest, the authorities can stabilise the market rate of interest at any level that they consider durable and appropriate for the economy, provided that their decisions are considered credible by the representative opinion.

THE EVIDENCE AFTER *THE GENERAL THEORY*

After the publication of *The General Theory*, Keynes dealt with the difficulty of reducing the long-term interest rate in three presidential speeches he gave at the Annual Meeting of the National Mutual. On 19 February 1936 he argued that, to reduce this rate, it was essential to affect the expectations on the future level of the short-term rate. He criticised the Treasury, which was not implementing a debt policy directed towards this aim, being preoccupied by the need to reduce its short-term debt. Keynes states:

> Short-term money to-day is extremely cheap. But it is confidence in the future of short-term rates which is required to bring down long-term rates. Now the policy of the Treasury is not calculated to promote such a confidence. They seem . . . anxious to reduce the short-term debt, in spite of the extraordinary cheap-rate with which it can be carried. They starve the banks and the money market of the type of security which the sound conduct of their business admittedly requires, and they pay a higher rate of interest than they need. . . . There can be no rational explanation of the longer-dated issue except that they themselves have no confidence in the short-term rate of interest remaining low. Since they largely control the situation, it is natural that humbler folk should be influenced by what the Treasury seems to expect. (Keynes, 1936b, p. 220)

He pointed out that the reduction of the long-term interest rate also required a larger increase of the supply of bank money than that allowed by the Bank of England and concluded that the monetary authorities tend to underestimate their own powers to achieve what they recognise as desirable (ibid., pp. 221–2).

Keynes's confidence in the ability of the authorities to control the whole structure of the interest rates was based on the evaluation that, although there were certain important limitations on their power, they were not operative. The external limitations were no more effective, owing to the abolition of the gold standard and to the founding of the Exchange Equalisation Fund, which had allowed the Bank of England to have a large control over the pace of its foreign issues (ibid., p. 222). The objective of the Fund was to avoid that the international gold movements, by changing the monetary base, could generate multiple variations in deposits and have substantial effects on the domestic credit and on the liquidity situation. The internal limitations come into operation when a state of full employment has been achieved:

> In such circumstances a further fall in the interest rate will merely stimulate a competition for current output, which will result in an inflationary rise of prices. Pre-war theory presumed that this was the normal state of affairs. Would that it were! But, in fact, this happy condition is not yet ours. When it is the rate of interest will have fallen far enough for the time being. (Ibid., p. 222)

In the speech given on 24 February 1937 he argued again that the British Treasury, following the American one, should have issued securities with a shorter maturity than it had done. This policy would have allowed the British government to reduce its total interest payments, given the large difference between short- and long-term rates, and would have made the yield curve similar to that of the United States, which was not as steep as that of the United Kingdom (Keynes, 1937, pp. 228–9).

In the speech he gave on 20 February 1938 he stated that the fall in the gilt-edged market, experienced in the previous months, had been caused by the way the Exchange Equalisation Fund had financed the purchases of gold due to the inflow of foreign capital. Basing his argument on information disclosed by the January Bulletin of the London and Cambridge Economic Service, Keynes claimed that the Fund had managed the situation in such a way as to strain the domestic credit situation. Instead of limiting itself to avoiding a situation whereby the inflow of gold would have resulted in a multiple rise of deposits and other liquid means, the Fund had operated in such a way as to keep these resources nearly constant. Since the vendors of gold desired to hold a portion of their proceeds in liquid form, the result had been a deflationary effect on the domestic credit situation and a rise in the interest rates (Keynes, 1938, p. 236). Keynes (ibid., pp. 234 and 236) complained that the policy of the Fund lacked transparency and concluded his speech by appealing to the government to lose no opportunity of adding to the knowledge of the essential facts and figures in order to avoid disastrous consequences by making the working of the economic system intelligible (ibid., p. 238).

In subsequent years, as Moggridge states (*The Collected Writings of J.M. Keynes*, vol. XXII, 1978, p. 408), Keynes's main contributions to discussions on borrowing policy and on the control of the interest rates almost entirely post-dated his appointment as a director of the Bank of England, following the death of Lord Stamp in an air raid. In some notes and memoranda written from 1941 to 1945, he again argued that the authorities can control the interest rate and its structure, as long as they select and persistently adopt a policy that is adequate for the current situation (Keynes, 1978, pp. 408–31). His confidence in the powers of the monetary authorities was not overcome by the difficulty he met in seeing his proposals successfully applied during the war.

In some documents, written between 1941 and 1943, he pointed out that, although the market preferred securities with shorter maturities, it was wise for the Treasury, given the large debt accumulated to fund the war, to attempt to issue, at the usual 3 per cent rate, irredeemable securities or securities with redemption possible over a longer period than was normally the case.[7] Keynes (ibid., pp. 415–16, date 23 October 1942) claimed that the Treasury had to take full advantage of the existing official controls of financial markets, and argued that it was necessary, in order to make the most of the controls, to persuade the public that they would not weaken in post-war conditions.

As Moggridge points out (ibid., pp. 412, 414, 416 and 419), the policy of the Treasury did not follow Keynes's proposals. None the less, as a letter to Robert Henry Brand of November 1944 shows, Keynes (ibid., pp. 419–20) did not lose his interest in the matter and his confidence that the authorities were able to control the interest rates by keeping them at a lower level than those which prevailed during the First World War.

Keynes's final concern with borrowing policy was the system of controls of new issues. On this topic he wrote two comments, one dated 7 January 1945 (ibid., pp. 421–4), and another dated 30 January 1945 (ibid., pp. 424–31). In them he argued that the controls had to be maintained if they were absolutely necessary and, in any case, they had to be carefully explained to the market and justified in terms of national security.

The evidence contained in *The Collected Writings* thus confirms that after the publication of *The General Theory*, Keynes maintained a pragmatic approach to the study of the borrowing policy and of financial markets. This approach was based on a detailed knowledge of the institutional mechanisms operating and led to some prudent, but confident conclusions as to the ability of the monetary authorities to control the whole structure of the interest rates.

CONCLUSIONS

Both in *A Treatise on Money* and in *The General Theory*, Keynes argued that the monetary authorities have the technical ability to control the amount of money in circulation and the interest rates. The control of the short-term rate is direct and effective; that on the long-term rate may be difficult, particularly during a period of crisis, but it should not be underestimated. These positions were maintained soon after the publication of *The General Theory* and during the Second World War.

The ability to control the money supply does not lead the central banks to fix this variable in a rigid way. On the contrary, Keynes claimed, monetary policy tends to accommodate the money supply to the demand for it coming at a rate of interest fixed by other national or international objectives.

Thus, Keynes's position appears incompatible with that of those authors who consider that the horizontal slope of the supply of money function reflects the technical inability of the monetary authorities to control the monetary issue. However, it is not in conflict with the idea that the money supply function should be assumed horizontal, because the monetary authorities tend to stabilise the interest rate at a specific level, by counteracting the effects of financial speculation and making the money supply accommodate the requirements of the economy.

The difference between *A Treatise* and *The General Theory* does not lie in the technicalities of the operation of monetary policy, but in the theory regarding the determination of the interest rate. In *A Treatise*, the level of the interest rate that the monetary authorities try to achieve is the 'natural' rate, which is determined by the traditional forces of productivity and thrift, as supposed by the contemporary neoclassical school. In *The General Theory*, the level of the interest rate is determined by a 'conventional' theory that underlines the relevance of some other historically prevailing factors.

Thus, the introduction of the notion of a monetary theory of production in 1932 and the consequent proposal of a new theory of interest, rather than his views on the technicalities of the operation of monetary policy, are the elements that mark Keynes's departure from the positions of the neoclassical school of thought.

NOTES

1. For an account of the role played by the money supply in these debates, see Musella and Panico (1995).

2. See Lavoie (1996) for a critical presentation of these positions, which are sometimes identified as the 'structuralist' or 'liquidity preference' versions of endogenous money.
3. Colin Rogers (2006) refers to Romer (2000), Svensson (2003) and others to underline that a large part of the monetary literature is now proposing macroeconomic models assuming a central bank that stabilise the interest rate and a horizontal money supply.
4. The differences between Kaldor's and Moore's positions are examined in Musella and Panico (1993).
5. In an article published in *The Nation and Athenaeum*, dated 10 May 1930, Keynes had already noticed that the chief obstacle for capital development at home 'is to be found in the fact that a rate of interest in the bond market, high enough to prevent our foreign lending from being excessive and to avoid a loss of gold, is too high to suit large-scale borrowers at home and is deterrent to domestic enterprise. To cure unemployment, therefore, we need either that the state should step in to supplement the lack of private enterprise, or that we should establish discriminating rates of interest for home purposes and for foreign purposes respectively, so as to maintain at the same time a rate of interest on foreign loans which keeps such lending within our capacity and a rate for home loans sufficiently low to make new domestic enterprises attractive' (Keynes, 1930b, p. 348).
6. Keynes had described what he called 'a crisis of liquidation' in a note on the economic conditions in the United States, written for the Economic Advisory Council Committee of Economists during the journey to England. 'A considerable number of the member banks and a fairly substantial proportion, measured in assets (perhaps as much as 10 per cent), are probably not solvent today, if their assets were to be valued strictly. They have purchased large quantities of second-grade bonds which have since depreciated in market price, and many of their advances to farmers and against real estate are inadequately secure. . . . The inevitable result is an absolute mania for liquidity wherever liquidity is possible. Bonds saleable at a reasonable price are sold; borrowers against good stock exchange collateral are pressed to liquidate; and new loans are not readily accorded. Thus for many ordinary people in small towns up and down the country, it is a travesty of the case to suggest that credit is easy. Here is to be found a large part of the explanation of the weakness of the bond market and of the failure of the cheap short-money to produce its normal reaction on the long-term rate of interest. When the less saleable bond improve a little in price and become more saleable, some bank takes the opportunity to get more liquid. It is, indeed, a vicious circle. The anxiety of the banks to get liquid keeps the second-grade bond market weak, and as long as the bond market is weak the position of the banks remain precarious' (Keynes, 1931c, pp. 568–9).
7. The first document, dated 15 September 1941, is titled, 'Loan policy' (Keynes, 1978, pp. 410–12); the second, dated 23 June 1942, is titled 'National war bonds' (ibid., pp. 412–14); the third, dated 1 October 1942, is titled 'The gilt-edge market' (ibid., pp. 414–15); the fourth, dated 23 October 1942, is titled 'Long and short borrowing' (ibid., pp. 415–16); and the fifth, dated 27 July 1943, is titled 'Tap issues' (ibid., pp. 417–19).

REFERENCES

Epstein, G. (1995), 'The illiquidity trap', *Eastern Economic Journal*, **21** (3), Summer, 309–18.

Keynes, J.M. (1929), 'Can Lloyd George do it?', in *Essays in Persuasion. The Collected Writings of J.M. Keynes*, vol. IX, edited by D. Moggridge, London: Macmillan and St. Martin's Press for the Royal Economic Society, 1972.

Keynes, J.M. (1930a), *A Treatise on Money*, 2 vols, London: Macmillan.

Keynes, J.M. (1930b), 'The industrial crisis', *The Nation and Athenaeum*, 10 May 1930, in *Activities 1929–1931: Rethinking Employment and Unemployment Policies. The Collected Writings of J.M. Keynes*, vol. XX, edited by D. Moggridge,

London: Macmillan and Cambridge University Press for the Royal Economic Society, 1981.

Keynes, J.M. (1931a), 'Addendum I to the report of the Committee on Finance and Industry', in *Activities 1929–1931:Rethinking Employment and Unemployment Policies. The Collected Writings of J.M. Keynes*, vol. XX, edited by D. Moggridge, London: Macmillan and Cambridge University Press for the Royal Economic Society, 1981.

Keynes, J.M. (1931b), 'Unemployment as a world problem: reports of Round Tables', 1931, vol. II, Harris Foundation Institute Round Tables, in *Activities 1931–1939: World Crises and Policies in Britain and America. The Collected Writings of J.M. Keynes*, vol. XXI, edited by D. Moggridge, London: Macmillan and Cambridge University Press for the Royal Economic Society, 1982.

Keynes, J.M. (1931c), 'Economic Advisory Council: a note on the economic conditions in the United States', in *Activities 1929–1931: Rethinking Employment and Unemployment Policies. The Collected Writings of J.M. Keynes*, vol. XX, edited by D. Moggridge, London: Macmillan and Cambridge University Press for the Royal Economic Society, 1981.

Keynes, J.M. (1932), 'A note on the long-term rate of interest in relation to the conversion scheme', *Economic Journal*, September, reprinted in *Activities 1931–1939: World Crises and Policies in Britain and America. The Collected Writings of J.M. Keynes*, vol. XXI, edited by D. Moggridge, London: Macmillan and Cambridge University Press for the Royal Economic Society, 1982.

Keynes, J.M. (1936a), *The General Theory of Employment, Interest and Money*, London: Macmillan.

Keynes, J.M. (1936b), speech to the annual meeting of the National Mutual, 19 February 1936, in *Economic Articles and Correspondence, Investment and Editorial. The Collected Writings of J.M. Keynes*, vol. XII, edited by D. Moggridge, London: Macmillan and Cambridge: Cambridge University Press for the Royal Economic Society, 1983.

Keynes, J.M. (1937), speech to the annual meeting of the National Mutual, 24 February 1937, in *Economic Articles and Correspondence, Investment and Editorial. The Collected Writings of J.M. Keynes*, vol. XII, edited by D. Moggridge, London: Macmillan and Cambridge: Cambridge University Press for the Royal Economic Society, 1983.

Keynes, J.M. (1938), speech to the annual meeting of the National Mutual, 20 February 1938, in *Economic Articles and Correspondence, Investment and Editorial. The Collected Writings of J.M. Keynes*, vol. XII, edited by D. Moggridge, London: Macmillan and Cambridge: Cambridge University Press for the Royal Economic Society, 1983.

Keynes, J.M. (1978), *Activities 1939–1945. Internal War Finance. The Collected Writings of J.M. Keynes*, vol. XXII, edited by D. Moggridge, London: Macmillan and Cambridge: Cambridge University Press for the Royal Economic Society, 1983.

Lavoie, M. (1996), 'Horizontalism, structuralism, liquidity preference and the principle of increasing risk', *Scottish Journal of Political Economy*, **43** (3), 275–301.

Moore, B.J. (1983), 'Unpacking the Post Keynesian black box: bank lending and money supply', *Journal of Post Keynesian Economics*, **5** (4), 537–56.

Musella, M. and C. Panico. (1993), 'Kaldor on endogenous money and interest rates', in G. Mongiovi and C. Ruhl (eds), *Macroeconomic Theory: Diversity and Convergence*, Aldershot, UK and Brookfield, USA: Edward Elgar, 37–63.

Musella, M. and C. Panico (eds) (1995), *The Money Supply in the Economic Process*, Aldershot, UK and Brookfield, USA: Edward Elgar.

Rogers, C. (2006), 'Exogenous interest rates in modern monetary theory and policy: Moore in perspective', in *Complexity, Endogenous Money and Exogenous Interest Rates, Festschrift for Basil J. Moore*, Cheltenham, UK and Northampton, MA, USA: Edward Elgar.

Romer, D. (2000), 'Keynesian macroeconomics without the LM curve', *Journal of Economic Perspectives*, **14**, Spring, 149–69.

Svensson, L.E.O. (2003), 'What is wrong with Taylor rules?', *Journal of Economic Literature*, **41** (2), 426–77.

Tobin, J. (1983), 'Comment on Kaldor', in J. Trevithick and D. Worswick (eds), *Keynes and the Modern World*, Cambridge: Cambridge University Press, pp. 28–37.

Tobin, J. (1991), 'On the endogeneity of money supply', in E.J. Nell and W. Semmler (eds), *Nicholas Kaldor and Mainstream Economics*, London: Macmillan, pp. 221–4.

11. Inflation targeting in Brazil: a Keynesian approach

Luiz Carlos Bresser-Pereira and Cleomar Gomes da Silva*

INTRODUCTION

Since the beginning of 1999, when the flotation of the real implied the abandonment of the exchange rate anchor, monetary authorities have adopted inflation targeting (IT) as the new nominal anchor, as if Brazil could not dispense with an anchor. Usually seen as a successful policy in so far as the inflation rate has been kept reasonably under control, IT policy has shown problems related to the achievement of its objectives and, principally, to the high fiscal and development costs involved. These problems are due to two main reasons. On one side, the Taylor rule – the simple model relating the target with the interest rate given the product gap – can only be accepted if it is combined with the consideration of other variables such as exchange rate and employment rate. The argument that the central bank can only have one target because monetary authorities have only one instrument is neither reasonable nor realistic. In practice, central banks do not work in this way.

The second one is related to a grave inconsistency dilemma. An IT policy is designed to 'manage' monetary policy, not to 'change' the 'monetary policy regime': it orients the policy maker to define the interest rate within a limited range, not to face an interest/exchange rate trap, characterized by an extremely high interest rate and an overvalued real prevailing in Brazil for many years.[1] An IT system implies in itself a monetary regime, and so it could be viewed as a 'regime', but we reserve the expression to designate inflation, interest rate and exchange rate patterns and the correspondent policies used to control such variables that possess a reasonable internal consistency. Monetary policy regimes persist for some time, but, in given moments, must undergo changes in order to deal with internal problems,

* We would like to thank Edwin Le Heron, Emmanuel Carré and an anonymous referee for their comments.

or because new structural facts impose changes. The IT system was adopted in Brazil, in 1999, ignoring that a previous reform of the monetary policy regime was required involving the end of indexation of public services and the de-linkage between the short- and the long-term interest rate. The result is that the government does not have any clear strategy to reduce the interest rate and it is far from starting a serious reform package and a deep fiscal adjustment.

Several works have analyzed the IT framework in Brazil. For instance, Bogdanski et al. (2000) wrote about the phase prior to implementing the plan itself and its first steps. Minella et al. (2003) studied the Brazilian inflation targeting policy and argued that emerging market economies may show high volatility in their main economic variables (exchange and interest rates, output growth rate and inflation rate), which brings problems to the system as a whole. As a result, conducting monetary policy in these countries is closely related to challenges such as trust building, reduction of the inflation rate, and resolution of fiscal, external and financial dominances. As inflation in 1999, after the exchange rate flotation, was smaller than many predicted, the quoted authors conclude that 'the Brazilian experience has been a successful stress test for the inflation targeting framework'. It means that they credited to the IT policy adopted in July (when the inflationary effects of the depreciation had already worked out) an outcome that was not due to the IT being implemented. This practice of overestimating the outcomes of the IT policy has been usual among conventional–orthodox economists. But, actually, the countries that adopted IT systems achieved neither better nor worse outcomes than the countries that do not use such a tool (Ball and Sheridan, 2003; Arestis et al., 2006).

The aim of this chapter is to offer a brief overview of the conduct of monetary policy in Brazil under IT and to show that it was adopted at an inappropriate moment. Second, we shall criticize the IT framework and show that it has been misused by the monetary authorities. It is not the aim of this chapter to pursue a theoretical discussion of the IT system. From a Keynesian point of view, IT will be acceptable if we see the equilibrium interest rate as just a 'changing convention', that is, if we see it theoretically as an empirical generalization of the way central banks work, and, in practical terms, if we combine the inflation target with either an exchange rate or an employment target – in the case of a small country like Brazil,[2] an exchange rate parameter might work better. In other words, in the framework of a pragmatic IT policy, the central bank is supposed to have a double mandate.[3]

Although IT was able to keep inflation relatively low, our claim is that it did that with extremely high fiscal and development opportunity costs.[4] Nowadays, inflation could be smaller and growth rates much higher in Brazil if the government had not hastened to import a monetary policy institution before the appropriate conditions had materialized. Thus, we shall not explore what is usually discussed in relation to IT: how ambitious should the targets be, which inflation index to use, which period to take into consideration, and so on. These are management problems. Here, we shall argue against the timing chosen for the adoption of the IT policy, and which are the preconditions for its success. We shall also be offering some indications of how to escape from the interest/exchange rate trap in which the Brazilian economy remains immersed.

INFLATION TARGETING POLICY

After a decade of frustrating attempts to adopt a monetary rule to control inflation, central banks in rich countries realized that a more practical policy had to be adopted in order to control directly the basic interest rate aiming at a low rate of inflation. This practical policy was IT. A number of countries started to adopt the system at the beginning of the 1990s. New Zealand was the first inflation targeter, in 1990, followed by Canada (1991), the UK (1992), Sweden and Finland (1993), and Australia and Spain (1994). Subsequently, many other nations implemented the policy, including Brazil in 1999. Although IT was adopted for pragmatic reasons, the theoretical approach often argued by orthodox economists for its justification is new classical 'credibility theory' (Kydland and Prescott, 1977; Barro and Gordon, 1983). Under this theory, if monetary authorities neglect the observation of rules, there will be a lack of credibility in their decisions and, therefore, higher inflation rates. Consequently, a reliable central bank is needed in order to eliminate the so-called 'inflationary bias' found in the conduct of monetary policy. Yet, this theory does not correspond to the practice of central banks. Adopting a historical instead of a hypothetical approach, Le Heron (2003) sees in the Canadian case the foundation of a new consensus on monetary policy – a Keynesian one. According to Le Heron, IT is in conflict with the credibility literature because it is actually based on confidence. There is an opposition between 'credibility' and 'confidence'. The credibility approach needs the full independence of the central bank, while IT requires just an operational independence, with the inflation target determined by elected politicians. Instead of emphasizing 'rules versus discretion', confidence emphasizes the anticipations of the economic agents, the behavior of financial markets and the price of assets. In a second paper (Le Heron and Carré, 2006), the authors emphasize that central bankers do not just follow rules assuming that they, and all economic agents, know the true model. Instead, central bankers gain confidence in so far as they act reasonably, sometimes just following the rule, sometimes changing it and offering justifications that economic agents understand, but always considering that structural shocks may require changes. In the whole process, communication and understanding are crucial to achieve confidence. Alan Greenspan was an example of a central banker who thought and acted according to the 'confidence' and not the 'credibility' principle (Aglietta and Borgy, 2005; Blinder and Reis, 2005).

Regarding both the optimal inflation and interest rates, what is commonplace nowadays is to analyze a central bank following Taylor's (1993) original formulation – the pragmatic equation known as the Taylor rule. In a more general form, the Taylor rule can be the following:

$$i_t - \pi_t = \bar{r} + b(\pi_t - \pi^*) + c(\ln Y_t - \ln \overline{Y}_t),$$

where i_t is the nominal interest rate, π_t is the inflation, $\ln Y_t - \ln \overline{Y}_t$ is the output gap and π^* is the target for inflation. In this case, $\bar{r}_t$ is the real interest rate that prevails when $Y_t = \overline{Y}_t$; thus, it is the equilibrium interest rate that is by assumption considered constant. Thus, this interest rate rule says that the central bank should raise the interest rate above its long-run equilibrium level when inflation exceeds its target and when output exceeds its natural rate. Some argue that a monetary policy rule under IT can be jointly attached to targets for other variables, such as the exchange rate, as long as they have a long-run consistency with the inflation target. The reason for such concern is that an appreciation of the exchange rate, just like an increase in the interest rate, reduces the interest rate but dampens economic activity (Romer, 2001).

IT theory was not the outcome of a concern for credibility, or of a neoclassical hypothetical-deductive reasoning about inflation, but it is the generalization of historical experience: how central banks are behaving in order to control inflation after they gave up monetary targets. Good macroeconomics adopts a method that is dominantly historical (Bresser-Pereira, 2006). The Taylor rule clearly has this historical and pragmatic origin. Central banks' behavior is also pragmatically based on a combination of several inflation theories and findings, among which is included the Phillips curve and an obvious confidence or credibility requirement.[5]

INFLATION TARGETING IN BRAZIL: AN OVERVIEW

The Brazilian economy changed abruptly when the 'Real Plan' started in 1994. Keeping a quasi-fixed exchange rate from the middle of 1994 up to the beginning of 1999 made the country run high current account deficits and, consequently it was, highly dependent on the inflow of international capital and extremely vulnerable to external shocks. Such weakness was confirmed when several crises hit the country, causing a rapid outflow of capital as a result of a chain reaction in the international market. The continuous loss of reserves forced the Brazilian government to float and accept the depreciation of its exchange rate, in January 1999.

The flotation of the real led policy makers to fear the return of high inflation. They raised the interest rate sharply, despite it being very high.[6] The fear of inflation was not confirmed by the facts. Indeed, the increase of the inflation rate after the flotation was much smaller than conventional economists expected. Nevertheless, the Brazilian monetary authorities started to work on achieving two goals: (i) a severe control of inflation in order to calm down financial market expectations and create credibility; and (ii) the implementation of an IT framework as a new nominal anchor for the economy.

Thus, six months after the adoption of a flexible exchange rate, the Central Bank of Brazil (CBB) put into operation a formal IT framework and set the targets for 1999 (8 percent), 2000 (6 percent) and 2001 (4 percent) (Figure 11.1). The broad consumer price index (IPCA)[7] was selected as the reference measure for the targets because it could be affected by seasonal factors as well as by temporary shocks. The overnight Selic rate (or short-term interest rate) was chosen as the policy instrument. Tolerance intervals of 2 percentage points[8] were allowed to take into account the

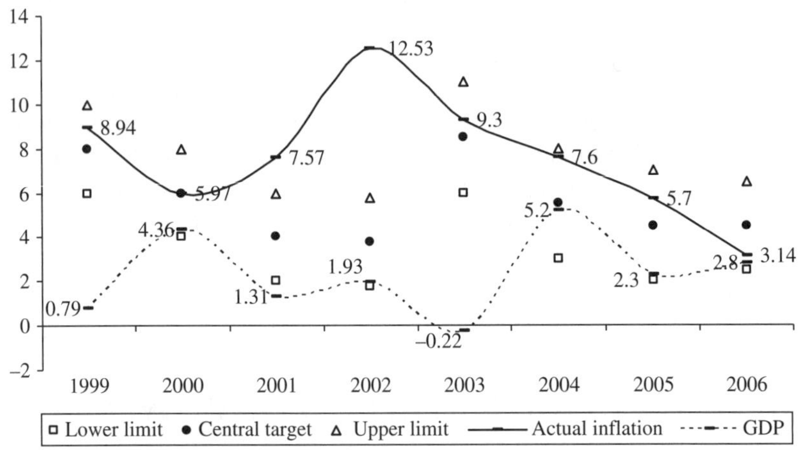

Source: Ipeadata.

Figure 11.1 Actual inflation rates, targets, tolerance intervals and GDP growth (1999–2006)

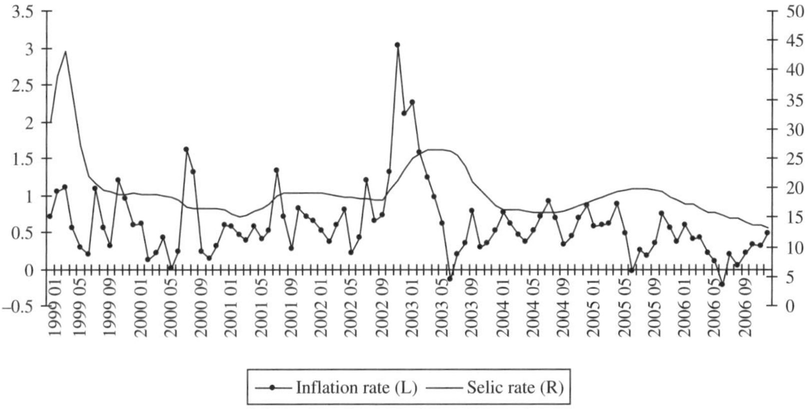

Source: Ipeadata.

Figure 11.2 Short-term nominal interest rate (Selic rate) and inflation rate (CPI)

importance of uncertainty about the inflationary process and also some unexpected temporary shocks and/or seasonal factors.

The exchange rate devaluation coincided with a period of slow economic growth, and this partially explains the behavior of inflation (Figure 11.2). The fact that indexation had been eliminated in 1994 is the main explanation. On the other hand, a reasonable control of government expenditures, and an increase in taxes led to a rapid growth of the primary surplus, which achieved 3.2 percent of GDP in 1999. This was combined with a strict monetary policy conduct. These facts, together with other important indicators, resulted in an inflation rate of just 8.9 percent in 1999 (Pinheiro et al., 2001). The year 2000 was more favorable to the Brazilian economy, despite the concerns regarding external factors. As a result, the 6 percent target was reached successfully even though there was a continuous realignment of monitored prices by the government (Figure 11.5) and some economic growth (Figure 11.1).

In 2001, the Brazilian economy was hit by a series of unfavorable shocks, such as the energy crisis, the end of the speculative bubble in stock markets throughout the world, Argentina's crisis and the terrorist attacks in the USA. These shocks made a great impact on international market expectations and, despite the high interest rates, it was difficult to attract foreign capital. On the other hand, the balance-of-payments deficit was even magnified by the outflow of capital, which was larger than foreign direct investment. At this point, the central bank, which had correctly been lowering the interest rate since 1999, made the mistake of increasing it, even though it was around

9 percent in real terms. Thus, the monetary authorities proved to be weak as they acknowledged a greater external vulnerability of the Brazilian economy than was actually the case, attracted the attention of foreign creditors, and passed the way for the balance-of-payments crisis that eventually occurred at the end of 2001. The inflation rate reached a yearly percentage of 7.7 percent (Figure 11.2), which meant that the target was breached. This rise in the consumer price index (CPI) was not the outcome of excess demand. Directly, it was related to the exchange rate pass-through to the prices, and indirectly, to the rise of administered prices. The fiscal side of the economy deteriorated in 2001, despite the government's primary surplus (3.75 percent of GDP).

In 2002, it was clear that the Workers' Party candidate, Luiz Inácio Lula da Silva, would be elected president. But there were some problems. First, the market did not know his real intentions. Second, there was the fiscal dominance problem related to the new increase in the interest rate. Third, there was a persistence of a high external vulnerability expressed in a high foreign debt/exports ratio. Together, these led to a greater likelihood of the probability of default on foreign debt.[9] As a result, there was a sharp increase in the interest rate on Brazilian government dollar-denominated debt. The real depreciated considerably against the dollar, which led to more inflation.

The fiscal dominance phenomenon was due to Brazil's great dependence on foreign capital, which tends to flow into emerging market economies when the interest rate is high. None the less, as real interest rates continue to rise, even those investors who trust the country's fundamentals start thinking twice. Consequently, new exchange rate depreciation can materialize. For that reason, an attempt to appreciate the exchange rate has an opposite effect, and this is characterized by the so-called 'fiscal dominance' (Bresser-Pereira and Nakano, 2002; Gomes and Aidar, 2004). According to Favero and Giavazzi (2005), Brazil's experience has shown how default risk may have a deleterious effect on the IT framework once the economy can move from a regime of monetary dominance to one of fiscal dominance. Under that condition, responding to higher inflation with real interest rate increases leads to a real exchange rate depreciation and, consequently, to a further increase in inflation. If this is the case, the right instrument to decrease inflation is fiscal (not monetary) policy.

After Lula's election, in October 2002, the government decided to maintain and deepen the previous monetary and fiscal policies, and also to continue microeconomic institutional reforms. As the market assessed that there would not be any significant policy change, there was a decrease in the probability of default, an appreciation of the real, and a decrease in inflation (Blanchard, 2005).

In 2003, with the new government in power and the orthodox conduct of monetary policy, Brazil's creditors started to calm down. By mid-year, the improvement of the country's foreign accounts and the recovery of confidence in public authorities opened an opportunity to the administration to engage in a strategy of lowering the short-term interest rate. Yet, the inverse decision was taken. The only concern was to signal to the financial markets that the priority continued to be the control of inflation. The interest rate continued at its absurdly high level, and the economy stagnated, despite the extremely favorable international conditions. The inflation targets in 2003 were changed from 4 to 8.5 percent, and, in 2004, from 3.75 to 5.5 percent (Figure 11.1). In addition to that, the tolerance intervals were modified from 2 to 2.5 percent.

In 2004, the Brazilian economy grew considerably (Figure 11.1), which was again attributed by the economic authorities to the 'correct' economic policies. In fact, it was the outcome of a major external adjustment that the economy underwent between 1998 and 2004 due to the joint effects of the depreciation of the real as a consequence of the 1998 and 2002 balance-of-payments crises, and of a great increase in the prices of Brazilian exported goods. The economy transited from a current account deficit of 5 percent of GDP in 1998 to a 1 percent surplus in 2004, while the investment rate was kept constant around 19 percent. Thus, there was an extraordinary substitution of domestic for foreign savings.[10]

The monetary authorities started 2005 with a similar monetary policy to the previous year, and the target was achieved. The inflation target was defined by the National Monetary Council up to 2008: 4.5 percent yearly, and this will probably be achieved. It is an inflation rate a little higher than the average of other similar medium-income countries. Administered prices are the main factor responsible for the inflation above international levels. According to Figure 11.4 (see below), between 1999 and 2003 these prices increased more than inflation, and after that they stabilized.[11] In 2005 and 2006, the inflation rate fell, and the target was achieved (Figure 11.1). By the end of 2006 the inflation rate was around 3 percent a year, and this rate was commemorated by conventional orthodoxy as its 'victory' against inflation. Actually, this low rate was the result of 'exchange rate populism', since it was achieved by a substantial appreciation of the real which artificially increased wages and consumption Figure 11.3. Given the fall in the inflation rate, the nominal interest rate fell, but the real interest rate remained above 10 percent at the beginning of 2007.

THE HIGH INTEREST RATE

The previous overview of IT in Brazil gives us the tools necessary to make an analysis of the Brazilian economy in the period. We shall discuss two

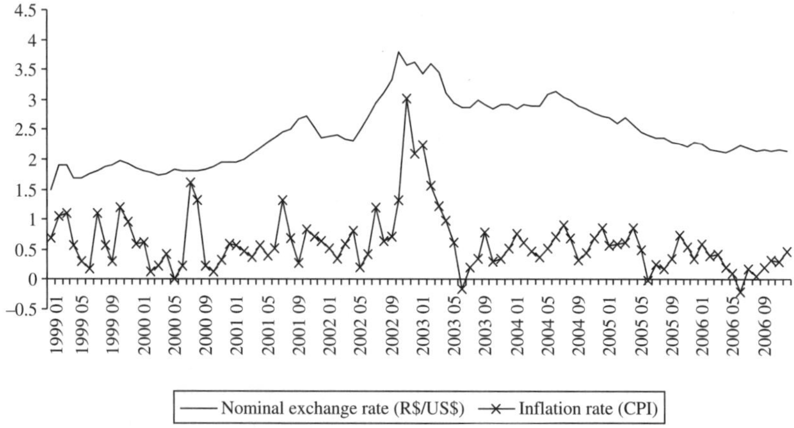

Source: Ipeadata.

Figure 11.3 Inflation rate (CPI) and nominal exchange rate (R$/US$)

Table 11.1 Selic interest rate, in real terms (a.a.)

Year	Nominal Selic rate (%)	Inflation (broad CPI)	Real Selic rate
1999	19.00	8.94	10.06
2000	15.76	5.97	9.79
2001	19.05	7.67	11.38
2002	24.90	12.53	12.37
2003	16.32	9.30	7.02
2004	17.74	7.60	10.14
2005	18.00	5.69	12.31
2006	13.25	3.14	10.11

Source: Banco Central do Brasil.

main issues: (i) the interest rate/exchange rate trap; (ii) the reasons why the interest rate is so high.

In simple terms, 'the interest/exchange rate trap' that has characterized the Brazilian economy since the 1994 Real Plan means that the short-term basic real interest rate does not go down below 9 percent a year in real terms (Table 11.1).[12] It means, additionally, that long-term interest on federal bonds pays the same Selic interest rate in so far as the National Treasury Bonds (LTNs) are indexed by the Selic rate and are often substantially higher than the interest paid by Brazilian bonds abroad.[13] Third, it means that the capital inflows, stirred up by this high rate, cause the overvaluation of the real. The process is stopped by a balance-of-payments crisis which provokes a sharp exchange rate depreciation, as occurred in the 1998 and 2002 balance-of-payments crises, but as soon as the crisis is over, the real appreciates again as has been happening in Brazil since 2002.[14] It is a trap because the monetary authorities fear lowering the interest rate below a given threshold. The IT policy reinforced the trap the moment when it defined the equilibrium interest rate in its model as being around 9 percent a year in real terms, thus formalizing the threshold. When the monetary authorities begin to reduce the interest rate, the exchange rate starts depreciating and inflation rises. It increases well before the lower interest rates could cause demand pressures, but, nevertheless, the CBB stops reducing the interest rate.

Why is the interest rate so high in Brazil? Essentially because the interest/exchange rate trap prevents it from being reduced. A secondary cause is the high level of state expenditures compared to the level of income per capita of the country. Third, the monetary authorities increase the Selic rate, trying (unsuccessfully) to lengthen the debt maturity (to build a long-term domestic credit market). Fourth, and this is probably the key reason, the Selic indexes most of the public debt as it links the short-term interest rate, the Selic, to the federal Treasury bonds (Barbosa, 2006). This is a legacy from the times of high inflation when policy makers kept the short-term interest rate high for fear of not being able to roll over the debt. In behaving in this way, they ignore that the players in the market – particularly the banks – have no alternative but to invest their short-term resources in government bonds. As Keynes showed in Volume 2 of his *Treatise on Money*, for monetary policy to work properly, an adequate yield curve must exist, so that policy decisions related to short-term interest rates can be transmitted to the interest rates that actually influence private agents' behavior. In Brazil, however, the Selic rate directly defines the long-run interest rate, that is, the rate that Brazilian Treasury bonds pay, which is the same as saying that there is no long-term interest rate. There is, however, a proxy: the interest rate paid by first-class Brazilian corporations abroad equals the Brazilian risk plus the interest rate on US Treasury bonds. In 2006, this rate is about half (that is, 5 percent) of the real Selic interest rate (10 percent). Fifth, the Selic rate is high because the CBB uses it as a tool to solve other sorts of problems, besides controlling inflation. For instance, it is used to: (i) attract foreign capital; (ii) reduce the current account deficit when it is increasing continuously; and (iii) increase public savings. Sixth, political economy plays a major role in explaining the abusive short-term interest rate in Brazil. The Selic rate is high because, since the end of the 1980s, the CBB has been 'captured' by rentiers who profit from high interest rates, by the financial sector which makes a living out of commissions/bonuses coming from rentiers, and by multinationals which increase their profit remittances with an overvalued real.

Seventh, there is an ideological hegemony cause: Washington, and specifically the International Monetary Fund (IMF), strongly supports the current Brazilian monetary policy – which is not surprising: the conventional orthodoxy that this agency and the international financial markets use to pressure medium-income developing countries is essentially a tool to neutralize their growth (Bresser-Pereira, 2005, Bresser and Gala, 2007).

However, government authorities should be making the term structure of interest rates the consequence of credit flows due to responsible macroeconomic policies. Some of these are: (i) a rigid inflation control (which they are implementing); (ii) a more competitive exchange rate; (iii) no current account deficit; (iv) reduction of the debt to exports ratio; (v) an interest rate cut; (vi) reduction of the public deficit with consequent reduction of the public debt to GDP ratio; and, principally (vii) de-linking the Brazilian Treasury bonds from Selic through a financial reform. These issues will be discussed more thoroughly in the fourth section.

There are other explanations. Economists offer a series of arguments, usually related to financial markets, for the high interest rate that recall the fable of the wolf and the lamb. The classical explanation for the high inflation rate was that Brazil's country risk was too high. Yet, Bresser and Nakano (2002) showed that since 1992, this was false: countries with the same or worse risk classification had much lower interest rates. In 2006 after the fall in Brazil's country risk, which has been taking place since the beginning of 2003, the short-term interest rate paid by the CBB, which indexes the whole public debt, is higher than the long-term interest rate paid by Brazilian enterprises. A second argument is that the interest rate is high because the country has a large public debt. But such public debt is not particularly high by international standards. It is extremely high only if we calculate the debt of the other countries discounting their nominal value by the Brazilian interest rate, and in this case we fall back into the interest rate trap. A third argument is that the interest rate is high because of the high budget deficit, which is not high by international standards. Another explanation is that a high interest rate is necessary to fight inflation. There is no doubt that the interest rate is the right instrument to do that. But the Selic rate does not fluctuate between 0 and 3 percent in real terms, as it does in rich countries, and not even between 2 and 5 percent, as it does in countries with similar risk classifications. Table 11.1 shows the real Selic rate for Brazil and Table 11.2 reports some basic interest rates of selected countries, which confirms what has been said.

A fifth explanation was offered by Arida et al. (2005). As justification for the high 'natural' rate in Brazil, or for the 'bad equilibrium', they cite the non-existence of long-term domestic credit, which is due to what they call 'jurisdictional uncertainty': the judiciary branch would not protect

Table 11.2 Selected countries: basic interest rates (2005)

Country	Real interest rates	Country	Real interest rates
Brazil	11.53	Mexico	4.42
Argentina	−3.36	Peru	1.66
Chile	1.22	Philippines	0.71
China	0.29	Poland	3.64
Colombia	1.49	Russia	1.10
Czech Republic	−0.16	Saudi Arabia	4.22
Egypt	5.00	Singapore	2.01
Hong Kong	2.13	South Africa	3.55
Hungary	2.86	South Korea	1.40
India	1.07	Taiwan	−0.55
Indonesia	−3.03	Thailand	−1.30
Israel	2.51	Turkey	7.01
Malaysia	−0.22	Venezuela	−1.77

Note: Real interest rates are short-term nominal interest rates minus consumer prices indices.

Source: *The Economist* (Emerging Market Indicators), February 2006.

creditors effectively and such action would bring negative consequences to private savings and investment. It is also misinterpreted as a consequence of market failures deriving from restrictions to currency convertibility, artificial term lengthening of public debt, compulsory saving funds, and forced savings through inflation. Thus, the country would have to live with a short-run real interest rate above 9 percent a year until a series of institutional reforms solve these problems and create 'jurisdictional certainty'. There is no doubt that a country like Brazil needs reforms. None the less, their absence cannot be blamed for mistakes in the country's macroeconomic policy, especially for the extremely high basic interest rate. In the past, Brazilian institutions were less developed, but the interest rate was much lower. Besides, the country's institutions are quite similar to, if not better than, those found in countries with equivalent (or worse) risk classification but with much lower interest rates. In fact, the 'jurisdictional uncertainty' argument makes no sense and nor is it sustained empirically.

Holland et al. (2006) formulate a methodology based on Arida et al.'s proposal and their results are highly unfavorable to the jurisdiction uncertainty argument. Their findings indicate that 'traditional monetary and fiscal factors are far more relevant to explain the level of short-term real interest rates than the binomial jurisdictional uncertainty/currency inconvertibility is'.

THE INTEREST–EXCHANGE RATE TRAP

Despite its high level, the movements in the basic interest rate in Brazil are quite similar to what is observed in other countries, that is, it increases in booms and decreases in downturns. However, the monetary authorities have not been able to consistently reduce this rate – and the result is the 'interest rate trap'. Our argument is that the Brazilian economy was not in a position to adopt an IT framework as a nominal anchor. And, as it ignored such a restriction, the trap became stronger.

The interest rate trap can be observed in many ways. First, whenever the CBB starts a process of interest rate reduction, the exchange rate depreciates, and the consequent changes in relative prices cause a rise in inflation. This is a threat to the IT framework, and the CBB reacts, increasing the interest rate again. Thus, paradoxically, a supply-side inflation is fought with a policy aiming at demand contraction. Every time the interest rate is reduced and there is some sign of economic growth, as the current account deficit increases,[15] the government authorities try to avoid a depreciation of the exchange rate by raising the Selic rate and, consequently, increasing unemployment rates. Raising interest rates makes both public deficit and public debt to GDP ratios increase (see Figure 11.3) and, accordingly, reduces the country's international credit, unless the primary surplus is correspondingly increased, usually through an increase in the tax burden.

This trap puts the country's economy in a short-term vicious cycle. At the beginning of 2003, for instance, the government decided to continue with the same macroeconomic policy adopted by the previous administration. As a consequence, credit flowed in again, the country risk lowered, and the exchange rate appreciated once more. But, at the same time, the financial market started to notice that there was no economic growth, that there were some social and political disturbances, and that the primary surplus began to decrease again.

The exchange rate is a particularly strategic macroeconomic price and it is the other side of the coin of the interest rate trap. Exchange rate depreciations can have a deleterious impact on inflation, whereas appreciations can affect negatively the national accounts via levels of exports and imports. A real appreciation can make domestic industry less competitive and, therefore, cause deficit in the current account. According to the conventional theory underlying IT, exchange rate targeting is likely to worsen the performance of monetary policy. Nevertheless, this does not mean that central banks should neglect the effects of the exchange rate movements on inflation and aggregate demand. In this case, the best solution is a transparent explanation of the exchange rate intervention as a way of mitigating potentially destabilizing effects of abrupt price changes (Mishkin and Schmidt-Hebbel, 2001).

MONETARY POLICY REGIME

Despite the low inflation rate that prevails in Brazil, our view is that the IT system is problematic because it contributes to maintaining a quasi-stagnant, economy and because the low growth rates are directly related to the fact that price stability is not the same as macroeconomic stability. Unemployment remains high in Brazil, the basic interest rate is absurdly high, and the exchange rate is overvalued. In addition, it co-exists with a high interest rate and keeps the exchange rate non-competitive. The economic policy that conventional orthodoxy proposes to medium-income countries and that the CBB faithfully adopts implies the overvaluation of the exchange rate. The Dutch disease and the growth under the foreign savings policy push up the exchange rate, overvaluing it. A competent macroeconomic policy must look at such tendencies, keeping the exchange rate competitive. Yet, as conventional orthodoxy defines macroeconomic stabilization as price stabilization, it uses the appreciation of the local currency to control inflation. It is impressive how the inflation rate accompanies the exchange rate in the Brazilian economy (see Figure 11.3).

The Brazilian economy was not really prepared for an IT framework, given the fact that such policy is designed to manage monetary policy, not to change the monetary policy regime. An IT policy will not apply if a country needs to change the monetary policy regime due, for instance, to its high and inertial inflation, as Brazil had between 1980 and 1994, or due to an absurdly high real basic interest rate and an overvalued exchange rate, as the country has been experiencing since 1994.[16] It must first address these problems that IT has not adequately solved. In fact, as argued in the paragraphs above, Brazil has been facing a high interest rate/overvalued exchange rate trap since 1994, which has kept the country out of its macroeconomic equilibrium. If the economic authorities believed that IT was a good route to be followed, they had to first face this trap.

In order to put the country on the right track again, several changes must be made. Indeed, a full strategy must be put into action. The aim is to reduce the basic interest rate (the Selic rate) so that it oscillates between 1 and 3 percent in real terms instead of between 9 and 15 percent. This reduction will only be possible with the end of the linkage of the long- to the short-term interest rate, that is, with the end of the indexation of the federal bonds by the short-term Selic rate. This practice is peculiar to Brazil (a legacy of high inflation) and it is the main institutional explanation for the high interest rate used to pay the servicing of the public debt. While the short- and the long-term interest rates remained, in 2006, around 12 percent a year in real terms, a proxy of the long-term interest rate (interest on US Treasury bonds plus Brazil risk) was around 5 percent a year. Instead of conducting reforms to end such distortions, in 1999 the administration adopted IT, and limited itself to managing it within the framework of an interest rate trap.

The government will also have to start a serious fiscal adjustment. The country has been obtaining considerable primary surpluses via tax increases – and not via public spending cuts – but this is not enough. While the interest rate is getting out of the trap, the authorities will have to reduce expenditures and, perhaps, generate a surplus. With this adjustment, not only will the government signal its rejection to any sort of populism but it will also control possible inflationary processes coming from a possible demand shock.

The reduction of the interest rate from its minimum 9 percent level, and of inflation from its 5 to 6 percent level will only be achieved with another important reform: the end of indexation of public services and, more broadly, the end of any indexation of contracts and administered prices in which the administration is involved as a provider or as a regulator.[17] As already mentioned, the broad CPI is the price index used for the definition of inflation, and the basket of administered prices amounts to 30 percent of the index. In terms of economic policy action, what is clear is that policy makers' actions affect considerably the price index variability because of monitored prices. As a consequence, the targets can be reached but there are high social costs involved, low economic growth as well as high interest rates. Monitored prices vary independently of demand factors and, as Figure 11.5 reports, the accumulated inflation related to the monitored prices increased much more than the other two indices (Gomes and Aidar, 2004).

Of course, when we say that administered prices should not be indexed, it does not mean that regulating agencies should neglect inflation processes in their price revisions. Like their counterparts in other countries, the Brazilian agencies will take inflation into consideration but without referring to a predetermined price index. Nor does it mean that the government would break existing contracts: it would just be strongly motivated to renegotiate them, and institutionally prohibited to make new indexed contracts.

Finally, government authorities should always bear in mind that these policies are aimed at bringing economic growth and, as consequence, less unemployment and fewer social disparities. Monetary policy rules should be seen as a guideline for decision making and not as a rigid rule. For unemployment specifically, the relationship between this variable and monetary policy is very important. Contrary to what is argued by some conventional theorists, monetary policy usually has positive and long-lasting effects on

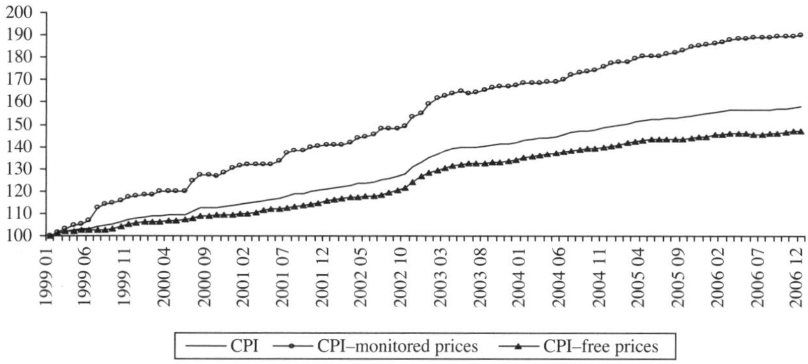

Source: Ipeadata.

Figure 11.4 Accumulated inflation rate (1999:01 = 100)

real interest rates and, consequently, on economic activity and unemployment. In other words, it influences unemployment rates, more than has been discussed in the current debate (Gomes and Aidar, 2005).

CONCLUSION

This chapter discussed the current inflation targeting policy adopted in Brazil and the interest rate/exchange rate trap the country is facing due to its high basic interest rate. First, we briefly reviewed the monetary policy in Brazil under inflation targeting, from the date of its implementation until the end of 2005. Second, we analyzed the problems faced by the Brazilian monetary authorities under the argument that the inflation targeting system faces some important theoretical problems and, more importantly, it has faced an inconsistency dilemma since it was designed to be used for purposes of 'management' of monetary policy, and not for 'changing' the monetary policy regime.

The 1994 Real Plan was a successful reform that de-indexed the Brazilian economy, thus neutralizing inflationary inertia. Yet, it was left incomplete in so far as administered prices and the public debt remained indexed. However, instead of working toward this objective, the Brazilian monetary authorities accepted the IMF recommendation and adopted an exchange rate anchor between 1995 and 1998. The outcome was catastrophic. Nevertheless, an inflation targeting policy was introduced in 1999 as a substitute for an exchange rate anchor. This monetary reform ought to have been preceded by reforms that ended all forms of indexation. Yet, instead of developing a strategy to reduce the interest rate, involving such reforms and deepening the fiscal adjustment, the government continued to define inflation as the main problem to be faced, and adopted a formal inflation targeting policy. The consequence was that, since 1999, the real interest rate has remained incredibly high: the Brazilian economy has been unable to escape the interest rate trap.

Perhaps, the best strategy should have been the search for a long-term convergence of inflation. For instance, Chile and Mexico acted similarly to Brazil before introducing their respective inflation targeting policies. They first pursued the equilibrium of their economies and began releasing inflation projections with long-term aims. In other words, they allowed inflation to converge smoothly and the result was a much smaller social cost, when compared to Brazil. In the case of Chile, which is a model of competent macroeconomic policy, the entire strategy started to be analyzed back in 1991. However, the full adoption of a mild form inflation target policy occurred only in 2000, when they started to release their inflation reports. For the Mexican case, the strategy was similar but in different periods.

In the Brazilian case, there was no proper preparation of the economy prior to the adoption of the system. In order to adopt the IT policy, authorities should have prepared the key variables of the economy in order for them to converge more smoothly. If they had first concentrated on getting rid of the interest rate/exchange rate trap in which the economy was immersed, they could, then have adopted an IT policy. Instead, excessively concerned with inflation, the authorities hastened to adopt a new nominal anchor. In consequence, the exchange rate remained highly unstable for several years and the economy failed to achieve its inflation target. Worse, the burden of interest on the public debt remained abnormally high – which involved high fiscal and development costs. Therefore, Brazil needs an urgent change in its priorities with regard to monetary policy: the high interest rate, not inflation, is the main problem to be faced. By just solving this problem, and lowering the interest rate to levels consistent with its countries risk, Brazil will be able to achieve international levels of inflation, instead of keeping it around 5 percent a year. To perform this action successfully, however, it will be necessary to involve not only the government but also the whole of society.

NOTES

1. An overvalued or non-competitive currency is a strong obstacle to growth since it hinders the export-oriented investment opportunities.
2. Small, as it represents around 1 percent of the world GDP.
3. We are speaking of a 'parameter', not a target, because it would not be explicit, but conventionally followed by the central bank and acknowledged by the financial market. Just

to include explicitly the exchange rate in the model and opt for a long-term inflation target, as proposed by Ball (2000), counting that, in this time, the movements of the exchange rate will be offset, is not enough.

4. The GDP growth rate of Brazil between 1999 and 2006 was just 2.3 percent on average – a rate substantially smaller than the one achieved by similar medium-income countries.
5. Credibility theory is either obvious or wrong. It is wrong when policy makers offer the 'credibility' of their policies as a substitute for economic fundamentals. This was what happened, for instance, in the classical Latin American Southern Cone stabilization experiments of the late 1970s (Diaz-Alejandro, 1981), or in the 1992 IMF-sponsored stabilization program in Brazil.
6. After the implementation of the IT regime there was a reduction of the real interest rate, but in 2001, when its real level continued very high, it was increased again.
7. The selected price index – IPCA – covers a sample of families with personal income between 1 and 40 minimum wages units and has a broad geographical basis (Bogdanski et al., 2000).
8. The tolerance intervals were widened to 2.5 percentage points after 2003.
9. The increase in exports and the improvement of the national accounts was beginning in this year but only became clear to creditors in 2003.
10. When a country follows the growth *cum* foreign savings strategy, large inflows of foreign capital takes place, the exchange rate appreciates, and (if the investment opportunities are not particularly favorable), the rate of substitution of foreign for domestic savings is high (Bresser-Pereira, 2004; Bresser-Pereira and Gala, 2007). In this case, given the depreciation of the real, the opposite occurred.
11. This behavior (high increase and stabilization) was mainly due to the use of the general price index (IGP), instead of the consumer price index, to define prices administered by contracts. Part of the IGP comes from wholesale price changes, which is closely related to exchange rate fluctuations.
12. Only in 2003 did it go down, averaging 7.02 percent. This was a recession year that followed the 2002 balance-of-payments crisis. The interest rate fell not due to but despite the central bank monetary policy.
13. In other words, they are often higher than the interest rate on Treasury bonds plus the Brazil risk, plus the difference between the American and the Brazilian interest rates.
14. In the worst moment of the crisis, the exchange rate was R$4.00 per dollar; in June 2007 it was below R$2.00 per dollar.
15. Since 1994, the current account deficit was close to zero on only one occasion – in 2002. This happened due to the exchange rate depreciation and a strong economic recession. However, this depreciation did not occur because of economic policies but because of a confidence crisis. In the first half of 2003, the exchange rate started to appreciate again, which might make the current account deficit reappear.
16. Actually, the real interest rate was high before 1994, but unstable, depending on the variations of inflation. Since inflation was incredibly high, all attention was directed towards it.
17. Administered (monitored) prices are those determined or influenced by government, either directly or through a government agency regardless of market forces. Some products which are part of the basket of administered prices are: water, electricity and sanitary fees, public transport, telephone calls, petrol, public transport, motor licenses and registration, health plans, and postage.

REFERENCES

Aglietta, M. and V. Borgy (2005), 'L'héritage de Greenspan: Le triomphe de la politique discritionnaire ['Greenspan's heritage: the triumph of discritionarity']', *Bouletim du Cepii*, **251**, December, 1–4.

Arestis, P., L.F. de Paula and F. Ferrari-Filho (2006), 'Inflation targeting in emerging countries: the case of Brazil', in *Proceedings of the 34th Annual Meeting of ANPEC* (Brazilian Association of Graduate Programs in Economics), December.
Arida, P., E.L. Bacha and A. Lara-Resende (2005), 'Credit, interest, and jurisdictional uncertainty: conjectures on the case of Brazil', in F. Giavazzi, I. Goldfjan and S. Herrera (eds), *Inflation Targeting, Debt, and the Brazilian Experience, 1999 to 2003*, Cambridge, MA: MIT Press, pp. 265–94.
Ball, L. (2000), 'Policy rules and external shocks', NBER working paper 7910, Cambridge, MA, September.
Ball, L. and N. Sheridan (2003), 'Does inflation targeting matter?', NBER working paper 9577, Cambridge, MA, March.
Barbosa, F.H. (2006), 'The contagion effect of public debt on monetary policy: the Brazilian experience', *Brazilian Journal of Political Economy*, **26**(2), 231–8.
Barro, R.J. and D.B. Gordon (1983), 'Rules, discretion and reputation in a model of monetary policy', *Journal of Monetary Economics*, **12**, July, 101–21.
Blanchard, O. (2005), 'Fiscal dominance and inflation targeting: lessons from Brazil', in F. Giavazzi, I. Goldfjan and S. Herrera (eds), *Inflation Targeting, Debt, and the Brazilian Experience, 1999 to 2003*, Cambridge, MA: MIT Press, pp. 49–80.
Blinder, A. and R. Reis (2005), 'Understanding the Greenspan standard', presentation to the Federal Reserve Bank of Kansas City symposium, Jackson Hole, WY, August.
Bogdanski, J., A.A. Tombini and S.R. Werlang (2000), 'Implementing inflation targets in Brazil', Banco Central do Brasil working paper series 1, Brasília.
Bresser-Pereira, L.C. (2004), 'Brazil's quasi-stagnation and the growth *cum* foreign savings strategy', *International Journal of Political Economy*, **32**(4), 76–102.
Bresser-Pereira, L.C. (2005) 'Macroeconomia pós-Plano Real: as relações básicas, ['Post real plan macro-economic policy: the basic relations']' in J. Sicsú, L.F. de Paula and R. Michel (eds), *Novo-Desenvolvimentismo: Um Projeto Nacional de Crescimento com Eqüidade Social*, Barueri: Manole; Rio de Janeiro: Fundação Konrad Adenauer: 3–47; also accessed at www.bresserpereira.org.br.
Bresser-Pereira, L.C. (2006), 'The two methods of economics', paper presented at the annual meeting of the European Association of Evolutionary Economics, Maastricht, 7-10 November 2004, revised in 2006 and accessed at www. bresser pereira. org.br.
Bresser-Pereira, L.C. and P. Gala (2007), 'Why foreign savings fail to cause growth', *Revista Economia Politica*, **27**(1) January, 3–19; in English at www. bressepereira.org.br.
Bresser-Pereira, L.C. and Y. Nakano (2002) 'Uma estratégia de desenvolvimento com estabilidade ['Economic growth with stability']', *Brazilian Journal of Political Economy*, **21**(3), 146–77.
Diaz-Alejandro, C. (1981), 'Southern Cone stabilization plans', in W. Cline and S. Weintraub (eds), *Economic Stabilization in Developing Countries*, Washington, DC: Brookings Institution, pp. 119–48.
Favero, C.A. and F. Giavazzi (2005), 'Inflation targeting and debt: lessons from Brazil', in F. Giavazzi, I. Goldfjan and S. Herrera (eds), *Inflation Targeting, Debt, and the Brazilian Experience, 1999 to 2003*, Cambridge, MA: MIT Press, pp. 85–108.
Gomes, C. and O. Aidar (2004), 'Metas de inflação: preços livres e administrados no Brasil' ['Inflation targeting: free and administered prices in Brazil'], paper presented to *the 32nd Annual Meeting of ANPEC* (Brazilian Association of Graduate Programs in Economics), João Pessoa, PB, December.

Gomes, C. and O. Aidar (2005), 'Cinco anos de metas de inflação no Brasil: sucesso ou Fracasso? ['Five years of inflation targeting in Brazil: success or failure?']', paper presented to *the 10th Annual Meeting of the Brazilian Association of Political Economy*.

Holland, M., F.M. Gonçalves and A.D. Spacov (2007), 'Can jurisdictional uncertainty and capital controls explain the high level of real interest rates in Brazil? Evidence from panel data', *Revista Brasileira de Economia*, **1**, 2–28.

Kydland, F.E. and E.C. Prescott (1977), 'Rules rather than discretion: the inconsistency of optimal plans', *Journal of Political Economy*, **85**, 473–92.

Le Heron, E. (2003), 'A new consensus on monetary policy?', *Brazilian Journal of Political Economy*, **23**(4), 3–27.

Le Heron, E. and E. Carré (2006), 'Credibility versus confidence in monetary policy', in R. Wray and M. Forstater (eds), *Money, Financial Instability and Stabilization Policy*, Cheltenham, UK and Northampton, MA, USA: Edward Elgar, pp. 58–84.

Minella, A., P.S. Freitas, I. Goldfajn and M.K. Muinhos (2003), 'Inflation targeting in Brazil: constructing credibility under exchange rate volatility', *Journal of International Money and Finance*, **22**, 1015–40.

Mishkin, F.S. and K. Schmidt-Hebbel (2001), 'One decade of inflation targeting in the world: what do we know and what do we need to know?', NBER working paper series 8397, Cambridge, MA.

Pinheiro, A.C., F. Giambiagi and M.M. Moreira (2001) 'O Brasil na década de 90: uma transição bem sucedida? ['Brazil in the 90s: 2 successful transition?']', BNDES working paper series 91, November.

Romer, D. (2001), *Advanced Macroeconomics*, 2nd edn, New York: McGraw-Hill/Irwin.

Svensson, L.O. (1998), 'Inflation targeting as a monetary policy rule', NBER working paper series 6790, Cambridge, MA.

Taylor, J.B. (1993), 'Discretion versus policy rules in practice', *Carnegie-Rochester Conference Series on Public Policy*, **39,** 195–214.

Taylor, J.B. (2000), 'Using monetary policy rules in emerging market economies', accessed at www.standford.edu/~johntayl/papers/Bank of Mexico Paper.pdf.

12. Eisner's radical approach to social security – tell the truth!

Stephanie Kelton

INTRODUCTION

Post Keynesians undoubtedly appreciate Robert Eisner for his contributions to investment, capital accounting and budgeting. In his later years, Eisner turned his attention to the issue of social security, laying bare the arguments of its so-called 'saviors', who sought to weaken (if not destroy) the system from within. Against the various calls to reform the system by slashing benefits, raising the retirement age, privatizing its contributions, and so on, he put forward the most honest and enlightening argument I have yet run across. His short book, *Social Security: More Not Less* (1998a), and his article in the *Journal of Post Keynesian Economics*, 'Save social security from its saviors' (1998b), have influenced my own work on the subject, and his name is always the first one I offer to those looking to understand my seemingly radical position on the issue.

Bob Eisner did not believe that social security was facing a crisis – not now, and not in the future. He rejected the idea that it could go 'bankrupt' and insisted that there were any number of easy accounting solutions to deal with what he perceived to be a simple accounting problem. He had a keen understanding of balance sheet accounting, and he was willing to explore the potentially mind-numbing institutional details of the system's inner workings. These characteristics allowed him to expose the weaknesses in the arguments of his opponents, while strengthening his own position, simply by demonstrating the way things actually work. These are the contributions I want to take up in this chapter, for there are still too many among us – Liberals, 'friends' of the system – who appear ready to concede ground to those who would nibble away at this most popular and important program. And although the Bush administration appears to have lost its battle to introduce 'personal retirement accounts', the assault on social security is likely to continue for years to come. Those of us who are disciples or admirers of Eisner must carry on his fight, exposing the truth about social security and protecting it from those who are committed to 'saving' it.

THE EISNER POSITION: THE IRRELEVANCE OF THE TRUST FUNDS AND THE POWER OF A SOVEREIGN ISSUER

I admired Eisner for comments like these: 'The fears and cynicism regarding Social Security, misguided as they are, should be met as fully as possible' (1998b, p. 85). Eisner addressed these fears head-on, questioning such universal 'truths' as: (i) payroll taxes finance social security benefit payments; (ii) the government cannot 'afford' to make good on future promises due to impending shortfalls in the trust funds; and (iii) at some point, we will be forced to raise taxes or cut benefits to deal with the problem. He realized that these beliefs were deeply entrenched in the American psyche, but he insisted that economists ought to tell the truth about the way things actually work. And this is just what he did – boldly and unapologetically.

'Social Security faces no crisis now or in the future', he said (ibid., p. 77). In fact, he called the 'whole problem . . . trivial', insisting that the 'projected shortage in the trust funds . . . is purely a matter of accounting, with any number of easy accounting solutions' (ibid., p. 83). These were brave statements, especially given that no one in the political arena has ever agreed with him and most ordinary Americans remain convinced that the system faces significant financial challenges in the not-too-distant future.[1]

But Eisner insisted that the truth be told: the government's ability to pay benefits is in no way dependent on the balance in the Old-Age, Survivors, and Disability Insurance (OASDI) trust funds. Indeed, Eisner considered the funds themselves to be simply 'accounting entities' with no *ex ante* significance (ibid., p. 80). He examined the disposition of Federal Insurance Contributions Act (FICA) contributions and explained that withheld payroll taxes do not 'go into' the trust funds (Eisner, 1997). Similarly, he explained that benefit payments do not come 'out of' the trust funds. Withheld payroll contributions flow into the same Treasury accounts as other governmental collections, and none of these payments yields a source of revenue that can be 'used' to finance benefit payments.[2]

As Eisner explained, benefits are always paid by writing a check on the Treasury's account at the Federal Reserve. And here Eisner makes a crucial point: the US government can always 'afford' to make these payments because it issues a sovereign currency.[3] To make his case, he cited Alan Greenspan, who has conceded that 'a government cannot become insolvent with respect to obligations in its own currency. A fiat money system, like the ones we have today, can produce such claims *without limit*' (emphasis added; Greenspan, 1997, p. 2).

Eisner understood the power that accrues to a government when it issues a fiat money. He knew that it did not matter whether the trustees declared the funds 'solvent' or not. In his words:

> The accountants can just as well declare the bottom line of the funds' accounts negative as positive – and the Treasury can go on making whatever outlays are prescribed by law. The Treasury can pay out all that Social Security provides while the accountants declare the funds more and more in the red. (Eisner, 1998b, p. 81)

When it comes to making payments, Eisner essentially said that the government simply needs to write the checks in order to make good on its promises to tomorrow's retirees. The government can 'afford' to pay promised benefits because it has the power to create money. It is that simple.

Because Eisner saw things in such simple terms, he was frustrated by those who sought to reduce the 'burden' of paying benefits in the future. He lashed out against the 'proposed nibbling away of Social Security, including that by some of its presumed friends', calling it 'disingenuous and misleading' (ibid., p. 77). He resented those who were willing to undermine our social insurance program in order to achieve a positive balance in the trust funds. And he was against any increase in the retirement age, calling it an 'insidious' reform (ibid., p. 77).

He also opposed reductions in the Cost-of-Living Adjustment (COLA), a reform that is frequently justified on the grounds that the consumer price index overstates actual inflation.[4] He also stood up against many Liberals, who argued in favor of means-testing – denying some or all social security benefit to those who are rich (or even moderately well off).[5] He argued that this kind of reform was 'likely to kill' rather than save social security, since means testing would 'convey the notion that Social Security is just for the poor, another form of "welfare" ' (ibid., p. 79).

Finally, he criticized proposals to allow workers to divert some of their payroll contributions into private retirement accounts, saying:

> [I]t is like asking us to forego our life insurance or health insurance premiums and turn them over to our brokers. If we could be sure that we will not need expensive medical care or that we will not die early and leave destitute dependents, that scheme might work out. But how many would consider this wise? (Ibid., p. 80)[6]

Let us discuss what Eisner *did* consider wise. He thought that Americans should do more to prepare for their retirement, and he supported the use of personal retirement accounts. But he insisted that these accounts be established as a supplement to, rather than a replacement for, existing social security benefits. He also believed that the government should increase, rather than decrease, promised benefits to retirees. He thought this could be accomplished by indexing post-retirement benefits to wages rather than inflation, so that retirees could share in the benefits of rising productivity.[7] And he recommended a number of technical changes to the way in which the funds themselves are credited and managed, but I want to leave these aside in order to move on to my next figure – Paul Krugman.

KRUGMAN'S POSITION: THE GOOD, THE BAD AND THE UNFORTUNATE

Few can dispute the influence of Paul Krugman. His op-ed pieces are read by millions, and he routinely appears on such television favorites as *The Daily Show*, *The Tonight Show* and *The Today Show*. He is quite possibly the most visible academic economist working today, and his message matters. On the issue of social security, he has spared no ink in his effort to convince ordinary Americans that President George W. Bush's plan to introduce 'personal retirement accounts' is a bad one. And I suspect that his efforts helped the Democrats in their mission to protect social security from this type of 'carve-out' reform. But for all of the good that has come from his efforts, Krugman also makes some unfortunate arguments that could make it difficult for Democrats to put forward sensible Keynesian policies in the future.

Unlike Eisner, Krugman *does* believe that 'there is a long-range financing problem' (2004b, p. 1). In an op-ed piece on March 5, 2004, he asked, 'Should we consider modest reforms that reduce the expenses or widen the revenue base of Social Security?', answering, 'Sure' (2004c, p. 2). In his view, the crisis could be managed simply by enacting the kinds of reforms that were implemented in the early 1980s, following the Greenspan Commission's recommendations (Krugman 2004c).[8] According to Krugman, the trust fund 'will run out in 2052' because the Greenspan Commission proposed an increase in the payroll tax that 'wasn't quite big enough' (ibid.). In other words, Krugman argues that pre-funding worked; we just did not increase payroll taxes enough to ensure solvency in perpetuity.

Having said that, Krugman did not recommend a hike in the payroll tax to alleviate the financial problems that he foresees in the long run. Instead, he has called for a 'rolling back' of the Bush tax cuts, which he believes threaten the government's ability to sustain social security in the long run. Time and again, he has used his op-ed column to try to persuade the American public that 'the Bush tax cuts are a much bigger problem for the nation's fiscal future than the Social Security shortfall' (2004c, p. 1). If the government were not losing 2.5 percent of GDP in revenue each year, he argues, it could easily cover the projected shortfall, which is estimated to be about 2 percent of GDP over the next 30 years (Krugman, 2004c).

Krugman's arguments are not only inconsistent with Eisner's, but they are also untenable in a balance-sheet sense. To see this, consider the following statement:

> It's interesting to ask what would have happened if the General Fund actually had been run responsibly – which is to say, if Social Security surpluses had been kept in a 'lockbox', and the General Fund had been balanced on average. In that case, the accumulating trust fund would have been a very real contribution to the government as a whole's ability to pay future benefits. (Krugman, 2005, p. 5).

According to Krugman, a 'lockbox' would have been a good idea, because it would have prevented the Treasury from 'spending' social security surpluses. He further argues that the rest of the government's budget should remain balanced, for otherwise the Treasury might still be tempted to dip into social security reserves. Others have questioned the logic of these arguments (Wray, 1999; Bell and Wray, 2000; Mitchell and Mosler, 2005; Mosler and Forstater, 2005).

Several of us have done so by analogy. Can a trust fund help to provide for future retirees? Suppose the New York Transit Authority (NYTA) decided to offer subway tokens as part of the retirement package it offers its employees – say, 50 free tokens per month (for life) upon retirement. Does this mean that the City should attempt to run an annual 'surplus' of tokens (on average collecting more tokens per month than it pays out) in order to accumulate a trust fund to provide for future NYTA retirees? Of course not.

When tokens are needed to pay future retirees, the City will simply issue more tokens at that time. Not only is it unnecessary for the City to accumulate a hoard of tokens, but it will not in any way ease the burden of providing subway rides to future retirees. Whether the City can meet its *real* obligation (to convert tokens into rides) will depend solely on the future carrying capabilities of the transit system. Eisner clearly understood this, saying:

> While we can save and invest now in more ovens that will be useful in the future, the bread dependents eat at any time must be baked by those working then. Retirees cannot eat balances in Social Security trust funds, or stocks and bonds or cash. In a real sense, for the economy as a whole, retirement benefits are thus always supplied on a pay-as-you-go basis. (1998b, p. 88)

Note, also, that the NYTA does not currently attempt to run a 'balanced budget', and, indeed, consistently runs a subway token deficit. That is, it consistently pays out more tokens than it receives, as riders hoard tokens or lose them. Attempting to run a surplus of subway tokens would result in a shortage of tokens, with customers unable to obtain them. Instead, the transit system always sets its price (say, $1.50 per token) and lets the quantity of tokens it issues 'float'.[9] Again, this typically results in a deficit, as more tokens are issued than are received, but this practice does not in any way jeopardize the Transit Authority's ability to make token payments to future retirees.

Why can't Krugman, as a Keynesian, see this? Why is he preaching the virtues of 'lockboxes' and fiscal responsibility? Surely he recognizes that budget surpluses reduce the demand for currently produced goods. But why does he not recognize that, 'as a matter of accounting between the sectors, a government budget *deficit adds net financial assets* (adding to non-government saving) and a budget *surplus has the opposite effect*' (my emphasis; Mitchell and Mosler, 2005, p. 5).[10] And why does he not recognize the power of a sovereign issuer? Why does he argue that 'the government's ability to honor future obligations' is in jeopardy because 'the General Fund has plunged into huge deficit' (2005, p. 4)?[11]

These are the unfortunate aspects of Krugman's contributions, for there really is no other economist with his visibility who can help the public to understand the choices that are available in a modern fiat money economy.[12]

CONCLUSION

Economists tell a lot of silly stories. Many teach their students that money was invented by utility-maximizing agents, who were trying to avoid the transactions costs associated with barter exchange. Others tell their students that the central bank is responsible for the amount of money and credit in the economy. Still others stare into the eyes of the uninitiated and assert that prices are determined by the forces of supply and demand in a competitive market environment. And the list goes on and on.

Post Keynesians (and institutionalists) typically fare better. But there is still considerable disparity among Post Keynesians on the issue of government finance and macro stabilization policy. Many still treat the federal government as if it were subject to the same constraints as a household or a private business. Only a handful of Post Keynesians (William Mitchell and Warren Mosler, Randall Wray, Mathew Forstater, Scott Fullwiler and Stephanie Bell) have embraced the modern money approach, which emphasizes functional finance and the irrelevance of concepts like government solvency. The rest should draw inspiration from the work of Robert Eisner, who took the time to learn how things really work and who had the courage to tell it like it was.

NOTES

1. I do not know of a single politician who has argued that social security faces no *financial* challenges due to the aging population and shrinking workforce.
2. Liberals inevitably misunderstand this point. For example, Ellen Frank argues that 'excess payroll taxes' yield 'cash [that] is turned over to the Treasury . . . [which] then spends the cash on welfare, roads, weapons, tax cuts' (1999, p. 1). Similarly, Krugman tells us that '[w]e take the payroll tax and it's used to pay benefits to retirees' (2004a). And Baker and Weisbrot (2000) treat the social security surplus as a loan to the federal government. See Bell and Wray (2000) for a detailed explanation of these misunderstandings.
3. Even Dean Baker and Mark Weisbrot (2000), who have contributed important and sound research on the subject, have made the mistake of treating payroll tax receipts as a constraint on the government's ability to pay benefits.
4. Instead, Eisner proposed that post-retirement benefits be indexed to wages (instead of prices), to allow retirees to 'share in growing productivity' (1998b, p. 78). Benefits would then rise at the rate of real wage increases.
5. Robert Samuelson supported means testing and also favored an increase in the eligibility age (Orr, 2005).
6. In defense of public insurance, he cited social security's ability to offer social insurance for all; actuarial fair annuities at retirement; automatic COLA adjustments; and extremely low cost/high efficiency (administrative costs are approximately equal to 0.8 percent of benefits).
7. The details are in Eisner's book, *Social Security: More, Not Less* (1998a).
8. The government implemented benefit cuts (in the form of an increase in the retirement age) and increased payroll in accordance with the Greenspan Commission's recommendations.
9. Although the federal government does not currently exercise the right to set prices, it certainly could do so. The NYTA is, in effect, buying dollars (that is, selling subway tokens for dollars). The difference between the NYTA and the federal government is that the former sets the price it is willing to pay for dollars (that is, 1 subway ride per 1.5 dollars) and lets the quantity of tokens it issues float, while the latter sets the quantity of dollars that will be issued (via the congressional budget) and lets the price of the goods and services it buys float (via market determination). The government's power to set prices is discussed in Wray (1999).
10. Krugman should realize this, since he uses the international accounting identity that shows that the public sector surplus is equal to the public sector deficit plus the balance of payments surplus in his textbook with Maurice Obstfeld (2004).
11. Eisner knew better, explaining, 'the federal government can always create what money it needs to service its debt. In this fundamental sense, then, federal debt is different from private debt or, for that matter, the debt of state and local governments, which do not have the power to create money. Thus the federal government has no reason ever to default on its debt or declare bankruptcy' (Eisner, 1993, p. 1).
12. Jamie Galbraith is an obvious alternative, but he has taken something of a Krugman-like position, arguing that minor adjustments to the trust funds may one day be necessary, but that the shortfalls can be covered by tapping other revenues to pay pensions (2004). Thus, Galbraith writes as if the government must locate an alternative revenue

source when benefit payments begin to outpace payroll tax receipts. This seems unfortunate, since the case could be made so much more easily by adopting the modern money view and emphasizing the government's full potential under a fiat money system.

REFERENCES

Baker, D. and M. Weisbrot (2000), 'Social security: the phony crisis', Center for Economic and Policy Research, accessed 5 March at www.cepr.net/columns/baker_weisbrot/2000_03.htm.

Bell, S. and L.R. Wray (2000), 'Financial aspects of the social security "problem" ', *Journal of Economic Issues*, **34** (2) June, 357–64.

Eisner, R. (1993), 'Federal debt', *The Concise Encyclopedia of Economics*, Liberty Fund, accessed 5 March 2000 at www.econlib.org/LIBRARY/Enc/FederalDebt.html.

Eisner, R. (1997), 'Whatever you call it, a tax goes to the Treasury', *Wall Street Journal*, 29 July, editorial page.

Eisner, R. (1998a), *Social Security: More, Not Less*, New York: Century Foundation/Twentieth Century Fund Report.

Eisner, R. (1998b), 'Save social security from its saviors', *Journal of Post Keynesian Economics*, **21** (1), 77–92.

Frank, E. (1999), 'The myth of the Social Security Trust Fund', *Dollars and Sense: The Magazine of Economic Justice*, May/June, accessed 5 March, 2000 at www.dollarsandsense.org/archives/1999/0599.html.

Galbraith, J.K. (2004), 'Schieffer was wrong, Kerry was right', accessed 10 December at http//dir.salon.com/story/opinion/feature/2004/10/14/social_security/index.html.

Galbraith, J.K. (2004), 'Social security scare campaign', 31 August, accessed 9 May 2008 at http://archive.salon.com/opinion/feature/2004/08/31/elderly/index.html.

Greenspan, A. (1997), remarks at the Catholic University of Leuven, January 17, *Bank for International Settlements Review*, accessed 5 March 2000 at www.bis.org/review.

Krugman, P. (2004a), transcript from an interview with Amy Goodman, *Democracy Now!*, website, accessed at www.democracynow.org/article.pl?sid=04/12/21/1535228.

Krugman, P. (2004b). 'Social security – inventing a crisis', *New York Times*, December 8, accessed at www.zmag.org/content/showarticle.cfm?ItemID=6823.

Krugman, P. (2004c), 'Social security scares', *New York Times*, 3 April.

Krugman, P. (2005), 'Confusions about social security', *The Economist's Voice*, **2** (1) The Berkeley Electronic Press, accessed at www.beepress.com.

Krugman, P. and Maurice Obstfeld (2004), *International Economics: Theory and Policy*, 6th edn, Reading, MA: Addison-Wesley Longman.

Mitchell, W. and W. Mosler (2005), 'Essential elements of a modern monetary economy with applications to social security privatization and the intergenerational debate', Center of Full Employment and Equity Working Paper No. 05-01, accessed at www.warrenmosler.com/docs/FebruaryWorkshop.htm.

Mosler, W. and M. Forstater (2005), 'Social security: another case of innocent fraud?', C-FEPS special report 05/01, Kansas City, MO: Center for Full

Employment and Price Stability, accessed 30 January at www.cfeps.org/pubs/sr/sr0501/sr0501.html.

Orr, D. (2005), 'Social security Q&A: separating fact from fiction', *Dollars and Sense: The Magazine of Economic Justice*, May/June, accessed 30 January at www.dollarsandsense.org/archives/2005/0505orr.html.

Wray, L.R. (1999), 'Subway tokens and social security', C-FEPS policy note 99/02, Kansas City, MO: Center for Full Employment and Price Stability, January, accessed 5 March, 2000 at www.cfeps.org/pubs/pn/pn9902.

PART V

Modern development and extensions of Keynesian economics

13. Investment finance and financial sector development

Bokhyun Cho*

INTRODUCTION

Keynes emphasized that the amount of real investment is the most important factor for determining the level of and the change in output and employment, and investment decision making and finance is mainly influenced by the activities in the financial sector. Although Keynes's argument sometimes involved debates, the arguments have been strengthened and developed by Post Keynesian economists.

Post Keynesians, following Keynes, argue that the expectation formation and liquidity preference under uncertainty in the financial sector have an important influence on the investment finance and investment decision making in the real sector. Banks control the amount and terms of money supply required for investment according to their liquidity preference. Financial markets influence the level of and the change in investment through their daily revaluation of investment project's prospective yield.

Post Keynesians, however, hardly discussed the effects of structural development of the financial sector on the change in expectation formation and liquidity preference in the financial sector, and hence on the investment finance and investment decision making.[1] A deeper investigation of the dynamics of the financial sector, therefore, is necessary in order to assess the workings of contemporary financial sector development and to search for a better financial system in line with Keynes's principle of effective demand.

This chapter aims to analyze the effects of the development of the financial sector on the changes in investment finance and investment decision making. We shall argue that the development of the financial sector following liberalization and innovation has made investment finance and investment decision making more unstable and insecure,

* I would like to thank Randall Wray, Eric Tymoigne, Tae-hee Jo and an anonymous referee for their helpful comments.

thus making investment expenditures become more stagnant and even decline.

The rest of the chapter is organized as follows. The following section reviews Keynes's arguments and the later discussions on the relation between investment and the financial sector. The third section explores the implication of financial liberalization and innovation during the past three decades from a Post Keynesian view. The fourth section examines the effects of financial sector development on investment finance and investment decision making. The final section concludes and discusses policy implications.

RELATIONSHIP BETWEEN INVESTMENT AND THE FINANCIAL SECTOR

Keynes on Investment Finance and Investment Decision Making

Keynes developed the argument that the level of output and employment as a whole depends on the amount of investment. It is 'not because investment is the only factor on which aggregate output depends, but because it is usual in a complex system to regard as the *causa causans* that factor which is most prone to sudden and wide fluctuation' (Keynes 1937a, 121). The major reason for the investment fluctuation, especially in the monetary production economy, is that investment is greatly influenced by activities in the financial sector, in which the formation of expectation and the liquidity preference have a definite role.

According to Keynes, the activities of the financial sector can influence investment through two different processes. The first process, which is relevant to investment decisions, is through the effects of the financial market at the investment expenditure level. The formation of and change in the expectation of future revenue determines the level and change of the price of securities, which, in turn, determines the level and change in the demand price of investment goods.

In *A Treatise on Money*, Keynes argues that the changes in the financial situation which are reflected in security prices can influence the attractiveness of investments and the amount of money available for the investment (Keynes 1930, pp. 225–7). The security prices are determined by the expectation of future profit and the opinion represented by the magnitude of a bear position. Thus, investment decision making is influenced by security prices which are determined in the financial market.

Also, in *The General Theory of Employment, Interest, and Money*, Keynes argues that the daily revaluation of the stock exchange exerts a decisive influence on the rate of current investment:

> For there is no sense in building up a new enterprise at a cost greater than that at which a similar existing enterprise can be purchased; whilst there is an inducement to spend on a new project what may seem an extravagant sum, if it can be floated off on the Stock Exchange at an immediate profit. (Keynes 1936, p. 151)

Therefore, the revaluation of the stock exchange is likely to be volatile because it is carried out by convention which is apt to be precarious. The precariousness is even amplified by some factors emerging in the process of the organized investment markets' development.[2]

The second process is associated with the supply of investment finance by the financial system, which was relevant to investment finance after the investment decision making was completed. Keynes emphasized that the finance, which is an advance provision of cash that is required by the current decision to invest, is mainly supplied by banks, not by *ex ante* saving, thus banks hold the key position in the transition from a lower to a higher scale of activity (Keynes 1937b, 1937c). While banks, along with individuals and financial markets, provide investment finance for firms, the supply of investment finance by banks depends on the existing state of liquidity preference of banks and the supply of money as governed by the policy of the banking system.

Apparently, the long-term issue market is also needed to fund a firm's short-term obligation in this process. Keynes states:

> [T]he entrepreneur when he decides to invest has to be satisfied on two points: firstly, that he can obtain sufficient short-term finance during the period of producing the investment; and secondly, that he can eventually fund his short-term obligations by a long-term issue on satisfactory condition. (Keynes 1937b, p. 217)

Keynes, however, did not explain about the long-term issue in detail.

Post Keynesians on Investment Finance

There have been various rebuttals and defenses about Keynes's arguments within the Post Keynesian camp. First, on the role of banks in providing investment finance, Moore raised questions about Keynes's argument that banks stood firm and refused to provide more cash to satisfy the finance, the interest rate must rise until sufficient cash is released from inactive balances. He argued against Keynes that banks in the overdraft system would not refuse the loan demand, and banks always accommodate the demand for credit by creditworthy borrowers without any effects on the interest rate. Banks have no reason to refuse the demand for a loan as long as borrowers remain within their allotted credit limits (Moore 1995).[3] Thus, banks do not have any direct control over the amount of finance or any influence on short-term interest rates; they only accommodate a loan demand at a constant interest rate passively.

Moore's refutation of Keynes is, however, too extreme and unrealistic, as Wray (1992, 1995) pointed out correctly. Wray developed the view that banks do not fully accommodate the demand for finance, or that the price of credit tends to rise with increases in its supply. This is because as loan expansion reduces bank liquidity and increases a risk of default, 'banks will use a combination of price and quantity rationing when supplying credit' (Wray 1992, p. 1162). According to Wray, banks control the money supply based upon their expectations, liquidity preference, leverage ratio, and upon the innovation and the competition among them. Thus, the argument that banks are always passive is misleading.

Banks hold the key position, not because they fully accommodate the demand for finance, but because they control the amount and terms of money supply required for investment. The important implication which must be derived from this discussion is how to change banks' attitude to finance supply and how to design the banking system to provide the investment finance under the changing financial environment in a stable and sufficient manner.

Second, Asimakopulos (1983, 1986) raised the question about how the investment expansion can be financed and funded without *ex ante* saving by households. Keynes argued that finance covering the interregnum is necessarily self-liquidating for the community taken as a whole at the end of the interim period. For Asimakopulos, however, self-liquidating is impossible as long as there is no increased saving. As firms obtain short-term finance with the expectation of being able to fund short-term obligations by long-term issue at reasonable terms, saving is necessary to purchase the long-term security. But,

> [T]his increase in desired saving does not occur simultaneously with the expenditure of the newly acquired increase in investment finance, even though *ex post* investment and *ex post* saving are always equal by definition. It takes place only when the full multiplier effects of an increase in investment have worked themselves out. (Asimakopulos 1986, p. 83)

Consequently, he concludes that the achievement of higher investment may, in certain circumstances, be contingent on the expectation of substantial increase in the flow of savings into the securities market (ibid., p. 88).

Some Post Keynesians, however, argue against Asimakopulos and state that the liquidity of a bank can be replenished without the multiplier process (Kregel 1984–5, 1986; Graziani 1986), and that the sale of long-term securities does not depend on the increased saving, but on the marginal propensity to purchase securities which is determined by savers' liquidity preference (Davidson 1986). According to Kregel (1984–5), as soon as finance expends, it increases the income of households and firms and the incomes return to the banking system if the demand of transaction balance by the public does not increase. Consequently the liquidity of the banking system can be restored immediately. Davidson (1986) also argues that although all new long-term securities cannot be sold at the original offer price, it is not because of the shortage of saving, but because of the shortage of willingness to purchase. If marginal propensity to purchase securities is less than unity, the new securities cannot be sold, even though desired household savings equals investment. Thus, the investment fund and the following investment finance are constrained by the liquidity preference determining the marginal propensity to purchase securities, not by the increased savings as Asimakopulos argued.

The discussion between Asimakopulos and others confirmed that Keynes's argument that the investment market can become congested through a shortage of cash, not through a shortage of saving, is valid and the shortage of cash is due to the liquidity preference of the public. Along with the first debate, this discussion gives us insight that the stable liquidity preference of banks and the public and banks' willingness to lending are necessary to finance and fund increased investment.

Third, it is still controversial whether the influence of the stock market on investment is negative or positive. While Keynes believes that the stock market has a negative impact on investment decision making and finance, Bernstein (1998) argues it has a positive one. Keynes argues that as the stock market develops, the revaluation of the stock exchange is very precarious and speculation is generalized. As a result, 'when the capital development of a country becomes a by-product of the activities of a casino, the job is likely to be ill-done' (Keynes 1936, p. 159). Contrary to Keynes, Bernstein emphasizes the benefit of the stock market as follows: 'the stock market is a vehicle for risk management as much as for risk taking . . . the institution of the stock market has encouraged a higher overall level of risk taking over time than would have been likely under other circumstances' (Bernstein 1998, p. 17). In particular, the liquidity, which is the dominant element in the stock market, enables investors to take the risk of making an investment.

There has been no significant discussion about this subject among Post Keynesian economists. However, the role of the stock market for investment decision making and finance is very important from the theoretical and practical perspectives. We shall investigate this in the following sections.

There are two implications of these discussions. One is that the expectation formation and liquidity preference in the financial sector have an important influence on the investment finance and decision making in the real sector. The other is that it is necessary to discuss further how the long-run development of the financial sector, that is, financial liberalization and innovation which has been developed during the past three decades, affects the change in expectation formation and liquidity preference in the financial sector, and hence investment finance and investment decision making. It is important to understand why real investment has been stagnant in most countries since the 1980s.

DEVELOPMENT OF THE FINANCIAL SECTOR

Financial Liberalization and Innovation

The financial sector in many countries has undergone widespread structural changes during the last three decades. Activities in the financial sector have followed the market principle rather than the regulation and direction of government. Furthermore, the pursuit of the financial sector's liquidity and profitability can be strengthened considerably due to the deregulation in this sector.

By the early 1970s, most countries had regulations governing the financial sector which included controls on long- and short-term interest rates and the allocation of credit, the issue of securities and the commission rates, and the line of business among financial institutions. These regulations had been imposed in many countries in order to stabilize the banking system by means of restriction of competition on the one hand, and in order to allocate the finance to preferred industries and to stabilize the security prices on the other.

The regulations in the financial sector achieved the desired goals to provide the funds and finance to firms sufficiently to stabilize the financial sector, even if they sometimes brought about corruption between government and firms in some countries. This was because the change in liquidity preference in the financial sector, which appeared as the fluctuation of interest rates, could be controlled appropriately and the activities of liquidity pursuit, which appeared as the short termism of lending, could be restricted adequately. From Keynes's point of view, it can be interpreted as follows: financial regulations allowed financial institutions to provide investment finance in a more stable manner and firms to make sound investment decisions through stabilizing the liquidity preference and controlling the liquidity pursuit appropriately.

During the past three decades, however, these regulations have been removed or mitigated in developed and developing countries.[4] Deregulation of the control on the lending and borrowing interest rates was generally taken in the 1980s in the developed countries and in the early 1990s in the developing countries. Deregulation of controls on allocation of credit also occurred between the 1980s and the early 1990s. In the security markets in many countries, access to the security industry, fixed commission rates and various other price and quantity controls were liberalized during the same period, and the regulation of bank activities and the separation of the banking and security business were also eliminated.

In addition to liberalization, new financial instruments have been introduced in order to avoid the interest rate regulation and to fund the liability of financial institutions. Moreover, new financial techniques in the management of assets and liabilities have been developed to enhance the liquidity of financial institutions. New financial instruments include commercial paper which has been issued since 1960 in the United States, and CD, RP, MMF and MMDA have been issued since the 1960s and 1970s.[5] The new financial technique of securitization[6] began with the development of mortgage-backed security in 1975 in the US, and it was introduced in 1987 in the UK and in 1992 in France. These financial deregulations and financial innovations have made the financial sector more market and liquidity oriented in setting prices, allocating credit and entering a new business line.

Development of the Financial Sector

The financial liberalization and innovation have brought about extensive structural and behavioral changes in the financial market and financial activities. First, the structural changes include the rise in the volatility of interest rates and stock prices, the shift of the center of financial activities from banks to stock market, and the growth of liquidity in the financial sector.

Interest rates and stock prices have risen and their volatility has increased since financial liberalization. Both the money market and the lending interest rates have risen persistently since the 1980s and the volatility of interest rates has become very high in both developed and developing countries (Honohan 2001). The volatility of stock prices has also increased substantially at the level of individual firms, although the market as a whole has shown a stable trend (Campbell et al. 2001).[7]

The center of financial activities has shifted from banks to capital markets. While the role of banks in the financial sector was weakened, the role of capital markets has grown and strengthened more and more during the 1980s and 1990s. Deregulation of the securities industry entry and of the commission rate in developed countries allowed individual investors to invest a larger part of their savings in the stock markets. Between 1983 and

1993, world stock market capitalization grew from $2 trillion to $10 trillion, which implies an average annual growth rate of 15 percent (Demirguc-Kunt and Levine 1995).

The liquidity in the financial sector increased dramatically in the 1980s and 1990s. The shortening of the maturities of bank loans and the rise in the trade value of the stock market greatly increased the liquidity in the financial market,[8] as did securitization.

Further, behavioral changes in the financial activities have occurred in the liquidity preference of banks and individuals and the lending pattern of banks. The liquidity preference of banks and individuals has fluctuated more rapidly and widely due to the increase of uncertainty which has come from the unstable financial market and the absence of government guarantees for financial institutions and firms. Financial liberalization increased the volatility of interest rate and stock prices, and freed banks to pursue liquidity and profitability. These institutional changes, which increased uncertainty, rendered the fortune of banks and individuals more dependent on their subjective expectations. Consequently the liquidity preference of banks and individuals has fluctuated more since financial liberalization.

Banks' lending patterns have changed markedly. Bank lending shifted from relationship lending to non-relationship (transaction) lending, and from industrial lending to proprietary investment lending. The management of a bank's assets changed to a more market-oriented approach, where bank lending was carried out based on the credit score of borrowers and the interest rate offered by borrowers rather than the long-run relationship with their customers. In particular, as became common in countries which experienced financial crisis after financial liberalization, banks increased their lending to speculators who invested their debt in real estate or equity.[9]

The structural and behavioral changes in the financial sector will have a considerable influence on investment decision making and investment finance. Since financial liberalization and innovation, banks have more power to control investment finance and the public have more ways of seeking liquidity. Also, firms have greater opportunities to obtain investment finance, but simultaneously they also encounter more unstable obstacles to acquiring finance, as well as a more uncertain and capricious basis from which to make investment decisions.

DEVELOPMENT OF THE FINANCIAL SECTOR AND INVESTMENT

As we examined above, financial liberalization and innovation have changed the financial market structure and the financial behavior of banks and individuals through the influence on the expectation formation and liquidity preference in the financial sector. They have also had an effect on the dynamic roles of the financial sector in making the investment decisions of firms, providing investment finance, allocating investment, and deciding investment objectives.

Rise in the Instability of Investment Finance and Decision Making

The changes in the financial sector have given rise to dynamic effects on investment in two areas: the rise in the instability of investment finance and the increase in the insecurity of investment decision making.

First, the rise in the instability of investment finance resulted from the increased volatility of the interest rate and the increased sensitivity of bank lending to the change in economic circumstances, which reflect the liquidity preference of banks and individuals. The increase in the volatility of interest rates is due to the amplified fluctuation in the liquidity preference of banks and individuals after financial liberalization. Minsky put forward an explanation for how the change in interest rates affects the size of investment finance. He analyzes how the demand price of capital assets has fallen as long-term interest rates have risen, and how the supply price of investment output has risen as short-term interest rates rise. These changes in interest rates lower investment demand (Minsky 1986, p. 195).

The increase in sensitivity of bank lending comes from the strengthened power and ability of banks to control the amount of lending according to their liquidity preference. In relation to this, Minsky argued that financial innovation is necessary for the banking system and corresponds to the changing business demand. This innovation, however, can amplify a boom and financial fragility, because a bank's lending and a firm's investment demand depend on the subjective expectation of future revenue. The optimistic expectation leads to the low evaluation of value of liquidity and to the acceptance of more aggressive financing practice. Thus 'banking and finance can be highly disruptive forces in our economy' (ibid., p. 249).

Although Minsky did not analyze the long-run change in the liquidity preference of banks after financial liberalization and the effects of liquidity preference of banks on investment finance, we can infer them from Minsky's arguments. Financial liberalization and innovation have amplified the change in the liquidity preference of banks and thereby have increased the volatility of the interest rate. If the interest rate fluctuates repeatedly and widely, investment demand and investment finance would fluctuate along with the fluctuation in interest rates, as argued by Minsky. The increased volatility of interest rates after financial liberalization, therefore, is likely to make the investment finance more unstable.

Financial liberalization and innovation also give banks the power to control the amount of lending according to their liquidity preference and the ability to expand lending with new financial techniques. Such power had been restricted by the regulation on banks' activities and the underdeveloped money markets before financial liberalization and innovation. Under the deregulated and developed financial environment, however, the movement of liquidity preference of banks can have an immediate effect on the amount of lending to firms, and make the investment finance more unstable.

Second, the rise in the insecurity of investment decision making is attributed to the increase in the volatility of stock prices, the rise of liquidity of the financial sector, and the shift in financial activities to the stock market. In combination, these increases have made expectation formation in the financial market more unstable. As we have seen above, the stock prices of individual firms have become more volatile during the last 30 years and the market as a whole has also been volatile since the mid-1990s.[10] In addition, the liquidity of the financial sector has increased as the secondary stock market has become more active. The liquidity increase in the stock market made its activity more speculative and more independent of real investment activity. According to Davidson, the deregulation of commission rates lowered the transaction cost during the last 20 years and brought about the rapid growth of day traders in the 1990s. Active financial market participants held securities only for capital gain rather than for income (Davidson 2002, p. 108).[11]

The increase in stock price volatility and stock market liquidity renders firms' investment decision making more unstable. Daily revaluation of investment projects and its independence from the fundamental value make investment decision making more insecure. With regard to this, Keynes states that 'enterprise', which is a term for the activity of forecasting the prospective yield of assets over their whole life, becomes 'the bubble on a whirl-pool of speculation' (Keynes 1936, p. 159). Then, the investment decision making becomes unstable and insecure, and investment expenditure stagnates.

Some authors argue that as the development of the secondary market increases liquidity, the volatility of stock prices becomes stable (Bernstein 1998; Davidson 2002, ch. 11). The increase in liquidity, however, cannot reduce the volatility of individual stocks, as Campbell et al. (2001) have shown. This is because the rise in liquidity does not increase the number of market participants with different opinions, but increases the number of ignorant individuals chasing mass psychology.

The instability of investment finance and the insecurity of investment decision making have caused investment to become stagnant and economic growth to become sluggish. Actually, the fixed capital formation as a percentage of GDP in the OECD as a whole shows a decreasing trend since 1970: 24.9 percent as an annual average in the 1970s, 22.9 percent in the 1980s, and 21.5 percent in the 1990s. Major developed countries like the US, Japan, Germany, the UK and France also show the same trend, not to mention the economic growth rate which has been decreasing in OECD countries as a whole – it shows 3.7 percent as an annual average percentage of GDP in the 1970s, 2.9 percent in the 1980s, and 2.6 percent in the 1990s.[12]

Changes in Investment Allocation and Investment Objectives

The changes in the financial sector have also given rise to an alteration in the investment allocation of the economy as a whole, as well as a shift in investment objectives of corporate management. The alteration of investment allocation occurred between industries and economic agents. The shift in the investment objective took place between the long-run productivity improvement and the short-run revenue maximization.

Financial liberalization enables banks to transform their lending freely from manufacturing industries to individuals who invest in real estate and equities, and from firm to consumer credits. Banks always want to increase profitability and liquidity, however, before financial liberalization, the lending line of banks was highly restricted. In many countries, governments directed banks to lend to preferred industries, but prohibited banks from lending to speculative or unproductive divisions. The regulation on banks' lending by the government restrained the banks from freely seeking profitability and liquidity. Since liberalization, however, banks have preferred short-run lending for real estate and equity investment rather than long-run lending or rollover of short-run lending for real investment of firms. Banks also prefer short-run consumer or service industry rather than firm or manufacturing industry lending in order to increase the liquidity and profitability of their assets.

But the transformation of lending allocation has brought about negative effects on the economy as a whole. Productive investment has been restricted due to the difficulty in accessing investment finance. Therefore, employment and economic growth did not increase faster than before financial liberalization. Furthermore, the increased lending in real estate and equity investment has led to a bubble and a burst in property prices, which often resulted in financial crisis.

The shift in financial activities to the stock market, as well as the development of institutional investors, has encouraged firm managers to replace their managerial goals and objectives with a focus on the maximization of shareholder value. They maximize a firm's stock value instead of maximizing market share or firm growth, because if they do not they would encounter the threat of takeover by others in the stock market and the intervention of management by institutional investors.

The development of the stock market can enhance a manager's control by subordinating the agent's to the principal's interest through takeover, in which case managers endeavor to maximize firm value. The institutional investors have a short-term horizon in assessing their financial investment performance, which forces the firm manager to have a short-term horizon for that performance. Actually, there are many external pressures on top managers from capital markets to adopt managerial short termism in determining their investment.[13]

The shareholder value maximization and the short termism of managers have resulted in the decrease in real investment through the shift from retention and reinvestment to the dividend distribution of profit on the one hand,[14] and through the growing financial investment out of profits instead of real investment on the other (see Stockhammer 2004). In addition, they have caused the redirection in investment to the short-run cost-cutting investment from the long-run productivity improvement investment.

The alteration in investment allocation and the shift in investment objectives have also contributed to the stagnant investment and the sluggish economic growth as much as the instability of investment finance and the insecurity of investment decision making. As we have seen above, the stagnant investment and the slow economic growth since the 1970s are caused by those factors which have intensified since financial liberalization.

CONCLUSION

We have analyzed the effects of the development in the financial sector on the dynamic changes in the decision making, finance, distribution, and objective of investment.

The development of the financial sector, that is, financial liberalization and innovation, has rendered investment decision making and investment finance more unstable and insecure due to the increase in the change of the liquidity preference and the expectation formation in the financial market. The development in the financial market has also brought about an alteration in investment allocation and the shift in investment objectives as a result of the pursuit of liquidity in financial activities and the institutional investors' enforcement of stockholder value maximization by the firm manager.

The increase in instability in investment finance and investment decision making and the changes in investment allocation and investment objectives, have led to stagnant investment and sluggish growth in the real sector.

From this discussion, we can see that it is necessary to construct an alternative financial system and macroeconomic policies which can stabilize the activities in the financial sector. An alternative system and policies should be designed to restrict excessive liquidity pursuing activities to stabilize the expectation formation and liquidity preference in the financial markets in order to stabilize and increase investment and economic growth. The excessive liberalization and innovation in the financial sector can only help the interests of financial capitalists, not the interests of the economy as a whole, especially with regard to the stability of employment and economic growth.

NOTES

1. Of course, Minsky (1986) and De Carvalho (1997) discussed these subjects. However, despite his emphasis on the effects of financial innovation on the financial fragility, Minsky paid little attention to the long-run change in tendency of investment finance and invest decision. While De Carvalho discussed this subject directly, he did not go forward beyond the confirmation that Keynes's argument is valid after financial innovation.
2. These factors are, according to Keynes, as follows: the increase in the number of stock owners who are ignorant about the management and the knowledge of circumstance of business; the excessive influence on market of daily fluctuations in the profitability of existing investment; a sudden fluctuation of opinion due to trivial factors; the behavior of a professional investor who foresees changes in the conventional basis of valuation a short time ahead of the general public; and the confidence of lending institutions (Keynes 1936, pp. 153–8).
3. If the liquidity of banks were not sufficient, banks could replenish it as they sell their assets and liabilities in the market in the case of an individual bank, or they go to the central bank which is always ready to supply the necessary liquidity in the case of the banking system as a whole (Moore 1988, p. 32).
4. On the concrete epoch or chronology of deregulation, see Williamson and Mahar (1998) or Kaminsky and Schmukler (2002).
5. Commercial paper issue has begun from 1960 in the US and Canada, 1985 in France, 1986 in the UK, 1987 in Japan, and 1991 in Germany (Edey and Hviding 1995).
6. Securitization used to refer to the process by which homogeneous, but illiquid, assets are pooled and repackaged, with security interests representing claims to the incoming cash flows and other economic benefits generated by the loan pool sold as securities to third-party investors (Lumpkin 1999).
7. According to Campbell et al. (2001), market and industry variances have been fairly stable, but firm-level variance displays a large and significant positive trend which has more than doubled between 1962 and 1997. The IMF (2003) also shows that the equity price volatility has experienced an upward trend since the mid-1990s and has been particularly high since 2000.
8. The increase in liquidity was outstanding in the stock market in particular. The trade value of stock has grown faster than the value of issue or the market value of stock. In the US, the trade value of stock to GDP during 1981–95 increased more than five times, while the issue value to GDP during the same period increased 1.3 times. Also in the UK, the former increased 14.5 times and the latter 1.4 times (Demirguc-Kunt and Levine 2001).

9. The increasing lending to real estate and equity investment was apparent in most countries experiencing financial crisis. See Radelet and Sachs (1998) on East Asia, and Drees and Pazarbasioglu (1998) on the three Nordic countries.
10. In fact, firm-level volatility may be more important than market or industry volatility in deciding investment for individual firms. So far, many authors have argued that stock market volatility has become more stable, but the influence on the investment of the individual firms may be the stock price of the individual firm, not the price of the market as a whole.
11. Arestis (2001) explains the increase of speculation in the stock market as follows: financial liberalization induced two types of speculative pressure – euphoric expectation and competitive – both of which contribute to the increased presence of short-term, high-risk speculative transactions.
12. These figures are calculated from *OECD Factbook 2006: Economic, Environmental and Social Statistics*, Paris: OCED.
13. For the case of the UK, see Demirag (1995, 1998); for the US, see O'Barr and Conley (1992).
14. Lazonick and O'Sullivan (2000) state: 'in the name of "shareholder value", the past two decades have witnessed a marked shift in the strategic orientation of top corporate managers in the allocation of corporate resources and turned away from "retain and reinvest" towards "downsize and distribute" '.

REFERENCES

Arestis, P. (2001), 'Recent banking and financial crises: Minsky versus the financial liberalizationists', in R. Bellofiore and P. Ferri (eds), *Financial Keynesianism and Market Instability*, Cheltenham, UK and Northampton, MA, USA: Edward Elgar, pp. 159–78.

Asimakopulos, A. (1983), 'Kalecki and Keynes on finance, investment and saving', *Cambridge Journal of Economics*, **7** (2), 221–33.

Asimakopulos A. (1986), 'Finance, liquidity, saving, and investment', *Journal of Post Keynesian Economics*, **9** (1), 79–90.

Bernstein, P.L. (1998), 'Stock market risk in a Post Keynesian world', *Journal of Post Keynesian Economics*, **21** (1), 15–24.

Campbell, J.Y., M. Lettau, B.G. Malkiel and Y. Xu (2001), 'Have individual stocks become more volatile? An empirical exploration of idiosyncratic risk', *Journal of Finance*, **61** (1), 1–43.

Davidson, P. (1986), 'Finance, liquidity, saving, and investment', *Journal of Post Keynesian Economics*, **9** (1), 101–10.

Davidson, P. (2002), *Financial Markets, Money and the Real World*, Cheltenham, UK and Northampton, MA, USA: Edward Elgar.

De Carvalho, F.J.C. (1997), 'Financial innovation and the Post Keynesian approach to the "process of capital formation"', *Journal of Post Keynesian Economics*, **19** (3), 461–88.

Demirag, I. (1995), 'Short-term performance pressures: is there a consensus view?', *European Journal of Finance*, **1**, 41–56.

Demirag, I. (1998), 'Boards of directors' short-term perceptions and evidence of managerial short-termism in the UK', *European Journal of Finance*, **4**, 195–211.

Demirguc-Kunt, A. and R. Levine (1995), 'Stock market development and financial intermediaries: stylized facts', Policy Research Working Paper 1462, World Bank, Washington, DC.

Demirguc-Kunt, A. and R. Levine (eds) (2001), *Financial Structure and Economic Growth: Cross-Country Comparisons of Banks, Markets, and Development*, Cambridge: MIT Press.
Drees, B. and C. Pazarbasioglu (1998), 'The Nordic banking crises: pitfalls in financial liberalization?', International Monetary Fund occasional paper 161, Washington, DC.
Edey, M. and Hviding, K. (1995), 'An assessment of financial reform in OECD countries', OECD Economics Department working paper no. 154, Paris.
Graziani, A. (1986), 'Keynes' finance motive: a reply', *Economic Notes*, 1.
Honohan, P. (2001), 'How interest rate changed under liberalization: a statistical review', in G. Caprio, P. Honohan and J.E. Stiglitz (eds), *Financial Liberalization: How Far, How Fast?*, Cambridge: Cambridge University Press, pp. 63–95.
International Monetary Fund (IMF) (2003), 'Financial asset price volatility: a source of instability?', Global Financial Stability Report, September, 62–88.
Kaminsky, G.L. and Schmukler, S.L. (2002), 'Short-run pain, long-run gain: the effects of financial liberalization', World Bank policy research working paper no. 2912, Washington, DC.
Keynes, J.M. (1930), *A Treatise on Money*, London: Macmillan.
Keynes, J.M. (1936), *The General Theory of Employment, Interest and Money*, London: Macmillan.
Keynes, J.M. (1937)' 'The general theory of employment', *The Quarterly Journal of Economics*, February, reprinted in *The Collected Writings of John Maynard Keynes*, vol. XIV, London: Macmillan.
Keynes, J.M. (1937b), 'Alternative theories of the rate of interest', *Economic Journal*, **47**, reprinted in *The Collected Writings of John Maynard Keynes*, vol. XIV, London: Macmillan
Keynes, J.M. (1937c), 'The "ex ante" theory of the rate of interest', *Economic Journal*, **47**, reprinted in *The Collected Writings of John Maynard Keynes*, vol. XIV, London: Macmillan.
Kregel, J.A. (1984–5), 'Constraints on the expansion of output and employment: real or monetary?', *Journal of Post Keynesian Economics*, **7** (2), 139–52.
Kregel, J.A. (1986), 'A note on finance, liquidity, saving, and investment', *Journal of Post Keynesian Economics*, **9** (1), 91–100.
Lazonick, W. and M. O'Sullivan (2000), 'Maximising shareholder value: a new ideology for corporate governance', *Economy and Society*, **29** (1), 13–35.
Lumpkin, S. (1999), 'Trends and developments in securitisation', in *Financial Market Trends*, no. 74, Paris: OECD.
Minsky, H. (1986), *Stabilizing an Unstable Economy*, New Haven, CT: Yale University Press.
Moore, B. (1988), *Horizontalists and Verticalists: The Macroeconomics of Credit Money*, Cambridge: Cambridge University Press.
Moore, B.J. (1995), 'The exogeneity of short-term interest rates: a reply to Wray', *Journal of Economic Issues*, **29** (1), 258–66.
O'Barr, W. and J. Conley (1992), 'Managing relationships: the culture of institutional investing', *Financial Analysts Journal*, September–October, 21–7.
Radelet, S. and J. Sachs (1998), 'The onset of the East Asian financial crisis', NBER working paper no. 6680, Cambridge, MA.
Stockhammer, E. (2004), 'Financialization and the slowdown of accumulation', *Cambridge Journal of Economics*, **28** (5), 719–41.

Williamson, J. and M. Mahar (1998), *A Survey of Financial Liberalization*, International Finance Section essays in international finance no. 211, Princeton, NJ: Princeton University Press.

Wray, L.R. (1992), 'Alternative approaches to money and interest rate', *Journal of Economic Issues*, **26** (4), 1145–78.

Wray, L.R. (1995), 'Keynesian monetary theory: liquidity preference or black box horizontalism?', *Journal of Economic Issues*, **29** (1), 273–82.

14. Keynes's theory of probability, investment behavior, and behavioral finance

Edwin Dickens

INTRODUCTION

This chapter is a contribution to the Post Keynesian literature (for example, Carabelli, 1988; O'Donnell, 1989; and Gerrard, 1992 (on the link between Keynes's theory of probability (that is, Keynes, 1921 [1973]: Part I) and his theory of investment behavior (that is, Keynes, 1936 [1964]: Book IV). My interpretation of this link is as follows: for any given investment project, Keynes shows that the probability of the payoff, and thus the expected profit, is less than the estimates of orthodox economists. To substantiate my interpretation, I make reference to the behavioral-finance literature on the winner's curse, betting quotients, preference reversals and loss aversion.[1]

For Keynes, the major problem with orthodox probability theory is the concept of risk that it implies. The orthodox concept of risk is derived from the definition of probability in terms of the principle of non-sufficient reason. However, orthodox economists assume, often implicitly, that it is also implied by the definition of probability in terms of the law of large numbers.[2]

In contrast, Keynes derives his concept of risk from the definition of probability in terms of the logical relationship between propositions, which opens the way for him to introduce the concept of the weight of arguments. Consequently, this chapter is structured as follows.

In the next section, I derive the orthodox concept of risk from the definition of probability in terms of the principle of non-sufficient reason. I then explain why the winner's curse invalidates this concept of risk, in so far as explanations of investment behavior are concerned. The third section will show how the orthodox concept of risk appears to follow from the definition of probability in terms of the law of large numbers. I then show that empirical data on betting quotients invalidate even this vitiated form of the orthodox concept of risk. The fourth section uses the definition of probability as a logical relationship between propositions to explain Keynes's concepts of risk and the weight of arguments. With reference to preference reversals and loss aversion, I then argue for the validity of these concepts. The final section provides a conclusion.

THE PRINCIPLE OF NON-SUFFICIENT REASON

Keynes (1921 [1973]: Part I) points out that risk is an ambiguous concept, its meaning depends on how we define probability. Probability has three distinct meanings, depending upon whether it is defined in terms of the principle of non-sufficient reason, the law of large numbers, or the logical relationship between propositions.

The first and most ancient meaning of probability is derived from the principle of non-sufficient reason. It can be traced back to James Bernouilli, who founded mathematical probability in the 18th century, and is the most easily refuted because, as Keynes (1936 [1964]: 152) points out, its application to human affairs 'leads to absurdities'.

According to the principle of non-sufficient reason, if we do not have a reason to assign different probabilities to a set of possible outcomes or events or propositions, then we must assign them equal probabilities. Starting with Markowitz (1959 [1991]), this principle has become the basis for the paradigmatic explanation of investment behavior among orthodox economists. We are asked to assume that investors ascertain all possible outcomes of an investment project (measured in terms of dollars of return). Investors are able to use the principle of non-sufficient reason to assign a probability to each possible outcome of an investment project, with the sum of assigned probabilities equal to one. The expected profit from the investment project is then taken to be the mathematical mean of the sum of the products of each outcome and its probability.

The orthodox concept of risk is derived from the principle of non-sufficient reason as thus applied to investment decisions. That is to say, orthodox economists define the risk of an investment project as the variability (or standard deviation), of the products of each possible outcome and its probability, around its mathematical mean.

Following Capen et al. (1971), the refutation of this explanation of investor behavior has come to be called the 'winner's curse'. Capen et al. examined the bids made by companies for oil-drilling rights on parcels of land in the Gulf of Mexico and the North Slope of Alaska in the 1950s and 1960s. Each bid for rights was unbiased and equally likely to be correct. Therefore, the principle of non-sufficient reason implies that the mathematical mean of the amounts bid by different companies for oil-drilling rights on each parcel of land represented the true value of those rights. But of course it was the highest bidder who received the rights in each case. Therefore, the winning bid was invariably higher than the true value of the rights, prompting Capen et al. (1971, pp. 652–3) to conclude as follows: 'He who bids on a parcel what he thinks it is worth, will, in the long run, be taken for a cleaning' (also see Bazerman and Samuelson, 1983 and Kagel and Levin, 1986).

In other words, instead of explaining investment decisions, the application of the principle of non-sufficient reason to them implies that no rational person would ever undertake an investment project. As Keynes said, this is clearly absurd. Consequently, the orthodox concept of risk is also refuted by means of *reductio ad absurdum*.[3]

THE LAW OF LARGE NUMBERS

The second meaning of probability is derived from the law of large numbers, or of statistical frequency. It can be traced back to Leslie Ellis in the 19th century, and there is a narrow class of cases to which it applies. However, investment projects which involve the purchase of capital assets are not members of that class.

According to the law of large numbers, we can define probability (p_o) as follows:

$$p_o = m/n, \tag{14.1}$$

where m is the number of occurrences of an outcome or event and n is the number of possible occasions for the outcome or event to occur.

The law of large numbers applies to games of chance, such as coin tosses or wheels of fortune. On the assumption that investment projects resemble games of chance, orthodox economists follow Markowitz (1959 [1991]: 39 ff) and define expected profit (E_o) as follows:

$$E_o = p_o A, \tag{14.2}$$

where A is the payoff from the investment project, if it is successful.

Since p_o implies a value derived from a large number of instances, E_o appears to still be the mathematical mean of the sum of the products of each outcome and its probability. Consequently, orthodox economists assume that the risk of an investment project has still been taken into account by the variability (or standard deviation), of the products of each possible outcome and its probability, around E_o.

For example, assume that people are asked the following question: how much are you willing to pay in order to receive \$1 in the event of the next toss of a coin turning up heads, but nothing in the event of the next coin toss turning up tails? The answers people give to this question give their betting quotients, and orthodox economists assume that a rational investor will use equations (14.1) and (14.2) to calculate them. That is to say, if n_1 is the number of coin tosses and m_1 is the number of times that heads occurs then, according to equation 1, $p_o = m_1/n_1 = 0.5$. It thus follows from equation (14.2) that the expected profit (E_o) from an investment in the next coin toss is E_o = 0.5 (\$1) = \$0.50. In other words, orthodox economists assume that rational investors will calculate a betting quotient of \$0.50 in this case (that is, they will be willing to pay \$0.50 for the right to receive \$1 in the event of the next coin toss turning up heads but nothing in the event of it turning up tails).

Unfortunately (for orthodox economists), Hershey and Schomaker (1985) found that, in this case, people typically calculate a betting quotient of \$0.40. In the fourth section, I argue that this is because people weigh equation (14.1), not as the determinant of the probability of the payoff from an investment project, but as one argument among others which must be considered in determining that probability.

PROBABILITY AS A LOGICAL RELATIONSHIP BETWEEN PROPOSITIONS

The third meaning of probability, and the modified meaning of expected profit implied by it, was first formulated by Keynes (1921 [1973]: 3–9) as follows:

$$p_k = a \mid h \tag{14.3}$$

$$E_k = p_k A, \tag{14.4}$$

where p_k is what we now call (post-) Bayesian probability (see, for example, Rottenstreich and Tversky, 1997); h is a set of propositions which constitute the premises of an argument; a is the set of propositions (or more often the proposition) which constitutes its conclusion; A is still the payoff, if the investment project is successful, but the probability (p_k) assigned to A in order to estimate the expected profit (E_k) is now obtained from equation (14.3) rather than equation (14.1).

Equation (14.3) can be read as 'proposition a on the hypothesis h has a probability p_k'. Alternatively, it can be read as 'the conclusion a can be inferred from the evidence h with a probability of p_k'.

If $a \mid h = 1$, then the hypothesis h implies the conclusion a with certainty. If $a \mid h = 0$, then hypothesis h implies that the conclusion a is impossible. If $0 < p_k < 1$, then there is a probability relation of degree p_k between a and h.

The concepts of the weight of arguments and risk will now be introduced as factors determining our degree of belief (p_k) in a conclusion (a) following from its premises (h).

The Weight of Arguments

The concept of the weight of arguments (w) can be formulated as follows (see Keynes, 1921 [1973]: 77–80):[4]

$$p_k = w\ (a \mid h), \tag{14.5}$$

where $0 < w < 1$.

For example, the data on betting quotients above can be explained as follows:

$$p_{o1} = a_1 \mid h_1 = 0.5;\ E_{o1} = p_{o1}\ (A_1) = \$0.50, \tag{14.6}$$

$$p_{k1} = w_1\ (a_1 \mid h_1) = 0.4;\ E_{k1} = P_{k1}\ (A_1) = \$0.40, \tag{14.7}$$

where a_1 is $A_1 = \$1$; h_1 is a set of propositions, including $m_1/n_1 = 0.5$; and $w_1 = 0.8$. In equation (14.6) the proposition $m_1/n_1 = 0.5$ is dominant, but in equations (14.7) other propositions in h_1 weigh against it.

In equations (14.6) and (14.7), the underlying causal structure, which determines the payoff from the investment project, is both knowable and known. It was thus possible to compare the estimates obtained from equations (14.1) and (14.2) with those obtained from equations (14.3) and (14.4) in terms of numerical values.

Unlike equations (14.1) and (14.2), equations (14.3) and (14.4) apply to two classes of cases which cannot be evaluated in terms of numerical values. None the less, it is shown below that a formal relationship of inequality can still be ascertained between the estimates obtained from equations (14.1) and (14.2) and those obtained from equations (14.3) and (14.4).

The two classes of cases are those in which the underlying causal structure is knowable but unknown[5] and those in which it is unknowable.[6]

For example, suppose that, while waiting to board an airplane, I consider investing in an insurance policy which costs \$1 and will pay \$250,000 if I die in an airplane crash. At first glance, the problem confronting me is as follows:

$$p_{k2} = a_2 \mid h_2 = 1/250{,}000, \tag{14.8}$$

where a_2 is 'I will die in an airplane crash' and h_2 is a set of propositions of which 'I can buy a $250,000 flight insurance policy for $1' is dominant.

However, there are other propositions in h_2 which may weigh against the dominant one. On the one hand, I may interpret my investment opportunity as a member of the class of cases with a knowable causal structure which is unknown to me. Consequently, I may re-formulate the problem as follows:

$$p_{k3} = w_2\ (a_2 \mid h_2) < 1/250{,}000, \tag{14.9}$$

where w_2 reflects the fact that the proposition in h_2 'the insurance company knows the statistical frequency of airplane crashes and expects to profit by offering the flight insurance' weighs against the dominant one. In other words, I suspect that:

$$a_2 \mid h_2 > a_2 \mid h_2 \cdot m_2/n_2, \tag{14.10}$$

where m_2 is the number of people who have died in airplane crashes and n_2 is the number of people who have flown in airplanes. As a result, I assign a weight (w_2) to the argument for a_2 in such a way that it becomes less probable (p_{k3}) than the probability implicit in the offer of the flight insurance (p_{k2}). In short, I will not buy the flight insurance.

On the other hand, I may interpret my investment opportunity as a member of the class of cases with an unknowable causal structure. Perhaps the growing threat of blowback from the Middle East conflict in the form of terrorist attacks implies that the statistical frequency (m_2 / n_2) of airplane crashes in the past no longer represents the causal structure which will determine the truth of a_2. I may thus re-formulate the problem as follows:

$$p_{k4} = w_3\ (a_2 \mid h_2) > 1/250{,}000, \tag{14.11}$$

where w_3 reflects the fact that the proposition in h_2 'the insurance company has failed to take into account the fundamental uncertainty of the current situation' weighs against the dominant one. In short, I will buy the flight insurance.

Risk

The problem with the orthodox concept of risk as the variance (or standard deviation), of the products of each possible outcome of an investment project and its probability, around the expected profit (E_o) is that it includes the possibility that the actual profit of an investment project will exceed the expected profit. Risk (R) only results from the possibility that the actual profit will fall short of the expected profit. For this reason, it can be defined as follows (see Keynes, 1921 [1973]: 348):

$$R = q\, E_o, \tag{14.12}$$

where $q = 1 - p_o$.

Equation (14.12) is formulated in such a way that risk (R) represents the cost of insurance against the loss of the money wagered on an investment project. The cost of re-insurance to the insurer (R_1) would then be $qR = q^2E_o$. If the re-insurance company buys re-insurance (R_2), and that re-insurance company buys re-insurance and so on, then the risk of loss is eliminated, but so is the expected profit (that is, $E_o + R_1 + R_2 + \ldots = E_o (1 + q + q^2 + \ldots) = E_o / 1 - q = E_o / p_o = A$). In short, equation (14.12) is formulated in such a way that it is only by bearing some risk of loss that potential investors can expect to profit.

Equation (14.12) can be used to show how risk, like the weight of arguments, is a factor determining the degree of belief (p_k) in a conclusion (a) following from its premises (h). That is to say, we can write (see ibid.: 348):

$$p_k = 2\, p_o\, w \,/\, (1 + q)\ (1 + w). \tag{14.13}$$

Equation (14.13) is formulated in such a way that two conditions are met: If $p_o = 1$ and $w = 1$, then $p_k = 1$; and if $p_o = 0$ and $w = 0$, then $p_k = 0$. It follows that, for any values of p_o and/or w between 0 and 1, $p_k < p_o$; therefore, $E_k < E_o$.

For example, Thaler and Tversky (1992) conducted an experiment based on the following two bets:

$$\text{Bet One: } a \text{ is `}A = \$4\text{' and } p_o = 8/9; \tag{14.14}$$

$$\text{Bet Two: } a \text{ is `}A = \$40\text{' and } p_o = 1/9.$$

What they found was a 'preference reversal'. That is to say, Thaler and Tversky found that people who owned the bets valued Bet Two more highly than Bet One, but when the same people owned cash and were offered the opportunity to invest in the bets, they valued Bet One more highly than Bet Two.

From the perspective of orthodox probability theory, the preference of the owners of the bets is easily explained. We simply plug the numbers from equations (14.14) into equation (14.2) and get:

$$\text{Bet One: } E_o = p_o\, A = 8/9\ (4) = \$3.56, \qquad (14.15)$$

$$\text{Bet Two: } E_o = p_o\, A = 1/9\ (40) = \$4.44.$$

In short, Bet Two has more value than Bet One (that is, the expected profit from owning Bet Two is \$4.44, as opposed to an expected profit of \$3.56 from owning Bet One).

However, for this very reason, the preference of the investors for Bet One is an unexplained anomaly from the perspective of orthodox probability theory. Behavioral economists attribute it to 'loss aversion', which they define as an asymmetry of value whereby people tend to judge the disutility of giving up something they own to be greater than the utility of acquiring it anew (see, for example, Kahneman and Tversky, 1984). Or, dropping the language of utilitarianism, 'loss aversion' denotes the fact that changes which make things worse loom larger in people's judgments of probability than changes which make them better.

As such, loss aversion is explained by plugging the numbers from equations (14.14) into equations (14.13) and (14.4). Since the weight of arguments (w) is not an issue in this case, $w = 1$. Therefore, equation (14.13) becomes: $p_k = p_o\ /\ 1 + q$ and we get:

$$\text{Bet One: } p_k = p_o\ /1 + q = 8/9\ /1 + 1/9 = 0.8; \qquad (14.16)$$

$$\text{Bet Two: } p_k = p_o\ /1 + q = 1/9\ /1 + 8/9 = 0.06.$$

$$\text{Bet One: } E_k = p_k\ (A) = 0.8\ (4) = \$3.20; \qquad (14.17)$$

$$\text{Bet Two: } E_k = p_k\ (A) = 0.06\ (40) = \$2.40.$$

In short, investors value Bet One more highly than Bet Two (that is, an investment in Bet One has an expected profit of \$3.20, as opposed to an expected profit of \$2.40 for Bet Two). This result not only explains the preference reversal but also suggests that equation (14.12) provides a formulation of risk understood as loss aversion.

CONCLUSION

In this chapter I interpret Keynes's theory of probability as encompassing the orthodox theory of probability. I provide evidence from the behavioral-finance literature which suggests that, for any investment project, Keynes's estimates of the probability of the payoff, and thus of the expected profit, are less than the estimates of orthodox economists.

Since Keynes's theory of probability applies to situations characterized by fundamental uncertainty (that is, the underlying causal structure is unknowable), it is not always possible to assign a numerical value to his estimates of the probability of the payoff from investment projects. None the less, even when there is fundamental uncertainty, I show that it is still possible to ascertain that Keynes's estimates of probability and expected profit are less than the corresponding estimates of orthodox economists.

NOTES

1. Fontana and Gerrard (2004: 628–31) also make reference to the behavioral-finance literature to substantiate Keynes's theory of probability.
2. Davidson (1996: 479; and also see Solow, 1985: 330) emphasizes the role of the law of large numbers in orthodox probability theory. My analysis of the role of the principle of non-sufficient reason amplifies his analysis.
3. Thayer (1992a: 52–3) extends the oil-drilling example to the hypothetical case of a company which has won oil-drilling rights to a parcel of land. He asks us to assume that, if the company fails to find oil on that parcel of land, then under current management it will be worth nothing – $0 per share. However, if the company finds all the oil that it anticipated when bidding, then the company could be worth as much as $100 per share. Consider an investor who is contemplating a takeover of this company. The investor assumes that his/her superior management skills will make the company 50 percent more valuable under his/her direction than it is under current management. The investor also applies the principle of non-sufficient reason and assumes that, given the range of exploration outcomes, all share values between $0 and $100 are equally likely. Therefore, the investor estimates the expected value of the company as $50 under current management and $75 under his/her management.

   The problem here is of course that the investor lacks a crucial piece of relevant information – namely, how much oil the company in question is finding. The company knows how much oil there is, and will only accept the takeover offer if it is in excess of its value based on this information. Therefore, the very fact of the offer being accepted will change the investor's calculation of expected value.

   For example, assume that the investor offers $60 per share for the company and the offer is accepted. The range of equally likely values for each share of the company thus falls from $0–$100 to $0–$60. The expected value of the company, including the 50 percent mark-up for the investor's presumed superior management skill, thus falls to $45, meaning that there is now an expected loss of $15 – and this would be true for any bid greater than $0: if it is accepted, the investor can expect to lose 25 percent of the amount bid.
4. See O'Donnell (1989), Gerrard (1992, 1994) and Dequech (1999) for alternative formulations of the concept of the weight of arguments. The fact of alternative formulations results in no small part from ambiguities in Keynes's analysis of this concept (see, for example, Runde, 1990). But, as Ellsberg (1961; and also see Camerer, 1994: 645) explains, ambiguity is often the consequence of situations in which a person does not know the relevant facts. My formulation of the concept of the weight of arguments is motivated by the belief that facts unknown to Keynes have now emerged in the literature on behavioral finance.
5. See, for example, Hacking (1975; and also see Dequech, 2000) who analyzes these cases in terms of an 'aleatory' dimension (that is, the knowable causal structure) and an 'epistemic' dimension (that is, the investor's degree of belief in that causal structure).
6. See, for example, Davidson (1991; and also see Keynes (1937a [1973]: 113–14, 1937b [1979]) who analyzes these cases in terms of 'non-ergodic uncertainty', as opposed to the 'ergodic probability' of cases with an underlying causal structure which is knowable.

REFERENCES

Bazerman, M.H. and W.F. Samuelson (1983), 'I won the auction but don't want the prize', *Journal of Conflict Resolution*, **27** (December), 618–34.
Camerer, C. (1994), 'Individual decision making', in J. Kagel and A. Roth (eds), *Handbook of Experimental Economics*, Princeton, NJ: Princeton University Press, p. 645.
Capen, E.C., R.V. Clapp and W.M. Campbell (1971), 'Competitive bidding in high-risk situations', *Journal of Petroleum Technology*, **23** (June), 641–53.
Carabelli, A.M. (1988), *On Keynes's Method*, New York: St. Martin's Press.
Davidson, P. (1991), '"Is probability theory relevant for uncertainty?" A Post Keynesian Perspective', *Journal of Economic Perspectives*, **5**, 129–43.
Davidson, P (1996), 'Reality and economic theory', *Journal of Post Keynesian Economics*, **18**, 479–508.
Dequech, D. (1999), 'Expectations and confidence under uncertainty', *Journal of Post Keynesian Economics*, **21**, 415–30.
Dequech, D. (2000), 'Fundamental uncertainty and ambiguity', *Eastern Economic Journal*, **26**, 41–60.
Ellsberg, D. (1961), 'Risk, ambiguity and the savage axioms', *Quarterly Journal of Economics*, **75**, 643–69.
Fontana, G. and B. Gerrard (2004), 'A Post Keynesian theory of decision making under uncertainty', *Journal of Economic Psychology*, **25**, 619–37.
Gerrard, B. (1992), 'From *A Treatise on Probability* to *The General Theory*: continuity or change in Keynes's thought?', in B. Gerrard and J.V. Hillard (eds), *The Philosophy and Economics of John Maynard Keynes*, Aldershot, UK and Brookfield, USA: Edward Elgar, pp. 80–89.
Gerrard, B. (1994), 'Beyond rational expectations: a constructive interpretation of Keynes's analysis of behavior under uncertainty', *Economic Journal*, **104**, 327–37.
Hacking, I. (1975), *The Emergence of Probability*, Cambridge: Cambridge University Press.
Hershey, J. and P.J.H. Schomaker (1985), 'Probability versus certainty equivalence methods in utility measurement: are they equivalent?', *Management Science*, **31** (October), 1213–31.
Kagel, J.H. and D. Levin (1986), 'The winner's curse and public information in common value auctions', *American Economic Review*, **76** (December), 894–920.
Kahneman, D. and A. Tversky (1984), 'Choices, values and frames', *American Psychologist*, **39**, April, 341–50.
Keynes, J.M. (1921 [1973]), *A Treatise on Probability*, New York: St. Martin's Press.
Keynes, J.M. (1936 [1964]), *The General Theory of Employment, Interest, and Money*, New York: Harcourt Brace Jovanovich.
Keynes, J.M. (1937a [1973]), 'The General Theory of Employment', in *The General Theory and After: Part II: Defense and Development*, London: Macmillan pp. 109–23.
Keynes, J.M. (1937b [1979]), 'Letter to H. Townsend: April 11, 1937', in *The General Theory and After: A Supplement*, London: Macmillan pp. 258–9.
Markowitz, H.M. (1959 [1991]), *Portfolio Selection: Efficient Diversification of Investments*, Malden, MA: Blackwell.
O'Donnell, R. (1989), *Keynes: Philosophy, Economics and Politics*, London: Macmillan.

Rottenstreich, Y. and A. Tversky (1997), 'Unpacking, repacking and anchoring: advances in support theory', *Psychology Review*, **104**, 406–15.
Runde, J. (1990), 'Keynesian uncertainty and the weight of arguments', *Economics and Philosophy*, **6**, 275–92.
Solow, R. (1985), 'Economic history and economics', *American Economic Review, Papers and Proceedings*, **75**, 328–31.
Thayer, R.H. (ed.) (1992), 'The winner's curse', in *The Winner's Curse: Paradoxes and Anomalies of Economic Life*, Princeton, NJ: Princeton University Press. pp. 50–62.
Thayer, R.H. and A. Tversky (1992), 'Preference reversals', in R.H. Thayer (ed.), *The Winner's Curse: Paradoxes and Anomalies of Economic Life*, Princeton, NJ: Princeton University Press, pp. 79–91.

15. Real exchange rate levels, investment and growth: a Keynesian perspective

Paulo Gala

INTRODUCTION

According to the 'development approach' to currency management (Williamson, 2003; Frenkel, 2004), relatively undervalued exchange rates have been a key factor in most East and Southeast Asian successful growth strategies. Chile, Uganda, Mauritius and Turkey in the 1980s and India and China in the 1990s have all benefited from competitive real exchange rates, which fostered exports and output growth. However, most Latin American and African countries have suffered from severe balance-of-payments crises due to exchange rate overvaluation. Chile and Mexico in the early 1980s, as well as Mexico, Brazil and Argentina in the 1990s are good examples.

Following the traditional Keynesian macroeconomic channel, an expansionary devaluation boosts exports, income and employment. Exchange rate management may also have strong impacts on savings levels as it determines paths of consumption and investment via real wage determination (Bresser-Pereira, 2004a). Also, an excessively overvalued currency could cause savings displacement. By stimulating the export sector, a relatively undervalued currency may help to avert financial crises and put the economy on a more sustained developmental path. It is an important tool to promote the development of the tradable sector, which is usually very dynamic and contributes to innovations and productivity increases. Numerous studies have argued that most balance-of-payments crises are related to overvalued or misaligned currencies (Goldfajn and Valdes, 1996; Palma, 2003a). If Purchasing Power Parity does not hold in the short run (see Sarno and Taylor, 2002 for a discussion) exchange rate policy may therefore have important developmental and growth effects (Frenkel and Taylor, 2006).

There is now an important empirical literature that relates per capita growth rates with real exchange rate levels. Since the 1970s, for a long list of developing countries, many works have found negative correlations between exchange rate misalignment and growth. The more overvalued the currency, the smaller the per capita growth rates (Cavallo et al., 1990; Dollar, 1992; Razin and Collins, 1997; Benaroya and Janci, 1999; Acemoglu et al., 2002; Fajnzylber et al., 2002). Other studies have found positive correlations between growth and undervalued currencies measured as accumulation of foreign exchange reserves, a result that seems to suggest an important relationship between growth and real exchange rate levels (Popov and Polterovich, 2002). A recurrent issue in this empirical literature is the relative undervaluation of the Asian currencies as compared to Latin American and African ones for the period from 1970 to 1999 (Dollar, 1992; Benaroya and Janci, 1999). In most works, a lower currency level for Asian countries emerges, which appears to be a regional pattern. For the Latin American and African cases, the pattern seems to be the opposite and overvaluation cycles are very common.

Following the discussion, the objective of this chapter is to explore the links between real exchange rate levels, investment and growth from a theoretical point of view. Based on Bhaduri and Marglin (1990), we analyze in a Keynesian macro model how an undervalued currency may contribute to investment and capital accumulation. The chapter is divided into four sections. Following this introduction, the next section briefly presents possible long-term effects of real exchange rate levels on growth through two main channels: technological upgrading and capital accumulation. The third section deals with the relationship between real exchange rate levels, real wages, and investment in the short run. Based on the Bhaduri and Marglin model, we show that, for given productivity levels, the real exchange rate may play an important role in determining real wages, profitability and thus investment levels. The final section reports brief conclusions with reference to the debate that deals with the Latin American and East Asian development strategies.

LONG-TERM EFFECTS OF REAL EXCHANGE RATE LEVELS

Two important channels through which real exchange rate levels affect long-term growth are related to accumulation of capital and technological change. Overvalued currencies have strong profit-squeezing effects in the tradable sector, which usually bring investment rates down. Undervalued currencies, on the other hand, tend to be associated with higher investment levels at the macro level. Based on Bhaduri and Marglin (1990), it is possible to show in a Keynesian macro model how an undervalued currency contributes to investment and capital accumulation. By defining an investment function that depends on capacity utilization, profit margins and a consumption function that depends on real wages, the authors indirectly introduce the real exchange level in the capital accumulation process.

For given productivity levels, the real exchange rate defines the level of real wages by setting the relative prices of tradables to non-tradables. A relatively appreciated currency, meaning lower tradable prices, higher real wages, lower profit margins, higher consumption and lower investment and a relatively undervalued currency means higher tradable prices, lower real wage levels, higher profit margins and investment. In the last case, an undervaluation would also contribute to more employment and investment by increasing capacity utilization through higher exports. With sufficiently elastic investment and export responses, the economy would get into an investment-led pattern of growth.

By affecting real wages, exchange rate levels also influence aggregate savings and foreign debt dynamics. As Bresser-Pereira (2004a) argues, in capital account liberalization processes with strong inflows, what usually happens is currency overvaluation which increases the consumption of tradable goods. The artificially high real wages caused by the appreciation of the currency stimulates consumption in the country that receives the inflows. Debt is used to finance consumption instead of generating resources to repay it, causing what became known in the literature as savings displacement (ibid.). The increase in external borrowing eventually generates unsustainable debt dynamics and the result of those cycles is a balance-of-payments crisis.

On technological grounds, an undervalued currency helps to stimulate the non-traditional tradable sector of developing economies, particularly the ones related to export manufactures. As Williamson (2003) argues in his 'development approach' to exchange rates, a relatively undervalued currency would provide stimulus for the development of a non-commodity dependent tradable sector, therefore avoiding Dutch disease problems and premature deindustrialization. By stimulating the production of industrial manufacturers for the world markets, a competitive exchange rate would help developing countries to climb up the technological ladder. Learning by doing and cumulative technological progress would depend heavily on the development of the manufacturing sector (Palma, 2003b; Williamson, 2003). This argument is especially relevant for resource-rich countries. Appreciated currency levels originating from high commodity exports would prevent the development of an industrial sector with its related economies of scale and technological spillovers. In this sense, by avoiding overvaluations, exchange rate policy could work as an effective industrial policy tool (Frenkel, 2004: 7).

Following those approaches, relatively undervalued real exchange rates would avoid savings displacement and contribute to capital accumulation by stimulating investment. On technological grounds, it would encourage the development of the non-traditional tradable sector, helping the countries to climb up the technological ladder. By increasing productivity, the development of a dynamic non-traditional tradable sector could also increase real wages, counteracting the negative effects of a weak currency for workers.

EFFECTS OF REAL EXCHANGE RATE LEVELS ON AGGREGATE INVESTMENT

One of the most important real effects of exchange rate levels in long-term growth is on aggregate investment. Based on Bhaduri and Marglin (1990) we can show in formal terms how a competitive currency may increase investment, savings and thus stimulate capital accumulation. By defining an aggregate investment function that depends on capacity utilization and on profit margins, and a consumption function that depends on real wages, it is possible to set up a macro model where savings and investment levels are a function of real wages and, thus, real exchange rate levels.

We start, following Bhaduri and Marglin, with a savings function S that depends on a fixed share s of capitalists' profits. Workers do not save in so far as they consume all their income.

$$S = sR = s(R/Y)(Y/Y^*)Y^*, \tag{15.1}$$

where R is the capitalists' income and Y^* potential output. By defining $h = R/Y$ as the capitalists' share of total income, $z = Y/Y^*$ as capacity utilization and normalizing potential output $Y^* = 1$, we have:

$$S = shz, \tag{15.2}$$

$$1 > h > 0, \tag{15.2a}$$

$$1 > z > 0. \tag{15.2b}$$

By following a traditional mark-up pricing rule, we can define profit margins or mark-ups as follows:

$$m = (p/bw) - 1, \tag{15.3}$$

where P is the price level, w the nominal wage, $1/b$ the productivity level and m a mark-up over labor costs. By defining W/Y as the labor share in income, N as the level of employed workers and $b = N/Y$, we have the labor share in income as a function of the mark-up level:

$$W/Y = wN/pY = bw/p = 1/1 + m, \tag{15.4}$$

and the capitalists' share in income $h = R/Y$ will be:

$$h = R/Y = (pY - wN)/pY = 1 - W/Y = m/1 + m. \tag{15.5}$$

Expressions (15.3), (15.4) and (15.5) give us the traditional distributive relations. For given productivity levels, there is an inverse relationship between mark-ups and real wages. The higher the mark ups, the lower the real wages and the higher the share of profits in income, h.

It is important to introduce at this point a crucial, but fairly ignored, issue: the role of real exchange rate levels on the determination of real wages and profitability in the short run and, thus, in the distributive relations. As discussed in the previous section, the more overvalued the domestic currency is, the higher real wages will be in so far as the prices of tradable consumption goods, especially commodities, will go down alongside the appreciation. If we assume that workers receive a nominal wage w and consume tradable and non-tradable goods, their cost of living will depend on the nominal exchange rate level and on the share of tradable goods in their consumption basket. According to this kind of reasoning, real wages and profits will, thus, depend on the level of the real exchange rate, besides the patterns of income distribution and productivity levels.

If we assume that the price level can be defined as an average of tradable pt and non-tradable pnt prices:

$$p = \alpha pt + (1 - \alpha)pnt, \tag{15.6}$$

and, further assuming that tradable prices in domestic terms are exogenously determined by the nominal exchange rate level e and international prices p^*,

$$pt = p^*e, \tag{15.7}$$

we can see how profitability and the real wage will depend on the real exchange rate level θ (defined as the ratio of tradable to non-tradable prices) using again the mark-up pricing rule (15.3):

$$m = \{[(\alpha p^*e) + (1 - \alpha)pnt]/bw\} - 1. \quad (15.8)$$

A devaluation of the exchange rate, causing increases in tradable prices as compared to the nominal wage, means a reduction in real wages and an increase in profits as long as eventual increases in w due to the devaluation are lower than the increases in the nominal exchange rate, for given international price levels. This usually happens if nominal wages remain constant or move more slowly than prices of goods. We are, thus, assuming here the hypothesis of nominal wage rigidity and real wage flexibility as opposed to nominal flexibility and real rigidity.

By assuming that workers do not save, as Bhaduri and Marglin do, we can then conclude that higher real wages and appreciated currencies are associated with lower saving rates and higher consumption levels. As a consequence, aggregate demand can increase or decrease because of higher real wages, depending on the effects of lower profit margins on aggregate investment. If, following Bhaduri and Marglin, we define an investment function that depends only on profit margins:

$$I = I(h), \quad (15.9)$$

$$\partial I/\partial h > 0. \quad (15.9a)$$

Equilibrium in the goods market is achieved by the traditional savings = investment identity, in other words an IS curve:

$$shz = I(h). \quad (15.10)$$

Capacity utilization levels will vary as a function of profit margins according to the following derivative:

$$\partial z/\partial h = (I_h - sz)/sh, \quad (15.11)$$

$$I_h = \partial I/\partial h > 0. \quad (15.11a)$$

As sh is always positive, capacity utilization will increase or decrease depending on $(I_h - sz)$. If investment is inelastic to changes in profit margins, real wage falls will be recessionary because decreases in consumption will not be compensated for increases in investment $(I_h < sz)$. This is the classical underconsumptionist thesis, where low real wages lead to low consumption and aggregate demand. On the other hand, real wage increases will be expansionary, compensating for low investment levels. This kind of 'consumption-led' growth, can, nevertheless, be problematic in the long run because of installed capacity constraints. If investment is elastic to profit margins, we have the opposite effect. Lower real wages will increase profit margins and investment, stimulating aggregate demand, capacity utilization and savings. Growth will then be 'investment led'.

Building up on this simple model, Bhaduri and Marglin introduce capacity utilization as a direct determinant of investment levels. Responses of aggregate investment depend now on capacity utilization z and on profit margins and profit shares in income h, which leads to a new goods market equilibrium:

$$I = I(h,z),\ I_h > 0,\ I_z > 0, \tag{15.12}$$

$$shz = I(h,z), \tag{15.13}$$

$$\partial z / \partial h = (I_h - sz)/(sh - I_z). \tag{15.14}$$

By imposing the Keynesian condition that equilibrium in the goods market is achieved through changes in savings rather than investment $(sh - I_z) > 0$, they arrive at the same qualitative conclusions of the simple case where investment depends only on profit margins and profit shares in income h. In the final step, Bhaduri and Marglin extend the model to the open economy case with real exports X_e and imports X_m that depend, respectively, on the real exchange rate θ and on capacity utilization z, with the following elasticities:

$$(dX_e/d\theta)(\theta/X_e) = \eta_e, \tag{15.15}$$

$$(dX_m/d\theta)(\theta/X_m) = -\eta_m, \tag{15.16}$$

$$(\partial X_m/\partial z)(z/X_m) = u. \tag{15.17}$$

In the new goods market equilibrium, total domestic savings plus imports in nominal terms M equals total investment plus exports in nominal terms E (ignoring interest rate, profits and remittance payments):

$$shz + M = I(h,z) + E. \tag{15.18}$$

The partial derivative of capacity utilization z with respect to profit margins and profit share h is very similar to the closed economy case (15.11):

$$\partial z / \partial h = (I_h - sz)(gu + sh - I_z), \tag{15.19}$$

where g represents the initial share of imports and exports over GDP and u is the elasticity of imports with respect to capacity utilization. By assuming that $(gu + sh - I_z) > 0$, we arrive again at the same conclusions of the simple case.

In the open economy case, a real devaluation decreases the real wage and increases profit margins, for given productivity levels. Income, exports and investment will increase as long as those two macro functions are sufficiently elastic. In the case of exports and imports, the overall effect on external accounts will be positive if the Marshall–Lerner condition holds, an assumption used throughout the whole chapter $(\eta_e + \eta_m > 1)$.

In summary, this simple model presents possible responses to a system of exogenous variations in real wages and exchange rates from a broad Keynesian perspective. The real exchange rate plays an important role in the capital accumulation process by defining real wages and profits, for given productivity levels.

LATIN AMERICA VERSUS EAST ASIA

According to the development approach to exchange rates, a central issue to understand the East and Southeast Asian successes, as compared to the Latin American and African failures, would be in the manner in which they have conducted their exchange rate policies and, thus, in their real exchange rate levels. For example, when discussing the impacts of the debt crisis in Latin America and Asia in the beginning of the 1980s, Sachs (1985) concludes that the superior adjustment of the Asian countries took place mainly because of their better exchange rate and trade regimes. Except for the case of the Philippines, none of the Asian high-performing economies has defaulted on external debt, a very different situation as compared to Latin America. According to the author, these two regions had three common and one distinct characteristic which were responsible for their rather smooth transition in the debt crisis. In terms of external debt, the Asian countries were near the Latin American levels. For example, South Korea had a total external debt over GDP of 27.6 percent in 1981, higher than the Brazilian level of 26.1 percent for the same year. When it comes to terms of trade, the author argues that some of the Asian countries had even worse shocks than the Latin Americans. Regarding state intervention, Sachs argues that both regions went through a process of some form of state-led development (for other interpretations, see Amsden, 1989; Wade, 1990; Rodrik, 1994; and Chang, 2003).

The great difference between these two macro regions is 'trade regime and exchange rate management'. While Latin America focused on an inward-looking industrialization strategy with a strong bias for currency appreciations, East and Southeast Asian countries pursued an export-led growth strategy, with heavy stimulus for the export sector through subsidies and competitive exchange rates. The reason for the better adjustment of East and Southeast Asia in the debt crisis is the existence of an ample and dynamic tradable sector, capable of producing the much-needed hard currency when the day of the reckoning came. This difference can easily be seen when we compare the exports over external debt ratio for both regions in the beginning of the 1980s. For example, Indonesia, South Korea, Malaysia and Thailand had on average an index of 0.821 in 1981 as compared to an average index of 2.715 for Argentina, Brazil, Chile, Mexico, Peru and Venezuela in the same year (Sachs, 1985).

While Latin American countries went through their well-known populist and stabilization episodes, East and Southeast Asian countries focused on their export-led growth strategy with a permanent stimulus for the export sector, avoiding episodes of strong appreciations. While the former have used exchange rates prominently as a populist or stabilization tool, the latter have used them in search of external demand, following their development strategy. Regarding the 1997 Asian crisis, the appreciation of some of the currencies in the region in 1996 and 1997 strongly contributed to the collapse. As Lim (2004: 67) puts it, those countries, 'in varying degrees, had a tendency to incur high deficits in their current account and overvalue their currency. This made the East Asian countries eventually "un-East Asian" since the earlier East Asian stereotype was a high saver and a high earner of foreign exchange'.

Another main difference between these two regions, then, is to be found in their savings and investment levels. East Asia is well known for its very high levels of investment and savings, whereas Latin American countries are famous for their excessive consumption and lack of savings. As we have shown above, it is possible to argue from a broad Keynesian–Kaleckian point of view that competitive currencies can also be associated with high levels of savings and investment. The stylized facts found in East and Southeast Asia regarding savings and investment patterns can, thus, be interpreted from Bhaduri and Marglin's point of view, provided that the conditions used in the model presented above hold. Undervalued currencies may have produced investment-led growth patterns in Asia, whereas overvalued currencies may have produced instability and consumption-led growth cycles in Latin America.

While the empirical literature on the impacts of overvaluations on growth is relatively rich, theoretical analysis of channels through which real exchange rate levels could affect economic growth and development are very scarce. Most works tend to concentrate on issues of exchange rate measurement, concepts of equilibrium and indications of misalignment, leaving the theoretical issues aside. The literature on exchange rate policy cases concentrates on country experiences, dedicating little attention to how overvaluations or undervaluations may impact on growth. The only literature that briefly mentions these theoretical aspects is a recent one that deals with policy advice. This chapter tries to contribute to the debate by bringing more theoretical elements to the connections between real exchange rate levels, investment and growth from a Keynesian perspective.

REFERENCES

Acemoglu, D., S. Johnson, Y. Thaicharoen and J. Robinson (2002), 'Institutional causes, macroeconomic symptoms: volatility, crisis and growth', NBER working paper no. 9124, Cambridge, MA.

Amsden, A.H. (1989), *Asia's next Giant, South Korea and Late Industrialization*, Oxford: Oxford University Press.

Benaroya, F. and D. Janci (1999), 'Measuring exchange rates misalignments with purchasing power parity estimates', in S. Collignon, J. Pisani-Ferry and Y.C. Park (eds), *Exchange Rate Policies in Emerging Asian Countries*, New York: Routledge, pp. 222–42.

Bhaduri, A. and S.A. Marglin (1990), 'Unemployment and the real wages: the economic basis for contesting political ideologies', *Cambridge Journal of Economics*, **14** (December), 375–93.

Bresser-Pereisra, L.C. (2004b), 'Exchange rate, fix, float or manage it?', Preface to M. Vernengo (ed.), *Financial Integration or Dollarization: No Panacea*, Cheltenham, UK and Northampton, MA, USA: Edward Elgar.

Cavallo, D.F., J.A. Cottani and M.S. Kahn (1990), 'Real exchange rate behavior and economic performance in LDCs', *Economic Development and Cultural Change*, **39** (October), 61–76.

Chang, H.J. (2003), 'The East Asian development experience', in H.-J. Chang (ed.), *Rethinking Development Economics*, London: Anthem Press, pp. 369–90.

Dollar, D. (1992), 'Outward-oriented developing economies really do grow more rapidly: evidence from 95 LDCs, 1976–1985', *Economic Development and Cultural Change*, **40**, 523–44.

Fajnzylber, P., N. Loayza and C. Calderón (2002), *Economic Growth in Latin America and the Caribbean*, Washington, DC: World Bank.

Frenkel, R. (2004), 'Real exchange rate and employment in Argentina, Brazil, Chile and Mexico', paper presented to the G24, Cedes, Buenos Aires, April.

Frenkel, R. and L. Taylor (2006), 'Real exchange rate, monetary policy and employment', United Nations Department for Economic and Social Affairs working paper 19, New York.

Goldfajn, I. and R. Valdes (1996), 'The aftermath of appreciations', NBER working paper 5650, Cambridge, MA, July.

Lim, J. (2004), 'Macroeconomic implications of the Southeast Asian crises', in K.S. Jomo (ed.), *After the Storm: Crisis, Recovery and Sustaining Development in Four Asian Economies*, Singapore: Singapore University Press, pp. 40–74.

Palma, G. (2003a), 'The three routes to financial crises: Chile, Mexico and Argentina [1]; Brazil [2], and Korea, Malaysia and Thailand [3]', in H.-J. Chang (ed.), *Rethinking Development Economics*, London: Anthem Press, pp. 297–328.

Palma, G. (2003b), 'Four sources of de-industrialization and a new concept of the Dutch Disease', in J.A. Ocampo (ed.), *New Challenges for Latin American Development*, Washington, DC: ECLAC-World Bank, pp. 71–116.

Popov, V. and V. Polterovich (2002), 'Accumulation of foreign exchange reserves and long term growth', mimeo, New Economic School, Moscow.

Razin, O. and S. Collins (1997), 'Real exchange rate misalignments and growth', NBER working paper 6147, Cambridge, MA.

Rodrik, D. (1994), 'King Kong meets Godzilla: the World Bank and the East Asian Miracle', in A. Fishlow, C. Gwin, S. Haggard, D. Rodrik and R. Wade (eds), *Miracle or Design? Lessons from the East Asian Experience*.

Sachs, J. (1985), 'External debt and macroeconomic performance in Latin America and East Asia', *Brookings Papers on Economic Activity*, **2**, 523–73.

Sarno, L. and M. Taylor (2002), *The Economics of Exchange Rates*, Cambridge: Cambridge University Press.

Wade, R. (1990), *Governing the Market, Economic Theory and the Role of Government in East Asian Industrialization*, Princeton, NJ: Princeton University Press.

Williamson, J. (2003), 'Exchange rate policy and development', paper presented at Initiative for Policy Dialogue Task Force on Macroeconomics, Columbia University, New York.

16. A reinterpretation, remedy and development of Keynes's liquidity preference theory

Wenge Huang

INTRODUCTION

Liquidity preference theory is always the most confused and controversial part of Keynes's *General Theory*. This results in the dissension on the mechanism of determination of interest rate in monetary economics. Liquidity preference theory was first introduced by Keynes in his profoundly influential *General Theory* in 1936. Before that, the classical theory of interest argues that the level of interest rate is determined by two real factors: the demand for investment and supply of saving.

In *The General Theory*, Keynes (1936) criticizes the classical theory of interest and presents a brand-new theory of interest, namely liquidity preference theory. In Keynes's opinion, interest rate is not determined by saving and investment, but by the demand for and supply of money. Demand for money, or broadly defined liquidity preference, is composed of transactions motive, precautionary motive and speculative motive. Among the three, transactions motive and precautionary motive mainly depend on the level of income; and speculative motive, or narrowly defined liquidity preference, mainly depends on the level of interest rate. The supply of money is the quantity of money determined by the monetary authority. Interest rate is a price that makes the quantity of money the public would like to hold equal to the quantity of money in existence.

Keynes's liquidity preference theory gave rise to many controversies soon after he introduced it. Most curiously, *The General Theory* holds that the change in propensity to invest (namely, a shift of the investment demand curve or Keynes's investment demand schedule) exerts only an *ex post* influence on interest rate indirectly via the change of transactions motive after income changes. Moreover, Keynes did not explain why. Ohlin (1932) and Robertson (1937, 1940), the two most famous loanable funds theorists, attacked Keynes's theory of interest effectively on this issue. Their criticism can be summarized as follows: if there is an increase in propensity to invest, according to Keynes, the multiplier effect can make the level of income rise, leading to investment equal to saving. However, in adjusting to the new equilibrium, desired investment and desired saving are not equal.

In his reply to Ohlin's criticism, Keynes (1937b [1973], 1937c [1973], 1938 [1973]) confessed his mistake and introduced a new and somewhat novel incentive for demanding money, namely the finance motive, in order to improve his liquidity preference theory. Keynes argues that during the period between the date when entrepreneurs make their investment decisions and the date when they actually make their investment, there is a demand for finance. Keynes stresses that the finance motive is an additional motive for demanding money and essentially a revolving fund, while an excess in demand for finance resulting from the increase in propensity to invest may lead to a rise in the interest rate.

In his debate with loanable funds theorists, although Keynes kept clarifying and improving his liquidity preference theory, the theory is still known for its oddity and its difficulty in being understood, resulting in a great deal of controversy in interpreting it. Most strangely, the finance motive is rarely found in the literature after Keynes until Davidson rediscovered it in 1965. Among the various interpretations, the IS–LM model is the best known.

The prototype of the IS–LM model was first presented by Hicks (1937) to elucidate the interrelationships between the theory of effective demand and the liquidity preference theory. But it is largely due to the work of Hansen that the IS–LM model became a popular model of the determination of the interest rate. In his book, *A Guide to Keynes*, Hansen (1953) points out that the interest rate is indeterminate in Keynes's theory of interest. Hansen's criticism can be summarized as follows: the interest rate is determined by the total demand for and supply of money, and the transactions motive for demanding money is determined by income; however, income is determined by investment, and investment is determined by the interest rate and the marginal efficiency of capital. Thus, the interest rate and income are all indeterminate. Therefore, Hansen develops the IS–LM model to solve this problem by making the goods and the money markets attain equilibrium simultaneously. Later, the IS–LM model developed from a model of determination of the interest rate to a dominant macroeconomic model of the neoclassical synthesis.

However, the IS–LM model has also been criticized by many economists. Among the various criticisms, the most fundamental and common attack is that the simultaneity approach does not apply to Keynes's theory, making the IS–LM model logically inconsistent. For example, Pasinetti (1974) has argued that Keynes's theory should not be analyzed simultaneously but rather sequentially. That is, Keynes's theory ought to be considered as a sequence of alternating decisions in the monetary and the real sectors. Davidson (1978) argues that the IS and LM schedules are interdependent when the finance motive is introduced. Chick (1983) also attacks the IS–LM model on the basis of its internal logic.

Which one is correct: the mainstream interpretation of liquidity preference theory or the criticism of it? Or is neither of them fully correct? Further, can liquidity preference theory be correctly interpreted without the finance motive? If not, what kind of role should the finance motive play in liquidity preference theory?

These questions inspired me to explore the essence of liquidity preference theory. The next section begins by analyzing the inherent logic of liquidity preference theory and presents a new interpretation of the theory in a more logical and clear manner. This new interpretation demonstrates that Keynes's finance motive plays a more fundamental role than the transactions motive does in determining the interest rate. It is the finance motive that transforms the flow demand for credit/fund to the stock demand for money, thus bridging the gap between the classical theory of interest and liquidity preference theory. The third section then argues that Keynes makes a crucial and yet unrectified mistake in his theory of interest, that is, interest rate is indeterminate, which is revealed by his introduction of the finance motive into the theory. To correct Keynes's mistake, the fourth section develops a new model of the determination of the interest rate on the basis of the liquidity preference analysis centered on a finance motive. In the new model, interest rate is not determined by the demand for and supply of money, but rather by the demand for and supply of idle money. Further, the fifth section adds the banking system into the above model and applies liquidity preference theory to the modern economy: considering the multiple expansion of bank deposits, the interest rate is determined by the demand for and supply of bank reserves. The final section provides a brief conclusion.

REINTERPRETATION OF LIQUIDITY PREFERENCE THEORY

After analyzing the previous literature on liquidity preference theory, I have found that the research approach adopted by subsequent economists may be inappropriate. They appear to limit themselves to Keynes's literature, and even follow the same sequence when they study the motives with respect to the demand for money, that is, they analyze the transactions motive first and the finance motive last. This approach makes it very likely that they will ignore the inherent logic of liquidity preference theory.

It is unlikely that liquidity preference theory was dreamed up by Keynes without any foundation. It reveals the objective law of the determination of the interest rate. Keynes does not create the law, but discovers it. The research that is confined to Keynes's literature may be misled by Keynes's mistake. Accordingly, by focusing on the internal logic of liquidity preference theory, I shall attempt to present a new interpretation of the theory to uncover its essence.

We can start from the problem of the classical theory of interest since Keynes tried to develop a new theory after he became aware that something was wrong with the classical theory. But when he criticizes the classical theory in his *General Theory*, Keynes creates confusion and conceals the essence of the problem by his unsuccessful attack. Given that the problem of the classical theory is still not clear, I feel that the following quotation from Keynes provides a clearer and more reliable point of departure:

> [A]s I have said above, the initial novelty lies in my maintaining that it is not the rate of interest, but the level of incomes which ensures equality between saving and investment. The arguments, which lead up to this initial conclusion, are independent of my subsequent theory of the rate of interest, and in fact I reached it before I had reached the latter theory. But the result of it was to leave the rate of interest in the air. If the rate of interest is not determined by saving and investment in the same way in which price is determined by supply and demand, how is it determined? (Keynes, 1937b [1973], p. 212)

It can be clearly deduced from this quotation that the initial divarication between the classical theory of interest and Keynes is whether the interest rate or income will change along with the change in propensity to invest (no matter which of them changes, saving would equal investment). When propensity to invest changes, the classical theory holds that the interest rate will change and income will not change, but Keynes holds the opposite view: that it is not the interest rate, but income that will change.

To settle the divarication, we shall analyze the *ex ante* situation first. If, for example, there is an increase in propensity to invest (namely, an outward shift of the investment demand curve or Keynes's investment demand schedule), desired investment will increase and exceed desired saving.

According to the classical theory, a rise in interest rate will decrease desired investment and increase desired saving. The interest rate will continue to rise until desired investment equals desired saving. Therefore, ultimately the interest rate changes, and income remains the same. Moreover, the interest rate is directly determined by desired investment and desired saving.

But how can Keynes's prediction that income will change be right? It is not difficult to see that income will change if the economy can draw idle money from somewhere to fill up the gap between desired investment and desired saving in the *ex ante* situation.

Thus, the debate on whether the interest rate or income will change is transformed into another equivalent debate: whether there is *idle money* outside the economic operation of the economy. If there is no idle money, income will not change, and the classical theory is right. If there is idle money, income will change and the interest rate cannot be determined by desired investment and desired saving.

Obviously, the idle money here is Keynes's 'inactive balances' or 'idle balances'. Why is there idle money? As Keynes argues, the reason why wealth-holders would like to hold money without gaining interest is the existence of the speculative motive for demanding money. Accordingly, the concept of liquidity preference is a logical extension. Is there any cost involved in drawing idle money into the economic operation? To make the wealth-holders give up their money, according to Keynes, requires a rise in the interest rate: the higher the demand for idle money, the greater the rise in interest rate. In this way, liquidity preference analysis is logically introduced into the determination of the interest rate in the *ex ante* situation.

When idle money exists, determination of the interest rate is related not only to the difference between desired investment and desired savings, but also to the interest elasticity of liquidity preference. In other words, the higher the interest elasticity of liquidity preference, the lower the cost of drawing idle money, the less the rise in the interest rate, the greater the increase in income. Contrarily, the lower the interest elasticity of liquidity preference, the higher the cost of drawing idle money, the greater the rise in the interest rate, the less the increase in income.

Here, I would argue that the difference between desired investment and desired savings as mentioned above, is equivalent to Keynes's excess finance motive that is a result of the increased propensity to invest. That is, the finance motive will increase first when propensity to invest increases. Only when the excess finance motive is satisfied by idle money is the excess investment realized and income can increase. When the multiplier effect causes the level of income to rise, idle money will become a revolving fund, which makes desired savings equal to desired investment if the increase in propensity to invest persists.

To clarify the concept of the finance motive, I would define the investment-realization period as the period between the date when entrepreneurs make their investment decisions (at the same time, they arrange their finance) and the date when they actually make their investment (at the same time, the payment is made). Figure 16.1 shows the role of the finance motive in a simplified investment-realization period.

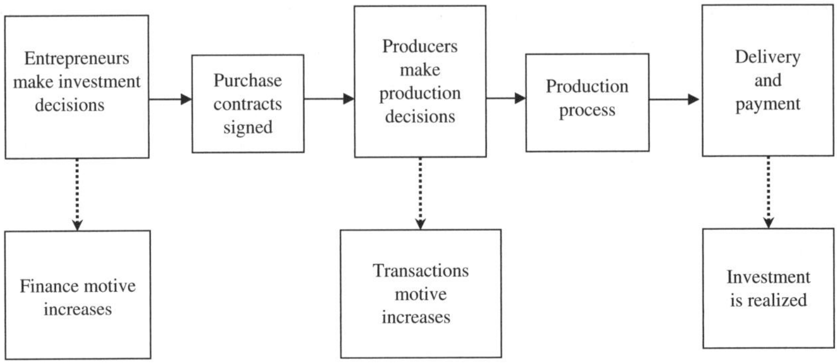

Figure 16.1 A simplified investment–realization period

A simplified investment–realization period begins when entrepreneurs make investment decisions. If the propensity to invest increases, the finance motive will increase simultaneously, drawing idle money from inactive balances into economic operation and leading to a rise in the interest rate. Then the purchase contracts of investment goods will be signed between entrepreneurs and producers. After that, producers will make production decisions and seek more working capital for producing more investment goods. Consequently, the transactions motive will increase, drawing more idle money from inactive balances into economic operation and leading to the rise in the interest rate once more. After the investment goods are delivered and payment is made, the investment process is completed, and the investment is finally realized. Moreover, if the increase in the propensity to invest persists, the increase in the finance and the transactions motives will continue in subsequent investment-realization periods.

The above analysis demonstrates two points: first, the finance motive exists not only when investment increases, *but also in economic operation at any time*.[1] When the economic operation is constant, the finance motive is a constant revolving fund, the amount of which equates to the amount of the desired investment or desired saving during an investment-realization period. When all the other conditions are the same, the amount of the finance motive depends on the length of the investment-realization period: the longer the investment-realization period, the more the finance motive for demanding money. In this way, the finance motive transforms the flow demand for credit/funds into the stock demand for money.

Second, the finance and the transactions motives are different demands for money and play different roles in the economic operation of the economy. They exist simultaneously in the economic operation of the economy and change at different times in the expansion or contraction of the economy. Therefore, the finance motive cannot be just a subcategory or addendum of the transactions motive.[2] Furthermore, I would argue that in determining the interest rate, the liquidity preference analysis based on the finance motive plays a more fundamental role than does the liquidity preference analysis based on the transactions motive because: (i) the finance motive bridges the classical theory of interest and liquidity preference theory, thereby illuminating the necessity of introducing liquidity preference analysis into the determination of the interest rate; and (ii) the finance motive is the starting-point of liquidity preference analysis since the finance motive changes first when the propensity to invest changes.

Thus, we arrive at a new interpretation of liquidity preference theory. Without the finance motive, liquidity preference theory is half-baked, or even false. However, it is very strange that the finance motive is rarely found in the literatures after Keynes, for example, the IS–LM model and most other interpretations of liquidity preference theory all overlook the finance motive.

It is likely that Keynes's mistake of initially overlooking the finance motive in *The General Theory* largely contributes to this phenomenon. Although Keynes later added the finance motive to correct his mistake, the strong first impressions of *The General Theory* persist, and most economists still consider that his initial mistake was the innovation of the theory. This misunderstanding results in them believing that the transactions motive plays a fundamental role in liquidity preference theory and that the finance motive is dispensable. Thus, the inherent logic and essence of liquidity preference theory are covered up, leading to much confusion and many misinterpretations. If Keynes had first introduced the finance motive with its *ex ante* effect on the interest rate, then brought forward the transactions motive with its succedent effect on the interest rate, liquidity preference theory would have become more logical and clear, and all the misunderstandings and controversies would have been resolved naturally.

KEYNES'S CRUCIAL AND UNRECTIFIED MISTAKE IN HIS THEORY OF INTEREST

After introducing the finance motive, Keynes summarized his liquidity preference theory in 'Mr Keynes' "*finance*" ':

> [T]he rate of interest is determined by the total demand and total supply of cash or liquid resources. The total demand falls into two parts: the inactive demand due to the state of confidence and expectation on the part of the owners of wealth, and the active demand due to the level of activity established by the decisions of the entrepreneurs. The active demand in its turn falls into two parts: the demand due to the time lag between the inception and the execution of the

> entrepreneurs' decisions, and the part due to the time lags between the receipt and the disposal of income by the public and also between the receipt by entrepreneurs of their sale proceeds and the payment by them of wages, etc. An increase in activity raises the demand for cash, first of all to provide for the first of these time lags in circulation, and then to provide for the second of them. (Keynes, 1938 [1973], p. 230)

Keynes may not be aware that a new problem arises after he adds the finance motive: the interest rate becomes indeterminate. Here, the interest rate is determined by the total demand for and supply of money, and the finance motive for demanding money is determined by desired investment. However, as desired investment is determined by the interest rate and the marginal efficiency of capital, the interest rate and desired investment have to be determined simultaneously. Thus, there is a circular logic in his theory of interest.

It would seem that I have arrived at a conclusion similar to Hansen's, that is, the interest rate is indeterminate in Keynes's theory of interest, but the basis of our reasoning is totally different. My reasoning is based on what I call the 'comprehensive liquidity preference theory', namely, Keynes's theory of interest, which includes both the finance and the transactions motives; whereas Hansen's reasoning is based on what I call the 'half-baked liquidity preference theory', namely, Keynes's theory of interest in *The General Theory* which merely includes the transactions motive.

Moreover, contrary to Hansen, I would argue that the interest rate is determinate in the half-baked liquidity preference theory. In *The General Theory*, there are two different incomes: one affects the transactions motive, the demand for money, and then the interest rate; and the other is determined by investment and then by the interest rate and the marginal efficiency of capital. The first income, or the *ex ante* income, is realized *before* the investment is made. The second income, or the *ex post* income, is realized *after* the investment is made. In *The General Theory*, although Keynes did not elucidate explicitly, he implied that the change in the propensity to invest does not directly exert an *ex ante* influence on the interest rate. Therefore, the *ex ante* interest rate is determined only by the supply of and the demand for money, the latter being determined by the *ex ante* income. This *ex ante* interest rate and the marginal efficiency of capital will then collectively determine investment and the *ex post* income. Accordingly, the interest rate and income are not determined simultaneously, but sequentially. This means that Pasinetti is right in his interpretation of the half-baked liquidity preference theory.

There is no circular logic in such a theory. The sequentiality of the theory makes the simultaneous IS–LM model logically inconsistent. It is the introduction of the finance motive that means that the interest rate and the desired investment have to be determined simultaneously, and then this results in the circular logic of the comprehensive liquidity preference theory. This is a crucial mistake in Keynes's theory of interest, but unfortunately he never became aware of it.

On the basis of the above analysis, it is not difficult to see that Hansen makes two mistakes: (i) he overlooks the finance motive and carries out research on the half-baked liquidity preference theory; (ii) he makes an incorrect interpretation of the half-baked liquidity preference theory. But by accident, based on his successive mistakes, Hansen arrives at a correct conclusion: the interest rate is indeterminate in Keynes's liquidity preference theory. The IS–LM model is logically inconsistent because the interest rate and income are determined sequentially in the half-baked liquidity preference theory.

REMEDY OF LIQUIDITY PREFERENCE THEORY

In order to correct the mistake in Keynes's theory of interest, I shall develop a new integrated model of the determination of the interest rate on the basis of the liquidity preference analysis centered on the finance motive.

If we regard the difference between desired investment and desired savings in an investment-realization period as the demand for idle money, the demand for idle money will increase along with the fall in the interest rate. When the interest rate falls, desired investment will rise and desired saving will fall, so the difference will increase.

If we regard the difference between the idle balance and the narrowly defined liquidity preference as the supply of idle money, this supply will increase along with the rise in the interest rate. When the interest rate rises, liquidity preference will decrease, that is, the money that the wealth-holders would like to hold will decrease; thereby, the supply of idle money will increase.

In this way, we arrive at a new model of the determination of the interest rate, or an integrated liquidity preference theory. In this model, the interest rate is not determined by the demand for and supply of money, but by the demand for and supply of idle money. The main features of the analysis can be illustrated in Figure 16.2.

In Figure 16. 2, the y-axis denotes interest rate, and the x-axis denotes the quantity of the demand for and supply of idle money. When the propensity to invest increases, the increase in the finance motive will make the demand for idle money curve move outward, leading to a rise in the interest rate from *a* to *b*. Later, when the producers make production decisions, the increase in the transactions motive will make the supply of the idle money curve move

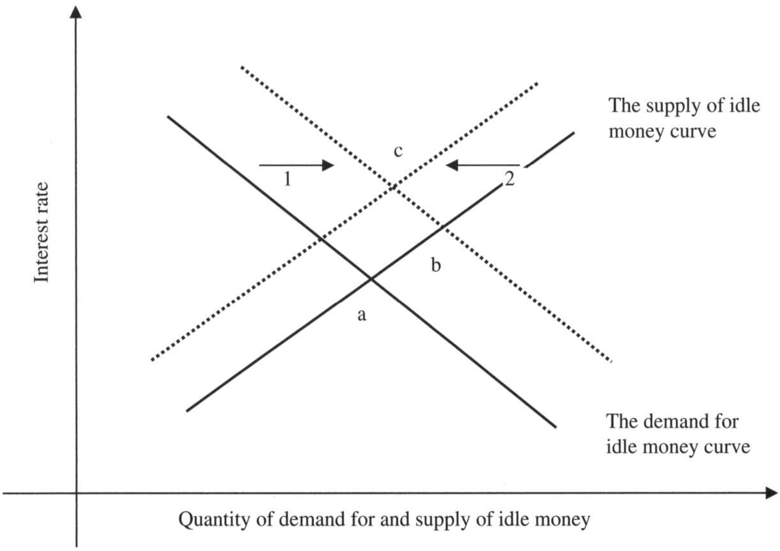

Figure 16.2 A new model of interest rate determination

inward, leading to a rise in the interest rate from *b* to *c*, since the increase of the transactions motive decreases the idle balance. This model is based on the relationship between the finance motive and the liquidity preference, namely, the liquidity preference analysis based on the finance motive; then the influence of the transactions motive is added to the model.

Compared with the IS–LM model, the new model is a logically consistent and stable model of the determination of the interest rate because the interest rate and the quantity of (demand for and supply of) idle money are determined simultaneously.

DEVELOPMENT OF LIQUIDITY PREERENCE THEORY

So far, we have not taken into account the modern banking system. In the above analysis, desired investment, desired saving and idle money all denote *cash*. This does not accord with the modern economy.

When adding the multiple expansion of bank deposits into liquidity preference theory, desired investment, desired saving and idle money all denote *check deposits*. Saving and wealth-holders giving up money mean transforming check deposits into *time deposits*, leading to the rise of *excess reserves* in commercial banks. This can be seen in Figure 16.3.

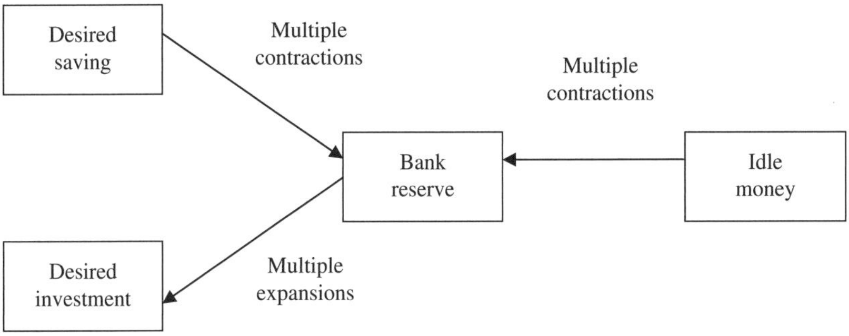

Figure 16.3. Adding the multiple expansion of bank deposits

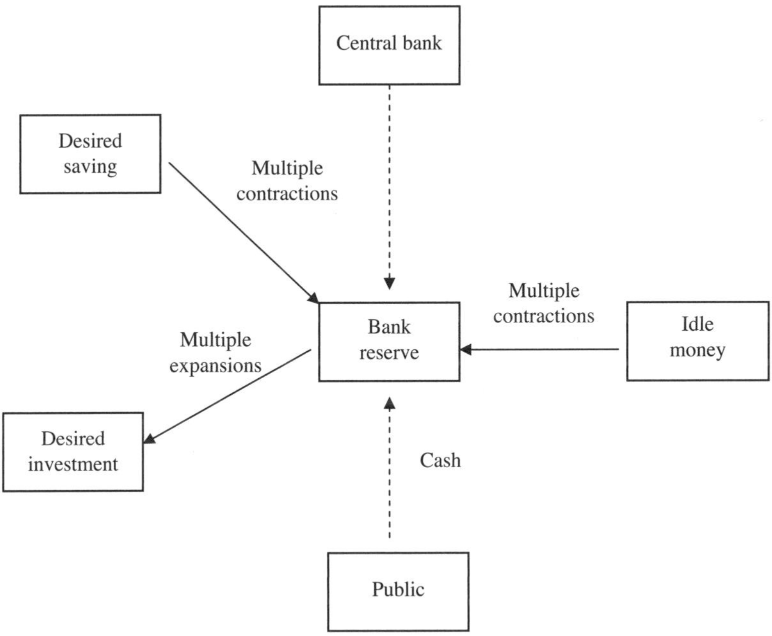

Figure 16.4 The whole picture of the modern banking system

The whole picture of the modern banking system is a little complicated. For a review, see Figure 16.4. From the figure we can see that there are two ways for commercial banks to satisfy a desire for more investment: first, without increasing reserves, commercial banks can increase excess reserves by attracting more savings and wealth-holders giving up money; second, commercial banks can increase reserves by obtaining more loans from the central bank or attracting more cash from the public.

Therefore, after adding the modern banking system, we can no longer say that the interest rate is determined by the demand for and supply of idle money. In the modern economy, the interest rate is determined by the demand for and supply of bank reserves.

Furthermore, liquidity preference theory reveals only the mechanism of how the interest rate is determined and does not tell us whether the central bank or market forces determine the interest rate; this depends on the central bank. For example, in fixed exchange rate regimes, the central bank cannot set the interest rate when it has to control the money supply; in floating exchange rate regimes, the central bank can determine the interest rate if it wishes. Moreover, the central bank can set the interest rate merely by utilizing the mechanism of how the interest rate is determined, which is revealed by liquidity preference theory.

CONCLUSION

With his profound and keen insight, Keynes creatively introduces liquidity preference analysis into the determination of the interest rate. However, he makes two mistakes in developing an integrated liquidity preference theory: (i) he initially overlooks the finance motive, and (ii) he wrongly insists that the interest rate is determined by the demand for and supply of money.

Although Keynes later added the finance motive to correct the first mistake, the strong first impressions of *The General Theory* exert a far-reaching influence on subsequent research: most economists erroneously consider his initial mistake to be the innovation of the theory. This huge misunderstanding results in the belief that the transactions motive plays a fundamental role in liquidity preference theory and that the finance motive is dispensable. Thus, the inherent logic and essence of liquidity preference theory are covered up, leading to much confusion and many misinterpretations.

The second mistake leads to an indetermination of the interest rate or a circular logic of Keynes's theory of interest. This mistake and its consequence are made apparent by the introduction of the finance motive into the theory. Unfortunately, Keynes never becomes aware of this problem. Hansen is right to argue that Keynes's theory of interest is indeterminate, but the basis of his reasoning is wrong.

This Chapter first clarifies the lasting misunderstanding resulting from Keynes's first mistake through analyzing the internal logic of liquidity preference theory, arguing that the liquidity preference analysis based on the finance motive plays a more fundamental role in determining the interest rate. It is the finance motive that transforms the flow demand for credit/fund to the stock demand for money, thus bridging the gap between the classical theory of interest and liquidity preference theory. Then the chapter points out Keynes's second mistake and reveals why the IS–LM model is logically inconsistent. We then develop a new model of the determination of the interest rate on the basis of the liquidity preference analysis which is centered on the finance motive. In the new model, the interest rate is not determined by the demand for and supply of money, but by the demand for and supply of idle money. Further, the banking system is added into the above model, making liquidity preference theory applicable to the modern economy by considering the multiple expansion of bank deposits; the interest rate is determined by the demand for and supply of bank reserves.

NOTES

1. This point of view is different from that of the structuralists.
2. This point of view is different from Bibow's (1995).

BIBLIOGRAPHY

Bibow, J. (1995), 'Some reflections on Keynes "finance motive" for the demand for money', *Cambridge Journal of Economics*, **19**, 647–66.

Chick, V. (1993), *Macroeconomics After Keynes: A Reconsideration of the General Theory*, London: Philip Altan.

Davidson, P. (1965), 'Keynes' finance motive', *Oxford Economic Papers*, **17**, 47–65.

Davidson, P. (1978), *Money and the Real World*, 2nd edn, London: Macmillan.

Hansen, A. (1953), *A Guide to Keynes*, New York: McGraw-Hill.

Hicks, J.R. (1937), 'Mr Keynes and the classics: a suggested interpretation', *Econometrica*, **5**, 147–59.

Keynes, J.M. (1936), *The General Theory of Employment, Interest and Money*, *The Collected Works of John Maynard Keynes* (*JMK*), Vol. VII, London: Macmillan.

Keynes, J.M. (1937a [1973]), 'The general theory of employment', *Quarterly Journal of Economics*, **51**, reprinted in *JMK*, Vol. XIV, 109–23.

Keynes, J.M. (1937b [1973]), 'Alternative theories of the rate of interest', *Economic Journal*, **47**, reprinted in *JMK*, Vol. XIV, 201–15.

Keynes, J.M. (1937c [1973]), 'The "ex ante" theory of the rate of interest', *Economic Journal*, **47**, reprinted in *JMK*, Vol. XIV, 215–23.

Keynes, J.M. (1938 [1973]), 'Mr Keynes' "finance"', *Economic Journal*, **48**, reprinted in *JMK*, Vol. XIV, 229–33.

McCallum, B.T. and E. Nelson (1997), 'An optimizing IS–LM specification for monetary policy and business cycle analysis', *Journal of Money, Credit, and Banking*, **31**, 296–316.

Ohlin, B. (1937a), 'Some notes on the Stockholm theory of saving and investment', *Economic Journal*, **47**, 53–69.
Ohlin, B. (1937b), 'Alternative theories of the rate of interest: rejoinder', *Economic Journal*, **47**, 423–7.
Pasinetti, L. (1974), *Growth and Income Distribution*, Cambridge: Cambridge University Press.
Robertson, D.H. (1937), 'Rejoinder to "Alternative theories of the rate of interest" ', *Economic Journal*, **47**, 428–36.
Robertson, D.H. (1940), 'Mr Keynes and the rate of interest', in *Essays in Monetary Theory*, London: Staples Press.

17. Keynes's 'revolving fund of finance' and transactions in the circuit

Steve Keen

INTRODUCTION

Keynes's primary motivation in writing 'Alternative theories of the rate of interest' (1937b) and 'The "ex-ante" theory of the rate of interest' (1937c) was to counter attempts by Bertil Ohlin and others to recast his liquidity preference theory as no more than a supply and demand model of the determination of the rate of interest. This rearguard action was ultimately unsuccessful, given the profession's ultimate acceptance of Hicks's IS–LM analysis as a summary of *The General Theory*. However, it also had a positive outcome, as tussling with Ohlin's arguments led Keynes to propose that investment finance was 'an additional demand for money' (Keynes 1937b: 247) to *The General Theory*'s triumvirate of transactions, precautionary and speculative demands.

Keynes's musings on the interplay between firms who wish to borrow to finance investment, and banks that provide that finance, is prescient of, and of course partly inspired, the circuitist school's later contribution. But Keynes's less formal logic also reached some conclusions contrary to current circuitist belief. Keynes was correct on these points, while recent circuitist literature is in error. Notwithstanding this however, the contributions of Graziani and others on the nature of a monetary economy are essential to the develoment of a proper model of Keynes's 'revolving fund of liquid finance' (Keynes 1937c: 666).

THE REVOLVING FUND

Keynes identifies three sources of confusion between himself and Ohlin, John Hicks and Dennis Robertson (Keynes 1937b: 241–6); the third of these – a confusion between the money needed to initiate an investment, and the money needed while investment is actually proceeding – led to the development of the concept of a finance demand for money:

> I proceed to the third possible source of confusion, due to the fact (which may deserve more emphasis than I have given it previously) that an investment *decision* (Prof. Ohlin's investment *ex-ante*) may sometimes involve a temporary demand for money before it is carried out, quite distinct from the demand for active balances which will arise as a result of the investment activity whilst it is going on. (Ibid.: 246)

Keynes emphasizes that, if a planned investment is to be turned into an actual one, then the investor will have a need for money that precedes the investment itself:

> Planned investment – i.e. investment *ex-ante* – may have to secure its 'financial provision' *before* the investment takes place; that is to say, before the corresponding saving has taken place . . . There has, therefore, to be a technique to bridge this gap between the time when the decision to invest is taken and the time when the correlative investment and saving actually occur. (Ibid.: 246)

This finance could be secured either by new equity or by new bank debt. In either case, there will be an imbalance between the market's commitments to finance these ventures, and actual savings at that point in time, which generates a 'finance demand for money'. Keynes argues that this should be considered a fourth, additional motive for desiring money in addition to the transactions, precautionary and speculative motives detailed in *The General Theory*:

> Investment finance in this sense is, of course, only a special case of the finance required by any productive process; but since it is subject to special fluctuations of its own, I should (I now think) have done well to have emphasised it when I analysed the various sources of the demand for money. (Ibid.: 247)

Keynes's discussion of how this demand might be met strengthens Dow's case, that Keynes viewed the money supply as endogenous (Dow 1997). Although he observes that additional finance demand for money might drive up the rate of interest – which is consonant with a fixed, exogenously determined money stock – he also countenances that the banking system might meet this demand with an additional supply – which implies an endogenous process of money creation:

> Now, a pressure to secure more finance than usual may easily affect the rate of interest through its influence on the demand for money; and *unless the banking system is prepared to augment the supply of money*, lack of finance may prove an important obstacle to more than a certain amount of investment decisions being on the tapis at the same time. (Keynes 1937b: 247; emphasis added)

Keynes continues that the decision to supply money as finance for investment is an important determinant of the level of economic activity. Thus while he rejected the 'classical' view that savings determined investment, he argued that finance determines investment, and investment in turn determines savings:

> It is the supply of available finance which, in practice, holds up from time to time the onrush of 'new issues.' But if the banking system chooses to make the finance available and the investment projected by the new issues actually takes place, the appropriate level of incomes will be generated out of which there will necessarily remain over an amount of saving exactly sufficient to take care of the new investment. (Ibid.: 248)

In making this case, Keynes also states unambiguously that banks control the supply of money:

> The control of finance is, indeed, a potent, though sometimes dangerous, method for regulating the rate of investment (though much more potent when used as a curb than as a stimulus). Yet this is only another way of expressing the power of the banks through their control over the supply of money – i.e. of liquidity. (Ibid.: 248)

Money is thus an endogenous variable, with its determination involving both the desire by firms to invest, and the willingness of banks to lend. Keynes starts his consideration of this process with a constant level of investment – that is, with a steady stream of investment projects coming forward over time, so that the rate of change of aggregate investment with respect to time is zero. In this case, Keynes argues that a constant stream of investment can be financed by a fixed pool of money, which turns over continuously:

> If investment is proceeding at a steady rate, the finance (or the commitments to finance) required can be supplied from a revolving fund of a more or less constant amount, one entrepreneur having his finance replenished for the purpose of a projected investment as another exhausts his on paying for his completed investment. (Ibid.)

This implies that a constant level of economic activity can be sustained by a constant stock of money – since investment in turn determines the level of income, and a constant level of gross investment implies a constant capital stock. Rising investment, on the other hand, implies rising capital and rising output, and here Keynes argues that there will be a rising demand for money for finance: 'if decisions to invest are (e.g.) increasing, the extra finance involved will constitute an additional demand for money' (ibid.: 247).

As noted above, Keynes countenances that this demand could put upward pressure on the rate of interest, if banks did not generate more money. But it could also lead to banks increasing the money supply 'if the banking system chooses to make the finance available' ibid.: 248. In tranquil times, banks would willingly supply additional finance when firms desired a rising level of investment, and this in turn would cause rising incomes over time. The demand for money would thus call forth its supply.

Keynes concludes with observations about the tendency of economists to confuse finance and saving, and stocks and flows. As he emphatically declared,

> 'Finance' has nothing to do with saving. At the 'financial' stage of the proceedings no net saving has taken place on anyone's part, just as there has been no net investment. 'Finance' and 'commitments to finance' are mere credit and debit book entries, which allow entrepreneurs to go ahead with assurance. (Ibid: 247).

Keynes's conjecture that confusion between stocks and flows was the source of important errors in monetary theory is worth quoting at length:

> It is possible, then, that confusion has arisen between credit in the sense of 'finance,' credit in the sense of 'bank loans' and credit in the sense of 'saving.' I have not attempted to deal here with the second. *It should be observed that a confusion between the first and the last would be one between a flow and a stock.* Credit, in the sense of 'finance,' looks after a flow of investment. It is a revolving fund which can be used over and over again. It does not absorb or exhaust any resources. The same 'finance' can tackle one investment after another. But credit, in Prof. Ohlin's sense of 'saving,' relates to a stock. Each new net investment has new net saving attached to it. The saving can be used once only. It relates to the net addition to the stock of actual assets. (Ibid.: 247; emphasis added)

Keynes's concept of a finance demand for money thus provides a link between a flow of demand for credit money, and the stock of credit money that is needed to meet that flow demand, given the time lags in the economy.

Unlike Keynes, the circuitist school has attempted to deal with 'credit in the sense of "bank loans" '. In so doing, they have reached several conclusions that implicitly or explicitly contradict Keynes.

Keynes implicitly argues that capitalists could make aggregate money profits, after borrowing money at positive rates of interest, when he speaks of 'one entrepreneur having his finance replenished for the purpose of a projected investment as another exhausts his on paying for his completed investment' (ibid.: 247). In contrast, circuitists explicitly allege that capitalists cannot make aggregate monetary profits, even if the rate of interest is zero:

> [I]n the basic circuit approach (describing a closed economy with no government expenditure), firms in the aggregate can only obtain the wage bill they advanced

> to workers (W_N) and, as a result, it is impossible for all firms to obtain money profits. (Bellofiore et al. 2000: 410)[1]

Keynes argues that constant economic activity could be supported with a constant stock of money, regardless of how workers allocated their wages. Circuitists claim that a constant level of activity requires an increasing stock of money if workers save, since with part of the borrowed money saved, firms are unable to repay their bank loans in full: 'If, as is likely to be the case, firms wish to continue their activities, they have to renegotiate bank loans equal to the net stock of money in addition to any lending necessary to start a new production process' (Fontana 2000: 35).

Crucially, Keynes sees money turning over indefinitely in a 'revolving fund of liquid finance' – so that money, once created, exists forever (though he did not consider the issue of bankruptcy). On the other hand, in circuitist literature, money is 'destroyed' when loans are repaid: 'To the extent that bank debts are repaid, an equal amount of money is destroyed' (Graziani 2003: 29–30).

In all these points of contradiction, Keynes is correct and the circuitists are wrong, for the reason Keynes gave in 1937: circuitists, like so many economists before them, have confused stocks with flows. However, circuitist insights into the nature of money, and of exchange in a monetary economy, play a crucial role in turning Keynes's accurate verbal insights into a workable mathematical model of a monetary production economy.

THE CANONICAL CIRCUITIST INSIGHTS

The three key contributions of the circuitist school are:

1. the proposition that a true monetary economy cannot use a commodity as money;
2. the insight that exchanges in a monetary production economy are three-sided, single commodity transactions; and
3. A logical definition of money that is free of the customary confusions that arise from defining money in terms of different types of bank deposits.

The first proposition is derived from the simple observation that 'an economy using as money a commodity coming out of a regular process of production, cannot be distinguished from a barter economy' (Graziani 1989: 3). From this it follows that true money is a token, which in turn gives rise to two further conditions, that:

> the use of money must give rise to an immediate and final payment and not to a simple commitment to make a payment in the future; and
> the use of money must be so regulated as to give no privilege of seigniorage to any agent. (Graziani 2003: 60)

These conditions lead to the second fundamental insight, that all sales in a monetary economy involve three parties: a seller, a buyer, and a bank which transfers the requisite number of units of account from the buyer's account to the seller's.

These in turn provide a definition of money that enables it to be clearly distinguished from credit – another confusion that Keynes notes. Money is as a unit of account whose transfer is accepted as final payment in all commodity and service exchanges; credit, on the other hand, enables a commodity or service exchange to occur, but involves a continuing debtor–creditor relationship between the buyer and the seller.

CIRCUITISTS AND CHARTALISTS

The state plays no necessary role in the above definition of money – though circuitists of course acknowledge the existence of 'fiat' money, and generally accept the chartalist or state theory of money position with respect to the origins of money and its modern legal framework (see, for example, Graziani 2003: 78–80). However, this school has attempted to build models which at the outset have no government sector – nor any explicit role for the central bank (ibid.: 26–32). In this sense, the circuit approach conflicts with the chartalist argument that 'It is thus impossible to separate the theory of money from the theory of the state' (Wray 2000: 50).

From the circuitist point of view, the production and enforcement of a unit of account by a tax-levying state is an embellishment to its fundamental concept of money. The circuitist starting-point of a pure credit economy is thus arguably closer to the essential nature of money, even if so-called 'state money' is the universal norm today, and even state enforcement of monetary obligations may be the only viable way to sustainably meet Graziani's anti-seigniorage condition in the real world.

However, the failure to date of circuitists to produce a coherent model of endogenous money could have implied that the chartalist position was correct, in that a tax-levying state was indeed an essential component of a functional model of money. In fact, as I show below, a functional model of a monetary production economy can be built without either a government sector or a central bank, so long as transfers between private bank accounts are accepted as making final settlement of debts between buyers and sellers.

THE BASIC CIRCUITIST MODEL

Graziani (2003) presents a canonical version of the circuitist verbal model of a monetary production economy. The model is described as having four classes of agents – 'the central bank, commercial banks, firms and wage earners' (pp. 26–7) – but despite this, the central bank is given no role in the model itself. The actual model therefore has only three agents.[2]

The model's monetary dynamics commence with 'A decision – by the banks to grant credit to firms, thus enabling them to start a process of production' (p. 27). Graziani argues that the amount of credit demanded by the firms (and supplied by the banks) equals the wage bill for the planned level of production.

Using the borrowed money, capitalists pay workers and put them to work to produce commodities. These are then sold, with consumer goods being sold to workers and investment goods to other capitalists (sales to bankers appear later).

Spending by workers on consumer goods (and also purchases of corporate bonds by workers) return money to the firms, who can then use this money to repay their debt to banks. This repayment of debt destroys money (Graziani 2003, pp. 29–30).

The repayment of debt closes the circuit, but this only happens '[i]f wage earners spend their incomes entirely' (including on purchases of corporate bonds). However, if they do not, then dilemmas arise: 'If instead wage earners decide to keep a portion of their savings in the form of liquid balances, firms are unable to repay their bank debt by the same amount' (p. 30).

The next cycle, if it involves an identical scale of production, therefore requires new money, so that the money supply must increase to finance a constant scale of production. The new quantity of money in this second circuit 'will be equal to the wage bill plus the new liquid balances set aside by wage earners at the end of the previous cycle' (p. 31).

The above, however, omits the problem of interest on debt! Graziani acknowledges this – in contrast to some circuitist papers that abstract from the problem, in a manner that is embarrassingly reminiscent of the neoclassical approach to logical conundrums (Bellofiore et al. 2000: 410, footnotes 8 and 9):

> It appears that firms are unable to pay interest: Even in the most favourable case [corresponding to workers spending all their wages], the firms can only repay in money the principal of their debt and are anyhow unable to pay interest. (p. 31)

The solution he proffers, in a monetary model, is a 'real' one, that banks are paid in commodities rather than money: 'the only thing they can do is to sell part of their product to the banks, which is tantamount to saying that interest can only be paid in kind' (p. 31).

At least bankers get their hands on the physical loot: capitalists, it seems, end up with neither goods nor money. Money profits in the aggregate are zero, and 'profits earned by one firm may simply be the mirror image of inefficiencies and consequent losses incurred by other firms' (p. 32).

A DYNAMIC MODEL OF THE CIRCUIT

Starting from precisely the same foundation, I reach contrary conclusions on almost every point above, and conclude instead that Keynes's 1937 insights were correct. A constant level of production can be financed with a constant stock of money (see also Andresen 2006); firms can easily pay the interest on debt with money; and firms in the aggregate earn money profits. Money is not destroyed by the repayment of debt (though bank deposits are 'destroyed' by loan repayment, and the stock of money available for transactions at any one time is reduced), workers can have positive bank balances without forcing firms to make losses; and, although it is related to the wage bill, the initial amount borrowed is in fact far smaller.

These contrary conclusions arise simply from applying the correct form of mathematical analysis to the circuitist school's logical insights into the nature of a monetary production economy. The circuit is fundamentally dynamic, and can therefore only be properly understood using dynamic analysis. Mathematical dynamics are essential here, partly because the interrelations between entities in a dynamic model are easily mis-specified in verbal analysis, and especially because it is easy, in a verbal exposition, to confuse stocks and flows. In what follows, I construct a skeletal dynamic mathematical model of the circuit, using balance sheets in which all entries are flows.

I also introduce a novel framework for developing a dynamic model that uses the familiar tool of the double-entry book-keeping ledger. The entries in Tables 17.2, 17.3 and 17.4, and on represent flows between accounts: each row in a table represents a particular class of transaction (payment of interest on the balance in the workers' account, for example), while the sum of each column gives the dynamic equation for the relevant system variable.

The model is, I stress, *deliberately* skeletal: causal factors of financial flows that are clearly variables in the real world are treated as constants – with the intention that these will indeed be made variables in a later model. However, just as much is learned in anatomy by studying skeletons, much can be learned about the actual monetary systems by studying a stylised system in which the causes of financial instability are absent.

Table 17.1 Loan issued

Time	Assets	Liabilities		
	Firm loan (F_L)	Firm deposit (F_D)	Banker deposit (B_D)	Worker deposit (W_D)
Start of loan	L	L	0	0

Graziani's model has three classes of agents – firms, banks and workers. Since this is a monetary economy, all three classes have deposit accounts which I indicate as F_D, B_D and W_D respectively. Prior to the making of a loan, all three accounts have zero balances, and a firm's debt to a bank's F_L is likewise zero (this is *not* a bank account as such: it does not contain money, nor can money be paid into it, but instead it records the outstanding obligation of the firm to the bank; it is, therefore, a record of account).

In step one of the model, a bank makes a loan to a firm. Since this is credit money, a debt obligation is created between the firm and the banks along with the creation of money. Using L to signify the magnitude of the loan, this results in the situation shown in Table 17.1. This clearly embodies the direct and causal 'loans create deposits' perspective of endogenous money.

A loan generates an obligation to pay interest to the lender, while a deposit obligates the bank to pay interest to the depositor. I use r_L for the rate of interest on loans and r_D for the rate on deposits (where $r_L > r_D$). These obligations therefore mean that the firm must pay the bank the amount $r_L \cdot F_L$, while the bank must pay the firm $r_D \cdot F_D$. These flows must be between the accounts in the system – since there is no other source of money. The firm must therefore pay the loan interest obligation out of its deposit account F_D, while the bank must pay its deposit interest obligation out of its deposit account B_D.

The flows occur between these two deposit accounts, and the payment of loan interest is recorded on the asset side of the ledger, so that the firm's debt remains constant at the level of the initial loan L. Since the interest payments flow between the firm's and the banker's deposit accounts, the overall sum of deposit accounts also stabilises at L; but since $r_L > r_D$, the balance shifts from the firm's deposit account to the banker's over time. This dynamic is shown in Table 17.2.

Equation (17.1), below, states this *incomplete* system as a set of coupled ordinary differential equations (ODEs). It is obvious that the level of debt will remain constant (at the initial value L), as will the sum of deposit accounts, but the money in the firm's account will over time be transferred

Table 17.2 Payment of interest

Flows	Assets	Liabilities			SAM
	Firm loan (F_L)	Firm deposit (F_D)	Banker deposit (BD)	Worker deposit (W_D)	Sum
Interest flows initiated by loan	$+r_L F_L$ $-r_L F_{L=}0$	$+r_D F_D$ $-r_L F_L$	$+r_L F_L$ $-r_D F_D$	0	0

to the bank's. At some point, the firm's deposit account will turn negative – which is of course an unsustainable situation.

$$\begin{aligned} &\tfrac{d}{dt}F_L = 0 \\ &\tfrac{d}{dt}F_D = r_D F_D - r_L F_L \\ &\tfrac{d}{dt}B_D = r_L F_L - r_D F_D \\ &\tfrac{d}{dt}W_D = 0. \end{aligned} \tag{17.1}$$

Figure 17.1 shows a simulation of this system. Given the set of example parameter values ($L = 100$, $r_L = 5\%$, $r_D = 3\%$) while the outstanding loan and the sum of deposit accounts remain at 100 throughout, all the money has been transferred from the firm's deposit account to the banker's after 30.5 years.

Given	Initial values	Flow dynamics
Firm loan account	$F_L(0) = L$	$\tfrac{d}{dt}F_L(t) = rL{\cdot}FL(t) - rL{\cdot}FL(t)$
Firm deposit account	$F_D(0) = L$	$\tfrac{d}{dt}F_D(t) = r_D{\cdot}F_D(t) - r_L{\cdot}F_L(t)$
Bank deposit account	$B_D(0) = 0$	$\tfrac{d}{dt}B_D(t) = r_L{\cdot}F_L(t) - r_D{\cdot}F_D(t)$
Worker deposit account	$W_D(0) = 0$	$\tfrac{d}{dt}W_D(t) = 0$

$$\begin{bmatrix} F_L \\ F_D \\ B_D \\ W_D \end{bmatrix} := \text{Odesolve} = \left[\begin{pmatrix} F_L \\ F_D \\ B_D \\ W_D \end{pmatrix}, t, Y \right]$$

This outcome possibly explains why circuitists have been loath to acknowledge the need to pay interest in their models of the monetary circuit: the situation seems hopeless for firms. However, this is only because

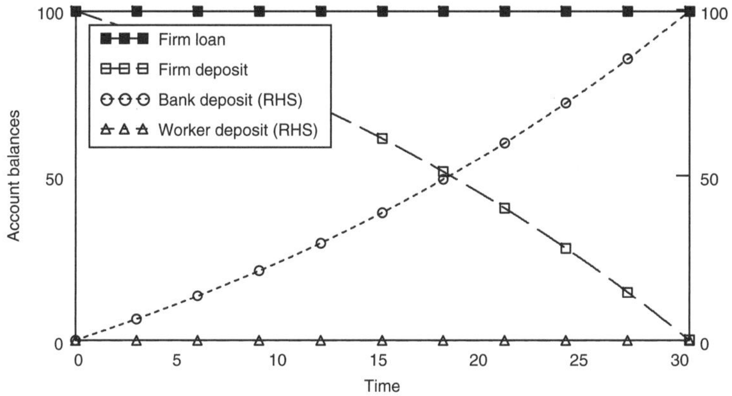

$F_D(Y) = 0 \;\; B_D(Y) = 100 \;\; W_D(Y) = 0 \;\; F_D(Y) + B_D(Y) + W_D(Y) = 100.$

Figure 17.1 Simulation of interest payment only model in Mathcad

firms have not yet done anything with the borrowed money. In fact, it has been borrowed to finance production, which involves both buying inputs from other firms, and paying wages to workers. This in turn is done in order to evoke a stream of purchases from other firms, workers and bankers from which the firms hope to make a net profit.

The issue of production, and the transactions enabling it and emanating from it, is another area of great confusion in circuitist writings. The key confusion is one of stocks and flows, starting from the proposition that the size of the initial loan (the *stock* L) is equal to the wage payments needed to hire the workforce (a *flow*). Instead, the wage bill is related, not to the initial loan, but to the rate of outflow of money from firms' deposit accounts that is used to pay wages. Calling this rate of outflow w, an amount $w \cdot F_D$ is transferred per unit of time (per year in this model) from firms to workers as wages.

The relationship between money and wages is thus not 'the credit initially granted [L, a stock] is totally turned into wages [$w \cdot F_D$, a flow]' (Graziani 2003: 29). Instead, in this skeletal model, wages equal a constant times the balance in the firm's deposit account.[3] Given the relationship between the initial loan and the balance in the firm's account, the annual wages paid can be substantially greater than the initial loan.

With workers now having a positive bank balance, they too are recipients of interest income. Though in the real world workers normally get lower deposit rates than firms, for simplicity I shall use the same rate of interest r_D here. A flow of $r_D \cdot W_D$ is therefore deducted from the banker's account and deposited into the worker's account.

Table 17.3 Transactions complete the basic model

Flows	Assets	Liabilities			SAM
	Firm loan (FL)	Firm deposit (FD)	Banker deposit (BD)	Worker deposit (WD)	Sum
Interest flows initiated by loan	0	$+r_D{\cdot}F_D$ $-r_L{\cdot}F_L$	$+r_L{\cdot}F_L$ $-r_D{\cdot}F_D$	0	0
Wage flow to initiate production		$-w{\cdot}F_D$		$+w{\cdot}F_D$	0
Interest income flows from wages			$-r_D{\cdot}W_D$	$+r_D{\cdot}W_D$	0
Flows from sale		$+\omega{\cdot}W_D$ $+\beta{\cdot}B_D$	$-\beta{\cdot}B_D$	$-\omega{\cdot}W_D$	0

To complete the model, we have to include the flow of transactions from workers and bankers to capitalists that purchase the goods flowing (implicitly in this model) in the opposite direction. Here I use ω for the rate at which spending flows from workers' deposit accounts to firms', and β for the corresponding rate of spending by banks. The amounts $\omega{\cdot}W_D$ and $\beta{\cdot}B_D$ are therefore deducted from the worker's and the bank's accounts, respectively, and credited to the firms' account.

The basic model is finally complete, and as shown by the sum column of the social accounting matrix (SAM) all transactions are properly accounted for and sum to zero – so that money is neither created nor destroyed. The components of the basic coupled ODE model can now be read down the columns of Table 17.3.

In coupled ODE form, the model is as shown in equation (17.2)

$$\begin{aligned}
&\tfrac{d}{dt}F_L = 0\\
&\tfrac{d}{dt}F_D = (r_D F_D - r_L F_L) - w{\cdot}F_D + (\omega{\cdot}W_D + \beta{\cdot}B_D)\\
&\tfrac{d}{dt}B_D = (r_L F_L - r_D F_D) - r_D{\cdot}W_D - \beta{\cdot}B_D\\
&\tfrac{d}{dt}W_D = w{\cdot}F_D + r_D{\cdot}W_D - \omega{\cdot}W_D.
\end{aligned} \tag{17.2}$$

The model can now be simulated (see Figure 17.2; the additional parameter values used here are w=3, $\omega = 26$ and $\beta = 0.5$), and since it is a linear model, its equilibrium can also be derived symbolically (see equation (17.3)).

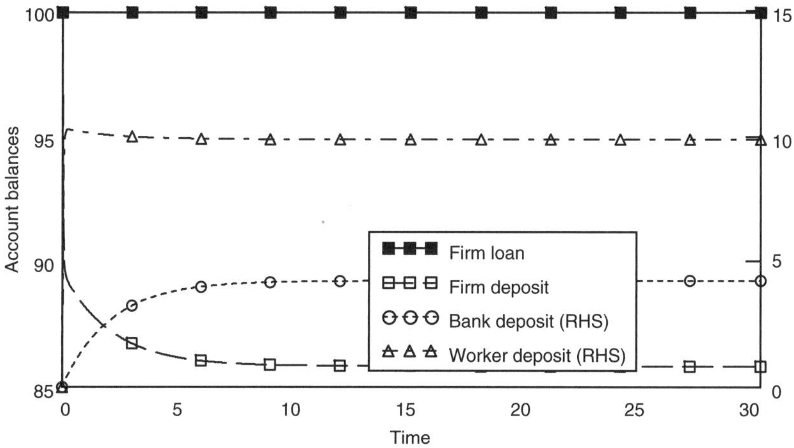

$F_D(Y) = 85.83$ $B_D(Y) = 4.255$ $W_D(Y) = 9.915$ $F_D(Y) + B_D(Y) + W_D(Y) = 100.$

Figure 17.2 Basic circuit model

As is now obvious, the basic circuit model with a single injection of endogenous money is consistent with sustained economic activity over time – contradicting the circuitists since an increasing supply is not needed to sustain constant economic activity, and confirming Keynes (1937b; see also Andresen 2006). However, the amounts shown here are transaction account balances: we do not yet know whether these are compatible with sustained incomes over time.

$$\begin{bmatrix} F_{L_E} \\ F_{D_E} \\ B_{D_E} \\ W_{D_E} \end{bmatrix} = \begin{bmatrix} L \\ \dfrac{L\cdot(\omega - r_D)\cdot(\beta - r_L)}{(w + \omega - r_D)\cdot(\beta - r_D)} \\ \dfrac{L\cdot(r_L - r_D)}{\beta - r_D} \\ \dfrac{L\cdot w\cdot(\beta - r_L)}{(w + \omega - r_D)\cdot(\beta - r_D)} \end{bmatrix} = \begin{bmatrix} 100 \\ 85.83 \\ 4.255 \\ 9.915 \end{bmatrix} \tag{17.3}$$

Income Dynamics

Fortunately, two income flows are easily associated with particular transactions in equation (17.2): wages and interest income. Annual wages are equal to $W\cdot F_D$ and gross bank interest income is r_L F_L (257.489 and 5 per annum, respectively, in this simulation). Wages and interest income are thus positive and sustained; what about profits?

To reveal profits, we need to consider what the term w represents. As well as being equivalent to wages, it also represents that part of the net surplus from production that accrues to workers. The net surplus – in monetary terms – itself depends on how rapidly money invested in production returns to firms. In Marx's terms, it represents the time lag between extending M and receiving $M+$ (assuming, as I do in this skeletal model, that the process occurs smoothly). This could be a period of, say, four months between financing production and receiving the complete proceeds of sale of output – again something that would be a variable in a more complex model. There are thus two components to w: the share of the net surplus (in Piero Sraffa's sense of the surplus, in which wages and profits are entirely paid out of the net surplus from the input–output process) from production going to workers, and the rate of turnover from M to $M+$, given by technical conditions of production and the time taken for the sale of physical commodities. I use s for the share of surplus accruing to the owners of firms (so that the share going to workers is thus $1-s$), and P for the lag between M and $M+$.[4] We therefore have the relation given by equation (17.4):

$$w = (1 - s)\cdot P \tag{17.4}$$

With w set to 3 in the simulation above, a hypothetical value of s of 0.4 (which corresponds to a 'rate of surplus value' in Marx's terms of 67 per cent) yields a value for P of 5 (which means that the lag between spending M and making $M+$ is one-fifth of a year or 2.4 months). The monetary value of net output per annum is thus $P\cdot F_D$ (which equals 429.15 in equilibrium, given the parameter values in the model) which is split between workers and the owners of firms in the ratio $(1 - s){:}s$. In this debt–finance only model, the owners of firms then have to pay interest on their outstanding debt to banks. Using Π, W and I to signify profits, wages and interest income, respectively, the income, flows of the model in equilibrium are:

$$\begin{bmatrix}\Pi_E \\ I_E \\ W_E\end{bmatrix} = \begin{bmatrix} s\cdot P - \dfrac{L\cdot(\omega - r_D)\cdot(\beta - r_L)}{[(1-s)\cdot P + \omega - r_D]\cdot(\beta - r_D)} \\ r_D\cdot L \\ (1-s)\cdot P - \dfrac{L\cdot(\omega - r_D)\cdot(\beta - r_L)}{[(1-s)\cdot P + \omega - r_D]\cdot(\beta - r_D)} \end{bmatrix} = \begin{bmatrix}166.66 \\ 5 \\ 257.49\end{bmatrix}. \tag{17.5}$$

Firms thus do make net profits, which, though related to the size of the initial loan, can be substantially larger than this amount (and profits are substantially larger than the servicing cost of debt). Economic activity also continues indefinitely at an equilibrium level with a single injection of endogenous money: additional money is not needed to sustain economic activity at a constant level. This contradicts Graziani's assertion that additional money would be needed if workers retained positive bank balances (Graziani 2003: 31), but confirms Keynes's intuition that a 'revolving fund of a more or less constant amount' can finance sustained economic activity (Keynes 1937b: 248).

The size of the initial loan L can also be related to the equilibrium value of wages generated by the loan:

$$L = W_E \cdot \frac{[(1-s)\cdot P + \omega - r_D]\cdot(\beta - r_D)}{(1-s)\cdot P\cdot(\omega - r_D)\cdot(\beta - r_L)} = 100. \qquad (17.6)$$

Two more issues remain to be considered: the modelling of money creation itself, and the impact of debt repayment.

Growth

At this stage, the model accords with Keynes's verbal analysis of the 'revolving fund of finance' without growth. The next problem is how to model endogenous money in a growing economy, when 'decisions to invest are (e.g.) increasing' and 'the extra finance involved will constitute an additional demand for money' (ibid.: 248).

Accounting for growth integrates Moore's 'horizontalism' into the circuitist framework (Moore 1988). As Moore argues, firms negotiate 'lines of credit' with banks that enable them to expand the available money, subject to the same sum being added to their outstanding debt. New money is thus created by an addition of an identical sum to the firm's deposit and loan accounts. Using n_M (for 'new money') to signify the rate, and relating this to the level of the firm's deposit accounts,[5] this introduces a new term $n_M \cdot F_D$ into the columns for F_L and F_D.

There is no offsetting transfer between income and capital accounts in this case, so that the term $n_M \cdot F_D$ causes a net increase in the money stock: it is an endogenous source of growth. As a result, rather than having a zero sum, the complete SAM has a positive sum, equal to the amount of new money being created each year.

Debt Repayment and Bank Reserves

According to Graziani – and almost all theorists in endogenous money – the repayment of debt destroys the money that was created with it (Graziani 2003: 29–30). I consider this by adding an additional term R_D to

Table 17.4 Complete system with new money, debt repayment and relending

Account Type	Assets			Liabilities			
	Loans	Reserves	Sum	Deposits			Sum
Name	F_L	B_R	Σ	F_D	B_D	W_D	Σ
Interest				$r_D \cdot F_D$ $-r_L \cdot F_L$	$-r_D \cdot F_D$ $+r_L \cdot F_L$		0
Wages				$-w \cdot F_D$		$w \cdot F_D$	0
Interest					$-r_D \cdot W_D$	$r_D \cdot W_D$	0
Consumption				$\beta \cdot B_D$ $+\omega \cdot W_D$	$-\beta \cdot B_D$	$-\omega \cdot W_D$	0
New loans	$n_M \cdot F_D$		$n_M \cdot F_D$	$n_M \cdot F_D$			$n_M \cdot F_D$
Repayment	$-R_D \cdot F_L$	$R_D \cdot F_L$	0	$-R_D \cdot F_L$			$-R_D \cdot F_L$
Relending	$R_R \cdot B_R$	$-R_R \cdot B_R$	0	$R_R \cdot B_R$			$R_R \cdot B_R$

represent the repayment of debt. If we relate this to the level of outstanding debt,[6] then the amount $R_D \cdot F_L$ is deducted from the firm's only source of money, F_D. Yet to where does it go?

Here Graziani's anti-seigniorage condition comes into play: 'the use of money must be so regulated as to give no privilege of seigniorage to any agent' (ibid.: 60). This repayment therefore cannot be made to the existing banker's deposit account B_D, since banks use this account to finance spending on commodities. It must therefore go to a separate, capital account: the bank's reserve account, which I call B_R.

Reserves, once created by the repayment of loans, will be re-lent at the rate R_R. This amount will be deducted from the bank's reserve account and deposited in the firm's deposit account – and a matching entry will be made in the firm's loan record of account. The complete relations are shown in Table 17.4. The repayment of loans therefore does not 'destroy' money, but transfers it out of income accounts – where it can be used for expenditure – to a reserve account. The proposition that money is destroyed when loans are repaid in part reflects economic conventions that money is the sum of active bank balances. If money is defined that way, then it is indeed destroyed; but the dynamics of endogenous money creation are more clearly illuminated if we define money in the fundamental circuitist sense as a token whose transfer settles all commitments between trading parties. That token can then reside in active accounts (deposits) or inactive accounts (reserves). Repayment of loans alters the balance between active and inactive accounts, and thus alters the amount of money in circulation, but it does not destroy the token itself.

Once there, it is an unencumbered asset of the banks which can then be relent – though not spent directly on commodities or services. This adds an important additional insight to the concept of endogenous money: not only do 'loans create deposits', but 'the repayment of loans creates reserves'.

The new parameters R_L and L_R were given the values of 2 and 3, respectively, while nM was set at 1/12.

The overall model, as shown in equation (17.7), is therefore 'dissipative', – in the language of modern dynamic analysis – rather than 'conservative', which has important implications for the feasible behaviour of any complete model built on this skeleton:

$$\begin{aligned}
\tfrac{d}{dt}F_L &= +R_R{\cdot}B_R - R_D{\cdot}F_L + n_M{\cdot}F_D \\
\tfrac{d}{dt}F_D &= (r_D F_D - r_L F_L) - (1-s){\cdot}P{\cdot}F_D + (\omega{\cdot}W_D + \beta{\cdot}B_D) \\
&\quad + (R_R{\cdot}B_R - R_D{\cdot}F_L) + n_M{\cdot}F_D \\
\tfrac{d}{dt}B_D &= (r_L F_L - r_D F_D) - r_D{\cdot}W_D - \beta{\cdot}B_D \\
\tfrac{d}{dt}W_D &= (1-s){\cdot}P{\cdot}F_D + r_D{\cdot}W_D - \omega{\cdot}W_D \\
\tfrac{d}{dt}B_R &= +R_D{\cdot}F_L - R_R{\cdot}B_R.
\end{aligned} \tag{17.7}$$

Although the amount of money and debt in this final model grow exponentially over time, the same relations hold between debt and income deposits, while the overall money stock includes both the sum of deposit accounts and the amount in banks' reserves. At the end of the simulation period (30 years), the endogenous money stock has grown from 100 to 379.13, 228.78 of which is in circulation between firm, bank and worker income accounts, and 150.35 of which is in the bank's reserve account (Figure 17.3).

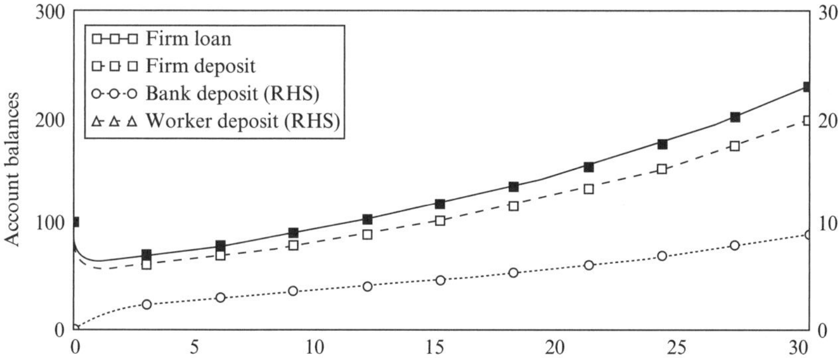

Figure 17.3 Model with growth

Deposit accounts	$F_D(Y) + B_D(Y) + W_D(Y) = 228.78$
	$F_D(Y) = 197.13$ $W_D(Y) = 22.73$
Bank assets	$F_L(Y) = 228.78$ $B_R(Y) = 150.35$
Income flows	$s \cdot P \cdot F_D(Y) = 394.27$ $(1 - s) \cdot P \cdot F_D(Y) = 591.4$
	$r_L \cdot F_L(Y) = 11.44$

From Parameters to Behaviours

Like a biological skeleton, this model is designed to have muscles attached, in that its fixed parameters can be replaced by nonlinear behavioural relations that mimic those of real economies. Two that deserve special mention are R_R and n_M, representing, respectively, the rate of relending by banks and the rate of new money creation driven by firms.

The latter provides the 'Horizontalist' aspect of this skeletal model, and in a general model would be a nonlinear function of firms' expectations of profits (see Keen 1995). The former reflects the structuralist emphasis on the active role of banks in the credit system. In a financial crisis, this would tend towards zero, while during a period of euphoric expectations the rate of relending would accelerate.

This illustrates another advantage of dynamic modelling over the conventional diagrammatic and static methods that Post Keynesian and circuitist economists have in the past applied. Diagrammatic methods are necessarily 'two dimensional', while static methods make it difficult, if not impossible, to examine causal relations – even when they are correctly specified, which is rarely if ever the case. On the other hand, this properly specified dynamic model enables the integration of the horizontalist and structuralist approaches (which could be further embellished by making the spread between r_L and r_D a variable).

CONCLUSION

Keynes was correct that a 'revolving fund of finance' can initiate an indefinite stream of production, and that this fund is a necessary prelude to production itself in a monetary economy. The circuitist formalisation of the concept of credit money plays an essential role in converting Keynes's vision from a verbal to a dynamic model, but at the same time, some prevalent circuitist concepts must be abandoned in favour of Keynes's accurate insights from 1937.

Both Keynes and circuitists gain from this model. Keynes is shown, once again, to have correctly identified the dynamics of a monetary production economy, even though he lacked the assistance of mathematical logic to clarify his argument. Circuitists gain an effective expression of their model, and lose only erroneous conclusions that shackled their capacity to achieve their real goal, of specifying the behaviour of endogenous money in a monetary production economy.

NOTES

1. Similar conclusions are reached in numerous other circuitist papers from Graziani (1989) on. Rochon puts the problem well: 'The existence of monetary profits at the macroeconomic level has always been a conundrum for theoreticians of the monetary circuit . . . not only are firms unable to create profits, they also cannot raise sufficient funds to cover the payment of interest. In other words, how can M become M'?' (Rochon 2005: 125).
2. The central bank properly enters the circuitist model when the banking sector is expanded, so that a seller can deposit the proceeds of a sale in a different bank from that of the buyer. This necessitates a clearing house between banks, which is the primary role of a central bank in the circuitist model. In this chapter, for the sake of simplicity, I omit inter-bank dynamics.
3. Later I apply Graziani's position that 'the demand for bank credit coming from producers depends only on the wage rate and on the number of workers that firms intend to hire' (Graziani 2003: 29) to calculate the size of the initial loan L as a function of the equilibrium wage bill.
4. Again, in a more complete model, each of these stages of the process would have their own equation with its own dynamics; here, for reasons of simplicity and exposition, they are all collapsed into the values of s and P.
5. It could as easily be related to the level of outstanding loans, and would doubtless have a more complex causal link in a full dynamic model.
6. It could equally be related to the level of F_D.

REFERENCES

Andresen, T. (2006), 'A critique of a Post Keynesian model of hoarding, and an alternative model', *Journal of Economic Behavior and Organization*, **60**, 230–51.

Bellofiore, R., G.F. Davanzati and R. Realfonzo (2000), 'Marx inside the circuit: discipline device, wage bargaining and unemployment in a sequential monetary economy', *Review of Political Economy*, **12**, 403–17.

Dow, S. (1997), 'Endogenous money', in G.C. Harcourt and P.A. Riach (eds), *A 'Second Edition' of the General Theory*, London: Routledge, pp. 61–78.

Fontana, G. (2000), 'Post Keynesians and circuitists on money and uncertainty: an attempt at generality', *Journal of Post Keynesian Economics*, **23**, 27–48.

Fontana, G. and R. Realfonzo (eds) (2005), *The Monetary Theory of Production*, New York: Palgrave.

Graziani, A. (1989), 'The theory of the monetary circuit', *Thames Papers in Political Economy*, Spring, 1–26, reprinted in M. Musella and C. Panico (eds) (1995), *The Money Supply in the Economic Process*, Aldershot, UK and Brookfield, US: Edward Elgar, pp. 1–26.

Graziani, A. (2003), *The Monetary Theory of Production*, Cambridge: Cambridge. University Press.
Keen, S. (1995), 'Finance and economic breakdown: modelling Minsky's financial instability hypothesis', *Journal of Post Keynesian Economics*, **17**, 607–35.
Keynes, J.M. (1937b), 'Alternative theories of the rate of interest', *Economic Journal*, **47**, 241–52.
Keynes, J.M. (1937c), 'The "ex-ante" theory of the rate of interest', *Economic Journal*, **47**, 663–9.
Moore, B. (1988), *Horizontalists and Verticalists: The Macroeconomics of Credit* Money, Cambridge: Cambridge University Press.
Rochon, L.-P. (2005), 'The existence of monetary profits within the monetary circuit', in Fontana and Realfonzo, pp. 125–38.
Wray, L. Randall (2000), 'What is money and where did it come from?' in J. Smithin (ed.), *What is Money*?, London: Routledge, pp. 42–66.

18. Monetary and fiscal policies in a Post Keynesian stock–flow consistent model*

Edwin Le Heron

LIQUIDITY PREFERENCE AND ENDOGENOUS MONEY: A RECONCILIATION

The theoretical approach of this chapter seems unrealistic, nevertheless, we shall attempt to reconcile in a model: (i) the liquidity preference theory with its endogenous interest rate (Keynes, 1936 [1973]: ch. 13; 1937), which focuses on the money stock and (ii) the endogenous money of effective demand with an exogenous interest rate (Keynes, 1936 [1973]: ch. 3; and the horizontalist approach of Kaldor, 1985 and Moore, 1988), which focuses on the money flow. Our solution generalizes the liquidity preference theory to the commercial bank sector, distinguishes the determination of the short- and the long-run interest rate, and analyzes the dynamic of flows and stocks in a Post Keynesian model.

In Keynes's *General Theory* and in the IS–LM model, the 'monetary authorities' should resolve all the problems regarding the creation and control of money. The banking system is analyzed solely in terms of central bank activities: the supply of money is fixed exogenously by the central bank. An endogenous theory of the demand for money coexists with an endogenous theory of the interest rate (liquidity preference).

But many Post Keynesians prefer to think of an endogenous money supply, determined by the demand for funds in the banking sector. They then use an exogenous theory of the short-term interest rate fixed by the monetary policy. This 'horizontalist' approach views banks as intermediaries between the central bank, which fixes the price of money, and borrowers, who adjust their demand according to industrial and financial

* A previous version of this model was written, notably for the Eviews modeling, with T. Mouakil (University of Bordeaux) in 2005. Our grateful thanks to W. Godley, M. Lavoie, J. Mazier, T. Mouakil, D. Plihon, E. Tymoigne and G. Zezza for their helpful comments on the previous drafts. The Regional Council of Aquitaine (France) financed this research.

needs. However, there is no place for banking behavior and for Keynes's theory of liquidity preference.

In my previous works (Le Heron, 1986, 2007), private banks can impose a monetary constraint independently of the central bank, in that they are producers of money within a framework of uncertainty. By their own anticipations of effective demand, commercial banks can influence growth and employment. The demand for money predetermines the money supply. While the money supply cannot be higher than the demand for it, it can be lower and thus restrain demand. Under the influence of the central bank and the effective demand of entrepreneurs, the money supply and the interest rate are endogenous; they are largely determined by banking behavior. These considerations require that the liquidity preference of banks should be integrated into the Post Keynesian framework.

Thus I have tried to make Keynes's approach (endogenous money and theory of liquidity preference) compatible with an endogenous theory of the money supply. The behavior of private banks determines the supply of money and, to a certain extent, the long-term interest rate. This application of liquidity preference to commercial banks[1] allows us to preserve the main part of the Post Keynesian theory of money: namely, that the demand for money is endogenous, the functions of money supply and demand are not independent and the short-term interest rate is exogenously determined.

From an examination of bank liquidity preference, the following phenomena become apparent: first, an insufficient supply of money can occur – that is to say, a supply that is lower than that which is demanded by firms. Banks can worsen unemployment by rationing the financing of demand and, hence, by slowing down growth. Second, endogenous long-term interest rates are determined not only by monetary policy, but also by the behavior of private banks. So the curve of interest rates becomes endogenous. Third, in a global economy with strong financial markets, well-structured accounting practices of banks often become essential. A more complex process of money creation can be introduced. Fourth, banking and financial instability often explains economic cycles and their crises (Minsky, 1975).

The channels of transmission of monetary policy originate in changes in the short-term interest rate. Usually, the focus of this subject is on the links between monetary policy and firms or households. Banks are considered merely as the 'drive belt' of these fluctuations in interest rates and are neutralized in the process. Nevertheless, banks, which may be regarded as entrepreneurs in the money production process, are also subjected to monetary shocks. Their reactions modify the quantity (flow) and the structure (stock) of financing as well as having a significant effect on the determination of long-term interest rates.

The aim is to analyze the consequences of a monetary policy shock on the behavior of banks and firms within three assumptions on the fiscal policy. First, we build a Post Keynesian stock–flow macroeconomic consistent model (Lavoie and Godley, 2001; Dos Santos and Zezza, 2004; Mouakil, 2006; Godley and Lavoie, 2007) with a private bank sector introducing more realistic features. For that purpose, we introduce the borrower's and the lender's risks from the Minskyan approach. The amortization of the circulating capital is introduced.

Second, we make simulations[2] to show the dynamic process that occurs between the monetary policy of the central bank and the reactions of commercial banks. We try to examine the consequences of a contractionary monetary policy on banks' and firms' behavior. For that purpose, we assume three assumptions and develop three versions of the model: first, a neutral fiscal policy; second, a weak contra-cyclical fiscal policy; and third, a strong contra-cyclical fiscal policy.

A POST KEYNESIAN STOCK–FLOW CONSISTENT GROWTH MODEL WITH A FULL BANKING SECTOR

Building a stock–flow consistent (SFC) model requires three steps: writing the matrices; counting the variables and the accounting identities issued from the matrices; and defining each unknown with an equation (accounting identity or behavioral equation). Five sectors form our closed economy: government, firms, households, private banks and the central bank. All production must be financed. However, current production is financed by the working capital of entrepreneurs (retained earnings) and by contracted revolving funds granted by banks at the current rate of interest. These two factors constitute a shock absorber to possible monetary rationing by banks. We are essentially limiting our study to the effects that monetary policy might have on new financing for investment and growth of production.[3]

Let us proceed to examine the gross supply (φ) and the net supply (ΔF) of finance by banks – that is to say, the new flow of money, as opposed to the existing stock of money (D). Also, there is a stock of money demand equal to transaction, precaution, finance and speculative motives, whereas the desired gross finance demand (ϕ^d) represents the new flow of financing required by firms (I^d) plus the redemption of the debt (amortization = *amort*) minus the undistributed profits (P^u). Thus the internal funds of firms (IF) represent the undistributed profits (P^u) minus the redemption of the debt (*amort*). Assuming a closed economy, this flow demand for money can be satisfied by banks, either by the stock markets or by credit. At the end of the period, net financing demand (ΔF_D) can be constrained by net money supply from banks (ΔF) (granted financing – paid off financing – amortization). ΔF determines monetary creation in the period. Following Minsky, we introduce the borrower's and the lender's risks.

We discuss here a closed economy without endogenous inflation. Firms issue equities, bonds with a fixed rate of interest and commercial paper, and borrow money from banks to finance investment but they do not hold deposits of money. They have excess capacity but no inventories.[4] Firms use two factors for producing goods (fixed capital and labor) but we deal with a vertically integrated sector and hence ignore all intermediate goods. Banks have no operating costs and they do not make loans to households. Contrary to Lavoie and Godley (2004), private banks own a net wealth and retain all their profits.

The central bank has neither operating costs nor net worth. The central bank pays back all its profits to the government, which collects taxes from households and finances its deficit by issuing Treasury bills. Government expenditures are only final sales of consumption goods: there is neither operating costs (like wages for state employees) nor transfers between households. The financial behavior of households is simplified: they hold only banking deposit accounts (current accounts and time deposits).

Godley's accounting method is based on two tables: a balance sheet matrix (stocks) and a transactions matrix (flows). Table 18.1 gives the transactions matrix that describes monetary flows between the five sectors of the economy. Every row represents a monetary transaction and every column corresponds to a sector account which is fragmented, except in the basic cases of the government and of the households, in a current and a capital account. Sources of funds appear with plus signs and uses of funds with negative signs, so every row must sum to zero as each transaction always corresponds simultaneously to a source and a use of funds. The sum of each column must also be zero since each account (or sub-account) is balanced.

Table 18.2 gives the balance sheet matrix of our economy. Symbols with plus signs describe assets and negative signs indicate liabilities. The sum of every row is again zero except in the case of accumulated capital in the industrial sector. The last row presents the net wealth of each sector.

Variables and Accounting Identities

Building a model that describes the monetary economy of production discussed above in a consistent way requires to be sure that the transactions matrix should be properly translated into equations. First, the model must contain the 26 variables of the matrix.[5] Each of these 26 variables can be associated with the behavior of one of the five sectors:

Table 18. 1 Transactions matrix

Operation \ Sector	Govt	Firms		Households	Private banks		Central bank (CB)		Σ
		Current	Capital		Current	Capital	Current	Capital	
Consumption		$+C$		−C					0
Government expenditures	−G	+G							0
Net investment		$+I$	$-I$						0
Wages		$-W$		+W					0
Taxes	+T			$-T$					0
Interest on Treasury bills	$-i_{b-1} \cdot B_{-1}$				$+i_{b-1} \cdot B_{-1}$				0
Interest on loans		$-i_{l-1} \cdot L_{-1}$			$+i_{l-1} \cdot L_{-1}$				0
Interest on comm. paper		$-i_{cp-1} \cdot CP_{-1}$			$+i_{cp-1} \cdot CP_{-1}$				0
Interest on bonds		$-i_{of} \cdot of_{-1}$			$+i_{of} \cdot of_{-1}$				0
Interest on bank deposits				$+i_{d-1} \cdot D_{-1}$	$-i_{d-1} \cdot D_{-1}$				0
Interest on CB advances					$-i_{cb-1} . REF_{-1}$		$+i_{cb-1} \cdot REF_{-1}$		0
Profits of firms		$-P$	$+P^u$		$+P^d$				0
Profits of banks					$-P_b$	$+P_b$			0
Profits of CB	$+P_{cb}$						$-P_{cb}$		0

Table 18. 1 (continued)

Sector / Operation	Govt	Firms		Households	Private banks		Central bank (CB)		Σ
		Current	Capital		Current	Capital	Current	Capital	
Δ HPM						$-\Delta H$		$+\Delta H$	0
Δ T bills	$+\Delta B$					$-\Delta B$			0
Δ equities			$+\Delta e \cdot p_e$			$-\Delta e \cdot p_e$			0
Δ loans			$+\Delta L$			$-\Delta L$			0
Δ commercial paper			$+\Delta CP$			$-\Delta CP$			0
Δ bonds			$+\Delta of \cdot p_{of}$			$-\Delta of \cdot p_{of}$			0
Δ bank deposits				$-\Delta D$		$+\Delta D$			0
Δ CB advances						$+\Delta REF$		$-\Delta REF$	0
Σ	0	0	0	0	0	0	0	0	0

Table 18 2 Balance sheet matrix

Sector / Assets	Government	Firms	Households	Private banks	Central bank	Σ
Capital		$+K$				$+K$
High powered money (HPM)				$+H$	$-H$	0
Treasury bills	$-B$			$+B$		0
Equities		$-e{\cdot}p_e$		$+e{\cdot}p_e$		0
Loans		$-L$		$+L$		0
Commercial paper		$-CP$		$+CP$		0
Bonds (fixed yield)		$-of{\cdot}p_{of}$		$+of{\cdot}p_{of}$		0
Bank deposits			$+D$	$-D$		0
CB advances				$-REF$	$+REF$	0
Net wealth	$-B$	$+V_f$	$+D$	$+V_b$	0	$+K$

Government: G, T, B, i_b;
Firms: I, W, P, P^u, P^d, e;
Households: C, D;
Private banks: $i_l, L, i_{cp}, CP, i_{of}, p_{of}, of, p_e, i_d, P_b$; and
Central bank: H, i_{cb}, REF, P_{cb}.

Second, we must use the accounting identities resulting from each row and each column in the model. We have nine accounting identities corresponding to the eight columns of the transactions matrix and to the non-ordinary row.[6] First, we just transcribe the identities (uses of funds on the left side, sources of funds on the right side) without stipulating how we shall use them in the model:

(i) $G + i_{b-1} \cdot B_{-1} \equiv T + P_{cb} + \Delta B$
(ii) $W + i_{l-1} \cdot L_{-1} + i_{b-1} \cdot B_{-1} + i_{of} \cdot of_{-1} + P \equiv C + I + G$
(iii) $I \equiv P^u + \Delta e \cdot p_e + \Delta L + \Delta CP + \Delta of \cdot p_{of} \equiv \varphi + P^u - amort$
(iv) $C + T + \Delta D \equiv W + i_{d-1}\, D_{-1}$
(v) $i_{d-1} \cdot D_{-1} + i_{cb-1} \cdot REF_{-1} + P_b \equiv i_{b-1} \cdot B_{-1} + i_{l-1} \cdot L_{-1} + i_{cp-1} \cdot CP_{-1} + i_{of} \cdot of_{-1} + P^d$
(vi) $\Delta H + \Delta B + \Delta e \cdot p_e + \Delta L + \Delta CP + \Delta of \cdot p_{of} \equiv P_b + \Delta D + \Delta REF$
(vii) $P_{cb} \equiv i_{cb-1} \cdot REF_{-1}$
(viii) $\Delta REF \equiv \Delta H$
(ix) $P \equiv P^u + P^d$

A feature of SFC models is that if there are M columns and N non-ordinary rows in the transactions matrix, then there are only $(M+N-1)$ independent accounting identities in the model. Due to this principle, which is very similar to Walras's law, one equation must be excluded, therefore we shall use exactly eight accounting identities in the model. It is a simpler matter with regard to the balance sheet matrix: we just make sure that initial values of stocks are consistent with the matrix. In the following periods, stocks will stay consistent since our eight identities will generate consistent flows. Now we must define every variable relative to the five sectors using an accounting identity or a behavioral equation[7]. When we introduce new unknowns into a behavioral equation we define them immediately so that our model should have the same number of equations as unknowns.

It is a growth model of a closed economy. The national income (Y) adds the household consumption (C), investment of the firms (I) and the public expenditure (G). The rate of growth of the national income is gr_y:

$$Y = C + I + G, \tag{18.1}$$

$$gr_y = \Delta Y / Y_{-1}. \tag{18.2}$$

Government: G, T, B, i_b

In the model, the government collects only taxes from households (on wages):

$$T = \tau \cdot W_{-1} \quad \text{with } \tau\text{: constant.} \tag{18.3}$$

The government finances any deficit-issuing bills, so that the supply of Treasury bills (B) in the economy is identical to the stock of government debt. In other words, it is given by the pre-existing stock of debt plus its current deficit (DG). The current deficit of the government includes the redemption of the national debt. Government bonds are considered to be zero default and liquidity risk ($r_d = 0$, $r_l = 0$). We assume that private banks give limitless credit to government at the current central bank key interest rate (i_{cb}):

$$B = B_{-1} + DG; \tag{18.4}$$

$$i_b = i_{cb}. \tag{18.5}$$

To analyze the consequences of a monetary shock, we assume three different assumptions for the fiscal policy.

Hypothesis 1 (H1): a neutral fiscal policy

First, to analyze a 'pure' monetary policy shock, the fiscal policy should be neutralized. We assume that a neutral fiscal policy corresponds to a constant ratio (r_{DG}) of government deficit to the last national income: DB/Y_{-1}, which is more or less the case in the Maastricht Treaty of the European Union. Article 104 of the Treaty decrees that 'Member States shall avoid excessive government deficits'. Compliance with this requirement is assessed on the basis of a maximum value for the government deficit to GDP ratio of 3 percent, and a reference value for the government debt to GDP ratio of 60 percent. With H1, the expansionist effect of the fiscal policy has always the same strength, whatever the growth rate. Then we use the first accounting identity to calculate the adequate public expenditure. Of course, we can modify the ratio (r_{DG}) of government deficit to the last national income to take into account a fiscal policy shock:

$$DG = r_{DG} \cdot Y_{-1}, \text{ with } r_{DG}: \text{constant}, \qquad \text{(H1: 18.6)}$$

$$G \equiv DG - (i_{b-1} \cdot B_{-1}) + T + P_{cb}. \qquad \text{(H1: 18.7–}i\text{)}$$

Hypothesis 2 (H2): an undetermined effect of the fiscal policy

Second, we assume that public expenditure (G) is growing at the same rate (gr_y) as the national income (Y). When we solve the model, this assumption makes it easier to find a steady state. With H2, public expenditure is procyclical, because G falls with the GDP. But the final effect of the fiscal policy is measured by the government deficit (DG). Public earnings fall at the same time as public expenditure, and with a contractionary monetary policy and its higher interest rate, the financial costs of the national debt increase. The global impact is not clear and can be pro- or countercyclical:

$$G = G_{-1} \cdot (1 + gr_{y-1}), \qquad \text{(H2: 18.6)}$$

$$DG = G + (i_{b-1} \cdot B_{-1}) - T - P_{cb}. \qquad \text{(H2: 18.7–}i\text{)}$$

Hypothesis 3 (H3): a strong countercyclical fiscal policy

Following a proposal of Godley, it would have been better to model the growth rate of public expenditure (gr_g) as an exogenous parameter. For Godley, the neutral fiscal policy corresponds to the gr_g adequate to the steady state. Then a strong countercyclical fiscal policy brings the economy back to the former steady state:

$$G = G_{-1} \cdot (1 + gr_g), \text{ with } gr_g: \text{constant}, \qquad \text{(H3: 18.6)}$$

$$DG = G + (i_{b-1} \cdot B_{-1}) - T - P_{cb}. \qquad \text{(H3: 18.7–}i\text{)}$$

With these hypotheses, we should better understand the links between monetary and fiscal policy. We shall make further simulations with these three hypotheses.

Firms: I, W, P, P^u, P^d, e

The investment function is the most important one in a growth model. The stock of capital increases with the flow of net investment (I) that is financed by the total of external funds from commercial banks (gross finance $= \varphi$) and by the internal funds of firms. The self-financing of firms corresponds to the retained earnings (P^u) minus the redemption of the debts of firms (*amort*). Amortization concerns only the debt: loans (L), bonds (OF) and commercial papers (CP).

$$K = K_{-1} + I, \tag{18.8}$$

$$I \equiv \varphi + IF, \tag{18.9–iii}$$

$$IF = \mathrm{P^u} - amort, \tag{18.10}$$

$$amort = a_1 \cdot L_{-1} + a_{of} \cdot of_{-1} + a_{cp} \cdot CP_{-1}. \tag{18.11}$$

In our model, we differentitate between the effective investment (I) and the desired investment of firms (I_D). The banks finance the latter totally or in part according their lender's risk (LR) (see equations (18.31), (18.32), (18.34). A monetary rationing on investment can exist ($\varphi < \varphi^d$ or $I < I_D$). The desired rate of accumulation (gr_{kD}) is a function of an exogenous state of confidence (γ_0), the capacity utilization rate (u) and of the borrower's risk, which is measured by the rate of cash flow (r_{cf}) and the financial condition index (FCI). The rate of cash flow is the ratio of retained earnings to capital and the financial condition index captures the sensitivity of investment to the long-term interest rate, to the short-term interest rate and to the financial capitalization ratio. The lender's risk and the borrower's risk come from a Minskyan analysis:

$$I_D = gr_{kD} \cdot K - 1, \tag{18.12}$$

$$\varphi^d = I_{D.} - IF, \tag{18.13}$$

$$gr_{kD} = \gamma_0 + \gamma_1 \cdot r_{cf-1} + \gamma_2 . u_{-1} - \gamma_3 \cdot FCI_{-1}, \text{ with } \gamma_i\text{: constant,} \tag{18.14}$$

where the rate of capacity utilization is defined as the ratio of output to full capacity output (Y_{fc}):

$$r_{cf} = P^u / K_{-1}, \tag{18.15}$$

$$u = Y / Y_{fc}. \tag{18.16}$$

The capital to full capacity ratio (σ) is defined as a constant:

$$Y_{fc} = K_{-1} \cdot \sigma, \text{ with } \sigma\text{: constant}, \tag{18.17}$$

$$FCI = \mu_1 \cdot i_1 \cdot L/K + \mu_2 \cdot i_{cb} \cdot CP/K - \mu_3 \cdot E/Y, \text{ with } \mu_i\text{: constants.} \tag{18.18}$$

Wages can be decomposed into a unit wage (w) times the level of employment (N):

$$W = w \cdot N, \tag{18.19a}$$

where employment is determined by sales given productivity (σ_2):

$$N = Y / \sigma_2, \text{ with } \sigma_2\text{: constant.} \tag{18.19b}$$

The full employment (N_{fe}) is :

$$N_{fe} = Y_{fc} / \sigma_2, \text{ with } \sigma_2\text{: constant.} \tag{18.19c}$$

The unemployment (Un) or the output gap (OG) are easily found:

$$Un = N_{fe} - N, \tag{18.19d}$$
$$OG = Y_{fc} - Y. \tag{18.19e}$$

The rate of unemployment r_{un} is:

$$r_{un} = Un/N_{fc}. \tag{18.19f}$$

Following Godley and Lavoie (2007), it is assumed, as is usual in PK models, that prices are set as a mark-up (ρ) on unit direct cost (UDC):

$$p = (1 + \rho) \cdot UDC, \text{ with } \rho\text{: constant}, \tag{18.19g}$$

where unit direct cost is the ratio of direct costs (that consist entirely of wages) on sales:

$$UDC = W/Y. \tag{18.19h}$$

Under these assumptions we have:

$$p = (1 + \rho) \cdot w / \sigma_{2.} \tag{18.19i}$$

In this model there is no inflation and prices are set exogenously to 1, so equation (18.19i) can be rewritten:

$$w = \sigma_2 / (1 + \rho). \tag{18.19i'}$$

Finally, equations (18.19a), (18.19b) and (i′) can be condensed in equation (18.19), which determines wages:

$$W = Y / (1 + \rho), \text{ with } \rho\text{: constant.} \tag{18.19}$$

Total profits (P) of firms are the difference between their sales and their expenditures (wages and interest payments on loans, commercial papers and bonds):

$$P \equiv Y - W - i_{l-1} \cdot L_{-1} - i_{cp-1} \cdot CP_{-1} - i_{of} \cdot of_{-1}. \tag{18.20–ii}$$

Distributed dividends (P^d) are a fraction of profits realized in the previous period:

$$P^d = (1 - s_f) \cdot P_{-1,} \text{ with } s_f\text{ : constant,} \tag{18.21}$$

and retained earnings (P^u) are determined as the residue:

$$P^u \equiv P - P^d. \tag{18.22–ix}$$

Equations concerning issues of equities by firms are usually oversimplified in SFC models. In this model we simply assume that the stock of shares grows at the rate of the GDP with a lag of one year (gr_{y-1}): $\Delta e / e_{-1} = gr_{y-1}$. The more the economy grows, the more firms issue equities. There are two explanations. First it is easier to sell new equities when the economy and thus the profits grow. Second, firms need new finance to follow the growth of the GDP. But alternative formulations would have been possible.

$$e = e_{-1} \cdot (1 + gr_{y-1}). \tag{18.23}$$

Households: *C*, *D*

We assume that households determine their consumption expenditure (C) on the basis of their expected disposable income and their wealth of the previous period (which consist entirely of bank deposits: current accounts and time deposits):

$$C = \alpha_1 \cdot Y_w^a + \alpha_2 \cdot Y_v^a + \alpha_3 \cdot D_{-1}, \text{ with } \alpha_i\text{: constants } 1 > \alpha_1 > \alpha_2 > \alpha_3 > 0, \quad (18.24)$$

$$Y_w^a = Y_{w-1} + \theta_h \cdot (Y_{w-1} - Y_{w-1}^a) \text{ with } \theta_h\text{: constant}, \quad (18.25)$$

$$Y_v^a = Y_{v-1} + \theta_h \cdot (Y_{v-1} - Y_{v-1}^a), \quad (18.26)$$

$$Yw = W - T, \quad (18.27)$$

$$Y_v = i_{d-1} \cdot D_{-1}, \quad (18.28)$$

$$Y_h = Y_w + Y_v, \quad (18.29)$$

where Y_w^a is the expected disposable income of workers, Y_v^a the expected disposable financial income and each α_i is a propensity to consume. In this model, the expected value of any variable for the current period (represented with the superscript *a*) depends on its value in the previous period plus an error correction mechanism where θ represents the speed of adjustment in expectations.

Following the Kaleckian tradition, we assume that wages are mostly consumed while financial income is largely devoted to saving ($1 > \alpha_1 > \alpha_2 > 0$). This class-based saving behavior is of importance in an SFC model where interest payments play a great role. With the same high propensity to consume ($\alpha_1 = \alpha_2$), an increase in the interest rates can move the economy to a higher growth path in the long run. The consumption decision determines the amount that households will save out of their disposable income Y_h:

$$D \equiv D_{-1} + Y_h - C. \quad (18.30\text{–iv})$$

Private banks: i_l, L, i_{cp}, CP, i_{of}, p_{of}, of, i_d, p_e, P_b

As in Lavoie and Godley (2004), we try to introduce more realistic features into the banking system. Bank liquidity preference operates on two levels: first, at the microeconomic level of the commercial banks; second, at the macroeconomic level of banks and between banks and the central bank.

Firms' financing is fundamental in a monetary economy of production. Firms begin by being self-financed then turn to external finance (ΔF_D). Banks only finance projects they consider profitable, but confidence in their judgment is variable and can justify various strategies. In deciding whether or not to make a loan, banks examine firms' productive and financial expectations and also their financial structure. This investigation is made according to their confidence in the state of long-term expectations of yields on capital assets, influencing what Keynes referred to as 'animal spirits'. After the study of expected production and of demand of financing that integrates the firm's borrowing risk (r_b), bankers can refuse to finance. The state of confidence of banks summarizes these factors.

Banks recognize a lender's risk (LR) when underwriting finance and creating money. A lender's risk is the sum of three fundamental risks. First, the risk of default (r_d) corresponds to the bank's perception regarding the borrower's likely failure to repay the claim. Second, the risk of liquidity (r_l) entails the ability to reverse a decision at any moment at the smallest possible cost. Third, the market risk (r_m) corresponds to unanticipated changes in the various financial markets (stock exchange, money market).

In equations (18.31), (18.34), (18.51) and (18.52), the risks of default and of liquidity are taken into account by the gap between the leverage ratio and a conventional leverage ratio. We also introduce Tobin's ratio and the cost of indebtedness for the risk of default. In our model, the market risk is taken into account by the expected capital gains on equities ($CG_e{}^a$) and on fixed-yield bonds (CG_{of}^a), but also with the central bank interest rate. Yet, a monetary policy shock strongly influences the market risk.

When the lender's risk is maximum ($LR=1$), commercial banks refuse to finance the net investment of firms: $\Delta F=0$. Desired investment (I_D) faces a serious finance rationing. The flow of net investment is only financed by self-funding, that is the retained earnings (P^u), minus the amortization of the debt, minus the capital losses of firms (CG) (see equations (18.9–10). Thus the money supply (in stock) can be reduced with the redemption of the debt. If the lender's risk is null ($LR=0$), desired investment is fully financed: $\Delta F=\Delta F_D$ or $\varphi=\varphi^d$. This is the horizontalist case. The capital losses of firms are also the capital gains of banks, measured by the capital losses on equities (CG_e) and on fixed-rate bonds (CG_{of}) (equations (18.43) and (18.49)):

$$\varphi=\varphi^d \cdot (1-LR), \text{ with } 0 \leqslant LR \leqslant 1, \tag{18.31}$$

$$\Delta F=\varphi - amort + CG, \tag{18.32}$$

$$CG=CG_e + CG_{of}. \tag{18.33}$$

In the model, the lender's risk (LR) is measured by the difference between the current leverage ratio and the conventional leverage ratio (quantity of indebtedness), by Tobin's q ratio and by the cost of indebtedness (i_{cb}). The higher the current indebtedness of firms ($(CP+OF+L)/K$) over the accepted indebtedness, the greater the lender's risk. The accepted indebtedness is conventional, but this conventional indebtedness can increase during a boom and decrease during a crisis. Tobin's q ratio is measured by the financial value of the firms on the capital K. The financial value is the value of the equities on the market:

$$LR = a_1 \cdot (lev_{-1} - lev_c) - b_1 . q_{-1} + c_1 . i_{cb}, \text{ with } a_1, b_1, c_1 \text{ and } lev_c\text{: constant,} \tag{18.34}$$

$$lev = (CP + OF + L)/K, \tag{18.35}$$

$$q = e \cdot p_e/K. \tag{18.36}$$

To avoid crises of liquidity and solvency, banks want to manage their uncertainty by choosing financing according to an arbitrage between yield and risk. They look for the easiest reversibility of their decisions at the smallest cost, which imposes a particular balance sheet structure. As such, the preference for short-term financing is one expression of strong liquidity preference of banks. The liquidity preference theory is generalized to the banks. The natural global constraint is that the yield on assets exceeds the costs on the liabilities. The asset side generates income from long-term interest rates (i_{LT}) while the liability side reflects the costs from short-term interest rates (i_{ST}). So, when the yield curve of the various interest rates takes its normal shape,[8] the spread ($i_{LT} - i_{ST} > 0$) should direct the mark-up of banks. Banks bought equities only with an expected high-risk premium ($i_e^a - i_l > 0$). In general, the hierarchy of the yields should be as follows:

$$i_{Assets} > i_{Liabilities}; \text{ Assets: } i_E > i_{OF} > i_l > i_{cp} > i_{cb};$$
$$\text{Liabilities: } i_{SS} > i_{CD} > i_{cb} > i_d.$$

The supply of bank financing depends on non-financial agents' demands (flow/ flow). On the other hand, the distribution of financing flows between securities and loans should take into account the desired structure of the balance sheet, and therefore the stocks. The liquidity preference of banks (LP_B) involves a portfolio arbitrage considered to be optimal among loans, bonds and equities to avoid crises while allowing the highest possible banking net profits.

We come to the equations defining the portfolio behavior of banks. We follow the methodology developed by Godley and Lavoie (2007) and inspired by Tobin. Banks can hold four different assets: bonds (with a fixed rate of interest) $OF = of \cdot p_{of}$, equities $E = e \cdot p_e$, loans at a variable long-term interest rate (L) and commercial paper (CP) at a short-term interest rate. The four asset demand functions described with the matrix algebra are:

$$OF = (\lambda_{10} + \lambda_{11} \cdot r_{of}^{a} - \lambda_{12} \cdot r_{e}^{a} - \lambda_{13} \cdot i_l - \lambda_{14} \cdot i_{cp}) \cdot F, \tag{18.37}$$

$$E = (\lambda_{20} - \lambda_{21} \cdot r_{of}^{a} + \lambda_{22} \cdot r_{e}^{a} - \lambda_{23} \cdot i_l - \lambda_{24} \cdot i_{cp}) \cdot F, \tag{18.38}$$

$$L = (\lambda_{30} - \lambda_{31} \cdot r_{of}^{a} - \lambda_{32} \cdot r_{e}^{a} + \lambda_{33} \cdot i_l - \lambda_{34} \cdot i_{cp}) \cdot F, \tag{18.39}$$

$$CP = (\lambda_{40} - \lambda_{41} \cdot r_{of}^{a} - \lambda_{42} \cdot r_{e}^{a} - \lambda_{43} \cdot i_l - \lambda_{44} \cdot i_{cp}) \cdot F. \tag{18.40a}$$

The λ_{ij} parameters follow the vertical, horizontal and symmetry constraints (Godley and Lavoie, 2007). Banks are assumed to make a certain proportion λ_{i0} of their financing in the form of asset i but this proportion is modified by the rates of return on these assets. Banks are concerned about i_l and i_{cp}, the rates of interest on loans and on commercial paper to be determined at the end of the current period, but which will generate the interest payments in the following period. We have further assumed that it is the expected rates of return on equities (r_e^a) and on bonds (r_{of}^{a}) that enter into the determination of portfolio choice.

As is the case with every matrix, we cannot retain all these equations in the model because each one of them is a logical implication of the others. We model commercial paper as the residual equation:

$$CP = F - OF - E - L. \tag{18.40}$$

Loans and bonds as a source of finance may seem very close. But in our model, the interest rates of bonds are fixed and those of loans are variable.

For the bonds, the expected rate of yield (r_{of}^{a}) is the fixed interest rate plus the expected capital gains on the market value of the previous period of these bonds (OF_{-1}). The market value of the bonds is the number of bonds (of) times their prices (p_{of}). The interest rate (i_{of}) is always the long-term interest rate of the first period applied to the initial price (in t_0, $p_{of} = 1$). But after the first period, the prices of the old and of the new fixed-yield bonds (p_{of}) are inversely proportional to the changes in the long-term interest rates (i_l).

The expected value of capital gains on bonds (CG_{of}^{a}) and on equities ($CG_e{}^{a}$) for the current period depends on its value of the previous period plus an error correction mechanism where θ represents the speed of adjustment in expectations. The capital gains (CG_{of} and CG_e) correspond to the variations in the price times the quantity of the previous period:

$$r_{of}^{a} = i_{of} + CG_{of}^{a}/OF_{-1}, \text{ with } i_{of}\text{: constant,} \tag{18.41}$$

$$CG_{of}^{a} = CG_{of-1} + \theta_b \cdot (CG_{of-1} - CG_{of-1}^{a}), \tag{18.42}$$

$$CG_{of} = \Delta p_{of} \cdot of_{-1}, \tag{18.43}$$

$$of = OF/p_{of}, \tag{18.44}$$

$$p_{of} = p_{of-1}\,(1 + i_{of})/(1 + i_l). \tag{18.45}$$

For the equities, the expected rate of yield (r_e^a) is the sum of the expected distributed profits (P^{da}) and the expected capital gains (CG_e^a), on the market value of the previous period of these equities (E_{-1}). As usual, the expected distributed profits (P^{da}) for the current period depends on its value of the previous period plus an error correction mechanism where (θ) represents the speed of adjustment in expectations. The only price-clearing mechanism of this model occurs in the equity market. The price of equities (p_e) will allow the equilibrium between the *number* of equities (e; see equation 18.21) that have been issued by firms (the supply) and the *amount* of equities (E) that private banks want to hold (the demand):

$$r_e^a = (P^{da} + CG_e^a)/E_{-1}, \tag{18.46}$$

$$P^{da} = P^d_{-1} + \theta_b \cdot (P^d_{-1} - P^{da}_{-1}), \tag{18.47}$$

$$CG_e^{\,a} = CG_{e-1} + \theta_b \cdot (CG_{e-1} - CG_{e\,-1}^{\,a}), \tag{18.48}$$

$$CGe = \Delta p_e \cdot e_{-1,} \tag{18.49}$$

$$p_e = E/e. \tag{18.50}$$

Monetary authorities determine exogenously the key rate on the money market (i_{cb}). Keynes (1936) asserts that this rate is widely conventional. While central banks fix the short-term rates, private banks' liquidity preference determines banking rates (short-, medium- and long-term interest rates). Significant rates for growth and financing (loan) are the long-term interest rates (i_l). The link between short- and long-term interest rates is complex. Macroeconomic banking interest rates (i_1) are the production costs of money plus a risk premium. The first element corresponds to functioning costs (wages, investment, immobilization); payment costs for monetary liabilities (subject to the firms' competition for households savings) and the cost of high-powered money determined by the central bank; and to a rate of margin (χ) corresponding to the standard profits of banks. The production costs of money are equal to i_{cb} plus a relatively constant mark-up (χ).

Risk premiums are not constant because they are the fruit of the banks' liquidity preference, which covers lender's risk (*lr*). Five expectations strongly influence risk premiums: anticipations about the productivity, economic evolution (growth, employment) and budget; expected inflation; the level of future short-term rates of interest; financial market evolution and capital asset prices; and the presence of foreign long-term rates. In the model, we use the same lender's risk as before, that is, a mix of leverage ratio and Tobin's q ratio. But with different coefficients, a_2 and b_2, lr can be negative and this reduces the mark-up. Therefore the long-term interest rate becomes endogenous and the spread between i_{cb} and i_l is not constant. Contrary to the horizontalist view, we introduce an endogenous curve of the interest rates. To explain the short-term interest rates (i_b or i_{cp}), i_{cb} and χ are sufficient. On the contrary, lr is the primary variable to explain long-term interest rates (i_l, i_{of}). Banks apply a spread (χ_3) between the key rate and the rate on deposits in order to realize profits:

$$i_l = i_{cb} + lr + \chi_1, \text{ with } \chi_1\text{: constant } \chi_1 > \chi_2, \quad (18.51)$$

$$lr = a_2 \cdot (lev_{-1} - lev_c) - b_2 \cdot q_{-1}, \text{ with } a_2, b_2, lev_c \text{ constant and } c = \text{convention on the 'normal' debt ratio}, \quad (18.52)$$

$$i_{cp} = i_{cb} + \chi_2, \text{ with } \chi_2\text{: constant } \chi_1 > \chi_2, \quad (18.53)$$

$$i_d = i_{cb} - \chi_3. \quad (18.54)$$

The initial structure of interest rates is as follows: $i_l > i_{of} > i_{cp} > i_b = i_{cb} > i_d$.

Banks try to maximize their net income. To make a profit, they finance the economy and agree to become less liquid. By making the almost irreversible decisions of financing, they are subject to the lender's risk. They can hope for big profits only by lowering their LP_B. Economic activity also depends on the animal spirits of banks. Finance scarcity can only be the consequence of a deliberate choice. 'Desired scarcity' of financing is the sign of banks' liquidity preference. From an optimal structure of their balance sheet, we can measure the profits of commercial banks (P_b) obtained by monetary financing:

$$P_b \equiv i_{b-1} \cdot B_{-1} + i_{l-1} \cdot L_{-1} + i_{cp-1} \cdot CP_{-1} + i_{of} \cdot of_{-1} + P^d - i_{d-1} \cdot D_{-1} - i_{cb-1} \cdot REF_{-1}. \quad (18.55\text{–v})$$

Central Bank: $H, i_{cb}, REF, i_b, P_{cb}$

It is assumed that banks are obliged by the government to hold reserve requirements (H) in high-powered money (HPM) that do not generate interest payments and that must always be a fixed share (the compulsory ratio η) of deposits:

$$H = \eta \cdot \mathrm{D}. \quad (18.56)$$

Since the central bank is collecting interest payment advances while paying out no interest on the notes, it is also making profits P_{cb}:

$$P_{cb} \equiv i_{cb-1} \cdot REF_{-1}. \quad (18.57\text{–vii})$$

It is assumed, in line with current practice, that any profits realized by the central bank revert to the government. Following the theory of endogenous money, we assume that the central bank is fully *accommodating*. The central bank fixes a key rate (i_{cb}) and provides whatever advances (REF) are demanded by banks at this rate:

$$REF \equiv REF_{-1} + \Delta H + \Delta B + \Delta F - CG - P_b - \Delta D, \quad (18.58\text{–vi})$$

$$i_{cb} = i_{cb0,} \text{ with } i_{cb0}\text{: constant.} \quad (18.59)$$

Our model is now closed. We have defined the 26 variables of the transactions matrix introducing 33 new variables[9] and we now have the same number of equations (59) as unknowns. Furthermore, we have managed to use the $M + N - 1 = 8$ accounting identities issued from the transcription of the transactions matrix. The missing identity is the one relative to the capital account of the central bank:

(viii) $REF = H$.

This identity reflects the fact that HPM is supplied to the economy through advances to private banks. Of course, this accounting identity must invariably hold. When we solve the model we have to verify that the numbers issued from simulations do generate $H \equiv REF$. As Lavoie and Godley (2001: 294) have underlined: 'it is only when an accounting error has been committed that the equality given by the missing equation will not be realized. With the accounting right, the equality must hold'. When we solve numerically our model, identity (viii) holds perfectly.

EXPERIMENTS ON A MONETARY POLICY SHOCK ON A FIRM'S INVESTMENT AND ON BANKING BEHAVIOR WITH THREE ASSUMPTIONS ON FISCAL POLICY

Given the complexity of the model, it would be difficult to find analytical solutions. We shall therefore conduct simulation experiments following the methodology used by Lavoie and Godley (2001: 296):

> First we assigned values to the various parameters using reasonable stylised facts. Then, we solved the model and found a steady-state solution through a process of successive approximations. Having found a steady sate, we conducted experiments by modifying one of the exogenous variables or one of the economically significant parameters of the model at a time.

Heterodox economists do not accept easily the notion of a steady state. We use it only as an analytical tool but we recognize that such a theoretical construct is never reached in practice because parameters and exogenous variables are actually changing all the time. That is why, when making a simulation, it is important to differentiate between the initial effects of some change (in the early periods of the dynamic response) and the terminal effects (in the steady state). These terminal effects will eventually arise as long as the structure of the model is left unchanged, although we know that this is unlikely. However, the final steady state, that is to say after the shock, is not the same as the initial steady state. There is no long-term predetermined equilibrium. This only signifies a kind of resilience in the economy. In the real life and despite shocks, the capitalist economies are not submitted to a full instability in the long term.

We shall increase the central bank key interest rate (i_{cb}) from 2 percent to 4 percent, to provoke a monetary policy shock. The simulations show the dynamic process that occurs between a contractionary monetary policy and the conditions of the investment financing. Behaviors of the commercial banks and of the firms, in particular, the lender's and the borrower's risks, have a wide influence on investment.

The simulations make three assumptions about the fiscal policy. With H1, we neutralized the fiscal policy, because we assume a constant ratio of the current deficit of the government (*DG*) to the GDP. Thus with H1, we can analyze the 'pure' effect of the monetary policy. With H2, we have a weak countercyclical effect of the fiscal policy. With H3, public expenditure continues to grow at the same rate gr_g, thus there is a strong countercyclical effect of the fiscal policy. With H1 and H2, the rise in the central bank key interest rate produced marked economic contraction. In the short term, the growth rate in the national income (gr_y) decreases strongly

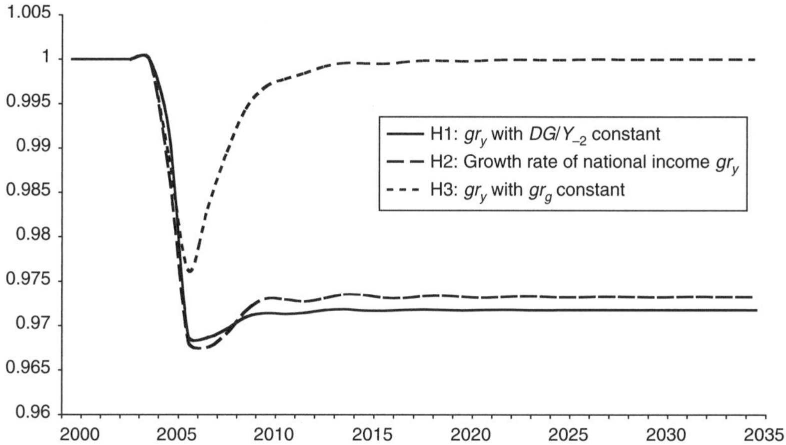

Figure 18 1 Higher central bank key interest rate: effects on the growth rate of the economy

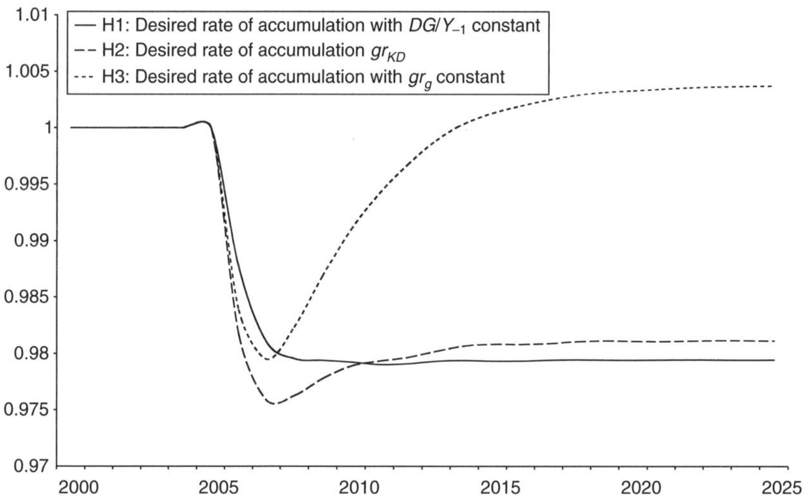

Figure 18 2 Higher central bank key interest rate: effects on the desired rate of accumulation

and then it goes up but to a lower steady state (Figure 18.1). The economic contraction is explained by the fall in the desired rate of accumulation (Figure.18.2) and therefore by the fall in investment. Investment responds with a lag to the rise in interest rates. In the short term, the economic

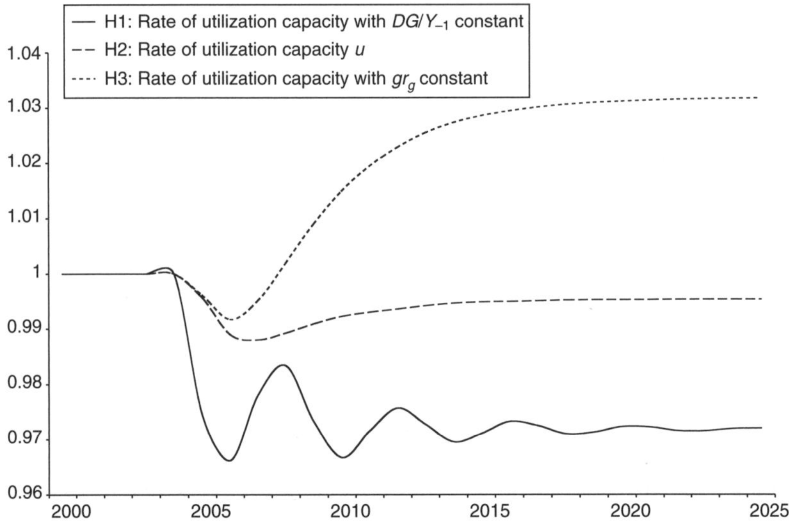

Figure 18.3 Higher central bank key interest rate: effects on the rate of utilization capacity

contraction involves a lower rate of utilization capacity (u). With the weak investment, the rate of utilization capacity increases in the medium term but under its initial level (Figure 18.3). The utilization capacity captures a crisis of investment.

With H3, the powerful countercyclical effect of the fiscal policy brings the economy back to the previous steady state (Figure 18.1) and explains the rise in the desired rate of accumulation (Figure 18.2) and the rise in the rate of utilization capacity in the medium term (Figure 18.3).

With H1 and H2, the financial behavior of firms largely explains these developments. The borrower's risk, measured by the rate of cash flow (r_{cf}) and the financial condition index (*FCI*), rises substantially. With higher costs of financing, the rate of cash flows drops in the short term. Interest payments on loans and commercial papers increase, and this reduces retained profits. But then, firms reduce the issue of equities to preserve the part of undistributed profits (P^u) and the rate of cash flow rises but is still less than its first position (Figure 18.4). The drop in Tobin's ratio (Figure 18.7) is a further negative effect. The financial condition index increases vigorously with the fall in financial capitalization (E/Y) (Figure 18.4). The commercial banks prefer to buy more commercial paper (preference for the short term) than to supply loans (see Figure 18.6). With the depressed *FCI* and the lower cash flow ratio, the borrower's risk increases seriously. Following the Minskyan approach, financial features explain the recession.

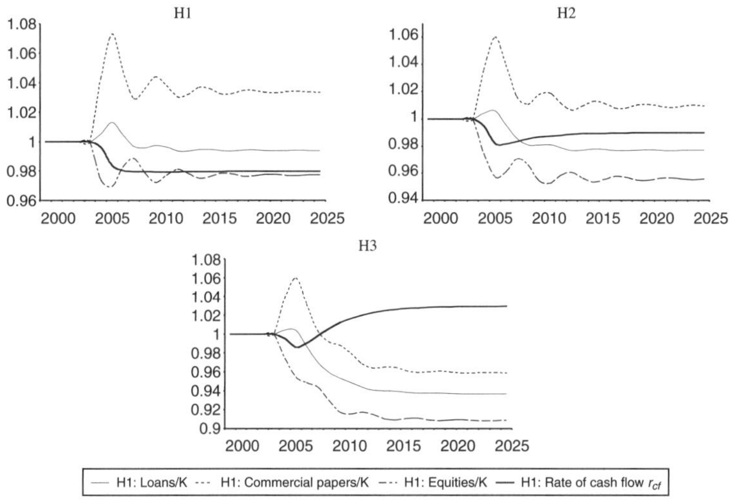

Figure 18.4 Higher central bank key interest rate: effects on the rate of cash flow and the determinants of the financial condition index

With H3, the higher government deficit allows an increase in the cash flow of firms. Their self-financing increases and their demand for external funds decreases. Then the contractionary monetary policy and the expansionary fiscal policy counterbalance each other. Government indebtedness substitutes firms indebtedness.

Now let us examine the impact of a monetary policy shock on banking behavior. The rise in the central bank key rate increases the interest rates on loans, on commercial papers and on deposits. The interest rate on the loan is now endogenous. The spread between the short- and the long-term interest rates is not fixed. In our simulation, this spread is weakly reduced with the three assumptions.

Demand for equities falls, generating a decrease in the price of equities. An additional negative effect on the demand for equities comes from the fall in distributed profits, which drives down the expected real return on equities. On the supply side, the fall in the GDP growth rate implies a fall in the issue of equities. The drop in the price of equities in turn has two opposing effects: first, it generates negative capital gains, proportional to the existing stock of equities; second it allows an increase in the yield of equities. In our simulation, the price effect is stronger, which is the reason for the increasing expected rate of return on equities in the long run, in particular with H3. On the other hand, the expected yield of

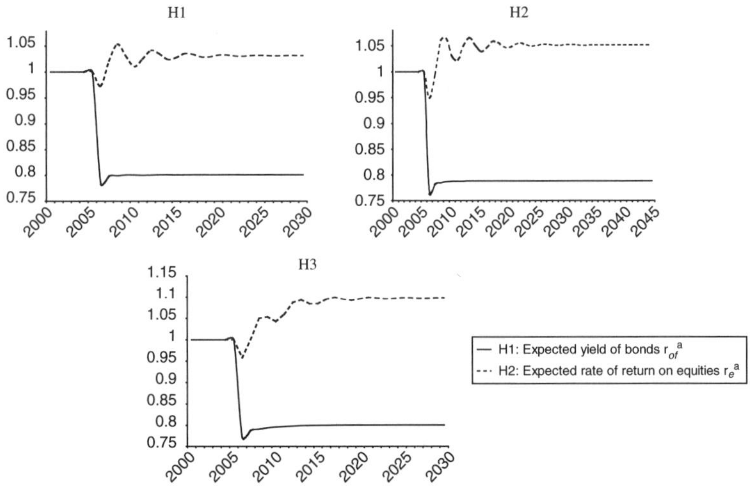

Figure 18.5 Higher central bank key interest rate: effects on the expected rate of return on bonds and on equities

bonds (with a fixed rate) is durably depressed by the rise in interest rates (Figure 18.5).

After the rise in interest rates, private banks reach a new equilibrium in their asset allocation. Their balance sheet structure clearly changes. The share of the bonds is reduced, in contrast to the loans and especially to the commercial papers. With H1 and H2, the share of equities is relatively stable and growing with H3 (Figure 18.6).

The rise in interest rates generates a positive effect on households' income, since interest payments on deposits increase. But with our Kaleckian consumption function, the benefits on consumption are very weak. However, bank profits decrease for the same reason, since the increase in interest payments on deposits and central bank advances is higher than the increase in interest receipts on loans.

But the key element of our simulation is the increase in the lender's risk. The fall in Tobin's ratio plus the lowest solvency of the firms following the rise in interest rates explain the rise in the lender's risk and the decreasing leverage ratio (Figure 18.7). With the assumptions on fiscal policy H1 and H2, our virtual economy stabilizes on a lower growth path, characterized by a lower rate of utilization capacity, a lower Tobin's ratio (q) and leverage (lev), and a higher lender's risk (LR) and a higher borrower's risk. The consequence is a credit rationing of the investment of the firms by the private banks: $\varphi < \varphi^d$ (Figure 18.8). The credit rationing of firms explains an increasing rate of unemployment.

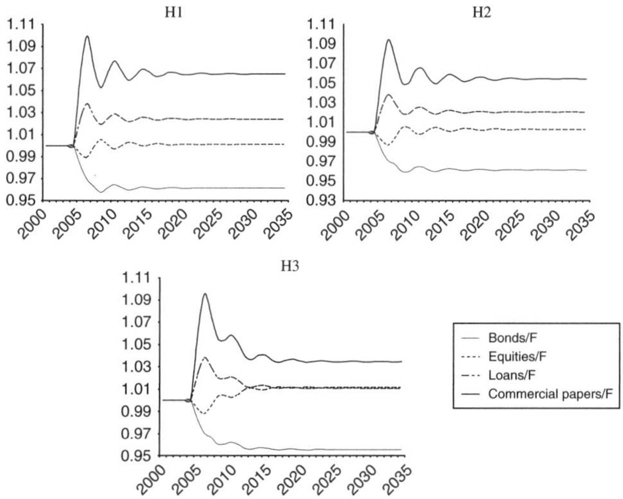

Figure 18 6 Higher central bank key interest rate: effects on finance structure

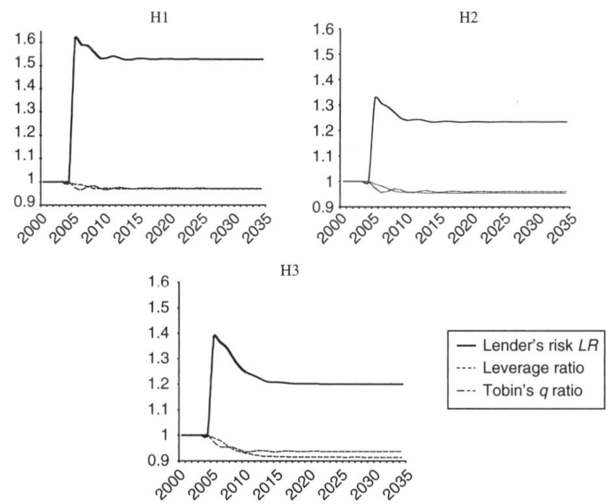

Figure 18 7 Higher central bank key interest rate: effects on lender's risk, on leverage ratio and Tobin's q *ratio*

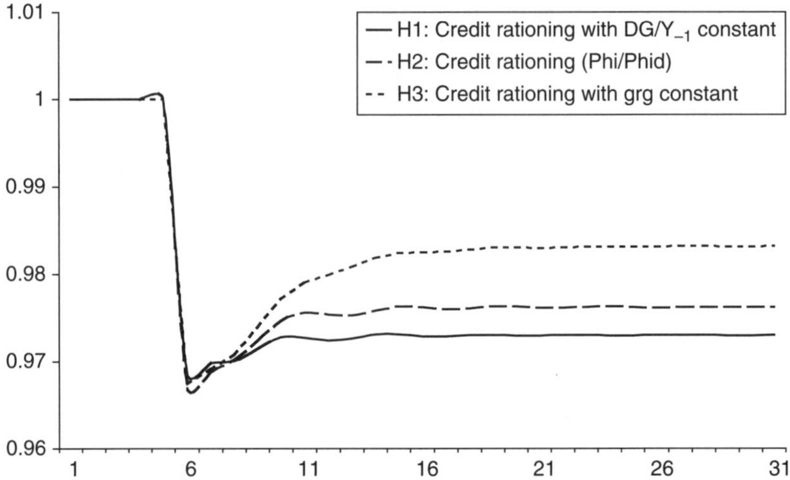

Figure 18.8 Higher central bank key interest rate: effects on credit rationing with H1, H2 and H3

With the powerful countercyclical effect of the fiscal policy (H3), the government spending counterbalances the effect of the credit rationing of the firms. Even with a lower Tobin's q ratio and leverage ratio, and higher lender's and borrower's risks, our virtual economy stabilizes on the previous steady state. The fact that private banks give limitless credit to government, explains this result.

CONCLUSION

All the measures aimed at ensuring safety and liquidity for bank financing go against both the 'animal spirits' of entrepreneurs and growth. The most adventurous entrepreneurs can even be completely excluded from financing. This 'desired scarcity' of financing is the result of the banks' liquidity preference and can restrict the level of production and employment. Growth requires not only confident entrepreneurs, but also confident banks, while a crisis can arise out of the pessimism of only one sector. That strengthens the possibility of underemployment in a monetary economy of production. To simplify, the quieter the situation is (accommodating monetary policy, growth and high profits, weak indebtedness, and weak borrower's and lender's risks), the closer we get to the horizontalist case. However, the more the situation is 'animated', the more banking behavior will have an influence on production and on the economic situation. Of course, we show that an expansionary fiscal policy without a limit of indebtedness can counterbalance a contractionary monetary policy.

By taking into account the behavior of the private banks, a more realistic creation of money and the financial risks of firms and banks, it is possible to make Keynes's approach of liquidity preference theory compatible with an endogenous theory of money in a Post Keynesian framework. The banks' state of confidence and their conventions are some important features in the understanding of a monetary economy of production. This stock–flow consistent model is only the first stage in this direction.

NOTES

1. For a detailed analysis of the generalization of the liquidity preference to the private banks, see Le Heron (2002, 2007).
2. We used the software Eviews 5.5 to manage the model and the simulations. The complete model (60 equations), the values of the parameters, the exogenous variables and the Eviews program are available from the author on request.
3. We follow the approach of Davidson (1972). But with the previous assumption, there is no radical opposition to those who take into account the financing of total production (Parguez, 1982). Again, for simplicity's sake, we do not study the financing of households by banks, which might be a significant factor in a more general model.
4. Excess capacity exists because of expectations of future demand, entry barriers, cost minimization, time-taking production, and so on. For the role of inventories, see Godley and Lavoie (2007: ch. 9).
5. The meaning of most of the symbols is made explicit in the left column of the matrix. See also the glossary of variables in Appendix 18.A
6. What we call the non-ordinary row is the row concerning profits of banks that includes three different variables (see ix).
7. When we use an accounting identity we often need to rewrite it, so we will always use its number (a Roman numeral) in order to enable the reader to recognize it easily.
8. The yield curve on interest rates is considered to be of normal shape when $i_{LT} > i_{ST}$. This curve is inverted when $i_{ST} > i_{LT}$.
9. These 33 new variables are the following:
   Government: *DG*;
   Firms: gr_y, gr_{KD} Y, Y_{fc}, K, I_D, r_{cf}, u, FCI, φ, φ^d, IF, $amort$;
   Private Banks: CG, CG_{of}, CG^a_{of} CG_e, CG^a_e, LR, lev, q, OF, E, r^a_{of}, r^a_e, P^{da}, lr;
   Households: Y^a_w, Y^a_v, Y_w, Y_v, Y_h.

REFERENCES

Davidson, P. (1972), *Money and the Real World*, London: Macmillan.

Dos Santos, C. and G. Zezza (2004), 'A Post-Keynesian stock–flow consistent macroeconomic growth model: preliminary results', working paper 402, Levy Economics Institute, Annandale-on-Hudson, NY, February.

Godley, W. and M. Lavoie (2007), *Monetary Economics: An Integrated Approach to Credit, Money, Income, Production and Wealth*, London: Macmillan, esp. chs 9 and 10.

Kaldor, N. (1985) *Le fléau du monétarisme* [*The Scourge of Monetarism*], Paris: Economica.

Keynes, J.M. (1936 [1973]), *The General Theory*, reprinted in *The Collected Writings of John Maynard Keynes*, Vol. VII, London: Macmillan.

Keynes, J.M. (1937), 'The "ex ante" theory of the rate of interest', *Economic Journal*, **47**: 663–9.

Lavoie, M. and W. Godley (2001), 'Kaleckian growth models in a stock and flow monetary framework: a Kaldorian view', *Journal of Post Keynesian Economics*, Winter, 277–312.

Lavoie, M. and W. Godley (2004), 'Features of a realistic banking system within a Post-Keynesian stock–flow consistent model', paper presented at the Basil Moore Festschrift conference, Stellenbosch University, South Africa, January.

Le Heron, E. (1986), 'Généralisation de la préférence pour la liquidité et financement de l'investissement', ['Generalization of liquidity preference and investment financing'], *Économies et Sociétés, Monnaie et Production*, (6–7), 67–93.

Le Heron, E. (2002) 'La préférence pour la liquidité des banques: une analyse post keynésienne du comportement bancaire' ['The liquidity preference of banks: a Post Keynesian analysis of banking practice'], *Cahiers Lillois d'Economie et de Sociologie*, (38), 97–131.

Le Heron, E. (2007), 'Dynamic analysis of monetary policy shock on banking behavior', in J. McCombie and C. Rodríguez (eds), *Institutions, Public Policy and Governance*, London: Palgrave-Macmillan, pp. 79–99.

Minsky, H. (1975), *John Maynard Keynes*, New York: Columbia University Press.

Moore, B. (1988), *Horizontalists and Verticalists: The Macroeconomics of Credit Money*, Cambridge: Cambridge University Press.

Mouakil, T. (2006), 'Instabilité financière et méthode stocks-flux: analyse critique de l'hypothèse de Minsky', PhD thesis, University Montesquieu Bordeaux 4, November.

Parguez, A. (1982), 'La monnaie dans le circuit: le voile déchiré' ['Financial instability and stock-flow method: analysis of Minsky's hypothesis'], *Économie Appliquée*, **35** (3), 231–65.

APPENDIX 18A GLOSSARY

Y	National income
Y_{fc}	Output of full capacity
gr_y	Growth rate in the income
N	Employment
N_{fe}	Full employment
OG	Output gap
Un	Unemployment
r_{un}	Rate of unemployment
L	Loans (variable rate)
CP	Commercial paper
B	Treasury bills
E	Equities
e	Number of equities
p_e	Price of equities
OF	Bonds (fixed rate)
of	Number of bonds
p_{of}	Price of fixed rate bonds

Central bank

P_{cb}	Central bank profits
REF	Reserve requirements (CB refunds)
H	High-powered money
i_{cb}	Central bank key interest rate

Commercial banks

P_b	Banks profits
V_b	Net wealth of banks
CG	Capital gains of banks
CGe	Capital gains on equities
CG_e^a	Expected capital gains on equities
CG_{of}	Capital gains on bonds
CG_{of}^a	Expected capital gains on bonds
i_{cp}	Interest rate on commercial paper
i_d	Interest rate on deposits
i_l	Interest rate on loans
i_b	Interest rate on treasury bills
FCI	Financial condition index
LR	Lender's risk
lr	Lender's risk for long-term interest rate
r_{of}^a	Expected yield of bonds
r_e^a	Expected return on equities
P^d	Expected distributed profits
lev	Leverage ratio
q	Tobin's q ratio

Firms

I	Net investment
I_D	Investment demand
W	Wages
K	Stock of capital
V_f	Net wealth of firms
u	Capacity utilization rate
gr_k	Growth rate in the stock of capital
gr_{kD}	Desired growth rate in capital
ΔF	Net finance
φ	Gross finance
φ^d	Desired gross investment
IF	Internal funds
$amort$	Amortization (debt redemption)
P	firm profits
P^d	Distributed profits
P^u	Undistributed profits
r_{cf}	Ratio of cash flow

Government

G	Government expenditure
DG	Government deficit
g_{dg}	Constant ratio of government deficit
P_{cb}	Central bank profits
T	Taxes

Households

C Consumption

D Bank deposits

Y_w^a Expected disposable income of workers

Y_v^a Expected disposable financial income

Y_w Disposable income of workers

Y_v Disposable financial income

Y_h Disposable income of household

19. Expectations and unemployment

J.W. Nevile and Peter Kriesler*

INTRODUCTION

Expectations have had a prominent role in macroeconomics ever since the publication of Keynes's *General Theory*. In that book, the word 'expectation' appeared in the title of two chapters, and the concept was used throughout. Expectations were central to the determination of both the interest rate and the level of investment and the trade cycle in the longer run. This is most clearly illustrated in chapter 5, 'Expectations as determining output and employment', where Keynes identifies the importance of expectations in determining the level of employment: 'To-day's employment can be correctly described as being governed by to-day's expectations taken in conjunction with to-day's capital equipment' (1936 [1973], p. 50).

By contrast, in Milton Friedman's version of monetarism, mistaken expectations explain the short-run trade-off between unemployment and inflation, while the correction of these mistakes leads to the long-run vertical Phillips curve. In the late 1980s and early 1990s new classical macroeconomics, with its emphasis on rational expectations, became very influential and the policy ineffectiveness theorem was widely accepted. However, neither of these two forms of monetarism lasted long as widely accepted theories useful for explaining short-run phenomena, though their conclusion that money was neutral and the Phillips curve vertical in the long run remained widely accepted.

This is well documented in a symposium in the May 1997 issue of the *American Economic Review*, where five eminent macro economists, Robert Solow, John Taylor, Martin Eichenbaum, Alan Blinder and Oliver Blanchard, addressed the topic 'Is there a core of practical macroeconomics that we should all believe?'. They all agreed that not only was money neutral in the long-run and that the long-run Phillips curve was vertical, but also that the long-run equilibrium position, or rate of economic growth, was not

* We would like to thank Geoff Harcourt and an anonymous referee for their helpful comments. The chapter was first presented at the 9th International Post Keynesian Conference: A Celebration of the Impact of Keynesian Economics and we would like to thank the participants for their helpful comments.

affected by the effects of short-run macroeconomic policy on real variables. They also all agreed that there was a short-run trade-off between unemployment and inflation, due, in varying amounts, to price and wage inflexibilities and other frictions in the system such as incorrect expectations. However, what they did not agree on was equally important. Two of the five, Solow and Blinder found it hard to say a good word about rational expectations, Eichenbaum thought it was useful but did not always apply and only Taylor generally accepted it. Blanchard said very little about expectations at all. Not one of them set out a coherent explanation of how the economy moved from disequilibrium in the short-run to long-run equilibrium. Solow explicitly said that this lack was one of the big weaknesses in generally accepted theory (Solow, 1997, pp. 231–2) and Blanchard made the point that we know very little about what determines the long-run equilibrium (1997, pp. 244–5). Yet despite this, no one thought that the changes brought about by short-run macroeconomic policy affected the long-run equilibrium position. In general, expectations were considered in the context of inflation and monetary variables. Their effect on real economic variables was not discussed.

This chapter agues that the consensus reached by the five economists and reflected in the textbooks is wrong, both with respect to the long- and the short-run situations. The long-un equilibrium positions of real variables are influenced by the short-run positions of both nominal and real variables. 'In fact, the long-run trend is but a slowly changing component of a chain of short-period situations; it has no independent entity', (Kalecki, 1968, p. 65). The reasons for this emerge when the weaknesses in the consensus position pointed out by Solow and Blanchard are addressed. The role of expectations, or lack of such a role, is important in the difference between the consensus view and that argued in this chapter. Moreover, this chapter argues that the effects of expectations on real variables are more important than their effect on prices.

THE CONVENTIONAL TEXTBOOK VIEW

According to the conventional view, the two most important and generally accepted results of macroeconomic theory are first that the long-run rate of unemployment is unaffected by macroeconomic economic policy, and second that money is neutral in the long run, unable to have any effect on real variables:

> There is substantial evidence demonstrating that there is no long-run trade-off between the level of inflation and the level of unused resources in the economy – whether measured by the unemployment rate, the capacity utilization rate, or

> the deviation of real GDP from potential GDP. Monetary policy is thus neutral in the long-run. An increase in money growth will have no long-run impact on the unemployment rate; it will only result in increased inflation. (Taylor, 1999, pp. 29–30)

In other words, according to this theory, unemployment tends towards the non-accelerating inflation rate of unemployment (NAIRU) in the long-run, irrespective of government (or other) macroeconomic intervention. Expectations, within this analysis, have no operational role in the long-run, except as part of the definition of long-run equilibrium, that is, when inflationary expectations are fulfilled. Expectations are assumed to be 'rational' in these models, in the sense that economic agents do not make systematic errors.

However, most commentators, although accepting that there is no trade-off in the long-run, allow for a trade-off between unemployment and inflation in the short-run, and hence allow for macroeconomic policy to have a short-run influence. Although economists should be neutral between policies, monetary policy, usually according to some rule, is often favoured (Kriesler and Lavoie, 2005).

Although the reasons given for the existence of the short-run trade-offs vary between economists, one of the most important is price and wage stickiness: 'The trade-off is due largely to temporarily sticky prices and wages' (Taylor, 2000, p. 90) so, even with rational expectations, such rigidities will allow some types of trade-offs, but only in the short-run. As a result, macroeconomic demand policies can have a short-run impact in pushing the economy towards its long-run position.

It is important to note that, within this analysis, the main type of expectations considered are inflationary expectations. These serve the role of allowing economic agents to disentangle nominal price changes from real price changes. Where inflationary expectations are incorrect, agents will be fooled into non-maximising actions. However, as soon as these expectations are revised to the correct level of inflation, real activity will return to its natural level, albeit with a different level of inflation built into the economy.

Even with rational expectations, similar mechanisms may operate if there are menu costs to price changes, or contracts setting prices or for labour services.

CRITIQUE OF THE TEXTBOOK VIEW

It is vital to note that the reason for these results is the specific shape of the long-run Phillips curve, and the underlying assumptions about the nature of markets, particularly the labour market, which is assumed to clear, except in the short-run where rigidities may prevent the market-clearing wage being achieved. In other words, if the long-run Phillips curve's existence is either denied, or has another shape, such as being horizontal, then the long-run ineffectiveness of policy and of expectations no longer holds, and many of the conclusions of the textbook view need to be revisited (Freedman et al., 2004; Kriesler and Lavoie, 2005).

Second, the modern textbook account errs in focusing on inflationary expectations. Expectations about output and future demand (in real terms) are not even mentioned. For example, in a typical Australian textbook – Gans et al. (2002) – there are a few lines about how expected prices affect demand and supply curves at the micro level, but the only extended discussion of expectations is in the context of the Phillips curve. Some principles textbooks are more sophisticated than this. Hall and Lieberman (2005) discuss expectations in four places: consumer expectations of future income in the chapter on the consumption function; expectations and the money market (that is, in the discussion of the determination of interest rates); some brief remarks about expectations in the discussion of the determinants of foreign exchange rates; and the role of expectations in ongoing inflation and the Phillips curve. However, neither book mentions expectations in relation to investment. Consumer confidence affects consumption, at least according to Hall and Lieberman, but business confidence is irrelevant to investment decisions. In the discussion of the determinants of investment, it is implicitly assumed that those who buy capital goods know in advance the actual stream of future returns from the goods so no discussion of expectations is necessary.[1] However, empirical evidence clearly shows that expectations and uncertainty play a major role in the determination of investment (Baddeley, 2003).

Of course, in the real world, expectations about future levels of economic activity undergird most investment decisions and are often of crucial importance in both the short and the longer runs. A simple example from Australian economic history illustrates this nicely. In the first 30 years after the Second World War, it was generally believed that the Australian government would ensure that any lapses of economic activity from the full employment level would be short-lived. There are no official quarterly estimates of national income and output for most of this period, but there was only one year, 1952–53, in which gross domestic product (GDP) was lower than in the previous year. In 1952–53, the government acted quickly and successfully to stimulate the economy, reinforcing the prevailing view that it could and would cut short any departures from full employment. Because any such departure was expected to be short-lived, it did not have a large effect on investment and became a self-fulfilling expectation.[2]

Third, in the event of path determinacy, where the short-run path of the economy influences its long-run position, expectations will play a vital role in determining both the path and destination of the economy with respect to the key variables of investment and income. Today's capacity and level of demand are the result of previous investment decisions, which were crucially dependent on expectations of future income, prices and demand. In other words, the current state of the economy is dependent on past expectations, both because previous investment decisions played a key role in determining current capital, costs and capacity, and because current investment decisions determine effective demand and, therefore employment and output. So, for example, if there is an improvement in animal spirits, so that a wave of optimism spreads throughout financial and investment markets, this will initially lead to increased investment, which, in turn, increases effective demand and the level of capacity utilisation. This validates the initial bout of confidence, influencing the economy's growth path. Self-fulfilling expectations of this sort can lead to expanding growth paths similar to Gunnar Myrdal's virtuous cycles of cumulative causation, or they can lead in the opposite direction to vicious cycles, where pessimistic expectations become self-fulfilling (Kriesler, 1999, 2003). However, it is important to stress that price expectations play a secondary role in these decisions, as it is output and demand expectations that are fundamental.

Fourth, the reason for the acceptance of the rationale expectations model is due to the underlying view of the economy as being inherently stable and relatively simple to model. In the light of these considerations, it is not surprising that the expectations process is also seen as relatively straightforward:

> A related determining factor in modelling expectations is the presumption, or otherwise, of market stability. If the theoretical framework is built on the premiss that parameters have values which ensure dynamic stability, it is natural to model individual behaviour as being based on the same presumption. But without the presumption of stability, i.e. if the theoretical framework allows for indeterminacy of outcomes, it is natural to model individual behaviour as reacting to that indeterminacy. Within a stable general equilibrium system, the nature of a new equilibrium state can be known from existing information combined with information about the exogenous shock which displaced the economy from its original equilibrium state. Thus individuals who acquire this information can in principle know what the equilibrium values of variables are. If, however, existing information is insufficient to determine the outcome of a shock to the system, because behaviour is creative, because there is no shared perception as to the stability of the system or its likely resting-place following the shock, or because expectations formation itself is indeterminate, then the actual outcome of the shock cannot be predicted deterministically. (Dow, 1996, p. 132)

However, if the underlying economy is seen as not tending to a stable equilibrium at full employment, then, *per se*, this would lead to major complications in the formation of expectations. If the underlying model is a simple one, then the formation of expectations can be relatively simple and quick. However, the more complex the underlying vision of the economy, the less likely it is that expectations can be as simply described as in the neoclassical model.

INFLATIONARY EXPECTATIONS

According to the conventional wisdom, the danger associated with inflationary expectations is that they are self-fulfilling. If economic agents expect inflation to rise, for example, then they will act on those beliefs. Workers will demand higher wages in anticipation of these price increases, while employers will, in view of their expectations, be more willing to grant them:

> Private agents' expectations about future monetary policy actions affect their current decisions. . . . For example, suppose that, for some reason, private agents come to expect future inflation. This expectation leads them to raise wages and prices immediately. (Eichenbaum, 1997, p. 238)

This view of the relation between inflationary expectations and the inflation rate is a key factor in the argument for the independence of central banks. This is due to the belief that independent central banks will be seen as being more credible anti-inflationary institutions, and therefore will have stronger inflationary dampening influences on expectations.

Despite the general acceptance of this view, it should be regarded as seriously deficient as no transmission mechanism from expectations to actual price changes is specified. If we accept that prices, particularly in the industrial sector, are a mark-up on costs, then, unless inflation has some impact on mark-ups, which is unlikely,[3] it must operate through costs, in particular wages. What the analysis requires, therefore, is that labour's wage demands are in terms of expected inflation. However, as far as we are aware, this has not been the case in any known labour bargain. Where inflation is explicitly acknowledged, it is usually the previous period's inflation, so that the negotiation is an attempt to recover real wages to the pre-inflation level, rather than to have them anticipate inflation. There does not appear to have been a significant instance of successful wage negotiations on the basis of expected inflation. In other words, because wage demands usually represent an attempt to regain previous losses caused by inflation, they do not attempt to anticipate inflation. If this is correct, then inflationary expectations play little role in wage bargaining. In this case, although inflationary expectations may influence other variables indirectly, there does not appear to be any direct channel of influence whereby they can affect inflation, and so the idea that they are self-fulfilling must be significantly revised. Although more work needs to be done on the 'inflationary expectations transmission mechanism', it appears that to simply assume that such expectations are self-fulfilling, without a detailed account of exactly how, is extremely problematic, to say the least.

EXCHANGE RATES

The foreign exchange rate is one of the most important prices in the economy. It directly affects the prices of exports and imports, and, therefore, the price of all goods and services which either use imports as inputs or which compete with imports and exports. From the point of view of employment, it is particularly export industries and import-competing industries that are important, though importers also create employment. Expectations about the exchange rates are crucial to the investment plans, and hence to the long-run health, of these industries.[4]

In this section, various ways in which expectations can and frequently do affect exchange rates are described. As many Post Keynesian economists have argued, the major influence on the determination of exchange rates, certainly since the last decade of the twentieth century, is expectations (see, for example, Harvey, 1999, 2003 and Taylor, 2004). However, no systematic theory about the relationship between the two is set out. While various theories have been put forward, none can be used confidently to predict or even consistently explain movements in actual exchange rates.

Elsewhere (Kriesler and Nevile, 2006), we examine the determinants of the exchange rate, concluding that 'exchange rates are, in the current international environment, mainly determined by expectations, which are not based on anything real' (p. 145). This view is reinforced by the well-known result within the mainstream showing that no model of exchange rate determination performs better than a random walk model (Meese and Rogoff, 1983). The beauty contest analogy Keynes used to describe the determination of prices in stock exchanges (Keynes, 1936 [1973], p. 156) fits today's foreign exchange markets very well.

Hicks's distinction between flex-prices and fix-prices is well known. He made a further distinction between two types of flex-prices which is helpful in this context. One type are those where prices are largely determined by producers and consumers of goods and services and the other those where prices are largely determined by the demand and supply of traders who hold large stocks of the goods and services (or financial assets). When prices are determined by traders who hold large stocks, the stocks must have a life long enough for expectations about their future value to be important, though with liquid assets this could be a very short period of time. The exchange rate is a prime example of this later type of flex-price. Capital transactions dominate the foreign exchange market and most of the capital account transactions are made by traders who usually have very short time horizons.[5]

Some trades are reversed more or less instantaneously through hedging and some are arbitrage, but the major influence on the rate of exchange in the short run is the positions taken by speculators. The very short-run expectations of these traders determine the exchange rate. The Bank for International Settlements (BIS, 2005) identifies two types of speculation as being important in recent years. One, which is called 'carry trading', has a rationale in economic factors. If a country has a high interest rate relative to other countries, textbooks suggest that this goes with an expectation of depreciation in its rate of exchange, but this is not always the case. When traders believe that no change or an appreciation is likely, carry trading occurs 'with investments in high interest rate currencies financed by short positions in low interest currencies' (ibid., p. 5).[6]

The other type of speculation, called 'momentum trading' has no economic underpinning. It occurs when a short-run trend is expected to continue and this becomes a self-fulfilling expectation. An example par excellence is the Australian experience in the year 2000. The Australian dollar was worth US$0.65 in December 1999 and US$0.51 in October 2000. The fall in the value of the Australian dollar of 20 per cent against the US dollar (and 15 per cent against the trade weighted index) was at a time when the economic fundamentals that the foreign exchange markets supposedly give weight to, were sound. The budget was in surplus. Apart from a one-off effect of the introduction of the GST (goods and services tax, a value-added tax), the rate of inflation was 2 per cent and not expected to rise significantly. Even the current account deficit was relatively low. There can be no doubt that the fall had little to do with economic fundamentals.[7]

When not ruled by the herd instinct in momentum trading, it is unclear exactly what speculators pay attention to. Some economists believe that expectations are based on 'economic fundamentals', which then are seen as playing a key role in the determination of exchange rates through these influences on expectations. However, this need not be the case. Harvey (2001) and Taylor (2004) question the existence of any such fundamentals, suggesting that, in fact, they represent nothing more than an *ex post* justification for actual movements, having no independent existence and, therefore, explanatory power: 'For all practical purposes fundamentals do not exist – except when market participants convince themselves that one or another of the many candidates truly matter' (Taylor, 2004, p. 307). This reinforces our earlier conclusion that there seems to be nothing real behind the determination of exchange rates.

There is not a great deal that can be said to sum up this discussion of expectations and the exchange rate. We have focused on expectations and the exchange rate in the short-run. This is because the long-run position of the exchange rate is strongly path determined. For example the depreciation–inflation vicious circle which is sometimes a feature of exchange rate crises can also take place slowly and determine the long-run trend. As far as the short-run is concerned, we can be confident about two points: exchange rate expectations are both important and volatile. However, the factors that determine them from day to day are far from clear. It is the reactions of speculators in the foreign exchange markets to events that directly affect exchange rates. Keynes's comparison of the determinants of share prices with those of the winner of a beauty contest is probably the most helpful analogy to use. It is not possible to give a convincing account of any systematic determination of exchange rate expectations.

Given the importance of exchange rates for domestic economic activity and employment, this discussion highlights another clear link between expectations and employment.

CONCLUSION

Rather than being concerned with the determinants of expectations, this chapter has concentrated on the role of expectations in determining economic activity. Except in discussions of the consumption function, consideration of expectations in today's conventional macroeconomics is confined to their influence on monetary variables and often goes no further than the Phillips curve. In particular, the role of inflationary expectations as being a key determinate of actual inflation is stressed. However, this analysis is lacking a coherent story of the expectations transmission mechanism whereby the influence of expectations on inflation is spelt out. In fact, it seems unlikely that inflationary expectations will have a significant impact on actual inflation rates. In the conventional story, long-run equilibrium is quickly reached with a vertical Phillips curve and the values of real variables unaffected by monetary influences. This chapter argues that this is an incorrect view of the role of expectations. Rather we have argued for a Keynesian vision where expectations are not only an important influence on real variables in the short-run, but that the effects of expectations on real variables in the short-run can have a major effect on long-run equilibrium which is path determined and not reached all that quickly.

The conventional focus on monetary variables when expectations are discussed is misplaced. Expectations about output and economic activity have a significant effect on investment and hence unemployment in the short-run. The very act of investment affects supply in the longer run and given the path-determined nature of long-run growth, the increase in employment associated with it also affects demand in the longer run.

A second major channel of the influence of expectations is through the exchange rate. This important price is largely determined by expectations and its value has major effects on the economy, sometimes benign when changes in the exchange rate help an economy adjust to external shocks and sometimes adverse as movements in it in effect produce external shocks or at least magnify their effects. Again the trend in the exchange rate is in part at least path determined so that short-run movements can have long-run effects.

Expectations, therefore, play a major role in the determination of the levels of output and employment in both the short and long runs. As a result, more serious attention needs to be paid both to this role, and to the determination of expectations themselves.

NOTES

1. It would be harder to find a more stark contrast to Keynes's view that '[t]he outstanding fact is the extreme precariousness of the basis of knowledge on which our estimates of prospective yields have to be made' (Keynes, 1936 p. 149).
2. For a more detailed discussion of the role of macroeconomic policy in this period, see Nevile (2000).
3. According to Fred Lee, the author of a number of important studies on prices and the determination of the mark-up, expected inflation has not played any role in any theoretical or empirical study of the determination of the mark-up (in conversation with the authors).
4. The importance of the exchange rate can be gauged by the fact that, for example, currently, in Australia, employment in actual or potential export and import competing industries (tradables) is estimated to be about two-thirds of total employment.
5. Total sales of the Australian dollar in traditional foreign exchange markets on a single trading day in April 2004 were, on average, nearly 20 per cent of the total annual value of Australia's GDP. This is a striking figure, but it does not contain much information except that the volume of daily foreign exchange transactions is great. There are not 365 trading days in a year, though there is trading on some Australian public holidays since nearly half of foreign exchange transactions involving the Australian dollar occur in markets abroad, notably in London; a conservative estimate of the number of trading days in a year is 250. The most meaningful comparison is not with GDP but with exports plus imports. Assuming that there are 250 trading days a year, the ratio of total annual foreign exchange transactions in the Australian dollar to exports plus imports is about 115, that is 11,500 per cent.
6. The Australian dollar was mentioned by the BIS as an example of a target currency in recent years with the US dollar as the funding currency example.

7. Some fall could be explained by an expected slowdown in the world economy and hence a fall in commodity prices, but the fall was much greater than can be explained by this factor.

REFERENCES

Baddeley, M.C. (2003), *Investment: Theories and Analysis,* London: Palgrave Macmillan.

Bank for International Settlements (BIS) (2005), *Triennial Central Bank Survey: Foreign Exchange and Derivatives Market Activity in 2004*, Basel: BIS Press and Communications.

Blanchard, O. (1997), 'Is there a core of usable macroeconomics?', *American Economic Review*, May, 244–6.

Blinder, A. (1997), 'Is there a core of practical macroeconomics that we should all believe?', *American Economic Review*, May, 240–43.

Dow, S. (1996), *The Methodology of Macroeconomic Thought,* Cheltenham, UK and Brookfield, USA: Edward Elgar.

Eichenbaum, M. (1997), 'Some thoughts on practical stabilization policy', *American Economic Review*, May, 236–9.

Freedman, C., G.C. Harcourt and P. Kriesler (2004), 'Has the long-run Phillips curve turned horizontal?', in G. Argyrous, M. Forstater and G. Mongiovi (eds), *Growth, Distribution and Effective Demand: Alternatives to Economic Orthodoxy*, Armonk, NY: M.E. Sharpe, pp. 144–62.

Gans, J., S. King, R. Stonecash and N. Mankiw (2003), *Principles of Economics*, Southbank, Vic.: Thompson.

Hall, R. and M. Lieberman (2005), *Economics: Principles and Applications*, International Student edn, Mason, OH: Southwestern.

Harvey, J. (1999), 'Exchange rates' in P.A. O'Hara (ed.), *Encyclopedia of Political Economy*, vol. 1, London and New York: Routledge, pp. 302–4.

Harvey, J. (2001), 'Exchange rate theory and "the fundamentals'", *Journal of Post Keynesian Economics*, **23**, 3–15.

Harvey, J. (2003), 'Exchange rates', in J. King (ed.), *Elgar Companion to Post Keynesian Economics*, Cheltenham, UK and Northampton, MA, USA: Edward Elgar pp. 131–5.

Kalecki, M. (1968), 'Trend and the business cycle', reprinted in J. Osiatynski (ed.), (1990), *Collected Works of Michał Kalecki. Volume 1: Capitalism: Business Cycles and Full Employment*, Oxford: Clarendon Press, pp. 65–108.

Keynes, J.M. (1936), *The General Theory of Employment, Interest and Money*, London: Macmillan, reprinted 1973 in *The Collected Writings of John Maynard Keynes*, Vol. VII, London: Macmillan.

Kriesler, P. (1999), 'Harcourt, Hicks and Lowe; incompatible bedfellows?', in C. Sardoni, and P. Kriesler (eds), *Themes in Political Economy: Essays in Honour of Geoff Harcourt,* London: Routledge, pp. 400–417.

Kriesler, P. (2003), 'The traverse', in J. King (ed.), *Elgar Companion to Post Keynesian Economics*, Cheltenham, UK and Northampton, MA, USA: Edward Elgar, pp. 355–9.

Kriesler, P. and M. Lavoie (2005), 'A critique of the new consensus view of monetary policy', *Economics and Labour Relations Review,* **16** (1), July, 7–15.

Kriesler, P. and J. Nevile (2006), 'Does the foreign exchange rate constrain full employment policy in Australia?', in G. Wrightson (ed.), The Constraint to Full Employment or Work Choices and Welfare-to-Work Conference, University of Newcastle, December 7-8, proceedings, refereed papers, Newcastle, Australia: Center of Full Employment and Equity, University of Newcastle, pp. 142–9.
Meese, R.A. and K. Rogoff (1983), 'Empirical exchange rate models of the seventies: do they fit out of sample?', *Journal of International Economics*, **14**(1), 3–24.
Nevile, J. (2000), 'Can Keynesian policies stimulate growth in output and employment?', in S. Bell (ed.), *The Unemployment Crisis in Australia: Which Way Out?*, Cambridge: Cambridge University Press, pp. 149–70.
Solow, R. (1997), 'Is there a core of usable macroeconomics we should all believe in?', *American Economic Review*, May, 230–32.
Taylor, J. (1997), 'A core of practical macroeconomics?', *American Economic Review*, May, 233–6.
Taylor, J.B. (1999), 'Monetary policy guidelines for employment and inflation stability', in R.M. Solow and J.B. Taylor (eds), *Inflation, Unemployment, and Monetary Policy*, Cambridge, MA: MIT Press, pp. 29–54.
Taylor, J.B. (2000), 'Teaching modern macroeconomics at the principles level', *American Economic Review*, **90**(2), (May), 90–94.
Taylor, L. (2004), *Reconstructing Macroeconomics: Structuralist Proposals and Critiques of the Mainstream*, Cambridge, MA: Harvard University Press.

Index